The Immigrant Divide

Are all immigrants from the same country of origin best understood as one political and social group? Or are generational differences more profound than we might imagine? Between Castro's rise to power in 1959 and the early twenty-first century more than a million Cubans immigrated to the United States. While it is widely known that Cuban émigrés have exerted a strong hold on Washington policy toward their homeland, Eckstein uncovers a fascinating paradox: the recent arrivals, although politically weak and poor, have done more to transform their homeland than the influential and prosperous early exiles who have tried for half a century to bring the Castro regime to heel. The impact of the so-called New Cubans is an unintended consequence of the personal ties they maintain with family in Cuba, ties the first arrivals oppose.

This historically grounded, nuanced book offers a rare in-depth analysis of Cuban immigrants' social, cultural, economic, and political adaptation, their transformation of Miami into the "northernmost Latin American city," and their cross border engagement and homeland impact. Eckstein accordingly provides new insight into the lives of Cuban immigrants, into Cuba in the post-Soviet era, and into how Washington's failed Cuba policy might be improved. She also posits a new theory to deepen the understanding not merely of Cuban but of other immigrant group adaptation.

Susan Eva Eckstein is Professor of Sociology and International Relations at Boston University. Author of *Back from the Future: Cuba under Castro*, as well as numerous other books on Latin America, she is also former president of the Latin American Studies Association and the New England Council on Latin America.

The Immigrant Divide

How Cuban Americans Changed the US
and their Homeland

Susan Eva Eckstein

 Routledge
Taylor & Francis Group

NEW YORK AND LONDON

First published 2009
by Routledge
270 Madison Ave, New York, NY 10016

Simultaneously published in the UK
by Routledge
2 Park Square, Milton Park, Abingdon, Oxon OX14 4RN

Routledge is an imprint of the Taylor & Francis Group, an informa business

© 2009 Taylor & Francis

Typeset in Galliard by
RefineCatch Limited, Bungay, Suffolk
Printed and bound in the United States of America on acid-free paper by
Walsworth Publishing Company, Marceline, MO

Trademark Notice: Product or corporate names may be trademarks or
registered trademarks, and are used only for identification and explanation
without intent to infringe.

Library of Congress Cataloging in Publication Data
Eckstein, Susan, 1942–
The immigrant divide : how Cuban Americans changed the US and their
homeland / Susan Eva Eckstein.
p. cm.
Includes bibliographical references.
1. Cuban Americans—History. 2. Cuban Americans—Social
conditions. 3. Cuban Americans—Politics and government. 4. Cuba—
History—Revolution, 1959. 5. Cuba—Emigration and immigration.
6. Cuba—Foreign relations—United States. 7. United States—Politics
and government. 8. United States—Emigration and immigration.
9. United States—Foreign relations—Cuba. I. Title.
E184.C97E27 2009
973'.04687291—dc22
2009016639

ISBN 10: 0–415–99922–7 (hbk)
ISBN 10: 0–415–99923–5 (pbk)
ISBN 10: 0–203–88100–1 (ebk)

ISBN 13: 978–0–415–99922–9 (hbk)
ISBN 13: 978–0–415–99923–6 (pbk)
ISBN 13: 978–0–203–88100–2 (ebk)

In memory of Maggie

Contents

List of Figures and Tables

Figures

Tables

Acknowledgments

Generous financial support helped make my research and writing possible. I am very grateful to the Andrew W. Mellon Foundation/MIT Program on NGOs and Forced Migration, the Cuban Committee for Democracy, the American Council on Learned Societies, the Ford Foundation/Institute for International Education (especially to Cristina Eguizábal), the John D. and Catherine T. MacArther Foundation, Boston University, and the Radcliffe Institute for Advanced Studies for support. The Radcliffe Institute provided far more than a salary and research stipend. As a scholar in residence at the Institute I benefited from intellectually inspiring colleagues. I am extremely appreciative of Drew Faust, Katherine Newman, and Judith Vichniac, at the time Dean of the Institute, Dean of Social Sciences, and Director of the Fellowship Program, respectively, for the exemplary work environment they created.

In working on the book, I benefited from exceptional assistance from Lorena Barberia, Tyler Johnston, Wendy Roth, and Zoua Vang. Although Lorena helped with interviewing, in the book I often insert myself as if I conducted all the interviews single-handedly. I do this to allow the book to read better, while fully appreciative of her contribution. In writing the book I also benefited from conversations over the years with Manuel Orozco, the leading expert on remittances to Latin America, and from data he generously shared with me. In addition, I benefited from critical readings of material included in diverse chapters and from conversations that I had while working on the book. I am especially indebted to Richard Alba, Emily Barman, Amy Bridges, Max Castro, Soraya Castro, Jorge Domínguez, Caroline Elkins, Anne Fernández, Luis Fraga, Rafael Hernández, Rosabeth Kanter, Riva Kastoryano, Catherine Krull, William LeoGrande, Dario Moreno, Emily Morris, Mae Ngai, Robert Pastor, Louis Pérez Jr., Jorge Pérez-López, Luciano Martins, Archibald Ritter, Ruben Rumbaut, Paolo Spadoni, David Swartz, Heike Trappe, and Graham Wilson. Gay Seidman and my husband, Paul Osterman, very generously commented on drafts of the entire manuscript. Their wisdom strengthened the book. In turn, Mark Rosenberg very generously provided me with invaluable contacts essential for my Miami interviews. And Alejandro Portes deserves a special note of thanks. He unwittingly inspired my interest in

xii   *Acknowledgments*

writing the book, when asking me to research and write a paper on the impact of family visits to Cuba, for the Committee for Cuban Democracy. Last but certainly not least, I am grateful to my daughters, Michelle and Rachel Osterman. Michelle helped with the preparation of the manuscript. I am also grateful to my mother, Ruth Eckstein, whose own lived experiences inspired my interest in immigrants and refugees, and who at age 92 anxiously awaited completion of the book and graciously withheld from calling me in the mornings because she knew that I dedicated the early hours to writing!

I would also like to acknowledge Michael Kerns who I was fortunate to have as an editor at Routledge. The superb staff at the publishing house who worked on my book included Felisa Salvago-Keyes, Sarah Phillips, and Sara de Vos, also my proofreader Anne Owen. I am most appreciative of all they did.

I dedicate this book to the memory of my sister, Maggie (Margaret) Loble. She suffered not merely the pains of forced migration as a child but as an adult the pains of a plague of our time, cancer, which took her life at an all too early age.

Introduction

As the US Congress deliberated whether to legalize or further criminalize the millions of undocumented workers on American shores, in 2006, immigrants nationwide took to the streets to make their desire for citizenship known. On May 1 of that year, some three-fourths of a million immigrants nationwide went so far as to absent themselves from work and participate in "A Day Without Immigrants." Immigrants wanted the non-immigrant American majority to recognize their often hidden contributions to the national economy.

The May event marked the first time in US history that immigrants of diverse backgrounds, though mainly from Latin America, had collectively taken to the streets to press for political inclusion. Some participants had worked in the country for as many as twenty years without legal labor rights and other protections. Not since 1986 had Washington granted illegal immigrants a path to citizenship.

The US is currently in the middle of one of the two main periods of immigration in the nation's history. Approximately 13 percent of the current population is foreign-born.[1] The previous period of large-scale immigration occurred around the turn of the twentieth century.

Although the US is a nation of immigrants, resentment toward the foreign-born festers. The preeminent political scientist Samuel Huntington, for example, set off alarm bells in 2004 with his book *Who Are We? The Challenges to America's National Identity.*[2] He argued that Hispanics, in particular, are eroding the country's core Anglo-Protestant values which he believes made America great, unified the country, and permitted immigrant upward mobility. Huntington expressed concern that immigrants from Latin America, who by the start of the new millennium accounted for approximately half of annual newcomers, and who together with their US-born progeny had become the country's largest minority group, were creating another America, one culturally and socially distinct.

At least as important as Huntington's overarching question, "Who Are We?," however, is the inadequately addressed question, "Who Are They?" "We" remain insufficiently knowledgeable about recent immigrants. Native-borns tend to concern themselves more with the "Americanization" of the foreign-born, with making them more like "us," than with appreciating immigrant differences.

This book addresses the question "Who Are They?" In particular, it focuses on the Cuban diaspora, how, when, and why it changed over the years, and the impact different émigré waves have had both in the US and in Cuba. By the dawn of the current millennium, Cubans constituted the second largest Hispanic immigrant group, second to Mexicans.[3] Indicative of how distinct "they" are, Cubans were not among the May 1 protesters, for reasons the book elucidates.

Cubans share a common language and common colonial cultural heritage with other Latin Americans. However, they tend to see themselves as different, and their experiences both in their homeland and their new land have been, in important respects, distinctive. Even Cubans who emigrated in different time periods will be shown to differ in their perceptions, experiences, and wants. They differ to the point that their policy preferences conflict.

Another aspect of the book is more theoretical. I argue that an understanding of immigrant adaptation is improved upon when taking the past of the foreign-born into account. First-generation immigrants who uproot at different points in time, as well as from different countries at the same time, may come to the US with different experiences, and with different values and views so formed, that influence their lives in their new land. Whilst studies of immigrants have contrasted first versus second-generation differences, variances among immigrants themselves have been insufficiently analyzed. While I am not the first to note that immigrants' homeland experiences impact on their new country adaptation, I am one of the few to trace the long-lasting, cross-border impact of those experiences and their macro-level consequences.

The Cuban Diaspora: How, When and Why it Changed, and with What Effects

I show that Cuban immigrants who uprooted at different points in time with different homeland lived experiences have different views on life, which have led them to adapt in various ways in the US and to relate differently to their homeland. At one extreme are the Cuban émigrés who left the island in the first years after Fidel Castro assumed power in 1959, who came of age before the revolution and who opposed the radical remaking of their country. I refer to them as the Exile cohort, because that is how they refer to themselves. Many of them grew up in a privileged world. They had some experience in civic life, but little tradition of democracy and political compromise. They left their homeland angry that the revolution had deprived them of their former way of life.

At the other extreme are the émigrés who knew life transformed both by revolution and the economic crisis the Soviet Union's dissolution caused. They also experienced the delegitimation of the political model on which their own country had, in many respects, been premised for thirty years. I refer to them as the New Cubans. These arrivals, in contrast, knew no luxuries, no civic culture, and little association life that was not state-based. They grew up heavily dependent on the state until the crisis made even their basic subsistence problematic. Against this backdrop, most New Cubans left their homeland to improve their material living standards, even when also politically disillusioned.

The weight of their different pasts is partly contingent on how old they were when uprooting. Within a cohort of arrivals, adults came with fully formed views which filtered both their new country adaptation and ties to their homeland. Child immigrants, in contrast, had both new and old country life-forming experiences.

With distinct pasts, the different émigré waves arrived with different perspectives on life in general and toward their homeland in particular, which remained consequential to them after years in the US. The first émigrés view their exodus through political lenses. They neither forgive nor forget Castro, whom they blame for depriving them of their lost life. Their outlook remains filtered through pre-revolution lenses, to the point that many of them continued committed from US shores to their generational battle against Castro and his supporters. From the US they tried to bring the Castro-led regime to heel, even as they successfully adapted to their new land.

The island crisis of the 1990s, in contrast, was the defining experience shaping the views on life of Cubans who uprooted in the post-Soviet era. The deep depression fueled a new, pragmatic family-focused outlook on life. Lingering belief in lofty revolutionary ideals that had captivated the hearts and minds of regime loyalists for decades withered.

The two sets of island-born Cubans represent contrasting archetypal immigrant types, one that viewed uprooting primarily as politically driven, the other as more economically driven. In between the Exiles and the New Cubans came another group of émigrés. Depending on their age, they experienced their homeland before the revolution as well as being revamped by it. However, they never experienced the subsistence crisis that New Cubans did. I refer to them as the Marielitos, named after the port in Cuba from which many of them exited. Because these arrivals include people with more varied experiences than those who left either in the first years of the revolution or after the post-Soviet era crisis, I focus less on them. As an immigrant group they do not constitute a distinctive archetype. They tend to interpret life through the same pre- and anti-revolution lenses as Exiles. However, they experienced more of Cuba transformed on which to base their views.

The two émigré cohorts that I mainly focus on, with their divergent pasts and perspectives on life, adapted differently to their new land. I will show that many of those who first fled the revolution built on homeland-attained social, cultural, and economic assets that enabled them to share in the American Dream, both economically and politically. But while assimilating and acculturating, they never forgot where they came from and why. They still retain, even if in transmuted form, homeland-acquired values, cultural practices, and commitments. They even learned to leverage US political institutions to advance their continued commitment to topple the Castro-led regime. With their goal in mind, they promoted a political wall across the Florida Straits.

In contrast, the New Cubans differ in their views toward cross-border ties. Their distinctive island generational formation predisposed them to covet the very transnational involvements the first post-Castro émigrés oppose. As a result, the émigrés who best knew Cuba under Castro most wanted to build a bridge across the Straits. Yet, politically weak, their concerns have gone largely unarticulated and unaddressed. Arriving without assets comparable to those of the first post-Castro arrivals, fewer of them have shared in the American Dream either economically or politically. And without significant homeland civic society experience to draw on, they have not established a civic associational life of their own in their new land that builds on, reinforces, and promotes their own values and concerns.

The different émigré views and involvements reflect, in turn, contrasting conceptions of Self. Whereas most of the first who fled the revolution perceive themselves as exiles and exiled, deprived of their homeland because of their political convictions, recent arrivals tend to view themselves as economic immigrants or merely as "having gone abroad." They see themselves as having moved to the US to earn money not merely for themselves but for their families still in Cuba. Differentiating themselves, these so-called New Cubans tend to accept the first émigrés' self-definition. They too refer to the first arrivals as exiles, or as the *historicos* and *viejitos*, the historical, old-timers and old folk. While I refer to the first émigrés as the Exiles, I do not wish to signify that their self-definition is accurate. The lives of some opponents of the Cuban makeover unquestionably were at risk. Many, however, left at their own volition, albeit not under conditions of their choosing. They uprooted as the country's social transformation stripped them of property and privilege and made demands of them that they resented. While having political grievances and framing their exit as politically induced, for most it was an assault on their lifestyle, not their lives, that led them to leave. But whether imagined or not, early émigrés' perceptions of themselves as exiles will be shown to be very real in its consequences.

Paradoxically, I will show that the New Cubans, with no organized political agenda of their own, have done more to transform Cuba under Castro than the rich and powerful earlier arrivals. The New Cubans unwittingly planted seeds of socialist transformation from the US side of the Straits, a byproduct, in the aggregate, of their transnationalized family commitments. Their social and economic ties across borders eroded socialism as islanders knew it. I trace the different homeland effects the émigré waves have had to their different pre-immigration lived experiences and perspectives on life so formed.

At the same time, the experiences of the émigré cohorts both in their new and old lands will be shown to be shaped by the broader context in which their lives transpired. The Cold War formed part of that context, with the first-generation émigrés experiencing it differently. The first islanders to come to the US in large numbers opposed Castro's alliance with the Soviet Union and the remaking of the island's political economy. They left in droves as Castro declared himself a Marxist-Leninist, oversaw the expropriation of their properties, and institutionalized a Communist Party-led government. For fleeing an anti-American, Soviet-allied country they were rewarded in their new country. In its global quest to win the Cold War, Washington gave those who fled the island's revolution a hero's welcome. They attained benefits extended to no other immigrant group.

The most recent émigrés, in contrast, fled the devastating effects that the Cold War's end had on the island economy. When Soviet aid and trade subsided, Cubans could no longer subsist on their once-adequate earnings. Although arriving in more need of help, Washington had lost interest in privileging Cubans over other immigrants, as it had by then won the Cold War. Accordingly, the Cold War's end disadvantaged New Cubans on both sides of the Florida Straits.

The different émigrés also arrived when different economic conditions prevailed in the US, associated with distinctive labor market options. And they settled in cities with different demographic bases and cultural milieus. The first émigrés contributed to the formation of an Hispanic-friendly environment that made the adaptation of later arrivals both easier and different. The first arrivals faced a nativistic backlash and a culture war, which, after winning first *de facto* and then *de jura*, transformed Miami, where most New Cubans settled, into the "northernmost Latin American city." But Exiles at the same time imposed their own conception of what cultural practices ought to be on the newer immigrants, which they interpreted through their politically based and biased lenses. Immigrant adaptation will be shown to be a by-product of such inter- and intra-ethnic struggles, filtered through pre-immigration formed views on life.

Outline of the Book

Books take on a life of their own, and mine is no exception. The book builds on earlier work of mine, as well as on my life history. Professional influences, for one, led me to write this book. I have devoted my scholarly career to the study of Latin America. Concerned about the poverty and injustices that so many people in the region unfortunately suffered, I first studied the urban poor in Mexico. Many of the city-dwellers were rural-born. They fled the countryside as economic opportunities there deteriorated, despite an agrarian revolution during the first decades of the twentieth century. Questioning why Mexico had as much poverty and inequality in the aftermath of a revolution as other Latin American countries that had never undergone a tumultuous social transformation, I decided to investigate the effects of diverse revolutions in the region, particularly in Bolivia and Cuba, as well as Mexico. Then, as ever more Latin Americans came to realize that neither rural-to-urban migration nor social revolutions were solutions to their plight, I became interested in learning more about those from south of the Rio Grande who in growing numbers came to view the US as their best hope. Steeped in an understanding of Cuba under Castro, I decided to focus particularly on Cuban immigrants.

My personal history further fueled my interest in immigration. While my family did not come from Cuba, unlike those of so many US-based Cuba scholars, my parents were refugees. They were stateless for some years, without a government guaranteeing them full rights and protections. I am the first in my family to be US-born. Had Hitler not made life impossible for Jews, I would not be a child of immigrants. Although my grandparents, parents, sister, and uncles successfully adapted to their adopted country, they suffered the pains of resettling shared with other foreign-born. My family made return trips to their homeland, in contrast to many of the first to flee Cuba under Castro whom I describe in the book. What my parents saw a decade after Hitler's defeat were places where they had lived and worked reduced to rubble. Much of the built environment of their past was nowhere to be found. To this day, when I see collapsed buildings, memories of those rubble heaps that they showed me on one of their first return trips come to mind.

Cuba today differs in many ways from Cuba before the revolution, and in more ways than in its built environment. The book is about these changes, in so far as they impact both on Cubans who emigrated and on their homeland ties. For this reason, the book begins and ends in Cuba. However, to discern aspects of the Cuban émigré experience that are unique and those that are more generalizable, in parts of the book I contrast Cuban with other immigrant group adaptation. I focus especially on comparisons with Dominican and Salvadoran immigrants, from countries with fairly similar sized populations that were similarly subjugated first to Spanish colonial rule and then to US influences. In the latter part of the twentieth century, all three countries also experienced the out-migration of a substantial portion of their populations. As Cuba alone underwent a revolution that instituted a state socialist economy, comparisons between Cubans, on the one hand, and the Dominicans and Salvadorans, on the other, help point to how diasporic experiences and their homeland impact are politically and economically contingent.

In Chapter 1, I describe the making of the Cuban diaspora. I detail the social, economic, and political backgrounds and pre-immigration lived experiences of Cubans who uprooted during different years, beginning with those who first fled the revolution and ending with those who lived through the revolution and its unraveling caused by the Soviet Union's demise. Based on different homeland experiences, I show that émigrés who uprooted at different times have differing life perspectives that they brought with them to the US.

The next two chapters examine Cuban immigrant adaptation in the US. Chapter 2 focuses on social, cultural, economic adaptation, Chapter 3 on political adaptation. I start with a brief overview of the assimilation and transnational conceptual frames through which immigrant experiences typically are assessed, and then offer a historically grounded generation thesis to address aspects that both frames leave unaddressed. My analytic frame takes into account the enduring cross-border effects homeland experiences may have on immigrant adaptation in a new country. Together these two chapters illustrate my thesis, that émigré experiences are best understood when taking their life before uprooting into account. In Chapter 2, I show the first émigrés not only to have assimilated and acculturated to the US milieu into which they moved, but also to have transformed the cities where they settled in largest numbers, Miami, and, second, Union City, New Jersey, in their own image. Their adaptation will be shown to be shaped by deliberate émigré initiatives, determination, and struggles. At the same time, their adaptation will be shown to be partly contingent on age at immigration. Child immigrants have more new, along with old, country experiences than their parents' generation on which they have drawn.

In Chapter 3, I document how in Miami the first arrivals in a short time joined the city's political class, benefited economically from their political influence individually and collectively, and leveraged local for national influence, to the point of setting in motion a foreign policy cycle linked to the presidential electoral cycle. Despite accounting for less than 1 percent of the nation's population, they managed to convince Congress, presidential candidates, and incumbent presidents to implement policies toward their homeland that they desired, between 1992 and 2004. All the while, the New Cubans remained without their own political representation.

The remainder of the book reverses the perspective, as it focuses on émigré dealings with their homeland. It addresses how and why Cubans who uprooted at different times with different experiences have related in various ways to Cuba from their adopted country. Chapters 4 and 5 point to émigré cohort differences in transnational bonding. Most Exiles will be shown to oppose cross-border people-to-people ties. In contrast, the New Cubans covet such ties. The different émigré cohort stances are traceable to their different views on life formed pre immigration. So different are their life perspectives that when émigrés of the different waves actually make trips back to their homeland, they see different Cubas. Described in Chapter 5, Exiles see a destroyed country, their ideal and idealized pre-revolution society nowhere to be found. Recent arrivals see a familiar country, filled with friends and family with whom their lives remain enmeshed. Child immigrants, who draw on both Cuban and US experiences, and values so formed, are more varied in their reactions to trips.

Chapter 6 focuses on cross-border income-sharing and Chapter 7 on the macro effects of such sharing. Although far poorer than earlier émigrés, the New Cubans are shown to remit the most money. In contrast to most Exiles who oppose infusing money into a country whose government they detest, the New Cubans wish to help the families they left behind materially. The moralities of the émigré cohorts differ, in line with their different lived experiences before uprooting.

In Chapter 7, I show how the interests of New Cubans in helping their island families dovetail with the Cuban government's interest in hard currency to finance imports, investments, and servicing of its foreign debt in the post-Soviet era. The government accordingly has initiated reforms to ease diaspora remittance-sending and to encourage its people to have family abroad income-share. I then show how the remittance interests of the state and of ordinary Cubans quickly came into conflict, as officials introduced measures to capture more of every dollar the diaspora remitted. Unable, however, to appropriate all diaspora dollars or to fully control their use, the state showed itself weaker and society stronger than theories of Communism and perceptions of autocratic rule under Castro suggest. Ironically, I show the humble New Cubans to have done more to change Cuba through their cross-border bonding and income-sharing than the rich, powerful Exiles who used their clout to make the wall across the Straits as impermeable as possible. New Cuban people-to-people cross-border ties have had the unintended effect of undermining the state socialist economy, the socialist system of stratification, socialist precepts, and the socialist normative and social order.

After briefly summarizing the US and cross-border experiences of Cuban émigrés detailed in the book, in the concluding chapter I reemphasize the theoretical importance of bringing the lived worlds of foreign-born prior to their uprooting into immigration analyses. I highlight how my theoretical frame provides a basis for understanding differences among first-generation immigrants both in their new country adaptation and transnational engagement that, in combination, other analyses have left inadequately addressed and analyzed.

The chapter ends with a brief discussion of how applicable my historically grounded generational thesis is likely to be for an improved understanding of other immigrant group experiences. And I address how US Cuba policy might be improved by taking into account the range of wants of émigrés who uprooted at different times.

The book, in sum, unequivocally demonstrates that knowing "who they are," that is, who immigrants are, improves our understanding of how foreign-born adapt and why. Such understanding can provide a basis for more informed policy-making.

Data Sources

In this book I make use of many information sources. I draw on published survey, electoral, census, and other statistical data, newspaper accounts, and secondary sources.

Both because Miami is home to most Cuban émigrés and because data is better for Miami than for the Union City area and other communities where Cubans have settled, I focus mainly on the diasporic experience in the Sunshine State city. However, I also examine the Cuban experience in "Havana on the Hudson," Union City, once home to the second largest Cuban community in the US.

In addition, I make use of semi-structured interviews conducted both in the US and Cuba. I interviewed most people between 2000 and 2006. Detailed more in the Appendix, these interviews were both with rank-and-file individuals and with well-placed persons. In total, in the US, I interviewed over one hundred rank-and-file individuals. I targeted persons who had emigrated in different periods. I asked them about their personal background, when they emigrated and why, their US associational involvements, their relationships with other émigrés, the nature of their transnational ties, and if, how, when, and why their cross-border views and involvements had changed. I asked them, in turn, for the names of others to interview, for snowball sampling purposes. In the text, I draw mainly on narratives from these interviews. However, in the Appendix, I summarize quantitatively some of this interview data.

In Florida and New Jersey, I also interviewed nearly eighty politicians, clergy, businesspeople, group leaders, and persons associated with travel agencies and income transfer agencies. These interviewees served as key informants about the émigré communities and about émigré homeland ties, and about how both had changed over the years. I asked these persons about views toward cross-border ties and US Cuba policy, organizational activities, intergroup relations, key community events, and differences among émigré waves in their backgrounds, involvements, and perspectives on Cuban matters. And when appropriate, I asked them the same set of questions about their personal experiences and views as I had asked rank-and-file Cuban American informants. I, in turn, asked them for names of other key persons in diverse institutional domains, as well as names of ordinary émigrés, to interview. In this manner I tapped into multiple networks in the two communities.

Some fifty-four ordinary Cubans, scholars, and government officials were interviewed in Havana between 2000 and 2002, in a similar open-ended manner.[4] The rank-and-file were queried about their lives in the post-Soviet era, how they viewed immigration and immigrants' impact in Cuba, their relations with the diaspora, and how, when, and why their relations had changed. Some people involved in entrepreneurial ventures that possibly made use of remittances were specifically targeted for interviews. The scholars and officials included persons informed about the diaspora, remittances, and studies of immigrants and immigration.

In relying on "open-ended" questioning, I established rapport with the people with whom I spoke, and allowed them to relate their experiences and perceptions through their own lenses. Nonetheless, in that I did not select the people I interviewed in a random fashion, and as I interviewed a relatively limited number of people, their narratives should be viewed as illustrative, and not necessarily as representative. For this reason, their stories provide only one of several sources of information on which I inductively base my analysis.

1 Immigrants and the Weight of Their Past

On January 1, 1959, Cuba's then-president, Fulgencio Batista, fled the country. He was a military man, whose government mainly protected and advanced the concerns of the upper and middle classes. His notoriously corrupt government was known to torture opponents. Disrespecting the 1940 Constitution and the country's 1944 election, Batista governed autocratically in the 1950s. The social order his government protected was conservative and highly stratified. Those who were born rich and poor, light- or dark-skinned, in the city or the countryside, had very different lifestyles, opportunities, and lived experiences.

Batista fled as Fidel Castro, an idealist young landowner's son, led a populist movement with urban and rural support that captured many Cubans' imagination. Riding to power as a nationalist and populist, within less than a decade he oversaw a radical makeover of the country.

The country's social transformation was all-encompassing. Within a few years Castro declared himself a Marxist-Leninist and allied with the Soviet Union. The new government nationalized most businesses, and transformed the polity and the country's values and norms. While the pre-revolution privileged classes lost their base of wealth and prestige, poor people benefited. Pre-revolutionary social classes thus experienced the country's makeover very differently.

Under Castro's rule Cuba underwent many changes that impacted islanders' lives. Periods differed in ideological intensity and emphasis, repression, hardship, and labor demands. However, no change after Castro's consolidation of power had as traumatic an impact on Cubans as the dissolution of the Soviet Union in 1991. At the time, the Cuban economy was so dependent on the superpower for aid and trade that in its absence Cuba experienced an economic depression from which it took about a decade and a half to recover.[1] Near-famine led most Cubans to rethink their perspective on life and to focus their concerns on family and survival. Many of them abandoned any lingering commitment they had to the utopian revolutionary project.

Islanders who left Cuba in different time periods thus had different experiences before uprooting. While I refer the interested reader to my book *Back from the Future: Cuba under Castro* for a detailed description of Cuba under Fidel Castro's rule,[2] the era on which the book focuses, in this chapter I summarize key features of the different periods. In turn, I note the social backgrounds of those who joined the diaspora during each period. First, though, I summarize Cuba-to-US immigration, including a cross-national perspective, to contextualize the discussion of the Cuban diaspora and how, when, and why it changed over the years.

This chapter, intended to provide a context for the focus of the remainder of the book, draws heavily on secondary sources.[3] I intend it to familiarize the uninformed reader with Cuban history under Castro, and how that history has shaped the diaspora. I also incorporate commentaries of Cubans whom I interviewed, to show how islanders who uprooted at different times saw themselves to have distinct experiences and different reasons, accordingly, for uprooting. And I draw on relevant official US and Cuban data on immigration.

Immigration Overview

Between the time that Castro assumed power and the early 2000s approximately one million Cubans emigrated to the US (see Figure 1.1 and sources). These Cubans account for an estimated 89 percent of the country's diaspora.[4]

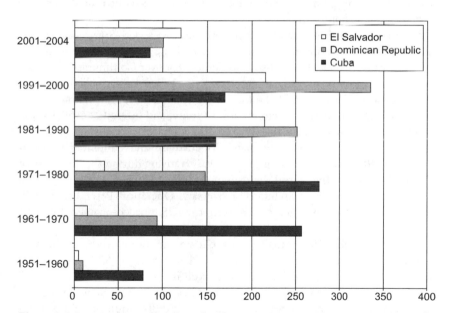

Figure 1.1 Immigrants officially admitted to the US by country of origin, 1951–2004

Sources: U.S. Bureau of the Census (USBC), *Statistical Abstract of the U.S., National Data Book* (U.S. Department of Commerce, Economics and Statistics Administration, U.S. Census Bureau, 1982–83), p. 90, and 1987, p. 11, and 2000, p. 10; U.S. Department of Homeland Security (USDHS), Office of Immigration Statistics, *2004 Yearbook of Immigration Statistics* (Washington, DC: USDHS 2005), pp. 8, 12, 13; and *2005 Yearbook of Immigration Statistics* (Washington, DC: USDHS, 2006), pp. 12, 13.

The first Cubans who arrived after Castro assumed power formed, along with Mexicans, the vanguard of the so-called new immigrant era.[5] But as Latin Americans increasingly replaced Europeans as the majority of US foreign-born, Cubans became less exceptional in their numbers. Before the twentieth century closed, most Latin Americans who moved north of the Rio Grande had emigrated from countries which had not undergone a socialist revolution and had never experienced Communist Party rule. Cubans also became less exceptional in what drove them to uproot. In the post-Soviet era, most Cubans, like most other Latin Americans at the time, emigrated to improve their economic lot, even when they also moved to escape a political regime they disliked (see Appendix).[6]

Cuban immigration to America depended not merely on who wanted to uproot; it also hinged on official Cuban exit and US entry policies. The Cuban government periodically permitted emigration to diffuse domestic discontent. But it was consistently reluctant to let young men leave before serving in the military and young professionals whose skilled labor the economy needed.[7] In turn, Washington most warmly welcomed Cubans when they served its Cold War geopolitical agenda. Once the US became the Cold War victor, US–Cuba bilateral crises, labor market priorities, and commitment to family reunification shaped its Cuban admission policy more. Its priorities contributed to a race and class bias to admission.[8]

With the revolution occurring in the throes of the US–Soviet contest for global domination, Washington initially turned the first émigrés into poster people for the virtues of capitalism and democracy over Communism. Cubans became the most privileged immigrant group. When Castro allied with the Soviet Union, US authorities exempted Cubans from country entry quotas then in effect, subsidized the emigration of some, and offered benefits to ease émigré adaptation.[9] Approximately 225,300 Cubans took advantage of the opportunities Washington immediately opened up and emigrated between 1959 and 1962. Anti-Communist fervor was so strong during the first years of the revolution that the State Department and the CIA even collaborated in a program that the Miami archdiocese oversaw, Operation Peter Pan, which brought more than 14,000 children to the US unaccompanied by their parents.[10]

After the October 1962 Missile Crisis, Cuban emigration to the US became more difficult. The number of entrants totaled 58,500 for 1963 and 1964, and about 9,000 for 1965 (before Castro allowed islanders to leave without US entry permission from Camarioca, described below).[11] Then, between the end of 1965 and 1973, Washington admitted over 260,000 additional Cubans on what US officials called Freedom Flights.[12] The name of the airlift spoke of Washington's Cold War stance toward Cuban émigrés. Following the sunsetting of the special flights, a mere additional 38,000 entered the US during the remainder of the decade.

In the late 1980s and early 1990s, Washington used immigration once again to advance its foreign policy agenda, but this time by clamping down dramatically on the Cubans allowed to enter. In doing so it sought to induce disenchanted islanders to press, instead, for change at home. Washington officials hoped Cubans would follow the example of their former East European comrades and take to the streets to bring their Communist regime to heel. As a result, the Reagan, Bush, and Clinton administrations, combined, issued as few as 11,222 immigrant visas between 1985 and 1994, even though an immigration accord that came into effect in 1984 specified that the US might admit nearly twice that number yearly.[13]

Yet, Washington did not always have the upper hand in controlling Cuban entrants. On three occasions—in 1965, 1980, and 1994—Castro unilaterally opened the door for islanders to leave, to defuse and deflect domestic discontent. In these instances the Cuban government lost control over who it let out and the US lost control over who it let in. Around 7,000, 125,000, and 33,000 islanders, known as Camariocans, Marielitos, and *balseros* (rafters), respectively, took advantage of these opportunities, before bilateral negotiations committed Cuban authorities to halt the unsanctioned Washington emigrations.[14] Camariocans and Marielitos were named after the Cuban ports from which they departed. The Cuban government allowed the Camariocan exodus to rid the country of islanders who previously had been unable or reluctant to emigrate but who opposed the country's radical transformation, which the other two exoduses occurred when the government faced outbursts of domestic unrest.[15]

In that the 1966 Cuban Adjustment Act, a legislative Cold War initiative, allowed almost any Cuban who touched US soil without an entry permit to qualify for residence status in a year and a day, and accordingly to qualify for work rights and a path to citizenship, the illegal 1965, 1980, and 1994 entrants could almost immediately adjust their status and enjoy legal immigrant rights.[16] Such unique entitlements help explain the notable absence of Cubans from the 2006 protests across the US, in which immigrants demanded economic and political rights.

Each of the three large-scale illegal exoduses induced Washington to sign special bilateral immigration accords with Cuba. US authorities agreed to the accords to restore order to who it permitted entry,[17] and as such reflected how Castro had orchestrated tumult in the Florida Straits to influence US immigration policy. The first agreement, a Memorandum of Understanding, established the previously mentioned Freedom Flights that brought more than a quarter of a million Cubans to the US between 1965 and 1973. The second accord, signed in 1984, entitled up to twenty thousand islanders yearly entry, while accords signed in 1994 and 1995 committed the US to accept a minimum of twenty thousand islanders yearly. The 1990s accords specified that a portion of admits be on the basis of a newly instituted lottery.[18]

With Washington having abolished individual country immigration quotas by the 1980s, the 1984 and 1990s accords formalized unique Cuban admission rights. And Cubans were almost unique among those admitted in being officially classified as refugees and asylum seekers.[19] However, in their effect the accords proved not to favor Cubans over other immigrants. Figure 1.1 shows that in the closing decades of the twentieth century the US admitted more immigrants from the Dominican Republic and El Salvador, countries of roughly Cuba's demographic size, and many more from far larger Mexico.[20] More Latin Americans from countries with market economies and (at least minimal) democratic polities than from Cuba moved to the US. They sought refuge from declining opportunities associated with neoliberal restructuring in their homelands. In the 1980s, Salvadoran émigrés also fled a civil war.

Washington, meanwhile, did not always honor the minimum Cuban entry allotment specified in the 1990s accords, after not having honored the maximum entitlement specified in the 1984 accord. In only half of the first ten years following the signing of the 1990s accords did Washington officially admit at least twenty thousand Cubans.[21] And the 1995 accord, which calls for the US and Cuban governments to collaborate in returning to Cuba islanders found at sea trying to emigrate without official permission, contributed to containing the number of illegal Cuban entrants.

In sum, immediately following the revolution an exceptionally large percentage of Cubans emigrated, and Cubans accounted for an exceptionally large portion of US admits. By the turn of the millennium, however, that was no longer true.

The Self-Defined Exiles: The Pre-Revolutionary Generation that Opposed Cuba's Radical Makeover, 1959 to 1980[22]

Despite widespread unemployment, underemployment and political repression, few Cubans emigrated before the revolution. At the time, US admissions policy favored Europeans, while US immigration had yet to become part of Cubans', and most other Latin Americans', repertoire of responses to difficult homeland conditions.[23] And the well-to-do had little reason to leave. They were a close-knit group, with strong family ties, who enjoyed a life of luxury. They typically socialized together at racially and socially exclusive clubs and married within their social class.[24] One of the island clubs was so exclusive that it had even refused Batista admission, because members considered him a mixed blood laborer's son.[25] They also participated together in civic groups. Batista's autocratic rule was not so complete as to prevent them from doing so.

The exodus from Cuba under Castro began with the emigration of Batista's close collaborators, known as Batistianos. The privileged classes soon joined them, in response to the new government's expropriation, first, of large and then of medium-sized landholdings, and then of everything but small businesses by 1963. They soon were joined by the politically engaged who became disillusioned with the radical and autocratic turn of the revolution. These émigrés form the core of the cohort who define themselves as exiles.[26] Most of them left when they lost the basis of their livelihood and lifestyle. Despite their definition of themselves as exiles, only a small number of them had actually suffered for their political convictions. An important minority, however, as I illustrate, suffered deeply for their opposition to the revolution. They came to the US to escape imprisonment, discrimination, and execution for their political commitments.[27] To all intents and purposes, this émigré wave, which filtered the country's social transformation through pre-revolutionary lenses and interpreted their uprooting as politically driven, ended with the last of the Freedom Flights in 1973. They constitute the cohort of arrivals I refer to as Exiles.

Their Class Base

Indicative that pre-revolutionary well-to-do quickly fled the country's radical makeover, Table 1.1 shows businesspeople, managers, and professionals, who had comprised 9 percent of the labor force under Batista, account for almost a third of the Cubans who moved to the US in the first three years of Castro's rule. These elite Cubans typically were conservative Catholics, and almost entirely light-skinned. For them the revolution represented a rejection of all that they stood for.

The new island government required those who uprooted to leave most of their economic assets behind. They could not take more with them than would fit into what Castro loyalists called *gusano* bags, worm-shaped duffle containers. "*Gusanos* for the *gusanos*," worms for the worms.[28] The new government pejoratively called the very émigrés who came to be viewed in the US as Golden Exiles as *gusanos*, crawling vermin.

Carlos Eire, in his eloquent memoir, *Waiting for Snow in Havana*, summarized the loss that drove his social class and race-based social world to flee. "[T]hat god-damned place where everything I knew was destroyed. Wrecked in the name of fairness. In the name of progress. In the name of the oppressed and of love for the gods of Marx and Lenin."[29] Eire remembers well the personal nannies he and each of his siblings had. So too does he remember the private Catholic school he attended, where *la crème de la crème* of Havana boys were educated, which closed in April 1962 because too few of its teachers and students remained. They "vanished without saying a word. One day they'd be there, and the next day they'd be gone."[30] Soon after the school shut, he too joined the exodus, at age eleven. He was one of the children who left in the Miami archdiocese-organized, US government-funded, Operation Peter Pan.

The pre-revolutionary privileged fled to an America they in many respects admired.[31] They knew the country from Hollywood movies and television shows they saw, from the cars they drove, from the clothes they wore, from the Coke and Pepsi they sipped, from the comics they read, and from the US tourists who visited the island. They also knew US investors and ex-patriots, with their lifestyle of luxury and country clubs, and conspicuous consumption. Privileged Cuban children even played American games and had American theme birthday parties.[32] Well-to-do Cubans, in turn, knew the US first-hand from their travels, and some from their studies at elite US schools.[33] They

Table 1.1 Cuban occupational structure and last job held in Cuba by émigrés to the US (select years, in percentages)

A. Cuban occupational structure

JOB IN CUBA[a]	1953	1975	1980	1989	2000	2005
Professional/ manager & Semi-professional	9%	9%	9%	6%	8%	8%
Technical	—	13	19	22	21	25
Clerical, sales	14	5	7	7	4	5
Skilled, Semi-skilled, unskilled[b]	27	57	52	52	50	37
Services	8	15	13	14	17	23
Agriculture, fishing	42	—	—	—	—	—
TOTAL PERCENTAGE[c]	100	99	100	101	100	98
TOTAL INDIVIDUALS[d]	1938	2600	3641	3843	4379	4723

B. Last job in Cuba held by émigré cohorts[e]

LAST JOB IN CUBA[a]	1959–62	1965–66	1970	1980	1990	1995	2000	2005[f]
Professional/ manager & Semi-professional	31%	21%	12%	11%	12%	19%	24%	14%
Clerical, sales	33	32	30	7	14	12	14	17
Skilled	17[g]	22	25	26	16	11	9	15
Semi-skilled, unskilled	8	12	16	45	35	41	34	31
Services	7	9	9	5	22	17	17	22
Agriculture, fishing	4	5	7	7	.01	.01	1	1
TOTAL PERCENTAGE[c]	100	101	99	101	99	100	99	100
TOTAL INDIVIDUALS	27,419	17,124	14,755	5,809	5,017	6,017	5,496	5,379

Sources: Silvia Pedraza-Bailey, 1985: 22, and references therein; U.S. Department of Justice (USDJ), Immigration and Naturalization Service (INS), *1990 Statistical Yearbook of the INS* (Washington DC: U.S. Government Printing Office, December 1991), p. 87, *1995 Statistical Yearbook* (Washington DC: U.S. Government Printing Office, 1997), p. 71, and *2000 Statistical Yearbook of the INS* (USDJ, INS, 2002), p. 79; USDHS, "Immigration Statistics 2006" (www.dhs.gov/ximgtn/statistics); Comité Estatal de Estadísticas (CEE), *Anuario Estadístico de Cuba 1989* (Havana: CEE, 1991), p. 126; Oficina Nacional de Estadísticas (ONE), *Anuario Estadístico de Cuba 2000* and *Anuario Estadistico de Cuba 2005* (Havana: ONE, 2001 and www.one.cu/anuariopdf, 2005), p. 123.

Notes:
a Officially reported occupational categories change after 1959 to worker, technical, administrative, service, and management, roughly equivalent, respectively, to worker (skilled, semi-skilled, and unskilled), technical (without equivalent), clerical and sales, service, and professional/manager in the 1953 census.
b Includes semi-skilled and unskilled workers.
c Total percentages do not always equal 100 due to rounding of occupational distributions to the nearest whole number.
d In thousands.
e Among people who worked in Cuba, for whom information is available
f Entrants according to year became permanent US residents.
g Includes operators and laborers, craft and repair workers

visited the US to shop, to vacation, and to do business, and moved between the two countries with considerable ease. They were "Americanized" without emigrating, and without displacing their ideas of old.

When they fled to the US after Castro took power, they presumed their stay in the US would be temporary, until the radical populist government was toppled. Some of them were determined to bring the regime to heel. The most notorious attempt was in 1961, when fourteen hundred of the self-defined exiles, mainly middle- and upper-class whites, invaded Cuba at the Bay of Pigs to reclaim their homeland. Cubans had a history of plotting revenge and political change from the US dating back to the days of José Martí, Cuba's most revered national hero. Martí had connived the island's late nineteenth-century independence movement from the US. While the 1961 invasion failed, the first émigrés remained committed to Castro's overthrow. Reflecting on how these émigrés held on to their past in anticipation of returning to their homeland, a retired actress, Diana, with whom I spoke in 2001, sadly conveyed, "What we thought would be six months turned into more than forty years . . . Cemeteries in the US are filled with the hopes of thousands of exiles who died yearning they would return soon to Cuba."

While the pre-revolution privileged class dominated the initial exodus, they continued to exit until the sunsetting of the Freedom Flights. Fewer of them uprooted as the years went on because fewer of them were left to leave. Nonetheless, some well-to-do initially had stayed, convinced that Castro's rule would be short-lived, after which they could resume the life and lifestyle they savored. Others initially stayed because they, for one reason or another, were unable to leave, or because they had not attained US entry permission. And still others at first supported Castro, but became disillusioned with the country's radical makeover.

To this day, some pre-revolution well-to-do remain on the island. Not forgetting their past, they still assess the revolution critically, through their pre-revolutionary-formed life perspective, even if they keep their thoughts mainly to themselves. Wendy Gimbel, in *Havana Dreams*, for example, portrays the world of an upper-class woman who stayed behind, who even after some thirty years of Castro's rule still resented and resisted the loss of her past.[34] For aristocratic ladies,

> immured among their remaining possessions, survival was in pretending pre-revolutionary Cuba would come back . . . Soon they would be shopping at the French salon . . . packing their Vuitton trunks for their trips to Paris, attending the New Year's Eve party at the Vedado Country Club, or the Christmas tea dance at the Havana Yacht Club.

She quotes one woman whose life she portrays: "We couldn't imagine ourselves going to another country. Who would we have become without our position or our possessions?" While her jewels became artifacts of a lifestyle no longer livable in a transformed Cuba, others from her social circle took a shared mindset with them when emigrating to the other side of the Florida Straits.[35]

The petty bourgeoisie also emigrated in large numbers, and there were more of them to uproot. Table 1.1 shows that one-third of émigrés until the Freedom Flights ended had held clerical and sales jobs. Never favorably predisposed to the revolution, government takeover of small businesses in 1968 fueled their ongoing exodus.[36] The 1968 expropriations marked the final state intervention to wipe out the private property base of pre-revolution social classes.

In smaller but increasing numbers, workers also left. Maurice Zeitlin found that workers reacted differently to the revolution depending on their generational experiences.[37] The workers most supportive of their country's radical remaking, whom he interviewed on the island in 1962, were of the so-called generation of 1953, the generation which, when reaching adulthood, experienced, and opposed, Batista's usurpation of power. His survey of workers accordingly found that even Cubans of the same social class, and of the class in whose name the revolution claimed to be made, viewed the revolution differently, depending on pre-revolution experiences when coming of age to interpret life for themselves.[38]

In contrast, few at the very bottom of the socio-economic spectrum left the island. This was largely because they benefited from new government-guaranteed employment, the improvement of earnings for low-wage workers, the expansion of free education and health care, and other reforms. When expropriating the largest landholdings in 1959, and so-called medium holdings four years later, the government gave sharecroppers title to land they tilled and wage workers rights to year-round employment. By the end of the 1960s the small farmers were the only remaining property owners. Benefiting from the government initiatives, agriculturalists, who constituted over 40 percent of the workforce, accounted for a mere 4 to 7 percent of islanders who uprooted between the time Castro assumed power and the final Freedom Flight (Table 1.1).

Before long, however, new government regulations limited agriculturalists' earnings and control over what they produced. This led some small private farmers to follow the example of the pre-revolution elite and leave the country.[39]

Thus, while the top echelon of the pre-revolutionary class order was overrepresented among Cubans who uprooted as the revolution radicalized, the lower echelon was underrepresented. The different social class proclivity to uproot revealed how emigration had economic underpinnings even when those who moved to the US rationalized their exodus politically. And their different proclivity reflects how different social classes tended to respond in opposite ways to the key event of their times. They viewed it through different lenses, with different interests and concerns.

But the class base to emigration hinged not merely on who lost and who gained with the revolution. It hinged also on US entry biases. In initially giving preference to Cubans who had acquired US travel visas before the revolution,[40] Washington institutionalized a class bias that continued in ensuing years. The well-to-do had attained most of the travel visas. With Washington subsequently prioritizing family reunification, relatives of the first émigrés enjoyed an admit advantage. Washington additionally reinforced the class bias by giving priority to islanders with skills.

Their Race and Age

Largely because of the class bias, there was also a racial bias to emigration. In pre-revolutionary Cuba, class and race were so intertwined that Eire noted how white his privileged island world had been before he emigrated in 1962.[41] The class bias to Washington's admission policy accordingly was racist in its effect, independent of intent. Indicative of how race-biased immigration was, 1970 census data, summarized in Table 1.2, show 97 percent of 1960s émigrés defined themselves as White. At the time of the last pre-revolution island census, in 1953, 73 percent of Cubans were classified as White.[42]

Table 1.2 Race, gender, and age of immigration among Cuban Americans in Miami and nationwide in census years 1970–2000 (percentage of cohort)

| Census year[b] | White[a] | Male | Age at migration | | | | |
			Under 18[c]	18–24	25–39	40–64	65+
A. National							
1970							
Pre-1960s	95	48	23	23	40	13	1
1960s	97	46	27	9	31	28	5
1980							
Pre-1960s	84	49	19	24	42	15	0
1960s	86	46	26	10	33	29	2
1970s	80	46	27	7	27	31	8
1990							
Pre-1960s	86	47	22	26	42	10	0
1960s	89	45	27	11	35	26	1
1970s	82	45	27	7	28	33	5
1980s	81	55	20	13	33	27	7
2000							
Pre-1960s	90	44	23	27	44	6	0
1960s	92	43	33	13	36	18	0
1970s	87	45	30	8	32	29	1
1980s	83	55	21	14	37	25	3
1990s	86	54	16	14	37	27	6
B. Miami							
1970							
Pre-1960s	99	47	24	17	41	17	1
1960s	100	46	26	9	29	31	5

1980							
Pre-1960s	91	47	18	21	42	18	0
1960s	89	45	23	9	32	33	2
1970s	84	45	24	6	27	34	10
1990							
Pre-1960s	95	46	22	25	41	12	0
1960s	94	44	23	11	35	30	1
1970s	90	44	23	6	29	36	6
1980s	91	52	20	11	32	29	8
2000							
Pre-1960s[b]	95	43	18	24	49	9	0
1960s	95	41	28	13	38	21	0
1970s	94	43	25	7	33	34	1
1980s	91	52	20	13	36	27	4
1990s	92	52	16	14	36	28	7

Source: Steven Ruggles and Matthew Sobek, et al., *Integrated Public Use Microdata Series* (*IPUMS*), Version 3.0 (Minneapolis: Historical Census Projects University of Minnesota, 2003, www.ipums.org).

Notes:
a Non-Whites mainly include census respondents who self-identified as mixed-race or Black.
b In all census tables in the book I classify immigrant children under age five as US-born, since most of their outside-the-home socialization occurred in the US. My conceptualization of second-generation immigrants accordingly is sociological, not specifically country-of-birth defined. Cuban ethnicity in the 1970 census derives from the Hispanic identity variable, while in the 1980 to 2000 censuses Cuban ethnicity draws on "Cuban ancestry" as well as Hispanic identity information.
c Total percentages on age-at-migration do not always equal 100 due to rounding up to the nearest whole number.

Table 1.2 further shows that age influenced who emigrated, separately and in combination with race and social class. Cubans who emigrated before the revolution were far younger, on average, than those who uprooted during the first decade under Castro. In strategically turning to youth to become both children and agents of the revolution, Castro won over their hearts and minds. Youth were integrated into the revolution first through a countrywide literacy campaign, and then through the radically revamped and expanded education system.[43] As a result, parents and grandparents sometimes packed up and left while their late adolescent children, by choice, stayed. Meanwhile, young children who emigrated mainly did so at their parents' choosing, as they were not old enough to decide for themselves whether or not to side with the revolution.

Their Political Leanings

Over time some Cubans who initially sided with Castro became disaffected. They opposed the revolution's increasingly Marxist-Leninist turn and demands made on them which they disapproved of. In the course of the 1960s the government and the Communist Party, reorganized as a Leninist "vanguard party," pushed to create what "Che" Guevara referred to as a "new man" with a new conscience committed to egalitarian precepts, selflessness, the collective good, non-material reward, hard work, self-improvement, and obedience.[44] The populace was expected to participate in new state-linked mass organizations and in popular militias, and to help out in agriculture, especially in back-breaking sugar harvesting. In the name of the utopian project, people were called upon to make material and other sacrifices. The committed believed in the mission and happily obliged, but those who objected faced castigation, assignment to labor camps, and, in some instances, imprisonment. In the name of the revolution, the government also cracked down on the religiously committed and on both political and cultural non-conformists.[45]

Patricio, whom I interviewed in Union City in 2001, demonstrates that not even all with the "right" age and class profile sided with the revolution, and that those who did not suffered for principles they believed in. He had a harrowing set of experiences before emigrating in 1970, which, to this day, filter his views toward the revolution. His family had been an immediate, but only short-term, beneficiary of the new Cuba. Thanks to the first agrarian reform, his grandfather, a sharecropper, received title to the land that he had tilled. However, the government controlled what he produced, and required that he sell his crops to the state at low, fixed prices. Disillusioned by his family's experience, in school Patricio refused to comply with government-mandated allegiance to the revolution. Disobedient, he was conscripted into the army. Refusing, in turn, to comply with pledges demanded of soldiers, he was sent to a "reeducation camp," along with homosexuals, Jehovah's Witnesses, Seventh-Day Adventists, dissidents, and pimps, to be socialized to the values of the revolution. At the camp he encountered cruel and inhumane treatment. He had to perform grueling, difficult work. And there he witnessed a firing squad shoot a friend of his in the genitals. When the government closed the camp, he was imprisoned for attempting to flee the country without an emigration permit. While cutting cane as a prison laborer he managed, however, to escape. He made his way to the US base in Guantanamo, where he gained US entry as a refugee. Patricio's experience reveals that repression did not necessarily succeed in compelling, when new state institutions failed to convince, young Cubans to adopt the revolutionary perspective for themselves.

Patricio was not alone among the Cubans who emigrated during the first two decades of Castro's rule with disconcerting experiences that remained part of their remembered Cuba. Two others whom I interviewed similarly exemplify the price those who opposed the revolution paid. One man who had been jailed in 1960 for attempting to subvert the revolution escaped five years later and fled immediately by speedboat to Florida. He felt that his name would have been on a black list had he remained in Cuba. And a couple fled in the mid-1960s after the wife's brother and two of his sons had been killed by what they defined as "Castro's army," and another of her brothers imprisoned for opposing the revolution. The couple fled, fearful that their own lives were at risk.

The very act of soliciting an exit permit caused suffering. In treating harshly those who sought to leave, the government gave others incentive to stay. Those requesting permits lost their jobs, and some of them were sent to perform forced labor for years before being allowed to depart. One man who emigrated in 1974 at age forty-one spoke to me of the harsh "psychological war which could drive you crazy" that he experienced after requesting permission to move to the US. These memories continued to shape his views toward the revolution after living for decades in the US.

Cuba Remembered

In their new land, Exiles continued to filter their homeland memories through shared, pre-revolution lenses. This was especially true of adult émigrés, who were old enough when they left to have interpreted life for themselves.

The wealthiest and most politicized Exiles tended to set the tone and norms for them all. They remained fiercely anti-Castro even though their conception of the country under Castro became mainly a construct of their imagination, given how little of the revolution they had personally experienced. They imagined their homeland through rose-colored pre-revolution lenses that blinded them to injustices which had prevailed in their midst. The little they experienced in Cuba under Castro they interpreted critically, with political spin. Many claimed to have suffered for their political convictions partly because they considered victimization under Castro a badge of honor. Speaking of the norms, views, and perspective that avid anti-Castroites took on in their new land, a businessperson who left Cuba before the revolution noted, when we talked in 2000, how Exiles in Miami frequently reinterpreted their past through their anti-Castro lenses.

> They claim to have been political prisoners and to have been treated unjustly for their political convictions, but when you have a conversation about what really happened to them, many experienced trivial problems ... They didn't have to leave ... Everyone claims to have had political problems.

Having never himself experienced the societal makeover, he never took on the Exile mindset for himself.

Antipathy towards the revolution remained so strong among émigrés who uprooted during the first two decades of Castro's rule that they identified with one another, especially on matters Cuban, despite class differences that divided them. And together most of them interpreted island emigration as politically driven.[46] A Cuba-born lawyer from a prominent pre-revolutionary family who moved to Miami in the late 1960s spoke on the point. He stated to me in 2000 that Cubans who emigrated during the first twenty years of Castro's rule collectively remained frozen in their past. While perceiving themselves as exiles, that identity, he admitted, had become increasingly tenuous with so many of them having opted for US citizenship and having made the US their home. He also acknowledged that only a minority of them were authentic political refugees, whose life, as opposed to lifestyle, would have been endangered had they stayed in Cuba.

In a similar vein, a Spanish-born priest whose family had emigrated to Cuba and who after fleeing the revolution ministered at a parish in Union City, reflected at the century's turn on how pre-1980 émigrés stayed wedded to life before Fidel, even after decades in the US "They live like in the old days, . . . as if in Cuba forty years ago." By way of example he noted that girls are chaperoned here, even if not as frequently as they were in Cuba, and rarely do girls have children out of wedlock. "Cuba has changed but Cuban Americans are living by traditions of pre-revolutionary Cuba." He added that "at least half of them are better off here, but they fantasize about what they had in Cuba . . . [and] they say they don't want to live in an atheist country [which Cuba under Castro officially was until a 1992 Constitutional reform], yet they don't go to church here." The priest accordingly alluded to how the life views of pre-1980 émigrés, rooted in their pre-immigration, pre-revolutionary past, were cultural and not merely political.

Both the lawyer and the priest point to what Lisandro Pérez refers to as an exile ideology, conservative and fervently anti-Castro.[47] The island-born who emigrated before 1980, especially those who maintain close ties with one another, live in a milieu that reinforces their old country mindset, even as they have adapted to the US. While most of them severed ties with their homeland physically, in their minds Cuba remained very much alive. They identified with a nation detached from the island transformed by revolution, with their nationalism taking on a life of its own, distinct from and in opposition to the nationalism the new government imbued in Cubans who stayed.

1980 Mariel Émigrés with Diverse Mixes of Pre-Revolution and Revolution Experiences

Following the ending of the Freedom Flights few Cubans emigrated during the 1970s, years when the government initiated a number of reforms that, in principle, made life easier, that improved living standards, and that made for a polity more responsive to ordinary people's concerns. It permitted more self-employment and set up worker-brigades to build much-needed housing. It also set about to institutionalize the revolution politically, through a system of local to national level governance known as Popular Power.[48] At the same time, it called upon late adolescent Cubans to partake in military and other overseas missions, mainly in Africa, with the goal of helping to bring about revolutionary change in other Third World countries as well.

Yet, neither the domestic changes nor the international solidarity initiatives won over the hearts and minds of all who remained in the country. First-ever émigré return visits on a large scale, in the late 1970s, sparked the 1980 exodus of over one hundred thousand Cubans from the port of Mariel.

Self-defined exiles visited determined to demonstrate how right they had been to leave. They lavished their island family with gifts and recounted stories of their prosperity and freedom in the US.

With whetted appetites to leave, some ten thousand Cubans stormed the Peruvian Embassy.[49] Envisioning no way to bring about domestic change, the disgruntled islanders en masse sought refuge abroad. To discredit them, Castro portrayed them as antisocial. He claimed that for this reason he wished them to leave.[50] He let it be known that officials would not stand in the way of families in the US who picked them up at the port of Mariel.

Who Emigrated and Their Experiences

The Mariel generation was also socio-economically diverse. It included some prominent intellectuals, with the author Reinaldo Arenas the most renowned. Having been unable to publish in Cuba since 1967, and having suffered repression and imprisonment, he had wanted to leave what he considered the "land of horrors" for many years.[51] Overall, though, Table 1.1 shows the Mariel cohort to be exceptionally working class, in comparison both to earlier émigrés and the island labor force. They were almost the class antithesis of Exiles. In leaving the island without either Cuban exit or US entry permission, official immigration biases did not stand in their way.

The Mariel cohort differed somewhat from earlier émigrés racially as well. The exodus included more who were dark-skinned (Table 1.2). Although only a minority were dark-skinned, their numbers were enough to convince the Exiles to see themselves as different and socially superior. In the process, pre-revolutionary racial, as well as class, divisions reasserted themselves on the US side of the Straits.

Castro contributed further to émigré cohort differences by loading mental patients and criminals onto the boats that took Cubans to the US from Mariel. Stigma toward some Marielitos tainted the image of others, even though 80 percent of the 1980 arrivals had no criminal record, and most of those with criminal records committed minor illegal acts, such as dollar-dealing, not recognized as a crime in the US[52] and decriminalized even in Cuba in 1993. Moreover, in conjunction with the 1984 bilateral immigration accord US authorities returned to Cuba so-called undesirables. In differentiating themselves, earlier émigrés referred to the new arrivals as Marielitos. I refer to them similarly, but with no condescension implied.

Beginning with the Mariel exodus the age and gender-base of those uprooting also changed. The percentage of young adults, 18–24 year-olds, among arrivals doubled (Table 1.2).[53] These young adults were the first émigrés to have been "children of the revolution" and to have not known pre-revolutionary life first-hand. Also, for the first time under Castro, men outnumbered women.

Having lived more years in Cuba-transformed, Marielitos had more basis than earlier émigrés on which to judge their country's makeover. Their very petitioning for permission to leave proved painful without precedent, and formed part of the island experience that they brought with them to the US. While officials castigated them, as they had people who solicited to leave in the past, for the first (and only) time they simultaneously galvanized neighbors and co-workers to turn on those opting out. The Party called on institutions of the new society, unions, and the Committees for the Defense of the Revolution, to mobilize the loyal against the new "turncoats." The politically committed staged *actos de repudio*, repudiation acts, against those who wanted to uproot. In night-time rampages, loyalists pelted the homes of those who had requested exit permits. And before applicants could depart, they had to sign documents in which they confessed to being social deviants and to having committed crimes against the state.[54] In discrediting those who sought to leave with the support of ordinary Cubans, the government sought to reaffirm the values of the new society, and keep others from leaving.

Cubans with whom I spoke confirmed the indignities Marielitos suffered. Anita, a doctor now living in Miami, for example, reported experiencing fifteen *actos de repudio* at the hospital where she worked and in the neighborhood where she lived. Upon announcing her wish to leave, she found herself treated like a social pariah. She was among Cubans branded "*escoria*," scum. Although relatives had come to pick up her family, officials only let one of them leave, and she was not the fortunate one. Denied permission to exit, she was forced to live amidst colleagues who had turned on her. Anita noted that when she returned to work in her hospital co-workers treated her like a criminal. "It was like a civil war," she reflected. She added that she knew fellow doctors who were thrown into trash cans, and who had feces thrown at them after announcing a desire to leave. "They didn't kill us, but they also didn't let us live." Branded a counter-revolutionary, authorities went on to punish her by assigning her to a rural hospital, and compelling her to leave her two-year-old son behind in Havana with family. "Eventually," she said, "the situation at work got so bad that I quit and I left the country." She found an opportunity to leave via Spain in 1985.

Beatriz, who emigrated to Union City in 1991 and who now works as a daycare provider, in turn, recalled how she paid a price in Cuba not even for her own but for her father's decision to leave during the Mariel exodus. "It was a very difficult time." In Beatriz's case, her prospects for career advancement ground to a halt after the Union of Communist Youth expelled her for ties she maintained with her father after he moved to the US. "To be accepted within Cuban society I had to give up contact with my father. The bitterness built up to the point that I couldn't stay." During Mariel times she also remembers witnessing a neighbor dragged through the streets naked because she made it known that she wanted to leave.

The age diversity among Marielitos meant, however, that the cohort varied in experiences before uprooting. Older émigré familiarity with life before the revolution filtered how they had assessed the country transformed. Some of them had previously wanted to leave, but were unable to do so for one reason or another. The younger, in contrast, could only filter the revolution indirectly through pre-revolutionary lenses, on the basis of stories that their parents and grandparents told them. Their first-hand experiences were entirely grounded in the country transformed. For this reason, age diversity made for an eclectic émigré cohort, in terms of experiences and views so formed, even when Marielitos together rejected the revolution.

At the same time, both the young and old of the Mariel generation understood the complexities of the revolution better than earlier émigrés. They were better positioned to recognize accomplishments, along with failures, of the island's makeover and to recognize differences among islanders in their commitment to the revolution. They had a basis on which to be more nuanced in their assessments.

Pulitzer Prize-winning reporter Mirta Ojito, who fled Cuba as a teenager during Mariel, illustrates how youth who left during Mariel filtered the revolution through values learned at home, from parents familiar with life before Fidel. But she was also exposed to values of the new society-in-the-making, at school and other institutional settings. In cases such as Ojito's, the two sets of values conflicted, and she found her parents' more compelling. In her memoir *Finding Mañana*, she describes how her parents had always raised her to know that one day they would leave Cuba.[55] They could not exit on a Freedom Flight because her father was ineligible. Under twenty-seven at the time, he had to complete military service before qualifying for permission to leave. Although born poor in the countryside, her parents were blinded to injustices under Batista, and they never believed that Castro would make a better world.[56] Her family made her sensitive to repression in her midst and wary of participating in political activity at school. Cognizant that "Anyone expressing desire to emigrate was ostracized, harassed and denied jobs and access to higher education," she kept her home-learned anti-Castro views to herself. Yet, she sensed that her private views were commonly shared. She knew others who similarly grew up "with two separate and distinct allegiances—to the revolution and to . . . families."[57]

Also illustrative of how island youth filtered their experiences through both institutions of the new society, as well as sometimes conflicting values learned at home, is Ricardo's experience. Now a retail store owner in Union City, Ricardo emigrated the same year as Ojito, and, similarly, as a teenager. He described how he grew up in a household that predisposed him to view hardships of his youth through anti-revolutionary lenses. His father had been a political prisoner. Rather than see school positively, as the training ground for building a new utopian society and new man, he instead focused on the negative aspects. School, for him, was repressive. He recollected how, after leaving home at 6:00 in the morning to make a thirty-mile trek to school, the director would not let him in if he were late. School officials would not allow him to complain about transportation problems, because they considered that a criticism of the revolution. He also remembered, and not happily, how teachers reprimanded his peers who wore sneakers and gold chains. Teachers suspected that the items came from *"gusanos,"* from family who had rejected the country's makeover. The government at the time emphasized that loyal revolutionaries were not to have contact with the *"gusanos."* Twenty years after moving to the US, such childhood memories kept him, like Ojito, critical of the revolution. Yet, he, along with his mother, also have positive memories of friends and family who stayed in Cuba. They distinguish the personal from the political.

Monica, a sixth grader during Mariel who emigrated eight years later, also reflected, when we spoke, on repression that she experienced as a child. A talented musician, she attended a very prestigious music academy. However, she suffered for her religious convictions. She was constantly reminded that as a practicing Protestant she had been admitted only conditionally, because it was "unjust for her to take the place of a talented, loyal *compañero*." Ultimately, she was indeed forced to leave the academy. Monica claims that her father was persecuted even more than she for his religious beliefs.

Yet, like Ricardo, Monica distinguished the personal from the political, with mixed feelings. She recalls how even to joke about emigration had been no laughing matter. She jocularly said to school friends that she planned to be a rafter and leave the country. The next day policemen came to her neighborhood looking for her family. They went to her representative of the CDR, the state-linked block organization, for assistance. She fondly recalls, however, how her block representative, a close family friend, chose to distract the police while sending someone to warn them that the police were coming. Alerted, her mother quickly burned documents that she thought were compromising, including religious papers and family passports that implied intent to emigrate. When the state agents came they found nothing incriminating.

An Incipient New Country Émigré Divide

While Marielitos never experienced in the US indignities comparable to the *actos de repudio* or the blatant discrimination they faced before departing, many of them did not enjoy the warm welcome they had anticipated. In distancing themselves, earlier émigrés spoke to me disparagingly about Marielito language, dress, and demeanor, and their "weird slang."[58]

The different Cubas Mariel and earlier émigrés experienced before uprooting filtered their views toward each other. Perceiving the recent arrivals through their anti-Castro pre-revolutionary-formed political lenses, earlier émigrés looked down on Marielitos not merely because of their lifestyle differences but also because they resented that Marielitos had stayed in Cuba so long. Mariel émigrés with whom I spoke reflected on how pained they were when relatives who left soon after the revolution rebuffed them upon their arrival in the US. One young Marielita, Justina, spoke of how her grandparents, who emigrated shortly after losing their land in 1959, with the first agrarian reform, refused to forgive her father, a teenager at the time, for siding with the revolution. Angry that she and her parents had stayed under Castro's spell as long as they had, her grandparents refused to meet them when they arrived in Miami.

But Marielitos, in turn, looked down on earlier émigrés, who suffered little under Castro and who were indifferent to their suffering. They also felt the early émigrés did not understand the transformed Cuba that they rejected. Both Justina and Monica expressed such complaints. Justina, for example, resented her grandparents' indifference to the price her father paid for staying in Cuba. Because he refused to participate in a pro-Communist march, Party cadre blocked his graduation from the university. She was also critical of her grandparents and others of their generation who were so stuck in their pre-revolutionary mindset that they refused to recognize that their idealized, remembered Cuba no longer existed. She noted when we talked in 2001 that her grandparents' generation had difficulty accepting anything that was a product of the revolution. "The older exiles feel it their obligation to rebuild the Cuba they knew rather than accept the reality that forty years have passed and there is a new Cuba." Monica disdained Exiles' arrogance, as well as their insensitivity to her own painful experiences.

Two other 1980s arrivals also spoke disparagingly to me of early émigrés who considered themselves superior. One, Anita, an island-trained doctor, noted that while Mariel arrivals "were looked down upon," she was proud of her generation. "We are more tolerant and more humane . . . Those who came in the 1960s are disconnected, but we who came in the 1980s know what it was like to grow up in Castro's Cuba." She held old-timers in contempt. She found them intolerant and prejudiced. In contrast, "We Marielitos care about freedom and think that it's a waste of time to be nostalgic, obsessed with the past." The other émigré, Natalio, who emigrated in 1981 at age thirty-two to Miami where he established a courier business, also viewed his generation (and more recent émigrés) as different and better than the first arrivals. He noted,

> The older generation and earlier migrants never knew and don't really understand Communism. However, we . . . understand the intention of the revolution was to improve the living conditions for the working class in Cuba—and we recognize the achievements in health and education. And unlike older exiles we know and understand the conditions under which our families struggled to survive, because we lived them ourselves.

By the time post-Soviet-era immigrants arrived, much of the initial stigma of Marielitos had faded.[59] However, my interviews reveal that even though Mariel and earlier émigrés shared opposition to the defining experience of their lifetime, they drew on somewhat different pre-immigration worlds. But Marielitos never established organizations of their own that reflected and reinforced their views. Having been blocked from organizing independent of the state in Cuba, they came ashore without a civil society experience on which to build. And as many were working class, they lacked comparable human and social capital to the first arrivals.

The Post-Soviet-Era Crisis and the New Cubans

Against the backdrop of the Mariel exodus and unresolved domestic problems, the Cuban national leadership in the late 1980s promoted a campaign to "rectify errors and negative tendencies." It claimed the campaign would correct ways the revolution had gone astray. The campaign attacked corruption and "bureaucratic tendencies." It also reemphasized Guevarist ideals somewhat akin to those promoted in the late 1960s, including prioritization of moral over material concerns and equality, linked to a diminution of earnings differentials through the raising of wages of the lowest paid. The campaign, in turn, reined in market features permitted since the mid-1970s, through promotion of collective forms of labor organization and a clampdown on an incipient housing market, self-employment, and private farmer markets that had been allowed following the Mariel exodus. At the same time, though, it reduced job and earnings guarantees and seniority rights, and it implemented consumer policies that caused the cost of living to rise. Then, as the 1980s drew to a close, Arnaldo Ochoa Sánchez, a popular military general, and three other high-level officials, were executed for alleged crimes against the state.[60] Thus, the reemphasis on lofty revolutionary principles concealed both reforms that, in part, worked to the disadvantage of ordinary Cubans and heavy-handed repression.

Nonetheless, before ordinary people could experience the full effects of the "rectification" campaign, Cuba's world collapsed. Soviet aid and trade, on which the economy had depended, abruptly ended. Concern with "rectification" became a luxury the government could no longer afford. Instead, it publicly announced a "Special Period in Peacetime," a euphemism for crisis and justification for policies it deemed necessary even if not ideologically defensible.

In the name of "saving socialism," the government reintroduced some market reforms and democratized governance somewhat (detailed in Chapter 7). At the same time, with Marxism-Leninism discredited in the countries with which it had allied itself for thirty years, Cuba turned increasingly to nationalism for legitimacy and loyalty. All the while, the crisis left an indelible mark on people's expectations, values, and social relations, and state influence over people's lives diminished.[61] Such was the trauma that Cubans' perspective on life changed, whether or not they emigrated. For most, survival became the primary concern.

The New Cubans

The crisis left its greatest mark on youth,[62] who came of age to interpret life for themselves in the context of the shattered revolutionary project. They were last to be hired in a state economy that offered diminished opportunities. Overrepresented among the unemployed and underemployed, they found little incentive to work or study.[63] Meanwhile, with much less invested in the socialist transformation than their parents' generation that came of age with Castro, youth also turned, as never before, to counter-cultural alternatives and to illicit activity.[64]

Cubans with whom I spoke reflected on how the crisis led not merely youth, but also the generation who had been children and beneficiaries of the revolution and regime loyalists for decades, to rethink their views and commitments. Facing difficulty addressing their most basic needs, they came to see socialism as no solution to their plight, a far cry from the utopia they previously imagined themselves building. Their disillusionment, in addition, built on the collapse of the international revolutionary project that they had believed they were helping to bring about and the failure of the Rectification Campaign to correct societal problems. At the same time, Cubans old enough to filter the revolution through pre-revolution formed lenses, experienced added confirmation of their views.

The shattering effect the crisis had on three former believers in, and beneficiaries of, the revolutionary project, who stayed in Cuba is telling. Two were among the dark-skinned whose lives had been much transformed by the country's radical makeover. One, Magdalena, a journalist in her late thirties when we spoke in 2001, noted that although she "had truly believed in the ideals of the revolution," she found herself in a quandary when her living conditions nosedived. "Without the revolution I would never have gone to college. I would never have done the things I wanted professionally . . . We were fighting for utopia . . . I believed in and worked hard for the utopia." But her suffering in the 1990s led her to question her belief in "the system." Her health deteriorated, as she deprived herself of food to feed her daughters. She developed asthma and suffered a neurological disorder. Although Magdalena had opted to stay in Cuba at age fifteen out of commitment to the new society in the making when her mother, putting politics above family, joined the Mariel exodus, the 1990s crisis led her to contemplate leaving and for the first time to identify with those who left. In the past, she had looked down on Cubans who rejected the revolution, as Party cadre had convinced loyalists to do.

The crisis also proved a turning point for Jesús, a child psychiatrist who had been a fervent revolutionary, a Party member, and a beneficiary of the Cuban revolution. The son of an illiterate poor farm laborer, thanks to the island socialist makeover, he had the opportunity to become a university-educated professional, while his mother became a textile factory manager. After Soviet aid and trade ended, though, they both experienced a reversal of fortune. The purchasing power of their earnings plunged to the point that they joined the ranks of Cuba's new poor. Despite working twelve-hour days in the hospital, his salary never exceeded the equivalent of about $20 a month, as the dollar informally gained value and the peso/dollar exchange rate caved. Constantly worried about where to get money for food, let alone for clothing and medicines, he and his family were depressed about their living situation. Nine of them lived in a run-down two-bedroom apartment.

Distraught as well as disillusioned, Jesús tried to leave on a makeshift raft that he built with materials he bought on the black market. Poorly constructed, it sank. Rescued by the Cuban coastguard, he was not penalized for illegally trying to leave because he was one of the tens of thousands of *balseros* who had attempted to flee in 1994 when Castro gave the green light for people to emigrate, if they wanted, without US entry permission. Jesús subsequently struggled to make do in the new Cuba, but without his former commitment to the revolutionary project. Around the turn of the century he managed to secure temporary work abroad.

Lourdes was another fervent revolutionary who became disillusioned during the Special Period. She continued to admire the ideals of the revolution. However, she was upset with, and stressed by, the extreme poverty in which she suddenly found herself living. Even though, in her words, she had been raised a Black Panther, with the view that the US was a racist society, she felt she had no option other than to move to the US. "Those who stay have no hope for improving or overcoming the crisis," she noted with dismay. "Everyone who leaves is able to send money to Cuba while those who stay have no hope of overcoming the crisis." At the start of the Special Period she left her state job, where she once believed herself to have a promising career, to take care of sick relatives. The only money she made was off-the-books, informally as a masseuse. When we spoke in 2001 she had no actual plans to emigrate. She only imagined her future more in leaving than in staying in Cuba.

The crisis, in essence, gave birth to a new generation grounded in a new set of experiences that impacted on both the young and old. While Cubans faced with crisis became more individualistic and family-focused in their life pursuits, some simultaneously turned to collective initiatives, such as community gardening, to address the new food shortages. Notwithstanding such initiatives, the new generation tended to concur that emigration was more promising than change at home. The Party and government continued to set parameters to islanders' ability and proclivity to organize on their own to bring about changes they might want. Under the circumstances, islanders also came to view the diaspora more favorably, despite three decades of government and Party condemnation of those who uprooted.

Socio-Economic Background of the New Cuban Immigrants

Initially, after the fall of the Berlin Wall, Washington admitted few Cubans, in hopes thereby of fueling a build-up of islander discontent to the point that Cubans would follow the example of their former Communist comrades to press for a market-democracy transition. But when unrest indeed erupted in 1994, Castro again manipulated the situation to his own advantage, and to the disadvantage of the US. He allowed islanders who wished to emigrate to leave by sea without US entry permits.[65] Against the backdrop of the exodus of some thirty-three thousand so-called "rafters," Washington agreed to sign the 1994 and 1995 bilateral immigration accords that officially permitted a minimum of twenty thousand Cubans US entry annually. As a result, and with old-timers gradually dying off, by the turn of the century 1990s arrivals outnumbered the core Exile cohort, the 1959 to 1964 arrivals, although by then US-born Cuban Americans far outnumbered both cohorts (see Table 1.3).

The social profile of the New Cuban differs somewhat in gender, race, and age from earlier émigrés. They differ especially from the first arrivals (Table 1.2), and most resemble the so-called new immigrants at the time from other Latin American countries. US censuses show post-Soviet-era entrants to include more men than women, and people in prime working years, the trend that began with Marielitos.

While emigrating less as families than the Exiles, the New Cubans, also like many other Latin American immigrants, tended to view individual emigration as part of a family project.[66] Those who uprooted were expected to share new country earnings. For this reason, employable-age islanders dominated the exodus more than in the past, with men seen as more employable than women and as breadwinners who would support women and children left behind. Men left more than in years past without their families because exit costs for multiple persons became unaffordable on official salaries which in the new economy no longer even covered basic subsistence needs.[67]

At the same time, the New Cuban immigrants were exceptionally diverse socio-economically (Table 1.1). Professionals/managers and clerical/sales workers exited far in excess of the percentage of the island labor force so employed, and service sector employees, central to the revolution-created cradle-to-grave welfare state, exited in far greater numbers in the post-Soviet era than before.[68] In contrast, agriculturalists, always a minority among émigrés, nearly disappeared from the ranks of those who fled across the Straits.[69]

In professional background the New Cuban and early Exile cohorts appear most alike. Of the years noted in Table 1.1, only immediately after Castro assumed power did professionals and managers account for a higher percentage of arrivals than in 2000. However, even when nominally similar in socio-economic background, their island class experiences differed markedly. Whereas the first arrivals had lived with bourgeois comforts of property and privilege, and had enjoyed exclusive social clubs and private schools, the New Cuban professionals and managers lived modest lives as state employees. Moreover, amidst the 1990s crisis they swelled the ranks of Cuba's new poor, entirely dependent on state salaries. The meaning of social class accordingly differed to the two émigré waves.

Meanwhile, the heterogeneity in New Cuban class background aside, the crisis had such a leveling effect that the majority of post-Soviet-era immigrants saw themselves similarly as emigrating for economic reasons. They continued to envision themselves as uprooting for economic reasons even as the economy rebounded from its 1993 nadir. Nearly half of the post-Soviet-era arrivals whom I interviewed in the early 2000s said they left for economic reasons; another 17 percent cited political along with economic reasons (see Appendix). Only one-fourth mentioned purely political reasons. In contrast, all

Table 1.3 Cuban Americans in 2000: Percentage US and foreign-born (by year of entry)

Year of arrival	Percent[a]
Before 1959	3
1959–1964	9
1965–1979	17
1980–1989	11
1990–2000	15
US born	46

Source: Steven Ruggles and Matthew Sobek, et al., *Integrated Public Use Microdata Series (IPUMS)*, Version 3.0 (Minneapolis: Historical Census Projects University of Minnesota, 2003, www.ipums.org).

Note:
a Total percentage does not equal 100 due to rounding up to the nearest whole number.

1960s and 1970s, and half of 1980s, arrivals whom I interviewed cited political reasons for uprooting.[70]

Alejandro typifies an economic immigrant of professional standing. He had held a responsible job in a state telecommunications enterprise until he was discharged when the economy went into a tailspin. He noted that he risked a raft voyage in 1994 with his three sons for "entirely economic reasons . . . Cuba became very, very poor, and my kids didn't want to stay. My choices were to leave with my children, or starve." Similarly, Marcía, a University of Havana professor, noted that she moved to Miami in 1999 "absolutely for economic reasons." Her professional salary no longer covered her family's basic needs. Until 1991 she had managed well, she said, raising two children as a single mother on her official salary.

At the other end of the socio-economic spectrum was Ophelia. She came from a poor family that in her words "definitely was much better off after than before 1959." In 2000, her family, however, decided to move to the US "because we thought that the only way to survive was to leave." Working in Cuba in the black market as a seamstress, she could not earn enough to feed her family. Her daughter, she noted with dismay, "became very skinny." Similarly, Orlandina, from a poor family of tobacco workers who "never earned enough to eat in a restaurant or see a movie" and whose mother suffered from depression, moved to New Jersey in the early 1990s to help island relatives. Despite her family suffering, she was not critical of the government "which gave her many good things." She felt different from the old-timers, who, in her words, "resent Castro and the revolution. They came for political reasons and remain political." She does not care who is in power in Cuba. For this reason she does not mind that her son serves in the Cuban military. She recognizes that her views are partly rooted in the fact that the revolution never took anything away from her.

Political Perspectives of the New Cuban Immigrants

Even the post-Soviet-era arrivals who claimed to leave Cuba for political reasons, exclusively or in combination with economic reasons, differed from the first who fled the revolution. They tended to differ in their political rationale for uprooting and in their political views of Cuba. Their differences built on their different lenses, formed pre-immigration, through which they view life. So different were the life perspectives and experiences of recent and first émigrés that they even at times looked down on each other when similarly emigrating for political reasons. Some New Cubans also resented that Exiles tried to impose their views. A number of New Cubans whom I interviewed spoke about the émigré differences and tensions.

Willy, for one, spoke of the political differences among the émigré waves. He was a journalist who moved to Miami in 1994. He noted that, "Whereas migration had essentially been politically driven during the first decades, today the political standstill has led to an economic crisis," to the point that "the two forces combined contribute to migration." The first émigrés had not left because they perceived a political standstill but because they opposed island political change.

Laurencio, a son of illiterate peasants, in turn, spoke of how he "was born after the revolution and didn't know anything else, and therefore became a Communist." Benefiting from opportunities the transformed country made available, he became a doctor. But having to struggle to survive during the Special Period, he "realized that Castro didn't want what was best for the Cuban people." Laurencio suddenly found himself without enough money to eat. "Keep in mind that I was a doctor earning 525 pesos per month, an extremely high salary for Cubans." State-rationed affordable food no longer covered his daily needs, and his state-job earnings were too meager for supplementary purchases. As his life became depressingly difficult, he found himself without the time, energy, or inclination to concern himself with the Party and the politics he previously believed in. Noteworthy, his main political grievance centered on the "corruption of the system." As he became disillusioned, he never focused mainly on Castro, Exiles' nemesis.

Even though he emigrated in 1999 disillusioned with the revolution, Laurencio did not identify politically with Exiles. He found them exceedingly intolerant. "You can express yourself to older exiles, but you must toe their line. I've had some difficult contacts with older exiles." He noted that on a Miami radio program on which he participated, he felt afraid to defend Cuba in any way because he might lose his job. "In Miami I feel liberty, except in places like Calle Ocho," the symbolic center of the Cuban community in Miami. "In Cuba, you have a choice of whether or not you want to be political. In Miami, you have to be political, especially to establish your legitimacy."

Alejandro, the former island telecommunications employee who left Cuba for "entirely economic reasons" also complained about how narrow-minded he found older émigrés to be. Although he had envisioned the US as a democracy, he found little of it in Miami, "Especially among the Cubans who have been here for forty years. They . . . want to force you to think like people thought forty years ago . . . They try to create in Miami pre-revolutionary Cuba." He also complained about how old-timers manipulated the local media. He would call to the radio talk shows, but "the opposition didn't let me express my opinions."

Even New Cuban refugees saw themselves different from Exiles. Julio Fernando, a prize-winning island novelist who moved to Miami as a refugee in 1999 at age twenty-one is a case in point. Although a dissident who suffered for his political convictions before leaving Cuba, he distanced himself politically from Exiles, of whom he was very critical. In Cuba, he had founded an independent literary society in his home town, and had worked for dissident radio stations, including for the US government funded Exile-run, Radio Marti. Police had routinely harassed him, and imprisoned him over a dozen times without ever charging him with a crime. He also had been expelled from the university for his "dissident record," and for one year before emigrating lived in hiding in Havana. His confrontations with authorities had been so wearing on him that after months in the US he still had nightmares about Cuba every night.

Yet, upon emigrating, Julio Fernando quickly became disillusioned with Miami Exiles. "Everything is political in Miami," he complained. He found, for example, a literary society meeting that he attended dominated by old-timers whom he felt inexcusably hijacked the meeting for their own political agenda. "Instead of talking about literature, we ended up talking about politics. This would never have happened in Cuba. In Cuba there is 'real' culture, and people have substance." This anecdote simultaneously reveals that after decades in the US old-timers still viewed even their professional lives through pre-immigration-formed anti-Castro lenses.

Julio Fernando also complained about how intolerant some Exiles were. When attending a party at the house of a friend from Cuba who had emigrated eight years before him, several, in his words, "*viejitos,*" old-timers, were there. Julio Fernando tried to play a tape of the popular island singer Silvio Rodríquez. Refusing to listen, the older émigrés turned off the cassette player. Julio Fernando tried a second time to play the tape, but they were equally intolerant. Then, his friend who had invited him and who himself secretly listens to and enjoys Rodríquez's music, said to the others, Julio Fernando's "problem is that he just came from Cuba and we haven't been able to cure him yet." In reflecting on the incident, Julio Fernando noted in outrage, "I came to the US so that I could listen to whatever I wanted. I don't care about Rodríquez's political views. I care that he is a good musician." Moving to the US because the Cuban government denied him freedom of expression, he was dismayed to find the older generation of émigrés in Miami equally repressive in certain respects.

To illustrate further, some recent political refugees from Cuba spoke at a Miami fundraiser that featured Vaclav Havel, the ex-dissident and former president of the Czech Republic, about their differences from earlier refugees. Both sets of former political prisoners had been invited to the fundraiser, where they were honored for the sentences they served. The recent arrival, Marco Torres, who had spent five years in Cuban jail, noted that "There are a lot of political differences in this room . . . We want concessions. The *Exilio* [Exile] is not putting the interests of Cuba first." And Maritza Lugo, who had been arrested more than thirty times before her recent move to the US, asserted that "I'm no *plantado*," no hardline ex-political prisoner from the early revolutionary period, opposed to dialogue and to an opening to Havana. The older generation of *plantados*, she added, "struggled for so many years, was jailed for so long, saw their families killed, their friends executed. These people don't know another route to power except through force."[71]

The *Émigré Cohort Social Divide*

Politics alone did not divide the émigrés. Exiles looked down on the New Cubans, as they had on Marielitos, and for reasons that transcended social class. Even workers, who emigrated soon after the revolution and who after decades in the US had no well-paying prestigious job to their credit, looked down on recent arrivals. Remberto, a retired construction worker who moved to Miami in 1962 at age twenty-nine, for example, spoke condescendingly of how recent arrivals "come with a different mindset. They are so different from us that they are not identified as Cubans. They even are confused with Central Americans and Mexicans." Considering themselves different from and superior to other Latin Americans, his generation viewed pan-Hispanic identity negatively except, as I indicate below, when entailing popular culture and elites from the region, under their sway. Remberto even perceived himself different from fellow workers among recent arrivals. For him, different generation-grounded experiences mattered more than class commonalities.

New Cubans felt looked down upon even when they adapted well economically. The experience of a 1994 rafter is telling. Although trained in Cuba as an electrical engineer, he felt stigmatized by older émigrés in the US. Old-timers referred to him as a rafter, even years after he resettled and had established himself anew professionally. The electrical engineer thought the rafter label implied that he was lazy, poorly educated, and of racially mixed blood. The stigma aside, he was proud to have been a rafter. To him a rafter signified a survivor.

The stigma, in point of fact, had little to do with his means of exodus and much to do with his and other recent arrivals' long-time association with the regime the first émigrés abhorred. Exiles considered the most recent newcomers, like Marielitos, guilty by association. Julia, who works for a social service agency, spoke of her cohort's stance. Recent arrivals, she noted, had lived under the "Hitler monster" for so long that even after coming to America they were afraid to talk. "They don't feel free to speak their minds. They still feel for the leader and the 'revolution.' Like the Nazis, once a Nazi always one.

They are like a fifth column in the US, here but still loyal to Castro." She presumed Castro responsible for their silence and reluctance to take on the Exiles' anti-Castro cause for themselves. She interpreted new immigrant behavior through her generation's lenses.

Some self-defined Exiles let their biases poison relations with family who emigrated in the post-Soviet era, as well as with Marielitos. New Cubans felt that Exile relatives looked down on them, which they deeply resented. The doctor Laurencio, for example, was both shocked and offended by the poor reception he received from relatives who had emigrated soon after the revolution. And Jaime Carlos, an accountant who emigrated in 1995 in his early fifties, attributed his difficult relationship with his uncles who had moved to the US in 1962 to his having chosen to remain in Cuba for so many years. His uncles do not call him and do not forgive him for having been "an apologist for the regime." Jaime Carlos added that "their views about Cuba haven't changed . . . There is a lot of bitterness and resentment . . . The old-timers want to erase those who remained on the island. They don't consider our viewpoint legitimate." Unlike his uncles, Jaime Carlos considers "family family," whatever their politics.

In contrast to the old-timers, Mariel-generation émigrés with whom I spoke felt they better understood, and were more appreciative of, post-Soviet-era arrivals. Having experienced revolutionary Cuba, they had a more nuanced understanding of it. By way of illustration, Natalio, the 1981 émigré owner of a messenger delivery service, noted when we talked that he does not hold Cubans who stayed for years in revolutionary Cuba in contempt. And Justina, who came to the US the same year as Natalio and who works as an assistant manager for a pro-life Catholic group, saw her generation more accepting than old-timers of recent arrivals. She noted that the Exile generation looked down on the new immigrants, and perceived them as less educated and less skilled. Justina believed racism also filtered their views. She added that the old-timers had difficulty accepting anything that was a product of the revolution. "The older exiles feel it their obligation to rebuild the Cuba they knew rather than accept the reality that forty years have passed and there is a new Cuba." She, in contrast, trusted the younger generation, the New Cubans, "They are more genuine . . . I feel they are the future of Cuba. They know what it is like in Cuba and they have a special outlook. I have never gotten the feeling of hope that I have gotten from the new exodus of people."

Whether or not they felt rebuffed, post-Soviet-era arrivals, with their shared island experiences, bonded among themselves. In this vein, Laurencio, critical of Exiles, lauded how "Recent arrivals always help you out without asking any questions. When they learn you just arrived they automatically lend you $100 or buy you new clothes." They are more generous, he noted, even though far poorer, than earlier arrivals. And Ernesto, a computer programmer who moved to Miami in 2000, speculates that the reception he received from fellow Cubans who emigrated not many years before him had roots in a culture of solidarity his generation established in Cuba.

We started out living with friends, the five of us sleeping on their living room floor. It's amazing how much people helped us. When you first arrive, even if people barely know you they make a special effort to help you out . . . Everything we have . . . is because of the solidarity of our friends.

He believed the people were so compassionate because "that's how we were raised in Cuba. There always was so much hardship, but we have a culture of helping each other out."

Conclusion

In sum, by the turn of the century, Cubans had emigrated in distinct waves with distinct pre-immigration experiences, and perspectives on life so formed. At one extreme were the self-defined Exiles who uprooted during the first decade or so of Castro's rule. They emigrated with a pre-revolution formed mindset that biased them against their homeland's social, cultural, political, and economic makeover. At the other extreme were the post-Soviet-era arrivals, the New Cubans, whose views on life were formed by the trauma of their country in crisis, against the backdrop of their international allies of thirty years rejecting Communism and Marxism-Leninism.

Cubans who emigrated in the intervening years, mainly the Marielitos, are a more mixed cohort. While together, critically, experiencing Cuba transformed by revolution, the older ones in the cohort viewed their lives through pre-revolution formed lenses. In contrast, the younger only experienced first-hand the country's makeover, although they often filtered it partially through their parents' pre- and anti-revolution lenses. With different mixes of experiences, they never constituted a cohort with a distinctive perspective that set them apart from earlier and later émigrés, and they never developed an organizational nexus of their own.

The ensuing chapters first focus on the US adaptation and then on trans-national involvements of these different émigré waves. If I am correct that the first-generation Cuban immigrants who uprooted at different times arrived with different homeland experiences, and life perspectives so formed, with enduring legacies, the chapters should reveal the following:

1   The émigré waves should differ in how they adapt to the US and how they relate to their homeland, in ways traceable to their different pre-immigration experiences. The self-defined Exiles and post-Soviet-era New Cubans should differ most. The Mariel cohort should be most variable in their new country adaptation and cross-border views and involvements. Yet, having lived in Cuba transformed by revolution, they should understand their country's makeover differently and with more nuance than the first who fled, who are frozen in their pre-revolutionary past.

2   While at any point in time immigrants of different social classes, races,

genders, and ages can be expected to have experienced life in their home-land somewhat differently, if they together shared meaningful gener-ational experiences they should differ in their new country adaptation, views, and cross-border engagement from others with their social attrib-utes who emigrated at other times with different life-defining experiences.

3   Immigrant status, and years since emigrating, in themselves should leave important aspects of the adaptation of the foreign-born unaccounted for and unexplained. Should immigrant adaptation rest first and foremost on length of time in the US, my historically grounded generation thesis would be shown not to be of significant explanatory import. The immi-grant assimilation thesis, summarized in the next chapter, would be borne out.

4   Immigrants' pasts would be expected to weigh especially on new country adaptation when those with shared backgrounds settle in close proximity, form groups of their own, and intermingle largely among "their own." Their social ties would likely reinforce views formed in the old country that filter their new life.

5   The adaptation of the foreign-born, however, would not be expected to be entirely determined by life before uprooting. Just as in their homeland, in their new land, their lives would be shaped by political, cultural, eco-nomic, and social conditions where they resettled and when. Moreover, they might become agents, and not function as mere subjects, of history, and accordingly change conditions in their midst. Yet, how they respond to opportunities should be influenced by their pre-immigration past. Depending on differences in social, cultural, and economic assets, émigrés would be differently positioned to impose their will and way on others. Nonetheless, those with limited assets can evade, quietly and covertly, demands of them. In the aggregate they might thereby bring about change which the powerful oppose.[72]

The remainder of the book explores the validity of these propositions. The next two chapters focus, respectively, on the new country social, cultural, economic, and political adaptation of the different émigré waves. The sub-sequent chapters center on émigré cohort differences in cross-border social and economic ties, lenses through which émigrés of the different waves experi-ence homeland visits, and the homeland effects émigré cross-border ties have.

2 Immigrant Imprint in America

How have Cubans of the different émigré waves adapted to the US, and how to explain their differences? This chapter traces differences, in part, to different pre-immigration pasts analytically ignored in existing theories of immigration. Where Cubans settled in large numbers they transformed their environs, at the same time that they assimilated and acculturated to their new milieu. But Exiles, who came with the most transferable assets and with a transnational political agenda, had the greatest impact. They transformed community cultural practices, civic associational and economic life, and, as shown in the next chapter, politics, which they imbued with their own homeland-formed shade of meaning. While capitalizing on opportunities in their new land, they embedded ideas of old anew. And they imposed their views on others, on subsequent immigrants as well as on non-Hispanics into whose midst they moved.

Toward an Improved Theoretical Understanding of Immigrant Experience

Long-standing theories of new country assimilation, acculturation, and incorporation, as well as more recent transnational theses that address how immigrant lives remain homeland-embedded, help account for important aspects of immigrant adaptation. But they fail to account for how and why immigrants who uproot at different times, including from any one country, may assimilate and acculturate differently and relate differently to their homeland, depending on lived experiences before uprooting, and perspectives on life so formed. After briefly summarizing the two main schools of thought regarding immigrant adaptation, and variants thereof, I offer a historically grounded generational thesis to further the understanding of immigrant adaptation. In my summarization I do not do full justice to either analytic frame, or to the fine scholarship in each tradition. I merely highlight key assumptions and arguments that have bearing on this and subsequent chapters, and point to matters they leave unexplained which my historically grounded generation thesis addresses.

Assimilation and Transnational Frames of Analysis

Since the large immigrant influx to the US a century ago, mainly from Europe, scholars typically have analyzed immigration through assimilation and acculturation lenses.[1] Building on the US adaptation ideal (without necessarily advocating it), their research focused on how extensively the foreign-born took on the language and culture of their new country, succeeded economically, participated in new country political and associational life, and mixed with native-born in their personal lives. They presumed that the longer immigrants lived in the US, and the younger they emigrated, the greater their assimilation and acculturation. The more years in the US, the more exposure the foreign-born have to the ways of their new land. And the younger they arrive, the better able they are to learn the language of their adopted country and take advantage of labor market opportunities where they settle, especially the more skilled they arrive.[2] By the same logic, assimilation is anticipated all the more among new country-born children of immigrants.

Studies in this frame of analysis note that immigrants may be incorporated in distinct ways, and that they may, in certain respects, hold on to their heritage while acculturating. The most nuanced studies in this tradition also point to the importance of institutional and locational context, for example, to economic and labor market conditions that set parameters to work options and economic mobility. The so-called old and new immigrants, namely those who came to the US in the last and most recent period of large-scale immigration, and new immigrants settled in different regions of the US, face different economic options.[3] With the shift from an industrial to a service economy, for example, low-skilled immigrants face fewer possibilities for economic advancement.

The most nuanced studies also point to how the macro-cultural milieu also weighs on immigrant adaptation. The post-1960s multicultural and diversity-friendly milieu into which new immigrants have moved may slow down acculturation, and contribute to greater home country cultural retention than in the era of the "old" immigrants, when the foreign-born felt pressured to bury their past. And the ongoing arrival during the new immigrant era of people with a shared country of origin further contributes to cultural retention.[4] Following the introduction of restrictive entry legislation in the 1920s, home country immigrant replenishment had come to a near halt among "old" immigrant groups. Studies also have pointed to "segmented assimilation," namely to foreign-born adaptation varying depending on the race, social class, ethnicity, etc., of the new country people with whom they associate.[5]

Also contextually conceived is the enclave thesis. It addresses how immigrant groups, where they live in substantial numbers, may turn "inward" and develop institutions and practices of their own that makes their assimilation distinctive.[6] Such enclaves rest on immigrants developing an economy by and for "their own." While the explanatory power of, and even the validity of the conceptualization, are disputed,[7] in that opportunities such enclaves can offer are inherently limited and not necessarily preferred by the immigrants them-selves, an ethnic economy might facilitate new country adaptation in the short run but not in the longer term. When they have the option, immigrants may prefer to work and live elsewhere, sometimes clustering in "niches" in the broader economy.[8] In that an enclave cannot be entirely autarchic, immigrant adaptation will always rest on broader societal dynamics that need to be accounted for.

These studies tend to view the assimilation and acculturation that transpire to be unidirectional, to entail immigrant adaptation to their new setting. Left undertheorized is the role power may play in shaping immigrant adaptation, and how immigrants may have sufficient formal or informal power, plus desire and determination, to transform their environs and subject others to their views and ways to the point that others assimilate and acculturate to them. Foreign-born may become the assimilators, as distinct from the assimilated, when they have force of numbers, organizations and institutional practices of their own, and the desire to impose their beliefs and practices on others. Also left under-theorized are conditions under which newcomers may not only pile new prac-tices and beliefs onto old but also combine them in new ways, and conditions under which views and involvements of old filter new country experiences.

In turn, assimilation-focused studies leave analytically unaddressed the homeland ties immigrants may maintain and their cross-border impact. The transnational conceptual frame developed since the 1990s fills this void.[9] It highlights how immigrant lives may become embedded across borders, and how immigrants and homeland people may accordingly influence one another. Homeland people may, as a result, be influenced by émigrés and their values and ways attained in the new country, whether or not they uproot or before they uproot. Some studies also point to the role governments and institutions, including immigrant-formed institutions, may play in shaping transnational ties and developments in both the new and native lands. Conditions prevailing in the new immigrant era, including the ongoing arrival of newcomers from a shared country of origin, the ease of cross-border travel and communication, and new homeland government interest in diaspora homeland engagement (including homeland investment), are especially conducive to transnational involvements.

However, transnationally grounded studies typically leave unaddressed and undertheorized historically grounded homeland experiences not embedded in cross-border ties that impact on immigrant adaptation. They also do not account for new country inter- and intra-group relations that weigh on immigrant adaptation. Yet, the simultaneity of transnational and assimilation processes has been noted.[10]

Generations Historically Grounded

In capturing different aspects of immigrant lives, the assimilation and trans-national paradigmatic frames, in combination, deepen the understanding of immigrant adaptation. However, if I am correct that Cubans who uprooted at different times have adapted differently to their new country in ways traceable to their variant pre-immigration pasts, neither paradigm accounts for how and why. A historically grounded understanding of the long-standing cross-border impact lived experiences before uprooting may have, fills the analytic lacunae.

Karl Mannheim provides a useful building block,[11] even though he never focused on immigration. Addressing generational dynamics in the context of a single country, he argued that people filter their lives through mindsets historically formed, especially in late adolescence. At that age individuals are old enough both to reflect on their past and to consider alternatives. Views then attained provide lenses through which later-in-life experiences are interpreted. By this logic, people of the same age born at different times, or at the same time in different places with different lived experiences, would likely differ in their perspectives on life. Even people who experience the same historical events, but at different ages, would be expected to interpret shared events differently. However, Mannheim also argued that each age group does not necessarily interpret life in a unique manner. An age group may take on the views of others, particularly when they perceive their experiences to differ little.

Mannheim adds, however, that not everyone of the same age, even in a single country, necessarily interprets shared experiences similarly. People may view life in opposing ways, for example, when of different social classes, races, or genders.

Inspired by Mannheim, Norman Ryder noted that as long-lasting as early-in-life experiences are, traumatic experiences, such as revolutions and economic crises, may lead people to rethink their past and modify their life outlook.[12] Also, generations are not necessarily equally free to form and express their views, and they do not necessarily have the same capacities and proclivities to organize or advance their concerns. This suggests that power relations be incorporated into the theoretical understanding of generations. Powerful people and groups may impose their beliefs and interpretive frames on others through the media, schools, and organizations, and through intimidation and repressive means. They can establish what is normatively acceptable, and penalize non-conformity.

In that the dominated do not necessarily believe what they are told or see the world through the lenses imposed on them, it is my contention that their views on life, and bases for their views, need be independently assessed. Those who are dominated can covertly resist the ways and wants of the more powerful, even if veiled behind outward loyalty and compliance.[13]

If perspectives formed early in life and in the context of trauma are enduring in impact, they might well remain consequential among immigrants. And if relations of power, of domination and subordination, and resistance, are of consequence, they may weigh on how foreign-born relate to non-immigrants and other immigrants, including immigrants from their same native country. They could also weigh on how immigrants relate to their homeland from their new land.

Accordingly, with the modifications I note, a Mannheimian historical generation frame can elucidate aspects of the immigrant experience that both the assimilationist and transnational theses overlook. If combined with the other frames of analysis, the understanding of immigrant adaptation can be improved upon. The weight of immigrants' pasts would be expected to be greatest when those with shared experiences settle in close proximity to one another, socialize and engage in group life together, and embed pre-immigration formed views anew.

This and the next chapter address new country social, cultural, economic, and political adaptation of Cuban émigrés who uprooted at different times, where they settled in largest numbers, and how their experiences before uprooting, and life perspectives so formed, impacted on their adaptation. The remainder of the book examines their transnational engagement, the relationship between their new country adaptation and cross-border involvements, and how pre-immigration formed views shape homeland ties and their effects. In this chapter I first describe Cuban American proclivity to settle among "their own" and the cultural war the first arrivals took on with Anglos into whose midst they moved, for Spanish-speaking retention rights, all the while that they gradually mastered English. I also address the group life and cultural practices the Exile cohort established, which they imbued with their own shade of meaning and imposed both on later arrivals from Cuba and on non-Cubans where they settled. While adapting to the Anglo world where they settled, so too did they assimilate and acculturate others to their ways.

I show Exiles to have transformed their key settlements into what Benedict Anderson called imagined communities that maintained meaning to them even after few of them lived there any more.[14] In the process of adapting they also created new identities, solidarities, and practices without precedent. I accordingly show assimilation and acculturation to be multifaceted and multidirectional, and to build on ideas and ways of old in new ways.

I conclude the chapter with an analysis of émigré success at living the American Dream. Many émigrés, Exiles above all, will be shown to have done well economically, partly by being in the right place at the right time, but also by creating opportunities above and beyond those confined to their ethnic group. They even contributed to the transformation and globalization of the Miami economy into whose center they moved. They had such impact without ever fully assimilating and acculturating to practices of the US-born, partly because they resisted burying their pre-immigration past.

The Cuban American experience accordingly will be shown to question theorizing, to date, about immigrant assimilation and acculturation, in ways my historically grounded generational frame of analysis will help elucidate. In this chapter I draw mainly on demographic, survey, and census data. I also draw on my interviews with group leaders and ordinary émigrés, archival material obtained from local groups, and secondary sources.

Exile Place Claims

Cuban immigrants have clustered together in their adopted county, and increasingly so over the years. They are among the most demographically concentrated of the new immigrant groups. In settling among "their own" they have magnified their impact.

The first who fled the revolution moved mainly to Miami. They knew the city from pre-revolution travels. In fewer, but significant, numbers they settled also in Union City, New Jersey, across the Hudson River from Manhattan. In the 1940s a man from Cuba's interior town of Fomento had settled there. After the revolution others from the town, and then from elsewhere, followed in his footsteps. Cubans had such a transformative impact on the two cities that they came to be dubbed the "Second Havana," and "Havana North" and "Havana on the Hudson," respectively.[15]

Indicative of their force of numbers, during the first decade of Castro's rule, the Cuban percentage of Union City's population surged from 20 to 80 percent,[16] even though only 14 percent of Exiles settled anywhere in New Jersey (Table 2.1). Because Miami was far larger, the influx associated with nearly half of the first arrivals settling there amounted only to 4 percent of the city's population (Table 2.2).

The popularity of Union City as a settlement destination declined, however, over the years. By the 1990s, only 4 percent of arrivals settled anywhere in New Jersey (Table 2.1), and by 2005 only 2 percent of newcomers informed the Department of Homeland Security of intent to settle in the state.[17] Cubans remained Union City's largest ethnic group, but by the first years of the new millennium they accounted for only 12 percent of its population.[18]

Cubans, instead, increasingly gravitated to Miami. Earlier émigrés who had settled in Union City and elsewhere in the US gradually relocated to the "Second Havana," with its more island-like climate and larger Cuban concentration. They defied US government pressure to disperse. To temper resentment in Miami to the flood of new Cuban arrivals, Washington had initially tied Cuban Refugee Program benefits to settlement elsewhere. But after the program ended, in 1973, the Sunshine State city became ever more a magnet for émigrés. By the turn of the century over half of the approximately 1.2 million in the US who claimed Cuban ancestry, and over 60 percent of the island-born, lived in the once small winter get-away for northern "snowbirds" and retirees (Table 2.1).[19] Cuban American presence in the city soared to 30 percent (Table 2.2). And by 2005 islanders were so drawn to the "Second Havana" that 84 percent of incoming arrivals noted their intention to settle there.[20] In due course, the percentage of island-born who resided anywhere besides Miami or New Jersey dropped to 32 in 2000, from 40 in 1970 (Table 2.1). Years in the US contributed to geographic concentration, not dispersion.

Exiles, the first to make Miami their home, were trendsetters for other Latin Americans as well. They contributed to the city's transformation into what became dubbed "the northernmost Latin American city." By the turn of the

Table 2.1 Residence of Cuban Americans in census years 1970–2000 (percent)[a]

	Miami	New Jersey	Elsewhere
1970 census			
US born[a]	40%	11%	49%
Emigrated 1960s	48	14	38
All émigrés	47	13	40
All Cubans	45	13	42
1980 census			
US born	34	9	56
Emigrated 1960s	52	10	38
Emigrated 1970s	53	15	32
All émigrés	50	11	38
All Cubans	45	11	45
1990 census			
US born[a]	40	8	51
Emigrated 1960s	61	8	31
Emigrated 1970s	59	11	30
Emigrated 1980s	67	7	26
All émigrés	61	8	31
All Cubans	53	8	39
2000 census			
US born[a]	37	7	57
Emigrated 1960s	60	7	33
Emigrated 1970s	58	10	32
Emigrated 1980s	65	6	29
Emigrated 1990s	66	4	30
All émigrés	61	7	32
All Cubans	52	7	41

Source: Steven Ruggles and Matthew Sobek, et al., *Integrated Public Use Microdata Series* (*IPUMS*), Version 3.0 (Minneapolis: Historical Census Projects University of Minnesota, 2003, www.ipums.org).

Note:
a Percentages do not always equal 100 due to rounding up to the nearest whole number.

Table 2.2 Racial and ethnic composition of Miami in census years 1970–2000 (percent)[a]

	Cubans	Non-Hisp White	Non-Hisp Black	Other Hisp
Year				
1970	4	79	14	3
1980	26	45	18	11
1990	31	31	19	20
2000	30	21	20	28

Source: Steven Ruggles and Matthew Sobek, et al., *Integrated Public Use Microdata Series* (*IPUMS*), Version 3.0 (Minneapolis: Historical Census Projects University of Minnesota, 2003, www.ipums.org).

Note:
a Percentages do not always equal 100 due to rounding up to the nearest whole number.

twenty-first century the city was home to the highest proportion of foreign-born residents nationwide, and to more immigrants in absolute numbers than all US cities besides Los Angeles and New York.[21] Unique to Miami, nearly all of the foreign-born came from south of the Rio Grande.[22] Cubans remained the largest Hispanic group, but they came to account for only half of all Hispanics (see Table 2.2).

As Cuban and other Latin American immigrants made Miami their home, Anglos, non-Hispanic Whites, became increasingly outnumbered. Their percentage of the city's population plummeted from 79 to 21 percent between 1970 and 2000 (Table 2.2). They were outnumbered both because the city grew dramatically with the arrival of Latin Americans, and because many non-Hispanic Whites under the circumstances, packed their bags and left. As a leading newspaper editor explained to me, "the Anglos disliked the city's new feeling of 'Otherness.'" Reflecting the sentiment their uprooting represented, a favorite Miami bumper sticker read "Will the last American out of South Florida please bring the flag."[23]

Cubans made their presence felt all the more by clustering in select neighborhoods and municipalities in Miami-Dade County, Greater Miami.[24] At the time of the 2000 census, Hialeah and Westchester were over 60 percent Cuban, while Hialeah Gardens, Sweetwater, Coral Gables, Miami City, and South Miami had smaller but still substantial Cuban populations.[25] Indicative of their "sticking to their own," when Florida International University's Institute for Public Opinion Research conducted a random sample of over eighteen hundred Miami Cuban Americans in 2004, only 14 percent reported living in neighborhoods where few Cubans lived (Table 2.3).[26] Even after forty or more years in the US, 40 percent of the first to flee the revolution lived mainly among co-ethnics.[27]

Émigrés' decision where to settle hinged on their social class, and not merely on their country of origin. In New Jersey, densely packed Union City, and neighboring West New York where many island-born also settled, remained working class, while the upwardly mobile moved to more posh communities in the New York/New Jersey metropolitan area. Within far larger Greater Miami, the working class gravitated to Hialeah, and the poorest to the City of Miami, while the moneyed made Coral Gables and other wealthy communities their home.[28]

The class-based ethnic residencies came to be associated, in turn, with different émigré waves. The well-to-do areas became home mainly to Exiles.[29] As a consequence, class differentiation familiar to Cubans before the revolution, but truncated by the social transformation, became newly embedded in the US.

In socializing mainly among "their own," the Cuban-born contributed further to reproducing their pre-immigration world. When I asked the rank-and-file Cuban émigrés about the ethnicity of their friends, two-thirds answered that most, like them, were from Cuba (see Appendix). Even after more than twenty to forty years in the US, half of pre-1980 émigrés socialized mainly

Table 2.3 Co-ethnic sociability in Miami among Cuban Americans in 2004

	Year of arrival					
	1959–64	1965–1974	1975–1984	1985–2004	US-born	Total
1. Live in neighborhood						
Mainly Cuban	40%[a]	37%	36%	44%	25%	38%
Mixed	45	51	50	46	51	48
Mainly Non-Cuban	15	13	14	11	25	14
2. Married to fellow Cuban						
Yes	78	80	76	84	60	79
No	22	20	24	16	40	21
3. Co-workers						
Mainly Cuban	17	21	25	32	19	25
Mixed	59	58	61	57	53	57
Mainly Non-Cuban	24	21	14	11	28	18
4. Work for Cuba-owned enterprise						
Yes	14	11	18	38	11	24
No	86	89	82	63	89	76

Source: FIU-IPOR, 2004 (www.fiu.org/ipor).

Notes:
N = 1,811
a Percentages do not always equal 100 due to rounding up to the nearest whole number.

with co-ethnics. And the 2004 Florida International University survey found that nearly 80 percent of the Cuban Americans in Miami who they interviewed had co-ethnic spouses (Table 2.3). Even 60 percent of the US-born had spouses of Cuban-origin. With the family the basic building block of society, Cubans as a group remained remarkably intact across generations, but especially among the foreign-born.

The co-ethnics with whom émigrés' lives remain enmeshed include former island neighbors, schoolmates, and co-workers. They resumed ties anew after resettling in the US. An early 1990s émigré described to me how Cuba-based his Miami social and cultural world was, and how it had become increasingly so over the years. He felt more of his former Cuba friends now lived in Miami than on the island. And to maintain bonds, about twenty to thirty of his former Havana co-workers get together twice a year. He added, "What's true for me is true for everyone." To him, "Miami was more Cuban than Cuba," and not merely because ties among the Cuba-born were so strong but because Cuban culture is more accessible in Miami than on the island. "You can find any Cuban music or book here, and more easily than in Cuba."

Émigré clustering among, and socializing with, "their own" contributes to their ongoing self-identification as Cubans, or as hybridized Cuban Americans, distinct both from other Latin American origin and mainstream native-born Americans. When I asked the rank-and-file émigrés I interviewed how they self-identified, over half of them claimed to be Cuban. Another 43 percent considered themselves to have double or hyphenated identities, namely as Cuban-American or Cuban and American. Only 5 percent viewed themselves as American, and even fewer as Hispanic. Despite the growing number of other Hispanics in their midst with whom they shared a common language and culture, and despite some limited initiatives by Cuban American leaders to forge ties with other Hispanics and to promote a pan-Hispanic culture, which I describe below, those of Cuban origin gravitated toward "their own" and considered themselves as distinctive.[30]

With most Cuban Americans settling in Miami, and with Union City a dying Cuban American city, I focus in the remainder of the chapter mainly on developments in the Sunshine State city. However, when relevant and when I have comparable data for Union City, I address how trends in the two cities compare.

Linguistic Acculturation? The Anglo-Exile Culture War

Clustering among "their own," and assuming initially that their US stay would be short-lived, until Castro's quick overthrow, Exiles took it upon themselves to use Spanish routinely in their everyday lives. Unlike immigrants in the past, Cuban émigrés relied on their home language in the public sphere and not merely in the confines of their private lives.

In transforming Union City into a majority Cuban city, Exiles met minimal resistance. But in Miami, where Anglos remained the numerical majority until around 1980, Cubans faced pressure to acculturate linguistically. The interethnic linguistic struggle that arose demonstrates how power and politics may, and in the Cuban case did, affect cultural adaptation. Exiles and Anglos each won some battles in their culture war, although they both also suffered defeats. Anglos who resented the Exile-led linguistic remaking of the city were among those who moved away. In defeat, they opted for exit. They left when they felt they lost their effort to maintain English as the city's dominant language. Their exodus shows how an immigrant group can impose their way on others into whose midst they move.

The culture war began when Anglos mobilized to insist on English as the city's official language. They tried both electoral and legal means. An English Only movement, the first in the country, successfully led a campaign in 1980 to repeal at the polls a Bilingual-Bicultural ordinance passed in 1973. Movement supporters also made it illegal to use county funds for activities in languages other than English and for promoting any culture "other than that of the United States."[31] The 1973 ordinance, which had reflected Exiles' growing political influence before the Mariel influx fueled a nativistic backlash, had designated Spanish as the county's official second language and called for the establishment of a Department of Bilingual and Bicultural Affairs, translation of county documents into Spanish, and recruitment of Latinos for county jobs.[32]

Exiles and then Marielitos were not the only Hispanics at the time who stirred Anglo rile. However, they were the most numerous, the most conspicuous, and the most publicly articulate. In that they dominated the city's ethnic makeover when the movement took hold, Anglos tacitly targeted them.

The English Only movement went on to win an amendment to the Florida Constitution in 1988 that specified English as the official language of the state of Florida. Eighty-four percent of state voters supported the amendment.[33] The movement also influenced electoral contests for public office. In 1989, for example, a candidate in the Democratic Party primary to replace Congressman Claude Pepper, who died in office, supported the English Only movement by advocating language tests for US citizenship. By then a surge of new arrivals from other Latin American countries plagued by debt crises and civil wars had further fueled anti-Hispanic sentiment.

Exiles mobilized to defeat the Democratic candidate who played the nativistic card, instead, electing one of "their own." And in 1993, they reversed a legal effort to demand their linguistic obeisance. The electorate, which by then included a small number of Marielitos, but many more Exiles (see Table 3.1 on p.91), contributed to the revoking of the 1988 amendment to the state constitution.[34]

By the early years of the new millennium, English Only supporters appeared also to have lost the linguistic battle *de facto*, in that Cubans continued to speak their native tongue in their everyday lives. Indicative of this fact, Florida International University found in its 2004 survey that a quarter-century after the launching of the nativist crusade, less than one-fourth of the Cuban Americans whom they interviewed in the city mostly spoke English in their public lives and preferred the English over the Spanish-speaking media for their news (Table 2.4).[35] Another of its surveys, three years later, which included fewer linguistic questions, found the percentage of Cuban Americans in the city who relied on the English media to have increased only slightly. The media question signified not merely homeland language retention but preference for Hispanic-filtered news, culture, and perspectives. Thus, the Exiles who led the movement to defeat English Only initiatives became role models for homeland language retention for later island arrivals.

Economic insecurities often fuel nativist movements, and Miami's was no exception.[36] The local economy had experienced a slow-down in the late 1970s, on top of which the Mariel influx exacerbated job competition. Moreover, Cuban Americans took over jobs Anglos until then had monopolized, especially in the garment, construction, hotel, and restaurant industries, and to a lesser extent in professional and executive jobs.[37] Cuban Americans also won out over local Blacks in the small business world, as I address further in Chapter 3. To the extent that these jobs provided goods and services for the city at large, and not specifically for fellow Cuban Americans, the enclave thesis fails to capture the Cuban American Miami economic experience. Relevant here, it does not reflect the economic basis of anti-Cuban Americanism during these years.

As Cuba-born made inroads to the citywide labor market, they saw Spanish language use to be advantageous. The English Only movement had failed to convince them otherwise. In the Florida International University 2004 survey, 70 percent of Miami Cuban Americans indicated that they felt command of Spanish facilitated job attainment (Table 2.4).[38] And the first arrivals, along with their US-born children upon reaching working age, were the most convinced. Eighty and 90 percent of them, respectively, felt that way. They viewed Spanish as cultural capital helpful in the work world. By the time of the survey, Exiles had established ethnic linguistic practices that permeated the labor market, and perceptions of it, to the point that the island-born had economic incentives to continue to speak their home country language and to teach it to their progeny. In Miami, valuation of Spanish proficiency did not decrease the longer Cubans lived in the US or across generations.

Cuban immigrants, under Exile tutelage, so transformed cultural norms and practices in Miami that by the early years of the new millennium most from the island felt they lived in a linguistically tolerant city. When queried in 2004 about whether they felt non-Spanish speakers were tolerant of Spanish speakers, most answered in the affirmative (Table 2.4). And most survey respondents reported that they had never experienced criticism or disparaging looks when speaking Spanish. The New Cubans were the most positive in their assessments. They had arrived after, and had benefited from, the Spanish-speaking culture war that the Exiles seemingly had won.

However, concealed behind the Spanish linguistic makeover of Miami are changes in language practices and preferences among Cubans. By 2004, most US-born Cubans lived their public lives mainly in English and felt more comfortable speaking English than Spanish (Table 2.4). The Anglos who had seemingly lost the culture war accordingly triumphed, among second-generation Cuban Americans.

Island-born, with time, also incorporated English into their everyday lives. This was most true among Exiles, in the US the longest. By 2004, a slight majority of them relied heavily on English in their public lives, while at the same time they continued to use Spanish in the confines of their homes. They accordingly had transformed themselves into bilingual/bicultural exemplars.[39] They had come to function in two cultural worlds, and helped sustain both. At the other extreme were the New Cubans. As of 2004 only one-third of them spoke mainly English outside the home, and only one-fifth of them preferred English over Spanish language news (although by 2007 86 percent of them claimed to rely sometimes on the English-speaking media).

Émigré cohort differences notwithstanding, Miami Cuban Americans show linguistic acculturation and homeland language retention not necessarily to be mutually exclusive. And as they have acculturated, their native language has undergone certain modification. Those born in Cuba are not abandoning their cultural past nor perpetuating it unchanged. At times they combine their new and old language in new ways, involving hybridization, popularly known as Spanglish.

Table 2.4 Cuban American linguistic acculturation in Miami in 2004 and 2007 (data for 2007 in parentheses)

	Year emigrated					
	1959–64	1965–74	1975–84	1985+	US-born	Total
1. Language primarily spoken in the home						
English	14%ᵃ	12%	7%	3%	34%	11%
Both about the same	19	19	14	7	17	14
Spanish	67	68	80	90	49	75
2. Language feel most comfortable speaking						
English	16	13	6	3	70	16
Both about the same	21	17	10	4	19	12
Spanish	64	70	85	94	10	72
3. Main language spoken outside the home						
English	21	21	15	14	68	23
Both about the same	35	22	20	18	27	23
Spanish	44	57	65	69	5	54
4. Language preference for news						
English	25 (28)	24 (17)	11 (9)	5 (5)	79 (85)	22 (25)
Both about the same	29 (39)	21 (63)	10 (71)	14 (86)	14 (3)	18 (20)
Spanish	46 (33)	56 (21)	79 (20)	82 (9)	7 (11)	61 (55)
5. In general, ability to speak Spanish makes it easier to get a job						
Easier	80	76	62	57	90	70
No difference	12	14	17	10	5	12
Harder	8	11	22	33	5	19

	Year emigrated					
	1959–64	1965–74	1975–84	1985+	US-born	Total
6. Number of Cubans who have not tried to learn English in South Florida						
Many	58	58	61	61	59	60
Some	22	22	20	20	27	21
Only a few	19	18	17	18	12	17
None	1	2	2	2	2	2
7. South Florida non-Spanish speaker tolerance of people speaking Spanish to each other						
Almost always understanding	31	36	36	45	13	35
Usually understanding	32	35	41	34	37	35
Often not understanding	26	22	18	15	40	22
Almost never understanding	11	8	4	6	10	8
8. Personally criticized or given disparaging looks for speaking Spanish						
Yes	35	32	31	26	51	32
No	65	68	69	74	49	58
9. Bilingualism in school: Best to start classes in Spanish and then shift to English or start immediately with most classes in English. Which do you think is better?						
Begin with Spanish	21	22	31	25	39	26
Begin with English	79	78	69	75	62	74

Source: FIU-IPOR, 2004 (www.fiu.org/ipor).

Notes:
N = 1,811 in 2004 and 1,000 in 2007.
a Percentages do not always equal 100 due to rounding up to the nearest whole number.

Even when holding on to their Spanish, Miami Cuba-born are committed to linguistic acculturation. That is how they perceive themselves. Only about one-fifth of the Cuban Americans Florida International University interviewed felt most of their co-ethnics resisted learning English (Table 2.4). Even the New Cubans, whose everyday lives transpired mainly in Spanish, perceived few of their co-ethnics to be linguistically recalcitrant. And three-fourths of the interviewees were so anxious for their children to learn English that they wanted their schooling to begin immediately in English, not in Spanish. This was almost as true of New Cubans as of the first émigrés. They all, no doubt, want what they perceive best for their progeny. Thus, as Exiles legitimated Spanish-speaking, they did not create a milieu discouraging subsequent arrivals from new country acculturation. And if the aspirations of the Cuba-born of the diverse émigré waves materialize, English acculturation will increase dramatically inter-generationally, even if not to the exclusion of children learning their parents' native tongue.

In sum, the Miami Cuban American experience demonstrates that acculturation can be partial, situational-specific, and subject to inter-ethnic power struggles, and be piled onto cultural practices of old. It also demonstrates that acculturation may result in a fusion of homeland and new country practices in new ways. Culture is not fixed in formation. Nonetheless, homeland language retention bound all Cuban émigrés together, despite differences among them, and set them partially apart from the broader society.

Exile Creation of Community in Their Own Image

Building on their homeland language retention, Cuban émigrés transformed the places where they lived. Here too Exiles took the lead. They imbued their new environs with their distinctive Cuba-formed perspective on life, they established themselves as ethnic gatekeepers, and imposed their beliefs on others in their midst, both on later Cuban arrivals and on non-Cubans. At the same time, they oversaw the formation of new pan-Hispanic cultural identities. They confined themselves neither to new country acculturation nor to old country cultural retention.

In both Little Havana and "Havana on the Hudson" the pioneer Exiles set up grocery stores, barbershops, cafés, and other small businesses, which gave the communities an ethnic economic as well as a social and cultural base. Both locales had been boarded up and full of abandoned stores when they first arrived.

The new ethnic enterprises created a milieu where island-born mingled, shopped, ate, drank, and "talked Cuba." Calle Ocho, Southwest Eighth Street, and Bergenline Avenue became the hubs of Little Havana and Union City, respectively. The areas maintained their Cuban flair and ethnic import, Exile-defined, even after they were no longer majority Cuban and after the Cuba-born became enmeshed in broader city life.

Exiles imbued the communities with their pre-revolution shade of meaning.

They accomplished this through a calendar of events, through social exclusion of challengers to their views, and through attaching symbolic significance to special sites. In so doing they reinforced pre-immigration values and customs to which they attached their own political spin, even as they assimilated and acculturated to mainstream America. The net effect was to give new country meaning to old ways and old country meaning to the new.

The émigré cohorts, and émigrés who uprooted as children and as adults, differed in their engagement in civic associations in their adopted country. Older Exiles brought groupings with them from Cuba, which they instituted anew, while child immigrants of Exile families drew also on new country associational life as they reached adulthood. In contrast, the more recent arrivals rarely were joiners, of their own groups, of groups Exiles formed, or of groups that were non-immigrant based. They established no civic associational life of their own.

Exile-Initiated Calendar of Celebrations

Exiles celebrated holidays in their new land that built on a calendar they brought with them from Cuba. To illustrate, each January, Exiles honor the anniversary of José Martí's birth. Martí is Cuba's most revered hero. He was a key player in the country's struggle for independence from Spain. The annual celebration of his birth affirmed Cuban national identity, commitment, and pride.

Exiles also commemorated the anniversary of the day Cubans had claimed their day of national independence before Castro assumed power, May 20. On that day in 1898, Cuba severed formal ties with Spain. Because the Castro-led government removed the day from its calendar of commemorations, as it reinterpreted Cuban history through lenses transformed by revolution, the date had most meaning to Exiles. Castro cancelled the holiday because he claimed true island independence from imperialist yoke came only with the revolution. Almost immediately following Cuba's break with Spain the US established "neocolonial rule." The new island leadership instead made July 26 the key day of national civic celebration. The July day commemorates the first armed effort by Castro and his fellow rebels to oust Batista, in 1953.

Thus, a day that nominally united all Cubans became an annual occasion for Exiles to affirm their opposition to the revolution. The annual event came to include not only a hoisting of the Cuban flag and a patriotic march, but also a tribute to former political prisoners who had suffered for their conviction to the anti-Castro struggle. They thus imbued a commemoration of old with new political significance. It came to be fused with their own Exile shade of meaning.

Participation in the annual celebration dwindled over the years. A local civic leader in Union City estimated, when we spoke, that in 2006 some five hundred to one thousand Cuban Americans attended May 20 events, down from thousands in the 1990s. Mainly only the first émigrés attended, and many of them gradually lost interest in the civic celebration, especially those who moved away and became enmeshed in the mainstream "American" world in which such civic celebrations had fallen out of favor.[40] And to the émigrés raised in revolutionary Cuba, the May day had little meaning.

Veterans of the 1961 Bay of Pigs invasion, in turn, each April commemorate their effort to reclaim Cuba, and pay homage to their martyrs, men who lost their lives during the island attack. At their annual gathering they play the "Star-Spangled Banner" along with the Cuban national anthem. In Miami, they also hold a special mass at the chapel that honors Cuba's patron saint. Their anti-Castro commemoration thus fuses patriotism and religion with US assimilation.

The commemoration each September of Cuba's patron saint's day is more important and popular among Cubans in the US than Exiles' civic celebrations. It affirms the religious base to Exiles' identity. But Exiles imbued this commemoration as well with their own shade of meaning. In both Union City and Miami, the celebration includes a procession and a special mass held around the same September day that Cubans on the island historically made pilgrimages to the provincial church named for the island's patron saint.[41] The same civic leader referred to above believed that five thousand Cuban Americans participated in the saint's day procession in Union City in 2006. However, émigré commitment to this commemoration has also declined over the years. In its heyday, four times as many had participated. Involvement used to be such that a procession ended with a service in the saint's name in a near-packed large stadium.

The commemoration of Cuba's saint's day is especially elaborate in Miami. For the occasion émigrés temporarily remove a statue of the saint that sits in the shrine in her name where Bay of Pigs veterans hold their yearly mass. Exiles raised funds to build the shrine. They place the icon on a festively decorated boat which a procession of sailboats and yachts escort through Biscayne Bay. The statue is then carried to a Miami stadium for an outdoor mass, where attendees wave Cuban flags and sing a hymn to the Virgen de la Caridad to the tune of the Cuban national anthem. But indicative of how the Exile Miami organizers of the commemoration also infuse the celebration with their own cohort's shade of meaning, is the fact that they call on attendees to pray collectively for the liberation of Cuba. In addition, they honor as special guests former island political prisoners.[42]

Exiles who immigrated when they were young adults added cultural events to the yearly calendar of celebrations, which were conceived in their new country but inspired by their old country. This occurred first in Miami, and later in Union City. The cultural festivities are far more popular in their appeal than the civic commemorations, including to other Latin Americans. More inclusive, they serve as a bedrock for the formation of an incipient pan-Hispanic identity and culture. In Miami, the Calle Ocho Festival, named for Little Havana's main thoroughfare, is loosely modeled on island annual *comparsas* street performances.[43] Sponsors of Miami's Calle Ocho Festival claimed the annual multi-day March event, with concerts, parades, youth entertainment, sports events, and stalls that sell ethnic foods, to be the biggest street party in the world. Musical groups associated with diverse Latin American countries perform. During the first years of the new millennium the festivities reportedly attracted more than a million people.

Inspired by the Calle Ocho Festival, in Union City Cuban Americans introduced an annual June Cuba Day Parade in 2000. In 2006, 350,000 people attended. The organizers of Union City's Cuba Day Parade and associated events intended their annual commemoration to improve public awareness of Cuban American contributions to public service, business, and the arts, as well as to celebrate Cuban Americans' cultural heritage, history, and traditions. The parade, well publicized by its media sponsors, includes participants carrying the Cuban flag who march down Union City's Bergenline Avenue.

While organized by and nominally for Cuban Americans, the Cuba Day Parade celebration, like the Calle Ocho Festival, is Latin American inclusive. It too serves as base for the formation of a new social and cultural identity, distinct both from Cubans' past and the Anglo-dominated US mainstream. But it is Cuban American at its core. Thus, while a star dedication honors *Latino* artists, and a gala affair associated with the Cuba Day Parade features both Cuban and other Latin American music, leading up to the event each year is a Celia Cruz Queen pageant. Honoring the Cuban American "Queen of Salsa," described in more detail below, the parade queen must have at least one Cuba-origin parent. Notably, she may be "mixed blood." Even the organizers of the June celebration, as well as event sponsors, are not exclusively Cuban American. Yet, here, as well as in Miami, Marielitos and New Cubans are nearly absent from the organizing ranks.

As the cultural festivities fostered a pan-Hispanic cultural identity and a basis of sociability, the Cuban American organizers established themselves as gatekeepers. They set politically defined boundaries to what was permissible. They considered island Cubans as well as Latin American artists who had visited Cuba to be *personae non grata*, irrespective of their talents and irrespective of whether their music had political content. In this vein, in 1989, the Little Havana Kiwanis Club that organized the Miami festival prohibited Puerto Rico-born Andy Montañez from performing because he had visited the island. The festival organizers used their institutional authority to serve as moral police and cultural boundary-setters. They punished Montañez for stepping foot in Cuba under Castro, and in so doing warned other musicians not to follow his example.

Exiles as Gatekeepers

The banning of Montañez from the Calle Ocho festival represented but one Exile effort to set boundaries to the culturally permitted.[44] The boundaries became implicitly understood, and when publicly challenged they became explicit. The boundaries were politically based and politically biased. Exiles imposed their standards both on other Cuban Americans and on non-Cubans. They tried to block artists and performers they perceived as "Castro sympathizers." They went so far as to try to leverage the law to institutionalize the boundaries they considered acceptable. And when their legal efforts failed they at times resorted to violence and intimidation to enforce their politically defined cultural norms.

In their effort to limit "Castro's" cultural influence, Exiles in 1996 successfully convinced the Miami-Dade county government to institute an ordinance to prevent the use of its funds for events that involved island artists. In that the ordinance received little public support from non-Cubans, and only partial support from Cuban Americans, it represented an effort by the hardliners to impose their standards on others, including on non-Cubans into whose midst they had moved. When Florida International University surveyed approximately fifteen hundred Miamians of diverse ethnic backgrounds in 2000, 75 percent of non-Cubans and half of Cuban Americans expressed opposition to the ordinance, which by then had been ruled illegal.[45]

Both when the ordinance was in effect and afterwards, hardline Exiles attacked co-ethnics who defied the cultural boundaries they set. A bomb, for example, was placed outside the Cuban Museum of Art and Culture in Little Havana in 1988, after a fundraising auction there included paintings by island artists.[46] Opponents also burned one of the controversial paintings, and hounded museum board members with death threats.

Hardline Exiles also imposed their standards on the performing arts. They prevented playwrights whom they defined as Castro sympathizers from staging theater performances, even when their work contained no political content. In this vein, a scheduled performance of a play by a New York-based Cuban American writer was cancelled in the 1980s after the organizers received threats.[47] The play had little to do with Cuba, but hardliners blackballed the playwright for his presumed pro-Castro views.

Hardline Exiles, moreover, tried to keep Miami free of island music, even as it gained popularity nationwide. They opposed local radio station broadcasts of Cuban music and live performances by Cuban musicians. In 1999, they tried to prevent a concert by Cuba's famed Los Van Van, a favorite among New Cubans from their pre-immigration days. Hardliners framed their opposition in terms of their unending opposition to Castro and the revolution. They leaned on the then mayor of the City of Miami, Cuban American Joe Carollo, to champion their cause. Carollo cancelled the scheduled local performance, while the group toured other cities in the country problem-free. Only when faced with legal pressure did the mayor concede to allow the concert. The American Civil Liberties Union threatened to sue the city for prohibiting the concert. The self-appointed cultural gatekeepers here experienced defeat, although they did not all acquiesce. Some of them protested at the concert. They shouted epitaphs and hurled cans, batteries, eggs, and other objects at concert-attendees. Fearful of revealing their identities, some Los Van Van fans came in disguise.

Exiles established themselves as political as well as cultural gatekeepers. They attempted to keep the city free of all "Castro sympathizers." A notorious example involved Nelson Mandela who received a hero's welcome in the US in 1990. But after acknowledging admiration for Castro on ABC News, Miami Cubans were incensed. They protested at his speaking in the city. Five Cuban American mayors in the county publicly proclaimed the South African *persona non-grata*.[48] Cuban American opposition so incensed African Americans that they retaliated by organizing a three-year boycott of the city's tourism and convention industry. Thus, the Cuban American political gatekeepers fueled inter-racial tensions.

Exiles Imbuing of Sites with Their Own Shade of Meaning

Exiles also imbued specific sites with their own shade of meaning. Later arrivals never did the same. For one, Exiles established memorials to their anti-Castro cause. Veterans of the 1961 Bay of Pigs invasion founded a museum to memorialize their failed effort to reclaim Cuba. And they installed what they call a Freedom Torch, which burns in the name of their martyrs, who lost their lives trying to overthrow Castro. Then, after the Cuban community failed in 2000 to keep the US government from returning six-year old Elián González to his father in Cuba after his mother died at sea while trying to enter the US illegally with him, the then Exile-dominated Cuban American National Foundation transformed the home of the Miami relatives with whom Elián had stayed into a museum to memorialize their struggle.

Exiles also renamed streets and parks after their heroes. A park where Little Havana men congregate to play dominoes was named after Máximo Gómez, a hero, along with Martí, of Cuba's struggle for independence from Spain. Their place-naming extended to heroes of their anti-Castro struggle. In this vein, they rebaptized several streets in Miami for co ethnics who were killed when the Cuban government in 1996 downed planes associated with the Exile group Brothers to the Rescue, and for Jorge Mas Canosa after he died the following year. Mas Canosa had been the most influential leader of the anti-Castro movement. And in Union City organizers of the Cuba Day Parade used the occasion of the annual celebration in 2003 to dedicate a local park in Celia Cruz's honor, after she passed away. The "Queen of Salsa" and winner of two Grammy awards was a 1960 émigré turned Cuban American icon.

In Miami, Exiles did not confine the sites they imbued with their own shade of meaning to Little Havana, which remained over the years their symbolic epicenter. La Ermita de la Caridad, the shrine of Our Lady of Charity, also known as the Shrine of the Virgin of Charity of Cobre, is one such site outside Little Havana. Exile values, views, and history permeate the church's very structure and design. The ninety-foot-high cone-shaped building, which casts a beacon toward Cuba, has as its centerpiece the statue of Cuba's patron saint used for the city's annual saint's day celebration. Some religious Catholics sneaked the statue out of the country when they fled the revolution in 1961.

And behind the altar rests a mural depicting the island's history up to the revolution, as if the revolution marked the end of Cuban history. Further denying revolutionary Cuba, the roof has six sides, representing the six provinces Cuba had until the Castro-led government reorganized the country into fourteen regions (plus the Isla de la Juventud as a special municipality). The six provinces are those that Exiles recognize. They refuse to recognize the new provinces, some named for symbols of the revolution.

The shrine serves as a gathering place for Cuba-born wherever in the city they live. But most who partake collectively in shrine activity left during the early years of the revolution. Many of them had been devout Catholics. More recent arrivals grew up in revolutionary Cuba where religion, until the 1990s, had fallen out of favor.

Another building outside Little Havana that Exiles imbued with their own symbolic meaning is the early twentieth-century Mediterranean-style building that initially housed the *Miami Daily News*. It subsequently became headquarters for the federal government refugee program. Before the program ended in the early 1970s, half a million Cuban arrivals had received refugee benefits there. Exiles considered the edifice their Ellis Island, their Freedom Tower.

With the intent of memorializing the building's historical import to the first arrivals, Jorge Mas Canosa purchased the structure, which had fallen into disrepair. He intended to turn it into a museum dedicated to documenting the Cuban American experience, comparable to the Holocaust Museum for American Jews. Dying before the project came to fruition, his US-born son, Jorge Mas Santos, restored the building's exterior, with Cuban American National Foundation support. Although Mas Santos had made public a commitment to create the museum his father had envisioned, within a short time he sold the building to a developer who planned a high-rise condominium for the site. In deference, the developer donated the tower to Miami-Dade College to build the museum Mas Canosa envisioned.

The Tower has no first-hand meaning either to 1980s or to more recent island arrivals because the government had shut down its refugee work there by the time they came ashore. However, Mas Santos ascribed broad ethnic import to it before selling the edifice. In July 2003, the body of Celia Cruz, one of the few Cubans with dark skin who fled the revolution early on, was flown from her home in Fort Lee, New Jersey, to lie in rest at the site. Considering Miami to be the exile heartland, her dying wish had been to be honored there.[49] From the Tower a procession proceeded to La Ermita de la Caridad for a special religious service in her name.[50]

Versailles Restaurant, meanwhile, serves as a Cuban American hang-out that Exiles have informally claimed for themselves. Cuban Americans from all over Miami patronize the restaurant. They go there not because it offers the best Cuban cuisine, but because it symbolizes being Cuban and because it has become *the* place "to see and be seen." Breaking island news can immediately be heard there, and reactions deliberated and disseminated. Politicians who wish to garner émigré group support know to go to Versailles, whether or not they themselves are Cuban American. Indeed, it is de rigueur for political candidates who seek Cuban American backing to make an appearance there. Even national politicians have been known to go there to meet with influential Exiles when considering a change in US Cuba policy, and when campaigning for office.

Exiles so dominate the culture of the restaurant that a Cuban American banker, one of the first and few outspoken proponents of cross-border dialogue in the 1970s, described to me what he felt the essence of the gathering place to be: "At Versailles you can see how controlled political speech and dissent in Miami are. Freedom for these people is the ability to sit in the restaurant. Versailles is where 1960s émigrés go."

Indicative of the social and political import Cuban Americans attach to Versailles, and to Calle Ocho where it is located, in August 2006, anti-Castroites congregated there immediately when they euphorically anticipated the Cuban leader's death following his intestinal surgery and his relinquishing of power to his brother, Raúl. Exiles went to celebrate what they assumed at long last to be their moment to reclaim their homeland. In what proved, at best, a dress rehearsal, someone paraded down the street with a Castro look-alike figure in a coffin on the back of a pick up truck. Someone else put a Castro manikin on a bench holding a personification of a baby Hugo Chávez, the President of Venezuela who was a "friend of Fidel."

Exile Cohort Domination of Group Life[51]

The first émigrés organized their ethnic calendar of events through groups they formed and preexisting groups they joined. Their groups had diverse social bases and different concerns. Some were nominally inclusively Cuban American, while others contributed to and reinforced the émigré social divide. And some groups served to assimilate and acculturate the foreign-born into mainstream America, while others served as bedrock for the incipient pan-Hispanic identity I described. Émigrés brought some of the groups with them from Cuba, while founding or joining others for the first time in their new land. No matter, taken together, the civic associational life mainly only involved the first émigrés. Marielitos and especially New Cubans were notably absent, both in leadership positions and as rank-and-file members. Accordingly, Exiles imbued their own shade of meaning into civic group life, and through groups strengthened social ties among "their own."

I illustrate a sampling of civic groups that émigrés formed and joined: their membership bases, activities they sponsored, and values they embedded. Florida International University found in Miami that as of the early 2000s Exiles were 2.5 times more likely than Marielitos, and 6.5 times more likely than New Cubans, to be involved in such civic and professional groups.[52] Exiles were even slightly more likely than their US-born children to be group affiliates.

Transplantation of Groups Formed in Cuba

The first émigrés reestablished island formal and informal group life after resettling in the US. This transpired particularly in Miami, among Havana's former well-to-do. In reestablishing groups through which they had bonded as a social class and through which they had reinforced their island class-based social and normative world, they embedded their former social and cultural world anew. Yet, in the new country context the groups never functioned entirely as in the past.

Formal Groups

La Liga Contra el Cancer (the League Against Cancer) is an important voluntary association that upper-class 1960s émigrés reestablished in Florida in 1975. Formed in Cuba in the 1920s, its formal mission is to serve cancer patients and to educate the public about cancer. In Cuba, wealthy doctors had donated their time, while society ladies did fundraising for La Liga.

In a similar fashion, the Miami association tapped into émigré generosity: doctors who donated free service to the needy, and individuals who donated funds to cover organizational overhead and other expenses. The tradition of charity that the Exiles brought with them provided occasions for the well-to-do to bond. In Miami, as in Cuba, La Liga activity reinforced class solidarity among wealthy supporters at the same time that they "did a good thing."[53] In the course of a year La Liga sponsors benefit dinner dances, fashion shows, a jewelry exhibition, and a presentation of Miss Universe contestants.[54]

The group initially targeted poor Cuban immigrants who were in need of care. By providing them with medical assistance in Spanish, the organization performed an important service. While Miami's La Liga thereby laid bedrock for inter-class émigré ties, and in Spanish, it did so in a manner that never challenged the socioeconomic hierarchy that the first arrivals brought with them from pre-revolutionary Cuba.

Miami's La Liga, however, became embedded in a new social setting that led its leadership ultimately to modify its mission. With émigré acquisition of medical coverage through Medicaid and Medicare, and through work,[55] the Cuban community in the city ceased to need La Liga services. Rather than dissolve the organization under the circumstances, its leadership decided to target needy immigrants from other Latin America countries and the Caribbean.[56] It also chose to broaden its revenue base by grass-roots fundraising and through sponsorship of an annual telethon on a Spanish television station. In 2004, the telethon brought in $3.9 million in pledges.[57] La Liga thereby adapted to the new *Latino/a* Miami. Noteworthy, it did not target poor non-Hispanics, such as African Americans. La Liga reinvented itself to assume meaning in the emergent pan-Hispanic Miami, in which African Americans remained at the sidelines.

Well-to-do first-wave émigrés and some of their economically successful US-born children dominated the organization and its fundraiser social events, even as La Liga served the needs of other Hispanics. In 2004, La Liga's thirteen-member Executive Board and forty-nine-member Board of Directors were Hispanic, most if not all Cuban American.[58] Both boards included prominent Cuban Americans, including former island elite. Board members have money to donate and contacts to mobilize.

Cuban Americans who lived the American Dream remained committed to their own cancer association at the same time that Anglos had their own Miami chapter of the American Cancer Society (ASC). The ASC typified how non-Hispanic Whites had a separate and distinct organizational world. While theirs pre-dated that of the Cubans, they resisted opening their ranks to Hispanics until the city had so demographically transformed that they, like La Liga, were forced to rethink their mission, as well as their fundraising strategy. Possibly, had the ASC leadership reached out to and incorporated Cuba's pre-revolution well-to-do into its ranks in the 1960s and early 1970s Exiles would not have reestablished La Liga. But once established, each cancer association promoted its own cause. The two do not communicate with each other or coordinate activity around their shared health concern. Indeed, in response to the city's ethnic makeover, the ASC launched its own Hispanic initiative. The drive resulted in *Latinos/as* accounting for approximately 30 percent of its volunteer staff as of January 2005. The ASC initiative was designed both to carry out its mission, to educate Hispanics about cancer prevention, and to target Hispanics for fundraising.[59]

Informal, Country Club Life

In their leisure life as well, wealthy Exiles tried to recreate their pre immigrant world. They sought to reestablish their former club life, which, as I noted in the previous chapter, had been restricted to people of the "right" racial stock, lineage, and income. In doing so, they set about to reconstruct the informal base to their race-based class life that the revolution had destroyed in their homeland.

In this vein, 1960s émigrés founded a club in Miami that built on pre-revolutionary Havana's five most exclusive ones. Its name, the Big Five, captures its island social essence. The new country club enabled the pre-revolutionary privileged class to continue to intermingle "among their own" in their new land. Former members of the elite island clubs automatically qualified for membership.

But as with La Liga, in their club life the pre-revolutionary elite never entirely succeeded in reinstituting their social world of old. Their children, in particular, did not gravitate exclusively to the Big Five, for they did not attach the same social meaning as their elders to the reincarnated club and they had other country clubs to choose from which were similarly elitist, though not confined to Cubans.

Rather than shutting down when faced with a shrinking Cuban American social base, the Big Five extended membership to other wealthy Latin

Americans who had come to make Miami their second, if not primary, home. At the turn of the century a club member estimated that 80 percent of all members were Cuban American, while all but 1 percent of the remainder were non-Cuban Hispanic.[60] The Big Five thereby came to provide yet another base for solidifying ties among elite of Latin American origin, separate from Anglo class equivalents. All the while, the more recent, more humble Cuban émigrés, who grew up in revolutionary Cuba in which the Big Five's social and class base had been obliterated, and without a club life, remained uninvolved.

Wealthy Anglos could, in principle, join the Big Five, but they preferred their own informal as well as formal social world. Around the turn of the century most non-equity members of the luxurious and exclusive Fisher Island Club, for example, were non-Hispanic Whites, although some Cuban Americans joined.[61] It was against the backdrop of such clubs that the Big Five lost the luster elite clubs had in Cuba before the revolution, where they alone brought the upper class together.

Thus, wealthy Exiles partially, though never fully, succeeded in reinstituting and reproducing their home country, class-based social world. For one, their US-raised children who had assimilated more to the new country had a broader range of options from which they could choose. And the Anglos who resisted joining the Exiles' elite club opened the doors of their clubs selectively to wealthy Cuban Americans. At the same time, Exiles opened their club to other Hispanics of their social class.

Wealthy Exile Schooling of Their Children

Cuba's elite, who had educated their children in select private schools before the revolution, also continued this tradition after resettling in the US. They thereby sought to pass on their race-based class world and advantages to their children, and their views on life, which Eire so eloquently recounted in his memoir (see p. 15). The first post-Castro arrivals even reopened some island schools in Miami that had shut down in Cuba, as faculty and students' families fled the revolution.

The most renowned island school, Belén Jesuit, had been based in Havana, with an affiliate in Santiago de Cuba. Castro was one of its illustrious island alumni.[62] The school in Cuba was "Groton, Andover, and Exeter all wrapped into one."[63] Pre-revolutionary well-to-do elites reopened the boys Catholic school in Miami, without paying homage to its famous graduate. After nearly two decades on Calle Ocho, it relocated to a suburb, this time following its wealthy second-generation, US-born Cuban American student body. Its new campus looked more like a college than a typical high school. At the same time, many Exiles sent their girls to a different single-sex parochial school.

Through such private schools children of the same socio-political, class, racial, religious, and ethnic background bonded, while acquiring a bilingual education filtered through the Exile view of the world. In 2001, a guidance counselor at Belén estimated that 93 percent of the school's students were Cuban. Four percent of the remainder were other Hispanics, especially Dominican, Colombian, Venezuelan, and Mexican. The students were uniformly light-skinned. Indicative, the class of 2004 included not one dark-skinned person.[64] Absent, however, were children of the Non-Hispanic White elite. They instead sent their children to prestigious non-denominational private schools that few Cuban or other Hispanics attended.

Most of the students of Cuban origin were second- and third-generation Americans, from families who emigrated before the Freedom Flights ended.[65] Commenting on how closely Exiles associated especially with Belén, a woman referred to the school as "living testimony to the Cuban exile movement."[66] Students were steeped in lore of pre-revolutionary Cuba, filtered through Exile lenses.[67] School reunions, which include Exiles who attended the Jesuit affiliates in Cuba, reaffirm Exile identity.[68] Children of more recent émigrés are notably absent. The later arrivals came without a tradition of private and parochial education that would predispose them to seek such schooling, even if they could afford it.

Thus, Exiles turned schooling into a vehicle through which to pass on their views on life and their class and race based advantages to their children, who in turn established ties among their own generation. Yet, in the new country context, the elite education subjected children to new country influences as well. Pre-immigration ways underwent change even when the foreign-born transplanted institutions of old.

Groups Formed in the New Country

After emigrating, Exiles formed many civic groups, with small memberships, that shared an anti-Castro agenda. Some allied in umbrella organizations: with Junta Patriótica and Unidad Cubana in Miami, and with Organizaciones Cubanas Unidos (OCU) in the Union City area.[69] In 2001, in Miami, over two dozen groups affiliated just with Unidad Cubana. Slightly fewer groups affiliated with OCU, the only umbrella group in New Jersey (with OCU leadership routinely rotating among its group members to help maintain inter-group unity). Miami, with its larger Cuban American population thereby had a denser and more coordinated associational life through which new country life was filtered.

Hometown Associations

Exiles in both Union City and Miami formed hometown associations, although in Union City, only a few. The association established by people from Fomento, the provincial island town from where the core of New Jersey Exiles came, became the main island community-of-origin group in "Havana North."

Miami, in contrast, gave birth to many Cuba-based hometown associations, which affiliated with the umbrella group, Cuban Municipalities in Exile

(Municipios de Cuba en el Exilio), and with Junta Patriótica, in turn. The first *municipio* group formed in 1962. The groups appealed especially to émigrés from provincial communities outside Havana who were less well-to-do.[70] In their class base, they were rather unique.

Exiles established *municipio* associations to help old-country townspeople regroup: to reestablish former acquaintances and maintain cultural practices of old, while also facilitating new country adaptation. They accordingly simultaneously both fostered and tempered assimilation and acculturation. The groups organized cultural and recreational activities, and they provided opportunities for émigrés with shared community origins to reminisce and collectively enjoy traditions of their past. At the same time, the groups addressed new arrivals' economic needs. They helped newcomers find jobs through group members' networks, they helped cover funeral expenses, and they offered small loans to those who lacked collateral to qualify for bank funds. In these respects, the *municipio* groups differed little from associations that both old immigrant groups, such as Italians, and other new immigrant groups, such as Mexicans and Salvadorans, formed.[71]

However, politically the *municipio* groups were distinctive. Initially they coordinated subversive activity designed to overthrow Castro, with tacit if not actual support from US intelligence agencies. The groups offered community-of-origin intelligence and island-based contacts who might serve as anti-Castro collaborators. While Washington put a halt to subversive interventions by *municipio* groups in the 1970s, because the leadership of the Municipalities in Exile remained anti-Castro, group members never routinely engaged in collective cross-border bridge-building as do affiliates of hometown associations of other new immigrant groups. Discussions at *municipio* group meetings focused on Cuban politics. Attendees would bicker among themselves over what they considered the best strategy to bring the Castro-led government to heel.[72]

Municipio groups fuse religion into their group life, which reinforces members' conservative Catholic Cuban outlook on life. Each *municipio* group visits the Shrine of the Virgin of Charity of Cobre on a set day each year, where they hold a special service in honor of their home community.

The *municipio* groups affirm the normative world of the first émigrés who fled the revolution, even though they, in principle, are based on homeland community and not émigré cohort. The Exile-dominated leadership of the umbrella organization tried to reach out to more recent arrivals, if for no other reason than that the association's future was at risk as the founding generation died off. It met with little success, however. The cultural milieu of the groups did not resonate with the newer Cubans. So dedicated were members to affirming their past that Mariel émigrés joked disapprovingly that the groups had created a time warp, of Cuba in the 1950s.[73] New Cubans, in turn, remained on the sidelines of *municipio* groups, even though they could benefit from the services the groups offered.

Socioeconomic Groups

The first émigrés also formed their own ethnic-based professional, business, and labor groups, associated with employment in their new country. In addressing socioeconomic interests, the associations heightened émigré class differences, alongside home country identity.

In Miami, Exiles formed, for example, unions, and lawyer, physician, and builder associations, plus their own Chamber of Commerce. Some of them affiliated with Junta Patriótica and Unidad Cubana. In formally naming groups when first forming as "In Exile," members demonstrated how they defined themselves in relation to their homeland and their opposition to the revolution which their generational opponents on the island championed. The professional groups typically involved the pre-revolutionary well-to-do (and their immigrant children), although the small business and builders' associations included upwardly mobile émigrés of more modest socioeconomic background.

Cuban émigrés initially formed these associations partly to defend their economic interests when excluded from their Anglo counterpart groups in their worlds of work. But as parallel mainstream US associations opened doors to them, the conditions that initially induced the formation of the ethnic-based groups no longer explained their continuation. Because the associations provided opportunities for co-ethnic sociability and for building ethnic-based social ties of economic worth, Cuban Americans maintained their separate associations while also, with time, joining the earlier "Anglo" equivalent functional groups.

Émigrés changed from perceiving their ethnic heritage as an economic liability to considering it an asset. Their associations served as bedrock for the change. Some of the groups even became influential local and state-wide power brokers, as detailed in the next chapter. This was true, for example, of the Latin Builders Association, which Cuban Americans formed in 1971 to ensure representation of their business interests in the building trades. And some groups, such as the association of Cuban American lawyers, came to envision their homeland as a potential landmine of economic opportunity in a post-Castro era, and tried to position themselves for the occasion. The significance of the groups to their members, in essence, changed over time.

Affiliations with Mainstream US Groups

The first émigrés also joined national and international organizations in which their local affiliates mainly only involved "their own." These groups served to assimilate and acculturate members to mainstream US associational life and norms while reinforcing ethnic solidarity, values, and identity. The Little Havana and Union City affiliates of the Kiwanis Club, which sponsor the popular pan-Latino cultural festivities, are illustrative. Around the turn of the century, membership in the Little Havana chapter of the formally "American" association was 100 percent Hispanic, 94 percent of Cuban origin.[74] While the Union City association similarly became pan-Hispanic in its social base, it was so dominated by Cuban Americans in numbers and influence that members referred to it jokingly as the Cubanis Club. Cuban Americans, Exiles in particular, imbued the "American" groups with their own shade of meaning.

Early émigrés remained committed to the Little Havana Kiwanis Club even after they lived and worked elsewhere in the city. They did so because Little Havana remained socially and symbolically important to them as they assimilated socially, acculturated, and shared in the American Dream.

Affiliates of mainstream American groups accordingly provided additional opportunities for Cuban Americans to build up and sustain social ties among "their own," including ties of actual and potential economic worth. But under first-wave émigré domination the groups embedded their anti-Castro view of the world. The groups thereby fused US with Exile-defined Cuban identities and norms.

Individual Bridge-Builders: Selective Exiles Tapped for Inclusion in the Elite Local Anglo-Dominated World

By the turn of the century, Miami's Anglo-dominated institutional world had opened up at the highest levels selectively to Cuban Americans. This rested on strategic Anglo rethinking, in light of the city's ethnic makeover. In the changed milieu Anglos tapped wealthy Cuban Americans to serve as chief administrative officers and as members of their boards of directors and boards of trustees. This was true of the United Way, the *Miami Herald*, and local colleges and universities.

Reflecting on the gradual inclusion of Cuban Americans in elite institutional circles, a wealthy, politically preeminent Cuban American businessman noted to me how he in recent years had come to see more fellow ethnics on the boards on which he served and at the high-level meetings to which he was invited. The Cuban Americans whom Anglos tapped were those who had emigrated in the first years of the revolution. In that they typically emigrated when young,[75] they were well schooled in US as well as Cuban ways. Meanwhile, because Anglos maintained control of the institutions, and because they did not simultaneously join Cuban American formed groups, inter-ethnic assimilation in these high circles, as in club life and private schooling, was unidirectional to the extent it occurred.

Yet, the early émigrés who were incorporated into the top circles of local institutional life never abandoned or repressed their ethnic identity and commitments.[76] They thus occasionally leveraged the Anglo institutions for ethnic causes they wished to champion. The preeminent Cuban American businessman, Carlos de la Cruz, for example, convinced the United Way, on whose board he served, to allot money to a Cuban American group that he helped form. The group worked with Cuban rafters who had been taken to the US

Guantanamo military base in 1994 after the Clinton Administration agreed to admit them, but before they gained US entry.[77]

In sum, émigrés' pre-immigration past influenced their civic life in their new country. They embedded their views, identities, and networks in their new associational world. They formed their own groups partly by choice, but also because initially they were excluded from Anglo groups. Whatever the origins, the groups served as a bedrock for sustaining views formed in Cuba, while simultaneously serving to assimilate and acculturate members into mainstream American life and to forge new pan-Hispanic identities that were Cuban American at their core. Notably, though, among the foreign-born, mainly only Exiles, the well-to-do in particular, became entrenched in US civic life.

Economic Adaptation: From the (Bilingual) American Dream to "The Other American"

Even when moving to the US unwillingly, most island-born émigrés improved their socioeconomic lot in their new land. They have been one of the most economically successful new immigrant groups.

I focus my economic discussion almost exclusively on Miami not merely because that is where most Cuba-born settled, but because data availability is best there.[78] In this manner, moreover, I can assess émigré adaptation within a single labor market milieu.

I shift my discussion here mainly to the individual level, as documented in census data from the first-decade Exiles who arrived through to the first-decade New Cubans who made the US their home. I examine census-based trends, however, in the context of community, national, and international developments, as reflected in material from my Miami interviews, the Department of Homeland Security (and Immigration and Naturalization Service), and secondary sources. My census analysis centers on high-end occupational and income attainment, and, at the other extreme, on poverty-level earnings. In that earnings are contingent on jobs held, the two aspects of economic adaptation are not entirely independent indicators of economic adaptation. And while I include information on all émigré cohorts by decade of arrival, my discussion mainly details contrasts between the first and most recent arrivals during the 1970 to 2000 census years. Because New Cubans had lived in the US at the time of the 2000 census too brief a time to discern any but their short-term economic adaptation, I discuss their labor market experiences in little detail, other than in relation to the adaptation of earlier émigrés during their first decade in the US, that is, during comparable years in the US.

Sharing in the American Dream

In tracing the economic adaptation of émigrés from the 1960s through the 1990s from the decade of their first arrival through the turn of the twenty-first century, I explore several forces that might possibly be in play:

1   *A possible assimilation effect.* If immigrant economic adaptation is so explained, each émigré wave should experience more economic mobility with years in the US and exposure to the US way of life.

2   *A possible age-of-immigration effect.* If of import, any assimilation effect should differ among the foreign-born depending on how old they were when they uprooted. Younger émigrés would be expected to confront less age-based labor market discrimination and to master English better, and to have better labor market options as a result. This thesis implies that Cubans who uprooted at the same age, independently of when, and independently of their experiences before uprooting, should have similar new country economic prospects.

3   *A possible age effect.* People's labor market experiences, whether US or foreign-born, may be expected to hinge on how old they are, and to improve from the time of first entry into the labor market through middle age.

4   *A possible émigré cohort effect.* If émigrés' lived experiences before uprooting impact on new country economic adaptation, the different émigré cohorts should differ in their labor market experiences, in ways traceable to their world before uprooting.

5   *A possible generational effect.* This would be reflected in differences between the foreign-born and native-born being more marked than differences among émigrés. The native-born would be expected to be more economically successful, in that they were entirely US educated and best positioned to make the school-to-work transition at an early age.

6   *A possible contextual effect.* How well émigrés do may be contingent on where they settle and when. Different labor markets offer different job and earnings possibilities, which may change over time, partly as a result of broader national and international trends, and of local niches developed and lost in the process. And government policies that change over time may influence immigrant options. Labor market participants, immigrants included, themselves may contribute to changed job and earnings options over time. Context by no means is static, and the foreign-born may shape and not merely be shaped by the labor market where they settle.

7   *A possible enclave effect.* If immigrant opportunities hinge not on overall labor market opportunities where they settle, but on those they create by and for "their own," economic adaptation would be more narrowly and ethnically contextually contingent than parameters set by the broader labor market where they live.

What do census data suggest? Overall, Cuban Americans have done well compared to the average American and average Latin American immigrant.[79] This is true both occupationally and financially.

Occupationally, during each decade in the US ever more Cuban immigrants attained top-level positions, which I define as employment in professional, managerial, and technical fields (Table 2.5). They were so successful that more

Table 2.5 Job and income attainment among Cuban Americans in Miami in census years 1970–2000

	Decade of arrival				
	US-born	1960s	1970s	1980s	1990s
OCCUPATION					
high-status jobs[a]					
1970 census	19%	11%			
1980 census	16	24	13%		
1990 census	29	31	22	14%	
2000 census	41	36	28	23	18%
worker—skilled (crafts)[b]					
1970 census	6	12			
1980 census	6	11	14		
1990 census	8	11	13	16	
2000 census	6	9	11	15	14
worker—semi & unskilled[b]					
1970 census	25	41			
1980 census	17	26	36		
1990 census	9	20	26	31	
2000 census	7	13	19	22	27
SELF-EMPLOYMENT (and unpaid family employment)					
1970 census	8	6			
1980 census	3	11	7		
1990 census	6	16	13	12	
2000 census	9	17	17	15	10
PERSONAL INCOME					
High (top tercile of US income earners)[c]					
1970 census	17	12			
1980 census	7	19	8		
1990 census	13	29	21	11	
2000 census	26	21	15	12	7
Poverty level					
1970 census	14	18			
1980 census	13	12	22		
1990 census	13	13	19	26	
2000 census	12	14	19	20	24

Source: Steven Ruggles and Matthew Sobek, et al., *Integrated Public Use Microdata Series* (*IPUMS*), Version 3.0 (Minneapolis: Historical Census Projects University of Minnesota, 2003, www.ipums.org).

Notes:
a Professional, managerial, technical.
b Skilled workers include crafts workers, semi- and unskilled workers include Op/Labor/ HH service workers.
c Cuban Americans are ranked high-income earners if they earn as much as the top tercile of all income earners nationwide.

Cubans held such jobs in Miami than in their homeland (see Table 1.1 on p. 16). Émigrés who went into business for themselves have also done well. Sales and receipts of Cuban American-owned businesses nationwide, most based in Miami, increased, for example, over 37-fold between 1969 and 1997 (in constant dollars), and reached $26.4 billion by 2001. Cuban American business revenue came to equal that of the entire island's gross domestic product measured at the official exchange rate, and substantially more at the unofficial exchange rate that the Cuban government itself recognized for island-based transactions.[80] The decadal job mobility suggests an "assimilation effect."

Occupational success, however, varies among émigré cohorts, which I delineate, according to census data, by decade of arrival (Table 2.5). While the number of top job holders increased over the years among all cohorts, 1960s émigrés were the most occupationally successful at the time of each census. In 2000, more than one-third of them held top jobs. And they tended to have more top job-holders than other émigré cohorts; even when controlling for years in the US. This proved especially true once settled in the US, beginning with émigrés' second decade in their adopted country. This suggests a cohort effect independent of an assimilation effect. The 1960s émigrés arrived with the best pre-immigrant work experiences, education, and social capital to draw upon. However, in that the first arrivals did not do so distinctively better than other émigré cohorts when controlling for years in the US, émigré life before uprooting alone does not determine new country success.

Noteworthy, Table 2.5 points to impressive accomplishments among Marielitos and New Cubans, as well as among Exiles. While remaining on the sidelines of civil society associational life, the newer émigrés individually took advantage of US economic opportunities. Marielitos' occupational achievements suggest the stigma they suffered was undeserved. By 2000, nearly a fourth of them had attained high-status jobs. My own survey, in which I asked émigrés about their homeland, job histories, as well as their new country, confirms that most 1980s arrivals improved their occupational status with their move to the US.

Moreover, within their first ten years in the US, census data show more 1990s cohorts than all preceding decadal cohorts to have attained top-level jobs. While it is too soon to see whether they will do better in the long run as well, New Cubans' immediate success, like that of the Exiles, built on pre-immigration skills and networks. But so too does it appear linked to the new opportunities the labor market opened up as Miami became increasingly Hispanic and developed, as I describe below, transnational reach. The job history of Elias, whom I interviewed, is telling. Although he speaks little English, the 2000 émigré landed a $40,000-a-year computer programming job just one week after arriving. This was about a one-hundred-and-sixty-fold increase over his yearly earnings in Cuba.[81] A friend of his from his Cuba days, who had moved to Miami just a couple years before him, found him the job. Thus, his pre-immigration social network took on economic worth in the US. Then, when Elias's employer realized how well he performed his work, and how his lack of command of English was not an obstacle, Elias received a $10,000 raise. Soviet trained during the years of Cuba-Soviet "solidarity," he moved to the US with Information Technology expertise that he could immediately put to use.[82] Elias adapted so well also because the Miami economy by the time he arrived had evolved to the point of opening up jobs in the high-tech sector for which English proficiency was not essential.

In every census except one, 1960s émigrés also included the highest number of self-employed (the exception was in 2000, when 1970 émigrés had an equal percentage of self-employed) (Table 2.5). Victor, who emigrated in 1964 after refusing to "take a revolutionary pledge," illustrates how after initial adjustment difficulties the first post-Castro arrivals put their pre-immigration entrepreneurial experiences to good use. He spoke to me about the farm his family had owned in Cuba before it was expropriated by the government. While he first worked after emigrating as an accountant in a factory, within five years he applied his island-acquired farm managerial expertise in his new urban setting. Starting his own business with three employees, by the early 2000s, he had seventy employees. He considered his import firm a "tremendous success."

Exile successes that built on human, social, and cultural, if not also economic, assets attained in Cuba are too many to cite. A few examples include the Fanjul brothers, Carlos de la Cruz, and Carlos Saladrigas. The Fanjuls, from an island sugar baron family, became major Florida sugar producers. De la Cruz came from such an upper-crust island family that he had been educated in an elite US prep school before the revolution. After emigrating, he became a wealthy Miami banker and then chairman of a number of major beer and soda bottler and distribution companies. And Saladrigas served as chairman of a bank and as CEO of the Vinca Group, which he co-founded. In 1998, the Vinca Group was one of the largest Hispanic-owned companies (before being acquired by ADP). Saladrigas also served on boards of directors and as advisor of several non-Hispanic companies. Influential and highly respected, as well as wealthy, de la Cruz and Saladrigas were among the few Cuban Americans tapped to serve on boards of directors and trustees (including as Chair) of Anglo-dominated universities, charity organizations, and other institutions.

Nonetheless, 1960s arrivals, steeped in Cuba's capitalist past, did not go into business for themselves more than later émigrés who grew up in socialist Cuba (Table 2.5). Once controlling for years in the US, the first émigrés have not gravitated more to entrepreneurial careers than émigrés who lived through the near obliteration of a market-based economy. Of course, people who go into business for themselves vary considerably in success, and Cuban émigrés are no exception.[83] Among entrepreneurs, the earlier émigrés earn substantially more. Portes and Shafer found, in 2000 in Miami, that the average personal income of pre-1980 émigrés was more than double that of later arrivals.[84] Their data adds credence to my cohort thesis. However, Portes and Shafer focus only on a single year. They do not control for years in the US, namely a possible assimilation effect, independent of cohort.

Unquestionably, 1960s émigrés have dominated certain fields of self-employment, some of which are very lucrative. They have prospered especially in the construction trades. By 1971, Cuban Americans owned roughly half of the main construction companies in Miami-Dade County, and soon thereafter 60 percent.[85] The first post-Castro arrivals took advantage of the construction boom that Miami's economic and demographic growth at the time fueled. They capitalized on being in the right place at the right time. Ironically, some of them went into business for themselves only after being denied the union membership essential for certain manual jobs. Jorge Mas Canosa, who became the most influential Cuban American leader, was one of the early émigrés to amass a fortune in the building trades. While the Cuban American experience in this sector suggests that context matters, why did Cuban Americans take greater advantage of it than others in Miami? Cuban Americans had the skills, determination, and contacts, including, increasingly, politically useful contacts that I detail in the next chapter, to prosper in the sector. The Cuban American experience also highlights how discriminatory practices by more established groups impact on émigré career paths, including in unanticipated ways.

However, not all émigrés, including Exiles, attained high-status, lucrative jobs. While the number of island-born émigrés who worked as laborers declined considerably over the years, at the time of each census, Exiles always had the fewest so employed (Table 2.5). But initially upon arrival, more Exiles than later émigrés worked at semi-skilled and unskilled jobs. Here too context mattered. Miami's late twentieth-century transformation into a post-industrial city closed down manufacturing job options, even for Marielitos with their working-class background. With the city's economic makeover, the percentage of Cuban Americans employed in manufacturing plunged from 34 to 19 percent in the 1990s.[86] The garment industry, which had employed Cuban immigrants in the 1960s, especially women, by the 1990s had all but disappeared.[87]

With varied occupational histories, émigré cohorts differ, in turn, in earnings. While the number of high-income earners, defined as people among the top tercile of income earners nationwide, increased among all cohorts until 2000, at the time of each census, Exiles had the largest number with top earnings.[88] And Exiles almost without exception also had the most top tercile income earners when controlling for years in the US (Table 2.5).[89] This again suggests a cohort effect, independent of an assimilation effect. The number of high 1960s income earners dipped, however, by 2000, as many of them reached retirement age.

But might cohort differences mask differences in economic success linked to the life cycle? Focusing only on émigrés in their prime employment years, ages 25–64, the younger Cuban Americans, aged 25–39, prove to do better than those over forty at accessing high-status jobs, across émigré cohorts (except among the 1960s émigrés in 2000) (Table 2.6). The older émigrés gravitate more to self-employment. Age accordingly impacts on labor market experiences, and among all émigré cohorts.

However, there appears to be a cohort effect above and beyond age-based

Table 2.6 Job attainment by age among Cuban Americans in Miami in census years 1970–2000

	Decade of arrival				
	US-born	1960s	1970s	1980s	1990s
HIGH-STATUS JOBS[a]					
1970 census, aged					
25–39	19%	13%			
40–64	30	11			
1980 census, aged					
25–39	29	32	15%		
40–64	28	21	14		
1990 census, aged					
25–39	39	40	30	15%	
40–64	34	29	18	14	
2000 census, aged					
25–39	48	36	39	31	19%
40–64	52	39	27	20	18
SELF-EMPLOYMENT					
(and unpaid family labor)					
1970 census, aged					
25–39	4	6			
40–64	16	7			
1980 census, aged					
25–39	7	9	8		
40–64	9	13	9		
1990 census, aged					
25–39	9	14	8	13	
40–64	11	18	17	15	
2000 census, aged					
25–39	11	13	11	13	9
40–64	14	17	18	17	11

Source: Steven Ruggles and Matthew Sobek, et al., *Integrated Public Use Microdata Series* (*IPUMS*), Version 3.0 (Minneapolis: Historical Census Projects University of Minnesota, 2003, www.ipums.org).

Note:
a Professional, managerial, and technical.

labor market sorting. Among the similarly aged, 1960s émigrés have done better than later arrivals at accessing high-level jobs, establishing businesses of their own (until 2000),[90] and attaining high incomes (Tables 2.6 and 2.7).

Age of emigration also has some bearing on economic success. At the time of each census typically more younger than older émigrés held high-level jobs and were top income earners. This was true after the émigrés' first decade in the US, once settled in the labor market (Tables 2.8 and 2.9). Yet, here too there appears to be a cohort effect. In each census year typically 1960s émigrés did better than later émigrés who uprooted at the same age (up to age forty). This was truer with respect to job than income attainment, however.

Table 2.7 Income by age among Cuban Americans in and outside Miami in census years 1970–2000

	Decade of arrival				
	US-born	1960s	1970s	1980s	1990s
A. Miami					
HIGH PERSONAL INCOME[a]					
1970 census, aged					
25–39	30%	18%			
40–64	28	15			
1980 census, aged					
25–39	33	30	11%		
40–64	25	21	13		
1990 census, aged					
25–39	50	52	37	15%	
40–64	43	35	24	15	
2000 census, aged					
25–39	39	40	34	21	9%
40–64	48	33	20	13	8
POVERTY LEVEL					
1970 census, aged					
25–39	3%	16%			
40–64	9	16			
1980 census, aged					
25–39	7	8	24%		
40–64	16	9	17		
1990 census, aged					
25–39	6	7	11	26%	
40–64	9	9	12	21	
2000 census, aged					
25–39	6	5	7	13	21%
40–64	8	9	15	18	22
B. Other-than-Miami					
HIGH PERSONAL INCOME[a]					
1970 census, aged					
25–39	36%	28%			
40–64	36	25			
1980 census, aged					
25–39	31	35	17%		
40–64	38	32	19		
1990 census, aged					
25–39	50	58	43	19%	
40–64	49	46	35	21	
2000 census, aged					
25–39	38	46	45	24	10%
40–64	44	42	28	16	12
POVERTY LEVEL					
1970 census, aged					
25–39	10%	14%			
40–64	12	11			

	1960s	1970s	1980s	1990s	2000s
1980 census, aged					
25–39	13	8	19%		
40–64	10	8	14		
1990 census, aged					
25–39	9	7	11	30%	
40–64	12	7	10	23	
2000 census, aged					
25–39	10	5	7	19	21%
40–64	12	8	11	26	21

Source: Steven Ruggles and Matthew Sobek, et al., *Integrated Public Use Microdata Series* (*IPUMS*), Version 3.0 (Minneapolis: Historical Census Projects University of Minnesota, 2003, www.ipums.org).

Note:
a Cuban Americans are ranked high-income earners if they earn as much as the top tercile of all income earners nationwide.

Table 2.8 Job attainment by age-of-immigration among Cuban Americans in census years 1970–2000

	Decade of arrival			
	1960s	*1970s*	*1980s*	*1990s*
HIGH-STATUS JOBS[a]				
1970 census, age-of-immigration				
under 18	9%			
18–24	13			
25–39	11			
40–64	11			
1980 census, age-of-immigration				
under 18	29	9%		
18–24	29	15		
25–39	22	14		
40–64	19	14		
1990 census, age-of-immigration				
under 18	42	30	12%	
18–24	32	26	13	
25–39	25	19	16	
40–64	22	16	12	
2000 census, age-of-immigration				
under 18	44	37	31	13%
18–24	35	29	25	17
25–39	28	23	21	21
40–64	25	17	17	16

Source: Steven Ruggles and Matthew Sobek, et al., *Integrated Public Use Microdata Series* (*IPUMS*), Version 3.0 (Minneapolis: Historical Census Projects University of Minnesota, 2003, www.ipums.org).

Note:
a Professional, managerial, technical.

Table 2.9 Income by age-of-immigration in and outside Miami in census years 1970–2000

	Decade of arrival			
	1960s	*1970s*	*1980s*	*1990s*
A. Miami				
HIGH PERSONAL INCOME[a]				
1970 census, age-of-immigration				
under 18	2%			
18–24	15			
25–39	21			
40–64	10			
1980 census, age-of-immigration				
under 18	23	2%		
18–24	31	6		
25–39	22	16		
40–64	11	8		
1990 census, age-of-immigration				
under 18	54	37	4%	
18–24	43	24	12	
25–39	27	26	17	
40–64	9	11	10	
2000 census, age-of-immigration				
under 18	44	34	19	2%
18–24	25	22	17	7
25–39	13	12	14	9
40–64	4	4	5	6
POVERTY LEVEL				
1970 census, age-of-migration				
under 18	19%			
18–24	12			
25–39	17			
40–64	18			
1980 census, age-of-migration				
under 18	7	17%		
18–24	9	21		
25–39	9	18		
40–64	19	24		
1990 census, age-of-migration				
under 18	6	8	24%	
18–24	7	18	25	
25–39	10	11	23	
40–64	23	27	26	
2000 census, age-of-migration				
under 18	6	8	12	26%
18–24	8	14	19	20
25–39	17	17	18	22
40–64	24	29	28	24

B. Other-than-Miami
HIGH PERSONAL INCOME[a]

1970 census, age-of-migration				
under 18	8%			
18–24	31			
25–39	28			
40–64	19			
1980 census, age-of-migration				
under 18	28	4%		
18–24	35	11		
25–39	34	22		
40–64	19	13		
1990 census, age-of-migration				
under 18	59	41	6%	
18–24	48	41	18	
25–39	41	37	22	
40–64	15	18	14	
2000 census, age-of-migration				
under 18	51	42	22	4%
18–24	34	30	18	7
25–39	16	18	18	11
40–64	5	6	10	10

POVERTY LEVEL

1970 census, age-of-migration				
under 18	20%			
18–24	8			
25–39	13			
40–64	12			
1980 census, age-of-migration				
under 18	9	18%		
18–24	8	22		
25–39	7	15		
40–64	13	18		
1990 census, age-of-migration				
under 18	7	11	24%	
18–24	7	15	31	
25–39	7	9	25	
40–64	16	18	26	
2000 census, age-of-migration				
under 18	7	8	19	26%
18–24	9	12	27	16
25–39	11	13	25	23
40–64	7	23	25	20

Source: Steven Ruggles and Matthew Sobek, et al., *Integrated Public Use Microdata Series* (*IPUMS*), Version 3.0 (Minneapolis: Historical Census Projects University of Minnesota, 2003, www.ipums.org).

Note:
a Cuban Americans are ranked high-income earners if they earn as much as the top tercile of all income earners nationwide.

And how well do the Cuban American US-born fare, compared to their immigrant parents' generation in Miami? Remarkably, in 2000, over 40 percent of the US-born held top-level jobs, more than 1960s émigrés in their peak year (Table 2.5). At the same time, their career path is somewhat distinctive. More are professionals, and fewer are entrepreneurs. Self-employment proves more an immigrant than native-born occupation. However, the native-born do not in all census years do better either occupationally or in earnings than émigrés. This is partly explained by age (Table 2.6). Among the similarly aged, the US-born typically do the best, except relative to 1960s émigrés in some years.

In sum, many Miami Cuban Americans have shared in the American Dream, and, generally, increasingly with years in the US. The data in this respect point to an assimilation effect, although one that is partly contingent on age and age at immigration. The data, however, also point to a cohort effect. The first émigrés, who knew island life before the revolution, have tended to do better economically than émigrés who grew up after the social transformation, in ways not explicable merely in terms of their greater number of years in the US.

Context: The Impact of Macro-Political and Economic Dynamics

Exile success rested not entirely on their skills, social capital, and perseverance. Exiles benefited from government support that was never offered on the same scale to later arrivals, and from economic opportunities that opened up not long after they arrived, for which they were well suited. They benefited from being in the right place at the right time in more than the building trades, while their pre-immigration background predisposed them to take advantage of extant opportunities.

The first who fled the revolution benefited, for one, from the federal government Cold War preoccupation at the time they arrived. Washington, as a result, made nearly a billion dollars worth of assistance available to them through the Cuban Refugee Program. The government invested in Cuban émigrés to demonstrate the superiority of capitalism over Communism. The program helped new arrivals adapt economically through employment placements, professional and other job training, English and bilingual education, and business and college loans (some of which were forgiven).[91] Although the government ended the program in 1973, Mariel and subsequent arrivals received some benefits that gave them an advantage over other immigrant groups if not over Exiles. Through special legislation they qualified for welfare, job training, Medicaid, food stamps, and Supplemental Security Income (SSI).[92] All Cuban émigrés also qualify for a "Green Card," immediately if they entered with an immigration visa, but almost without exception also after a year and a day if they entered without such a permit. Cuban illegal as well as legal entrants can accordingly quickly access jobs requiring legal status.

The first who fled the revolution also benefited from employment and business opportunities tied to Washington's regional security agenda when they first arrived, which centered on preventing "other Cubas" in the backyard of the US. In the 1960s, the CIA and other intelligence agencies employed some twelve thousand Exiles in Miami as case officers and agents.[93] The agencies appreciated both the Cuban newcomers' command of Spanish and their antipathy to Communism. Émigrés who arrived in subsequent decades had no comparable employment options. By the 1980s, intelligence agencies had refugees from the Central American civil wars to hire, and by the time the 1990s émigrés arrived, the Cold War had ended and Washington's security concerns had shifted elsewhere, especially in the aftermath of September 11, 2001.

Beginning in the late 1960s, the Exile cohort benefited, and more so than subsequent arrivals, also from Small Business Administration (SBA) loans.[94] The SBA is a federal program designed to help the entrepreneurial ambitious in general, regardless of ethnicity. The SBA does not lend money itself. Rather, it guarantees loans made by private banks. Hispanics received nearly half of all SBA loans in Miami-Dade County between 1968 and 1980. In that Cubans at the time accounted for about two-thirds of the county's Hispanic population (though only for 4 percent of the city's residents in 1970 and for 26 percent ten years later [Table 2.2]), and for most Hispanic self-employed (see Table 3.5 on p. 104), they undoubtedly were the main Hispanic beneficiaries of SBA-backed loans.[95] By definition, Cuban émigré recipients between 1968 and 1980 only involved 1960s and 1970s arrivals. A quarter-century later, when Hispanics received around one-third of all SBA-backed Miami Dade loans, a high-level Miami SBA officer told me that Cuban Americans received about half the Hispanic loans. Yet, the officer also noted that recent Cuban arrivals received few of the loans, because they lacked the requisite credentials, collateral, professional and managerial experiences, and resources to be considered good credit risks. Thus, over the years the SBA in Greater Miami maintained a bias toward early émigrés. Differential access to financing may contribute to the differential earnings among Cuban Americans who went into business.

In the 1960s, émigrés also developed and benefited from the formation of an ethnic enclave economy. They patronized co-ethnic businesses, and employers hired co-ethnics. Small Exile-formed banks, for example, financed co-ethnic start-up businesses before the SBA loan program went into effect, with bankers making so-called character loans to émigrés without collateral based on their reputation in Cuba.[96] Even as Exiles became loan officers and managers at non-Cuban-owned banks, they continued to favor others of their cohort whose reputation they knew from their Cuba days. Consequently, while the government under Castro had prohibited émigrés from taking much money with them when they left, and forced them to leave fixed assets behind, it could not keep them from taking their social ties as well as skills with them. The first émigrés drew upon economically useful homeland social assets when they resettled in Miami.[97]

Pre-immigration high-class social networks lost their capital-generating worth in the US in the 1980s. The practice of extending loans based on pre-revolution island reputation wound down with the ending of the Freedom Flights, because, as a banker explained, Exile bank-lenders no longer knew the people who were arriving.[98] But later arrivals had their own Cuba-based networks to draw upon that at times had substantial economic worth, as the story of Elias, the computer programmer who landed a $40,000-a-year job in his first week in Miami through a former friend from Cuba illustrates. Their networks, however, built on different homeland experiences. The New Cubans grew up in a socialist, not private, market-based economy.

In Miami, the 1960s émigrés also benefited from being in the right place at the right time from a global economic vantage point. Aside from accessing manufacturing jobs before they moved overseas, these émigrés were able to benefit from the city establishing a hemispheric niche.[99] The city's transformation began in the 1970s and deepened in the decades that followed. The city underwent economic restructuring, diversification, and expansion, and took on regional reach to the point that it was dubbed the "Gateway to the Americas." The city became a center of regional trade, banking, multinational corporate activity, and tourism. Trade became Miami's number one industry.[100] With the development of freight-forwarding facilities, the city also became an entrepot. Concomitantly, Miami became the fourth most important international banking center in the US.[101] Banking, like trade, was hemispheric focused. Multinational corporations of diverse sorts, in addition, set up headquarters for their Latin American operations in Miami. The city became a preferred base for Latin American business as increasing crime, kidnappings, and civil strife south of the US border made living there unsafe for management.[102] A businesswoman closely associated with a freight-forwarding zone in Miami estimated that 90 percent of locally based international activity dealt with Spanish-speaking countries.

The first post-Castro émigrés, with ingenuity and determination, as well as human, social, and economic assets, contributed to, as well as benefited from, the city's economic metamorphosis. Their knowledge of Spanish proved a source of cultural capital. Bilingual and bicultural Cuban Americans helped promote and negotiate hemispheric economic activity. Although the early émigrés were not alone in retaining command of their mother tongue, they were the most inclined among the foreign-born, as I previously noted, also to master English. In that they had other economically useful assets as well, as large national and multinational businesses squeezed out smaller Cuban American-owned firms, they hired Cuban Americans for middle and top management positions. Businesses with a focus on the Americas located in Miami over other border cities in no small part because Cuban Americans there offered the range of assets useful for hemispheric dealings.

However, the community context also set a ceiling to Exiles' as well as later Cuban immigrants' economic success. Big business remained mainly Anglo-owned and Anglo-controlled. Chief executive officers of the top banks, law, accounting, and other firms, and members of corporate boards, remained, as one of the most successful Cuban American businessmen explained to me, largely "old [Anglo-] boys' networks."

The "Other Cuban Americans"

Government support and economic restructuring did not enable all first-wave émigrés, much less subsequent arrivals, to share in the American Dream. There is an "Other Cuban American,"[103] an impoverished émigré. However, overall, fewer Cuban Americans than other Hispanics live in poverty. Elderly are the one exception.[104]

Among all émigré waves the poverty rate in Miami declined with years in the US (Table 2.7). The biggest drop occurred during émigrés' first decade in their new country. Their rate dropped until reaching retirement age, at which point it spiraled, to levels high even in comparison to other Hispanics.[105] The poverty rate reached nearly 50 percent among some cohorts of elderly.

However, in that the 1960s émigrés' poverty rate began and remained lower than other cohorts', and was lower after controlling for years in the US, a cohort effect impacts on low as well as high earnings (Table 2.5). Also indicative of such an effect, the poverty rate differed among émigré waves after controlling for age (Table 2.7). The first post-Castro arrivals had the lowest, and the most recent émigrés the highest, poverty rates among the similarly aged. And when also controlling for age at emigration, 1960s arrivals had the lowest poverty rate (Table 2.9).

Some émigrés, in addition, suffered severe loss of status with their move to Miami, even when not falling into the ranks of "the Other Cuban American" and even when their earnings, over the years, improved. Island-trained professionals, in particular, had difficulty practicing in the US. Several émigrés I interviewed complained of professional disappointments after resettling in the US. The island-trained doctor, Anita, for example, became *déclassé*. Without US medical credentials she worked at eleven different jobs in fourteen years. The single mother was so depressed with trying to make do in Miami that she almost had a nervous breakdown. Another island-trained physician, lacking US credentials, took a job a family friend offered. She complained that the work was "very manual labor-intensive and didn't follow labor standards, things that were basic in Cuba." In turn, a former university professor who emigrated in the late 1990s reported working at three part-time jobs: as a store clerk, a housecleaner, and an accountant at a pizza parlor. She could not find work enabling her to draw upon her professional training. She felt that all she does in the US is work for money, and for very little. She noted that she no longer worked for professional development, as she had in Cuba. And yet other former island professionals found the manual work they were forced to take on beneath their dignity, given their education and pre-immigration work experiences.

Alejandro, a 1994 rafter who lives in a room he rents in a trailer, is also illustrative of New Cubans who, despite emigrating mainly for economic reasons, struggled to make do in their new milieu. Having become disabled, he lives, with difficulty, on government support. His room rental absorbs 80 percent of his monthly disability stipend. He depends also on food stamps. Even his children, who emigrated in prime employment years, have not fared well. Two were unemployed. Alejandro never expected life in the US to be so difficult. Whether New Cubans will overcome such disappointments once they are more settled in the labor market remains to be seen.

Does Miami Offer Cuban Americans an Economic Advantage?

Does living in Miami among "their own" help or hinder Cuban immigrants' economic success? Scholars differ in their opinion on the subject. At one extreme, Portes (and collaborators) have argued that the enclave economy that the first arrivals established benefited the émigré community, at least the pre-1980 arrivals.[106] Huntington, at the other extreme, claims that such ethnic "stickiness," which he believes to be distinctively Hispanic, impedes immigrant economic mobility.[107] Although Portes and collaborators, as well as Huntington, focused on Miami, and on Cuban Americans there, they differed in their arguments and assessments.[108]

Huntington might appear to account for Miami's "Other Cuban Americans," for those who live at or below the poverty level. However, as I noted, Cuban American poverty rates are relatively low, except among the elderly, and are low relative to other Hispanics. They also declined among each cohort over the years. Moreover, Huntington's thesis cannot explain why more Cuban Americans than other Hispanics have shared in the American Dream, and why, on balance, Cuban Americans have done well relative to the US population at large.

Consistent with the enclave thesis, I showed how Miami Cuban Americans created economic opportunities for themselves and for each other. But I also showed Cuban American economic options not to be contingent merely on the local community context. Global restructuring opened up certain options while closing down others, beyond what the enclave thesis can account for. The new Miami has rested on the development of a hemispheric niche in which Cuban Americans play a key role, at the same time that the move of low-skilled manufacturing to poorer countries where labor is cheaper reduced worker job options. The Miami labor market in general, and for Cuban Americans in particular, needs to be understood in this broader context.

In highlighting the Miami Cuban American success story, I made no claims that the ethnic group did better in the city than elsewhere. Indeed, comparisons between Cuban American earnings in Miami and elsewhere suggest that the Sunshine State city did not, overall, give the Cuba-born émigrés who settled there a financial edge over those who resided in other places (Tables 2.7 and 2.9). Although the aggregate data undoubtedly conceals considerable locational variation, more émigrés of the same age, age of immigration, and arrival cohort were top income earners outside Miami than inside, in census years 1970 to 2000. Moreover, in 2004, Cubans living outside Florida had a higher median income than those in the state: $44,000 versus $36,000.[109]

Meanwhile, poverty rates among the Cuba-born appear not to be contingent on location. Yet, when controlling both for age, age of immigration, and year (decade) of arrival, fewer who settled outside than inside Miami lived at or below the poverty level at the time of the 1970 to 2000 censuses (Tables 2.7 and 2.9). And among the US-born, poverty rates were higher outside than inside Miami. This was true when controlling for age.[110]

Thus, even though the comparative data does not control for locational differences in living costs, the Cuba-born émigrés did not necessarily do better in earnings when settling in Miami. And US-born Cuban Americans did not necessarily do better if they settled outside Miami, where most took up residency (see Table 2.1). Either Cuban Americans are oblivious to their variable locational earning power, or non-economic considerations had greater bearing than economic ones on their decision where to live. Whatever opportunities the formation of an enclave economy and then a hemispheric "gateway" city offered, they prove not necessarily financially more advantageous to Cuban Americans than labor market options elsewhere.

Explanation of the locational differences goes beyond the scope of my study. But my research suggests some possible explanations, none of which support Huntington's ethnic "stickiness" thesis. One reason for low Miami earnings may be intra-ethnic exploitation.[111] I know New Cubans in Miami who took advantage of ethnic contacts and worked for Cuban American employers when they first settled in the US. However, dissatisfied with their earnings, they went on to take other jobs, for example, in the public sector, when able to do so. Émigrés who work for co-ethnics may thus do so by default and not merely by choice. Business owners' ethnic loyalty in hiring also may have declined over the years, to émigrés' labor market disadvantage. In this vein, Cuban American businesspeople with whom I spoke in the early 2000s, although few in number, noted limited commitment to hiring co-ethnics. They tapped into a broader labor market network, which they believed to be in their business interests. They talked of prioritizing worker qualifications over ethnicity, and they perceived Cuban émigrés not necessarily to have the best credentials. In addition, one businessman noted that he deliberately hired ethnically and racially diverse workers, to broaden the market for the goods he retailed. Against the backdrop of the large influx of Latin Americans besides Cubans, the Miami labor market became more competitive.

Meanwhile, the comparative data suggests that the enclave thesis exaggerated all along wage-earning benefits accruing to Cuban émigrés, including before the large influx of other Latin American immigrants. Dating back to 1970, Cuban Americans who settled outside, as opposed to in Miami, typically earned more (see Table 2.9). And by the turn of the twenty-first century the Miami economy, overall, had been transformed into a heavily low-wage service economy, as it took on global reach. The broader economic context in which earnings options are embedded dramatically changed over the years, and not necessarily, in the aggregate, to the advantage of Cuban Americans who settled there rather than elsewhere in the US.

Immigrant economic adaptation thus hinges on a combination of individual, cohort, and contextual factors. None alone explains how well Cuban Americans have done in Miami, much less in comparison to fellow émigrés who settled elsewhere.

Conclusion

On balance, the Cuban experience suggests that the better the economic, social, and human capital assets with which immigrants arrive, the greater the state assistance received upon emigration, and the better the labor market and creatable labor market opportunities they face, the more economically successful they will be. Such immigrants are also more likely to acculturate to mainstream America, although not necessarily while abandoning homeland cultural practices.

Focusing on three domains of immigrant adaptation, social, cultural, and economic, at the institutional, group, and individual levels, this chapter demonstrated that:

1   Assimilation and acculturation may be selective and transpire at the same time that immigrants transplant homeland solidarities, norms, and cultural practices. Assimilation and acculturation also are not necessarily unidimensional, involving immigrants taking on the habits of the native-born into whose midst they move. The foreign-born émigrés may transform life where they settle, including in ways that build on new practices and not merely on the transplantation of ideas of old. Accordingly, a full understanding of immigrant assimilation and acculturation requires a historically grounded, nuanced frame of analysis that takes immigrants' past and modes of embedding in the new country into account.

2   Émigré cohorts differ in how they adapt, in ways partially traceable to experiences before uprooting. Life before emigrating does not predetermine how foreign-born émigrés will adapt, but émigrés with a repertoire of organizational experiences and with greater assets to draw upon are best able to take advantage of their new environs. Among Cubans, Exiles had the greatest individual and organizational resources both to draw upon and on which to establish their life anew, imbued with their distinctive cohort shade of meaning. How Exiles adapted is not adequately understood in terms of their greater number of years in the US, as the assimilation thesis would suggest.

3   Context was shown to matter. Cubans adapted differently partly depending on where they settled and when. Government support helped the first émigrés adapt better than later arrivals, and Cubans in Miami at the time of its growth boom and neoliberal era restructuring enjoyed opportunities

on a scale later arrivals did not. How émigrés drew on individual assets and cohort experiences partly was contextually contingent, and must be understood accordingly.

4   Immigrant adaptation was shown also to hinge on treatment by established groups, and immigrants' capacity and determination to impose their ways on others in their midst. Among Cuban Americans, inter- and intra-ethnic struggles varied by cohort. Assimilation and acculturation resulted not merely from some "invisible hand," but from use of power, and shifts in how power was exercised over time.

5   The Cuban experience suggests, in turn, that, overall, foreign-born émigrés do not inherently do better or worse when settling in close proximity to, intermingling mainly with, and depending economically heavily on "their own," as the enclave thesis and Huntington's "ethnic stickiness" thesis, respectively, suggest. Émigré waves with different lived experiences, and with different predispositions thus formed, experienced the same social and cultural milieu and the same labor market conditions differently, and not in a patterned, consistently different way than émigrés who settled more dispersed.

The émigré cohorts also differ in their political adaptation and in their development and use of political capital, with economic success proving partly to be politically contingent. Exiles most effectively leveraged votes, personal contacts, and interest group politics to both their personal and cohort advantage. These matters are the focus of the next chapter.

3 Immigrant Politics: For Whom and for What?

If immigrants' pasts shape their new country adaptation, that should be true politically as well as socially, culturally, and economically. Political involvements should be filtered through pre-immigration lenses, with Exiles and New Cubans accordingly differing. This should be especially true of adult immigrants. But child immigrants would be likely to be influenced by politics learned at home, combined with experiences in the new country.

Indeed, Exiles have shared in the American political along with the economic Dream, in ways shaped by their pre-immigration world. They have joined the political class where they have taken up new country roots, and successfully used politics for their own individual and collective gain, from the local to the national level. Anglos who continued to dominate the highest circles of the business world at the local level, in effect, conceded political power.[1]

When sharing in the American political Dream, Exiles built on political practices and perspectives familiar to them and their families from their Cuba days. The better-off Exiles, in particular, had a tradition of civic engagement in Cuba to build on. Their past predisposed them to use politics to promote their anti-Castro mission which they refused to concede. In the post-Cold War world their mission centered on maintaining and tightening the embargo, to debilitate the Cuban government to the point of collapse. Their pre-immigration background also led many in their ranks to have low tolerance for political compromise.

The New Cubans, at the other extreme, remain on the political sidelines. Even as they increasingly take advantage of citizenship rights and vote, they remain unrepresented in the Cuban American political class and uninvolved in politically influential groups. As a result, their commitment to a life across borders received little political representation. Their political marginality built on their past, different from that of the Exiles who knew little of Cuba transformed by revolution. New Cubans had no familiarity with political life independent of the state, and many disliked the state-directed political life they knew. Meanwhile, their situation in the US reinforced their political marginality. The economically humble lacked the socioeconomic attributes typically associated with political engagement in the US.[2] Under the circumstances, New Cubans accepted political representation by Exiles and their US-born children, even when they disagreed with the Cuba policies the politicians promoted.

Marielitos, the mixed cohort that includes older émigrés whose generational formation typically had roots in life before the revolution, and young as well as old who had lived as many as two decades in revolutionary Cuba, also remain on the political sidelines. They too are uninvolved in political organizations and without representation in the Cuban American political class, even though by the turn of the twenty-first century they had lived in the US as long as Exiles had when they first became politically active and influential in their adopted country.

Children of the first émigrés, in contrast, have joined the political class. Brought up exposed to mainstream US institutional life and not merely to views learned at home, they are more eclectic in their views. Views learned at home, and reinforced by community norms and the Cuban American-dominated media, incline them to concern themselves with Cuban matters from an Exile vantage point, even though they do not know the island first-hand. At the same time, their US upbringing has made them more supportive of the politics of compromise than their parents' generation.

I will show how the emergent political class, both the Cuban and the US-born, have promoted hardline Exile interests, in the name of all Cuban Americans. They leveraged US political institutions from the local to the national level for the causes they sought to champion. Hardliners favored policies that they hoped would destabilize the Castro-led government to the point of collapse. In this vein, they advocated an embargo as all-encompassing as possible, to block political, economic, and social, as well as cultural life across borders. Through the turn of the century the political class spoke almost exclusively in a single voice. They kept challenges to their views at bay.

Although Exiles shared certain concerns with all island-born émigrés, on tightening the wall across the Straits they and the New Cubans were poles apart. The New Cubans, who experienced the post-Soviet-era crisis with friends and family on the island, favored cross-border bridge-building policies. While their views at first went unrepresented, hardline hegemony began to fracture after 2000. Changing demographics of the Cuban American community contributed to the fracturing, but so too did some influential Cuban Americans, by rethinking their stance toward Cuba after experiencing a major political defeat. The death of Cuban Americans' most powerful and influential leader also created a power vacuum hardliners never managed to fill. Meanwhile, in the post-Cold War era national lawmakers became more open to lifting, selectively, the wall across the Straits.

Below, I first detail how Cuban Americans took advantage of their new country voting rights in the new country to elect "their own" to office. Then I show how Exiles used politics for both ethnic group and private gain, operating on both sides of the law. Afterwards, I show how they masterfully organized, lobbied, and leveraged political donations to create what I call an ethnic political field, from the local to the national level and across the partisan divide, and involving more than "their own." Even in the post-Cold War era, when Cuba no longer presented a national security threat, they convinced Congressional representatives and Presidents to institute hardline policies toward their homeland, especially in years of presidential elections. I conclude the chapter with a discussion of how and why the hardline hegemony fractured by the time of the 2008 presidential cycle.

In this chapter I draw mainly on census, survey, and political contribution data. I also make use of organization documents, my interviews with politicians and top officers of key political groups in the US, news articles, and secondary sources. I focus mainly on Miami, from where Exiles built up political influence to the highest levels of national policy-making. However, I show how Cuban Americans also made political inroads in the Union City area, and at the New Jersey state level in turn, with ties to influential Miami Exiles who helped finance their campaigns.

Exile Domination of Voting and Office-Holding[3]

Nearly all Cuban émigrés qualify after five years for US citizenship, and therefore for the right to vote. Even illegal entrants enjoy such rights, after an additional year, owing to the 1966 Cuban Adjustment Act implemented during the Cold War.

Census data summarized in Table 3.1 show Cuban Americans to have taken advantage of their citizenship rights in growing numbers between 1970 and 2000. As of the turn of the twenty-first century 73 percent of Cuban Americans nationwide, and 67 percent in Miami, were citizens (Table 3.1).[4] The longer in the US, the higher the citizenship rate. Exiles accordingly have the highest rate. However, when controlling for years in the US, their rate is not distinctively higher than that of later arrivals. This suggests an assimilation, independent of cohort, effect. Until 2000 a "contextual effect" also was at play. Among each cohort of arrivals, more who settled away from, than in, Miami, took advantage of citizenship rights. Quite possibly, in recreating Miami in their image Exiles kept the belief in a homeland return alive longer there than elsewhere in the US, and accordingly for more years resisted becoming US citizens.[5]

Florida International University's Miami surveys, in turn, show that Cuban Americans who become citizens take their voting rights seriously. In 2004 and 2007, 90 and 91 percent, respectively, of Cuban American age-eligible citizens were registered voters (Table 3.2). Registration rates were high among all émigré cohorts. But in that they were highest among Cubans who emigrated before the Freedom Flights ended in the early 1970s, in exercising citizenship rates, there is some "cohort effect." The first who fled the revolution registered to vote in larger numbers even than age-eligible US-born Cuban Americans.[6]

Cuban Americans used their vote to elect "their own" to political office. A former mayor explained to me, "Cubans vote Cuban." But the Cubans they

Table 3.1 Citizenship rates among Cuban Americans in Miami and nationwide in census years 1970–2000

	% citizens	% who are eligible for citizenship[a]	% potential voters 18+ years old among those citizen-eligible	% actual citizens among those of voting age (18+ years old)	untapped voters[b]
A. Miami					
1970s census					
all Cuban Americans	33	64	68	39	6_
emigrated 1960s	15	49	89	21	7_
1980 census					
all Cuban Americans	51	94	77	47	53
emigrated 1960s	49	100	100	49	51
emigrated 1970s	14	73	88	18	82
1990 census					
all Cuban Americans	59	94	80	55	45
emigrated 1960s	64	100	100	64	36
emigrated 1970s	38	100	100	38	62
emigrated 1980s	12	72	95	15	85
2000 census					
all Cuban Americans	67	87	86	74	26
emigrated 1960s	91	100	100	91	9
emigrated 1970s	82	100	100	82	18
emigrated 1980s	53	100	100	53	47
emigrated 1990s	14	43	95	25	75

(Continued overleaf)

Table 3.1 Continued

	% citizens	% who are eligible for citizenship [a]	% potential voters 18+ years old among those citizen-eligible	% actual citizens among those of voting age (18+ years old)	untapped voters [b]
B. Nationwide					
1970s census					
all Cuban Americans	39	64	67	47	53
emigrated 1960s	19	47	89	29	71
1980 census					
all Cuban Americans	60	95	75	56	44
emigrated 1960s	52	100	100	52	48
emigrated 1970s	18	77	88	21	79
1990 census					
all Cuban Americans	68	95	78	63	37
emigrated 1960s	67	100	100	67	33
emigrated 1970s	44	100	100	44	56
emigrated 1980s	15	73	95	18	82
2000 census					
all Cuban Americans	73	89	82	78	22
emigrated 1960s	90	100	100	90	10
emigrated 1970s	83	100	100	83	17
emigrated 1980s	51	100	100	51	49
emigrated 1990s	14	41	95	24	76

Source: Steven Ruggles and Matthew Sobek, et al., Integrated Public Use Microdata Series (*IPUMS*), Version 3.0 (Minneapolis: Historical Census Projects University of Minnesota, 2003, www.ipums.org).

Notes:

a Cuban Americans who emigrated in the first four years of each decade, or earlier, were eligible for citizenship at the time of decadal census, in accordance with the 1966 Cuban Adjustment Act. The legislation allows Cuban immigrants rights to citizenship after six years in the US.

b Untapped voters are persons 18 or older who are eligible but are not citizens.

Table 3.2 Political participation, partisan preferences, and ethnic representation among Cuban Americans in Miami in 2004 and 2007 (data for 2007 in parentheses)

| | Year of arrival | | | | | |
	1959–64	1965–74	1975–84	1985–2004	US-born	All
Citizens	96 (97)	90 (97)	71 (81)	24 (1985–94: 56) (1995–2007: 19)	98 (99)	67 (66)
Registered voter if citizen and age-eligible	95 (97)	93 (98)	86 (92)	82 (1985–94: 85) (1995–2007: 60)	86 (94)	90 (91)
Registered Republican[a]	74 (77)	80 (73)	68 (73)	67 (1985–94: 66) (1995–2007: 61)	42 (50)	69 (66)
Candidates' position on Cuba important in determining how vote	75	75	74	78	69	75
Satisfaction with Congressman representing interviewee's views on Cuba	85	92	85	84	77	86

Sources: FIU-IPOR 2004 and 2007 (FIU-IPOR 2004 and 2007 www.fiu.edu/orgs/ipor/cuba2004/years.htm and www.fiu.edu/orgs/ipor/cuba8/pollsresults.html).

Notes: N = 1,811 in 2004, and 1,000 in 2007.
a In 2004 7 percent and 14 percent of the 1959–64 and post-1984 émigrés, respectively, and 26 percent of the US-born were registered as Independents. In 2007 12, 13, 17, 10, and 13 percent of 1959–64, 1965–73, 1974–84, 1985–94, and 1995–2007 émigrés were registered as Independents, as were 22 percent of the US-born.

elected were almost without exception from families that had fled the revolution early on, and, increasingly, their US-born children.

In that most of the Cuba-born politicians emigrated when they were young, during Castro's first years of rule, and the second-generation Cuban American politicians never stepped foot on the island, the emergent political class mainly imagined Cuba under Castro. Although imagined, it was very real in its consequences. Regardless of which side of the Straits they were born, the emergent political class very publicly opposed Castro. Politicians found it paid for them to do so, to win votes at the polls and to attract Cuban American financial contributions to their campaigns.

Cuban Americans began to be elected to political office in the 1980s. They joined the political class in working-class communities, but also in wealthy areas where class considerations might have been expected to trump ethnicity in shaping voter preferences.[7] While they first won offices in municipalities where many émigrés lived, they subsequently also won offices in areas where Cuban Americans were a numerical minority. They won with support of non-Cubans.

As Cuban Americans joined the political class, they became mayors of Miami-Dade municipalities. Raúl Martínez won office, for example, in Hialeah where many working-class and lower middle-class Cuban immigrants live. First elected in 1981, he held the position for more than 20 years, until forced to resign after the turn of the century when term limits went into effect. The City of Miami, in turn, had a succession of Cuban American mayors, beginning in 1985: first the Harvard-educated lawyer Xavier Suárez, then Joe Carollo, followed by Manny Díaz. The three were Cuba-born child immigrants. With their families having fled during Castro's first years of rule, in opposition to the revolution, the Cuba the mayors knew was filtered more through anti-Castro views learned from their parents' generation than first-hand.

Cuban Americans attained other public posts as well, both elected and appointed. They serve as City Managers, Fire and Police Chiefs, and City Council members. Minimally in their public lives they, like mayors, demonstrated themselves to be no friends of Fidel.

Cuban Americans also made political inroads at the county level. In 1996, Alex Penelas became Miami-Dade's first Cuban American mayor. Eight years later Carlos Álvarez succeeded him. While Penelas was the US-born son of early Castro-era émigrés, Álvarez emigrated at age eight in 1960. The county mayor is one of the most influential positions in the state.

As of 2000, Cuban Americans held one-third of the top appointed positions in the county, more than any other ethnic group. And indicative of how influential they were perceived to be, 75 percent of eight hundred Miami-Dade residents polled that year by the *Miami Herald* said they felt Cuban Americans to be the most politically powerful of the county's ethnic groups.[8]

The first to flee the revolution and their US-born children also made inroads in state politics. In 1982, the first Cuban American was elected to the state legislature, and within little more than a decade Cuban Americans held half the state legislature seats, mainly as representatives of South Florida districts.[9]

Then, at the beginning of this century, a Cuban American, Marco Rubio, became the first Cuban (and first Hispanic) Speaker of the State House. The Cuban American state legislators also had either emigrated when young at parental initiative, or were born in the US. In either case, they came from families who had fled the revolution early on.[10] Embedded in shared ethnic networks, the Cuban American legislators knew each other well, shared similar values, caucused together, and voted as a bloc.

By 2002, three Cuban Americans also attained Miami Congressional seats: Lincoln and Mario Díaz-Balart, and Ileana Ros-Lehtinen. The three previously had served in the Tallahassee legislature. Then, in 2004, Florida elected its first Cuban American Senator, Mel Martínez. They, too, came from families who had emigrated during the first years of Castro's rule. Martínez was the one exception. His parents sent him to the US on his own, at age 15, as part of Operation Peter Pan, the Miami archdiocese-run program that airlifted children from Cuba. Thus, his family also opposed the revolution, though it took them longer to uproot. While Mario was born in the US, both his older brother, Lincoln, and Ros-Lehtinen emigrated when young. Thus, for the three Congressional Representatives, in particular, Cuba under Castro was mainly an imagined country, filtered through parental lenses.

The Díaz-Balarts background is especially noteworthy. They are scions of a prominent pre-revolutionary political family.[11] Their father, Rafael, boasted that he raised his sons to be both "100 percent American and 100 percent Cuban."[12] Rafael purportedly groomed them to be political leaders, in the hope that they would one day return to Cuba and fulfill his own ambitions there.[13] US born Mario went even further than his father in his public defin ition of himself. He claimed to be 150 percent Cuban as well as 150 percent American.[14]

Although I focus my political discussion on Miami, where most Cuban Americans live, Hudson County, New Jersey, also elected two Cuban American Congressman during these years. The first, Robert Menéndez, built his political career in New Jersey, but with ties he cultivated in Miami. He is a former Union City mayor, who, after serving in Congress between 1992 and 2005, became, like Martínez, a Senator. US-born, Menéndez came from the minority of families who emigrated before the revolution. As such, he was an exception among the Cuban American political class. The second, New Jersey Cuban American Congressional Representative, Albio Sires had been mayor of West New York, adjacent to Union City, home also to many who fled the revolution early on. Cuba-born, he emigrated at age eleven in 1962. He was elected to the Congressional seat vacated by Menéndez when he became Senator.

The Cuban American electorate supported politicians who addressed their Cuba concerns. In Miami, three-fourths of the Miami Cuban Americans that Florida International University surveyed in February 2004 acknowledged that the stance of candidates on Cuba influenced how they voted. Even more of them felt well represented by their Congressional legislators on Cuban matters (Table 3.2). Such sentiments were shared by Cuban Americans no matter when they emigrated, and almost as widely among the US-born émigrés as the island born. The first who fled the revolution passed on to their progeny a commitment to Cuba such that US policy on Cuba became a multi-generational concern, even in elections for local office that had no foreign policy authority. As to the New Cubans, they settled for Congressional representatives who concerned themselves with Cuba even when, as I detail below, the lawmakers did not promote policies they wanted.[15]

Cuban American hardliners capitalized on the ethnic constituency in their midst, and marginalized challengers to their views. They achieved hegemony through a two-step process. First, Cuban American candidates beat other ethnic group contenders. Some elections were especially inter-ethnically contentious. Illustrative of this was when Republican Ros-Lehtinen first ran for Congress in 1989, in the election for the seat vacated by the death of New Deal Democrat Claude Pepper, and racial and ethnic tensions flared. Only Chicago around that time had witnessed an election in which voters divided so clearly and intensely along ethnic lines.[16] The Anglo Democratic candidate played to the festering nativistic sentiments associated with the English Only movement. He claimed the contest to be for an "American seat." He received the support of 88 percent of non-Hispanic Whites and 96 percent of Blacks. But Ros-Lehtinen won, with the Cuban community voting almost monolithically and in large numbers for her. She was helped in her campaign by the Cuban American-controlled media that staunchly supported her candidacy. She captured 94 percent of the Cuban American vote in her district, with 70 percent turnout in some precincts.[17]

The second step in hardliner consolidation of power involved intra-ethnic contests in which hardliners defeated Cuban American candidates who favored cross-border bridge-building. Both Ros-Lehtinen when she ran for reelection in 1992, and Mario Díaz-Balart when he first ran for Congress a decade later, faced opponents who advocated removal of US–Cuba trade barriers and US–Cuba dialogue. Ros-Lehtinen's and Mario Díaz-Balart's victories gave hardliners a lock on the South Florida Cuban American Congressional delegation, unchallenged until 2008. Lincoln Díaz-Balart, first elected in 1992, shared their hardline stance.

The Cuban American electorate expected their political representatives not to forget where their families came from and why. When speaking to me in the early 2000s, a second-generation chief officer of the Cuban American National Foundation summarized Cuban Americans' unrelenting political commitment to Cuban matters even as they otherwise assimilated. He made an analogy with US Jews for whom politicians' stance on Israel mattered. He added, "Our tragedy binds us and makes us politically powerful. We are fighting a war with Castro and not winning it. The fact that we are engaged in this struggle makes us strong here."

The embargo symbolized the "war with Castro." It was especially important to the Cuban Americans in the US the longest, even after they recognized it to be ineffective. To them, the embargo symbolized opposition to the

Table 3.3 Foreign policy preferences among registered and non-registered Cuban American voters in Miami in 2007

	Registered voters	Not registered to vote
Favor permitting US companies to sell medicine to Cuba	67%	79%
Favor permitting US companies to sell food to Cuba	55	73
Support US government military intervention to overthrow the Cuban government	55	45
Support military action by exiles to overthrow the Cuban government	69	73
Favor expanding agricultural trade to Cuba	28	43
Favor continuation of the embargo	66	45

Source: FIU-IPOR 2007 (www.fiu.edu/orgs/ipor/cuba8/pollsresults.html).

Note: N = 1,000

government under Castro. They therefore believed in supporting it on principle. With two-thirds of registered Miami Cuban American voters in 2007 still favoring continuation of the embargo, and somewhat more of them favoring Exile military intervention to overthrow the Cuban government (Table 3.3), politicians did well if they touted a hardline on Cuba.[18]

Nonetheless, the Miami Cuban American electorate became increasingly divided in their views, against the backdrop of selective embargo-loosening Congressional initiatives. By 2007, a slim majority of registered Cuban American voters approved of US companies selling food to Cuba, and two-thirds of them approved of sales of medicines (Table 3.3), exports Washington had permitted since 2000.[19] But Cuban American support for the one-way embargo opening varied by émigré cohort and generation. Exiles remained most opposed. They wished especially to stop food sales. They also most disapproved of cross-border dialogue and establishing diplomatic relations with Cuba under Castro (Table 3.4). They only approved, in the majority, of sales of medicine.

At the same time, the Cuban American electorate was not focused on a single issue. They looked to politicians also to address their everyday concerns. As a US-born Cuban American state legislator on the rise politically explained to me in 2000, opposition to Castro was "a threshold issue," after which politicians needed to address bread-and-butter preoccupations of constituents. Especially in local campaigns, voters took into account the stance of candidates on the same range of daily issues as other citizens, such as taxes, employment, and social services.[20]

Use and Abuse of Power for Material Gain

When Cuban Americans stormed the Miami political scene, poor Blacks, Jews, retirees, and newly arrived farmers from other parts of the South were vying for

Table 3.4 Views toward US Cuba policies among Cuban Americans in Miami in 2004 and 2007 (data for 2007 in parentheses)

	Year of arrival				US-born	Total
	1959–64	1965–74	1975–84	1985+		
1. Favor reestablishing diplomatic ties	29%	26%	38%	61%	56%	43% (57%)
2. Believe that embargo overall does not work	68 (71)	70 (65)	73 (70)	81 (1985–94:79) (1995–2007:83)	78 (82)	75 (77)
3. Favor continuation of embargo	75 (78)	77 (79)	68 (68)	56 (1985–94:48) (1995–2007:41)	54 (54)	66 (58)
4. Favor dialogue among exiles, dissidents & Cuban government	45 (43)	41 (49)	54 (50)	68 (1985–94:66) (1995–2007:79)	71 (83)	56 (65)
5. Support direct US military invasion to overthrow Cuban government	62 (61)	67 (51)	64 (55)	50 (1985–94:46) (1995–2007:41)	69 (64)	60 (51)
6. Support military action by exile community to overthrow Castro government	66 (74)	65 (66)	60 (75)	52 (1985–94:71) (1995–2007:72)	64 (69)	60 (71)
7. Should stop agricultural trade with Cuba	65 (63)	69 (52)	56 (51)	35 (1985–94:36) (1995–2007:26)	33 (30)	51 (40)
8. Favor allowing companies to sell medicine to Cuba	61 (59)	58 (64)	64 (69)	80 (1985–94:69) (1995–2007:85)	79 (68)	69 (72)
9. Favor allowing US companies to sell food to Cuba	42 (37)	39 (46)	50 (56)	72 (1985–94:62) (1995–2007:78)	65 (69)	55 (62)
10. Favor return to Bush policies until 2003	(36)	(52)	(49)	(1985–94:71) (1995–2007:86)	(64)	(64)

Sources: FIU-IPOR (www.fiu.edu/orgs/ipor/cuba8/pollsresults.html).

Note: N = 1,811 in 2004 and 1,000 in 2007.

political influence. They each sought to advance their own interests.[21] Cuban Americans took advantage of the fragmentation to centralize power. They benefited individually and collectively. Exiles benefited most.

When leveraging politics for their own ends, Cuban Americans operated on both sides of the law, much as the Irish, among other immigrant groups, had a century earlier, in the heyday of city machine politics. But Exiles embedded political practices common in Cuba before the revolution. Their dense social networks described in the last chapter served as the bedrock for exchanges of favors. Although in wrong-doing they were not alone, building on their networks they took advantage of illegitimate along with legitimate opportunities for gain. Of course, not all of them abused public office for private and group gain.

Illustrative of abuse of office, some Cuban American legislators used state offices for personal profit. Havana-born state senator Alberto Gutman, for example, was indicted in 1999 on charges of medical fraud and conspiracy.[22] And more than most other state lawmakers, those of Cuban origin allowed lobbyists to curry their favor. A 1998 investigation of Tallahassee lobbyists found that the by then large South Florida Cuban American contingent, along with the smaller Black delegation, received a disproportionate share of the gifts costing more than $25 which lobbyists must report. During the two month period that state legislators met that year the 1,900 lobbyists spent nearly $1 million just on wining and dining the lawmakers.[23]

Cuban American state legislators also pressed for special benefits for co-ethnics. In particular, they pressed to waive internship and hospital residency requirements for island-trained doctors who settled in the state. They also lobbied to institute a separate, less rigorous training course for Cuban émigré medics. When most of the island-born doctors failed the qualifying exam twice, the Cuban American delegation in Tallahassee pushed for the right of the émigrés to skip the test altogether.[24] They tried to bend legislated professional standards only for "their own."

At the local level, the 1960 child immigrant, Raúl Martínez, exemplified in Hialeah how Cuban Americans used and abused office, without suffering community retribution. Known in Hialeah as a strongman who got things done, the charismatic mayor supervised everything from buying street lamps to filling potholes.[25] Following indictment on racketeering and extortion charges, he was dismissed from office for three years, beginning in 1991. Martínez was charged with providing zoning favors to developers in exchange for money and land deals.[26] Afterwards, he returned to office relatively unscarred. Even during the years when he was barred from office, the City Council and Chief of Police remained loyal to him and he maintained informal power. Cuban Americans continued to support him because they liked what he did for them and the personable manner in which he served them. Martínez also knew when to prioritize ethnic concerns, such as in the battle to give Miami relatives custody of six-year-old Elián González when the President and his Attorney-General sought to return the motherless boy to his father in Cuba. In that battle the

Democratic mayor sided with Cuban Americans against the Clinton White House.

The first Cuban-born mayor of the City of Miami, Xavier Suárez, from a family who emigrated in the first years of the revolution, also did not take long to misuse the top municipal office and earn the nickname "Mayor Loco," Crazy Mayor. Suárez had attended the prestigious Belén Jesuit Preparatory School that opened in Miami after closing in Cuba. Initially elected mayor in 1985, he was reelected four years later. Although his first two terms of office were wracked with charges of corruption and erratic behavior,[27] both on his part and by his close associates,[28] he was reelected to the top municipal office again in 1997, or so it seemed. In March 1998, he, along with a city commissioner and thirteen staff members, were removed from office because an appeals court ruled Suárez's victory to have rested on registering fraudulent absentee ballots, some cast in the names of deceased people and residents who had moved away.[29] Meanwhile, the dismissed commissioner was charged with covering up the voter fraud, after winning his own reelection when under indictment on federal charges of mortgage fraud and money-laundering.[30]

While Suárez left office in disgrace, he did not disappear entirely from the local political scene. In 2000, the Republican Party, considering him more an asset than a liability, tapped him to serve on its county-wide Executive Committee, and in that capacity had him help mobilize absentee votes for George W. Bush in the contentious presidential election that year. Suárez was rewarded for his generous financial contributions to the party. He became one of the select so-called "Billionaires for (George W.) Bush."[31] But Suárez also benefited from the Republican Party having become, in the words of two political analysts, "little more than a front organization for the interests of the Cuban community."[32]

Wrong-doing in Suárez's administration also involved the city's long-term City Manager, Cuba-born César Odio. Odio was accused of taking a kickback in conjunction with awarding a city insurance contract. He went to jail on charges of malfeasance. And while lining his own pockets, he also used his office to help the Exile-formed Cuban American National Foundation consolidate power. Suárez's successor discovered that Odio had spent thousands of dollars of city funds on events sponsored by the anti-Castro group.

Carollo, Suárez's successor, who had emigrated at age fifteen in 1970, in turn took little time in office to be nicknamed Crazy Joe. Although his supporters had hoped that he would erase the Banana Republic image of the city that Suárez had reinforced, if not created, Carollo also lent no moral dignity to the top City of Miami office. Carollo came to be viewed as ruthless, demagogic, and bankrupt of conscience, in his private along with his public life. Early on as mayor he got into a spitting match with the City Commission, and his entire term of office was wracked with disputes with commissioners. Further tainting his image, the media made much ado about alleged physical abuse of his wife,[33] which led to his arrest while in office. After spending a night in jail he was released on bond and ordered to turn over to his attorney guns he kept in his home. Carollo owned a semi-automatic rifle and two 9MM semi-automatic pistols at the time.[34]

Carollo ultimately lost support even among fellow Cuban Americans. When running for reelection he faced contenders who pledged to put a plug on police corruption and embarrassing city scandals.[35] The near-political novice, Manny Díaz, won. Díaz, who emigrated at age seven in 1961 and who, like Suárez, had attended Belén Jesuit Preparatory School, won because he masterminded an ethnic, not ethical, crusade. He had led the community's legal battle with the White House the year before to give Miami relatives custody of Elián. That he lost the case mattered less than the fact that he defended the latest of causes Cuban Americans took on.

Díaz's victory, nonetheless, ushered in a turn toward seemingly good governance, from which many Cuban Americans benefited. By the time of his reelection, in 2005, Díaz had transformed the City of Miami both in image and form.[36] During his first term, crime, poverty, and unemployment rates all dropped. He streamlined city bureaucracies, hired a new police chief to improve the department's reputation in the wake of corruption scandals, rescued the city from the edge of bankruptcy, and oversaw the city's biggest real estate boom, linked to the largest urban renewal project nationwide other than the rebuilding of lower Manhattan post 9/11.[37] Cuban American developers in construction, real estate, and banking, who helped finance Díaz's and other pro-development candidates' campaigns, duly benefited from business deals. Twenty billion dollars in development projects were under way or in the planning stages when Díaz ran for reelection.[38] Builders had parlayed political contacts for contracts in the past, but under Díaz the scale of pay off reached new proportions. Business people in real estate and finance also benefited. African Americans at the time were the big losers, in that they were not awarded contracts, and they could no longer afford to live in their old neighborhoods.[39]

By 2007, however, the real estate boom entered a downturn. The city had overbuilt. Units were left unsold and unoccupied, and real estate prices fell. Díaz had allowed an unsustainable bonanza. The 2008 national recession compounded the local investment crisis.

County-level governance, in turn, became wracked by use and abuse of office. When elected to office in 1996, Penelas inherited a county bureaucracy known for wrong-doing; however, he did little to right the wrong. In the 1990s, before he became mayor, more than 270 county public employees, including police officers, had been charged with crimes ranging from falsifying records to ties with drug dealers. County officials had also become the focus of fury when construction scandals came to public light as Hurricane Andrew stormed Miami in 1992. Mother Nature tore off roofs, toppled walls, and exposed serious construction flaws that were attributed to lax building code enforcement. Then, five years later, under Penelas' watch, the county's building inspection department again was accused of corruption. Building inspectors allegedly pressured by their bosses, allied with contractors and overlooked construction flaws.[40] Many of the contractors were Cuban American. Also under Penelas' watch, Cuban Americans aggressively fought zoning regulations that impeded their profiteering.[41]

County corruption was so rampant that it became a way of life.[42] Economic development in Greater Miami, and not merely in the City of Miami under Manny Díaz, created a myriad of opportunities, including for illicit dealings in a milieu devoid of political-moral constraints. With a multi-billion dollar budget, a booming airport and seaport, and need for new infrastructure to keep pace with the county's demographic growth, and much of the economic growth government-linked, opportunities for deal-making abounded. The weak system of government, meanwhile, contributed to poor law enforcement. County, along with city, commissioners were poorly paid part-time officials who often took the civil service jobs not merely to serve the public good but to access opportunities for private gain. In turn, as political campaigns became increasingly expensive, candidates became beholden to the interests of those who helped them compete for office.[43]

Political connections and influence opened up economic opportunities for honest Cuban Americans, and not merely for those willing to evade laws. As the economy expanded, opportunities on both sides of the law increased, and in the public as well as private sector.

The previously noted Miami mayor, with whom I spoke in 2005, explained how Cuban Americans in the private along with the public sector benefited from what he referred to as the Miami machine, a machine which he believed operated somewhat differently from US urban machines of the past. He viewed the local political machine as similar to the old in its employment effect, but somewhat different in how its wheels were greased. The Miami machine, he said, was more sophisticated while less structured. But it also was less flexible and more constrained in how it awarded work, in that it had to comply with state and federal guidelines that were non-existent in the days of the old machines. Aside from offering government patronage jobs, on a four-year electoral cycle, the government had some $25 billion of county contracts to dispense. "A large industry of people benefit from the government expenditures," he added. Even national firms that secure contracts subcontract to locals.

Many Cuban Americans own businesses that benefit from contracts, not merely in construction but also in landscaping, cleaning, and the like. Despite the minority rights guidelines now in effect, the former mayor claimed that "fifty to sixty times more contracts go to Cuban than to African Americans." By way of example, "If you look at contracts that have been awarded for airport and seaport development, Cubans have been the main beneficiaries." In business as well as in housing, African Americans lost out as Cuban Americans gained. While the former local chief official felt Cubans attained deals more because they were aggressive and skilled than because they were corrupt and corrupting, he also felt that they made political contributions that won them favors. Then, because "Cubans hire Cubans," yet more Cubans benefit. Firms with county contracts subcontract to many small firms that more often than not are also Cuban-owned—for example, for testing and engineering work. "The Cubans benefit from a lot of networking." Countywide, Cuban American social, economic, and political capital became mutually reinforcing.

Employment figures speak to the former mayor's perception, in ways that go beyond Cuban American entrepreneurship noted in the last chapter. Since 1980, censuses record an exceptional number of Cuban Americans going into business for themselves (Table 3.5). In Greater Miami, the percentage of Cuban Americans who were self-employed, persons who created labor market opportunities for themselves partly with government contracts, spiraled from 3 in 1970 to 35 at the turn of the twenty-first century, years during which the overall portion of the labor force that was self-employed barely increased. Meanwhile, during the interim years non-Hispanic Whites' percentage of self-employed nosedived, from 89 to 29, although in 2000 they still accounted for a slightly higher percentage of the self-employed than their share of the population. The contrast with Blacks is also noteworthy. Blacks accounted for a mere 6 percent of the labor force that worked for themselves in 1970, and for only 8 percent thirty years later, a period during which their percentage of the population rose from 14 to 20. This and other labor market marginalization contributed to the African American resentment of Cuban immigrants.[44]

The Small Business Administration (SBA) contributed to the ethnic entrepreneurial disparities; it favored Cuban Americans,[45] a bias that did not go unnoticed. Blacks, along with Anglos, resented SBA favoritism of Cuban Americans.

Some Cuban Americans leveraged all levels of government to accumulate business fortunes. The Fanjul brothers, who fled Cuba soon after the revolution, are especially notorious. From a wealthy island sugar family that controlled much of the American sugar industry in Cuba before the revolution, they became renowned US sugar barons after resettling in Florida. Associated with Florida-Sun, they benefited handsomely from lobbying and strategic campaign contributions.[46] While major donors to the influential Cuban American National Foundation, and to campaigns of the South Florida Cuban American Congressional delegation, the Fanjuls targeted most of their over $900,000 in political contributions in the 1990s to national power wielders, in order to have federal policy bent in their favor. With one brother associated with the Democrats and the other with the Republicans, together they influenced both sides of the Congressional aisle.[47]

Other Cuban Americans attained public sector jobs that offered secure salaries and social benefits, even if they did not thereby become rich. Cuban Americans' representation among Miami-Dade public sector employees rose from 1 to 27 percent between 1970 and 2000, years during which the percentage of the labor force so employed declined (Table 3.5). During the thirty-year period Cuban Americans experienced a far greater rate of increase in public sector employment than other Hispanics and Blacks, while the number of non-Hispanic Whites holding such jobs dropped off as much as

Table 3.5 Type of employment, labor force participation, and population by ethnicity in Miami in census years 1970–2000

	1970		1980		1990		2000	
	% of worker-type by ethnicity	% of labor force	% of worker-type by ethnicity	% of labor force	% of worker-type by ethnicity	% of labor force	% of worker-type by ethnicity	% of labor force
A. Employment[a]								
Self-employed:		9%		9%		11%		12%
Cuban Amer.	3%		28%		37%		35%	
Other Hispan.	2		8		16		28	
Non-Hisp. White	89		59		39		29	
Black	6		5		7		8	
Total	100		100		99		100	
Wage, non-gov't:		72		77		76		76
Cuban Amer.	5		30		33		33	
Other Hispan.	3		11		22		32	
Non-Hisp. White	80		44		29		19	
Black	12		15		16		17	
Total	100		100		100		101	
Wage, gov't:		18		13		12		12
Cuban Amer.	1		16		24		27	
Other Hispan.	2		6		10		17	
Non-Hisp. White	86		48		37		24	
Black	11		30		29		33	
Total	100	100	100	99	100	99	101	100
B. Population								
Cuban Amer.	4%		26%		31%		31%	
Other Hispan.	3		11		20		28	
Non-Hispan. White	79		45		31		22	
Black	14		18		19		20	
Total	100		100		101		101	

Source: Steven Ruggles and Matthew Sobek, et al., *Integrated Public Use Microdata Series* (*IPUMS*), Version 3.0 (Minneapolis: Historical Census Projects University of Minnesota, 2003, www.ipums.org).

Note:

a Data on unpaid family workers excluded from the table.

Table 3.6 Type of employment among Cuban Americans in Miami in census years 1970–2000[a]

	Self-employed	Wage, non-gov't	Wage, gov't
1970 census			
all Cuban Americans	7%[b]	88%	5%
1960 émigrés	6	91	3
1980 census			
all Cuban Americans	10	83	8
1960 émigrés	11	81	8
1970 émigrés	7	86	6
1990 census			
all Cuban Americans	13	78	9
1960 émigrés	16	73	11
1970 émigrés	13	78	9
1980 émigrés	12	83	5
2000 census			
all Cuban Americans	13	77	10
1960 émigrés	17	70	13
1970 émigrés	16	74	10
1980 émigrés	15	77	8
1990 émigrés	10	85	6

Source: Steven Ruggles and Matthew Sobek, et al., *Integrated Public Use Microdata Series* (*IPUMS*), Version 3.0 (Minneapolis: Historical Census Projects University of Minnesota, 2003, www.ipums.org).

Notes:
a Data on unpaid family workers excluded from the table.
b Percentages do not always equal 100 due to rounding up of numbers.

among the self-employed. In the public, as in the entrepreneurial, sector Cuban Americans captured the void left when non-Hispanics fled the city's ethnic makeover. Cuban Americans thereby were the main beneficiaries of the White flight.

Nonetheless, in the public sector, unlike in the entrepreneurial sector, Blacks, along with Cuban Americans, gained job access. In 2000, even more Blacks than Cuban Americans held public sector jobs. This was partly because so few of the dark-skinned went into business for themselves, but possibly also because they benefited in the public sector from enforcement of the minority guidelines to which the former mayor alluded.

Yet, to speak of Cuban American employment success conceals differences in émigré job attainment (see Table 3.6). In each census between 1970 and 2000, more 1960s arrivals than later arrivals were not only self-employed, as noted in Chapter 2, but were also employed in the public sector. Thus, while Cuban Americans as a group enjoyed labor market advantages over others in Miami, and increasingly so over the years, the Exiles were the prime Cuban American beneficiaries.

Exile Leveraging of US Political Practices for Ethnic Gain: What Organization and Money Attained

Cuban Americans exacted ethnic concessions up to the highest levels of national policy-making not merely for personal but for collective ethnic gain. Their success rested on the ethnic-socio-political field they created, based on their rich network of mutually reinforcing social, cultural, economic, and political ties. Exiles dominated this politicking as well. Their success rested on crafty targeting of revenue they raised while maintaining discipline within their ranks.

Exiles organized, lobbied, and made political contributions that extended their domain of influence beyond "their own," beyond their territorial base in Florida, and across the partisan divide even as they became predominately Republican in their personal preferences. They prioritized their collective ethnic concerns, as they defined them to be, over their private party loyalty. They wielded influence through the Cuban American National Foundation, commonly called the Foundation, under the sway of its charismatic leader, Jorge Mas Canosa, beginning in the early 1980s. Through the early 2000s, no other Cuban American group matched the Foundation in power-brokering.

Mas Canosa masterfully leveraged Foundation-raised funds for the agenda that he and his close collaborators set. He became so successful at power-wielding that he became the main enemy of Castro. While their opposition to one another rested on their differing stands on the revolution, they both personalized their stands.

Formally, the main goal of the Foundation was to advance freedom and democracy in Cuba.[48] The leadership defined this goal as conditional on Cuban regime change. With the goal in mind, Mas Canosa and Foundation staff lobbied for legislation and helped elect politicians whom they entrusted to further their cause. A top Foundation officer described the organization to me as "the keeper of Cuba, the keeper of the flame of what a potential Cuba could be, the repository of the future Cuba." Its goals were ambitious, with transnational implications.

Ronald Reagan, when President, gave the Foundation its initial boost. He understood that Cuban Americans could be an asset at the polls, not merely to help him win reelection but to further the Republican's new strategy to win over the South.[49] Reagan also recognized that with their wealth attained in the US, Cuban Americans could be a source of campaign financing, and that, given their antipathy to Communism, they could be counted on to help defeat Left-leaning political movements then in the hemisphere, especially in Central America.[50]

Prior to the Foundation's formation, Exiles had created scores of small organizations that differed somewhat in strategy but shared a common anti-pathy to the Castro-led regime. From the US side of the Straits they continued the battle they had lost in Cuba. Some groups favored violence to promote their cause (initially with CIA support), drawing on practices familiar to them from their Cuba days. And some of the groups reconstituted themselves in the US after defeat in Cuba, while others were new country creations. Violent, partially clandestine, groups included Omega 7 and Alpha 66.

In encouraging the Foundation's formation, and what proved to be consolidation of Cuban American political group life, Reagan courted Mas Canosa. Mas Canosa had participated in the 1961 Bay of Pigs invasion that militant anti-Castroites had masterminded, with CIA backing. He had also been involved in other groups that had sponsored violent actions to try to topple the regime Castro led.[51] While Mas Canosa had been well on his way toward establishing himself as one of the immigrant group's most influential and charismatic leaders and as patriarch of the anti-Castro movement by the time he attracted Reagan's attention, the President helped solidify his preeminence by legitimizing, and overseeing the financing of, an institutional base to his power. Reagan also strengthened Mas Canosa's influence by granting him White House access. In the process, Reagan transformed the once-proponent of violence into a born-again influence-peddler. He coopted the charismatic émigré, and his supporters in turn, to play according to the political practices the US system permitted. Exiles accordingly developed an institutional base to their political incorporation that had the highest level of political backing. This development was not a byproduct of some invisible forces of political assimilation operating on their own.

Reagan gave the Foundation an important initial financial boost through the channeling of hundreds of thousands of federal dollars to a Foundation-affiliated organization, via the National Endowment for Democracy (NED). Congressman Dante Fascell, a Florida Democrat, introduced the enabling legislation to form the NED, and became the NED's first director. The Foundation, using NED funds to help finance political campaigns, demanded support for its anti-Castro crusade as a quid pro quo.[52]

But the Foundation quickly established a revenue base of its own. Mas Canosa convinced fellow Exiles who shared in the American Dream to make large annual contributions to the organization. He served as exemplar. He proved himself a late twentieth-century Horatio Alger, although not a Horatio satisfied with economic success alone. Beginning his life in the US as a dishwasher, shoe salesman, and milkman,[53] Mas Canosa went on to acquire a small construction firm that under his tutelage became one of the two largest Hispanic-owned businesses, a telephone cable company he named Mastec. He accumulated his fortune working on both sides of the law. As a result of the illicit source of some of his wealth, his company became the subject of a 1998 Florida investigation of a $58 million paving contract that county officials contended overcharged taxpayers by millions.[54]

By the early 1990s the Foundation was claiming fifty thousand members, and by the twenty-first century's turn 5,000 more, with 170 directors, trustees, and associates reputedly contributing $1,000 to $10,000 annually to the organization.[55] The Foundation included the by then "who's who" of the

Miami Cuban American community, and the top political donors of Cuban descent. But one example was Armando Codina, CEO of the Codina Group, who became a business partner of George H. W. Bush in the Codina Bush Group.

The wealthy contributors were early émigrés. By the early 2000s, the Foundation also included, in small numbers, US-born children of Exiles in their ranks. When coming of age, the US-born initially took on their parents' views on Cuba for themselves.

As Mas Canosa guided the Foundation to leverage influence in Washington, he oversaw the formation of both a formally autonomous lobbying organization, the Cuban American Foundation (CAF), and a political action committee (PAC), the Free Cuba PAC. He formed these spin-off groups to comply with official US regulations, to accommodate to the accepted US way of politicking in the halls of high-level policy-making. The Free Cuba PAC accounted for all but 1 percent of Cuban American PAC contributions between 1982 and the turn of the twenty-first century. During these years it took in nearly $1.7 million, and made $1.3 million in political donations.[56]

The Foundation began in Miami where most of its membership, leadership, and financial contributors lived. And it was in Miami, and in Florida more broadly, that it built up its initial influence-peddling political base. It did so by publicly endorsing and privately funding campaigns of candidates sympathetic to its anti-Castro mission.

Mas Canosa proved himself a power broker in his own right, to the point that he came to be regarded as kingmaker in local politics.[57] He dominated, for example, Mayor Xavier Suárez's administration.[58] This helps explain why Suárez's administration subsidized Foundation activity. Locally, Mas Canosa's influence rested on charismatic and not merely institutional rule. And institutionally, he solidified his influence, and support for his hardline Cuba stance, through a radio station, *La Voz de la Fundación* (The Voice of the Foundation), that the Foundation founded. His cohort brought a tradition of radio-listening with them from Cuba, which he capitalized on.

Under Mas Canosa's tutelage, Foundation influence came to extend to the state and national levels. The same top Foundation officer to whom I previously alluded noted to me in Miami in 2000 that "Cuba policy begins here," in that "Foundation decision-making occurs here."[59] He saw Washington as where Cuba policy was implemented, Miami as where it was crafted!

The Foundation established itself as one of the most effective ethnic lobbies. It modeled itself after the influential pro-Israel lobby, with the political contributions it collected exceeding that raised by all ethnic groups besides the pro-Israeli.[60] In the 1990s, the sixty-seven pro-Israeli PACs contributed approximately twice as much to federal campaigns as did Cuban American PACs, but the third largest ethnic lobbyists at the time, Albanian-Americans, contributed half as much as Cuban Americans.[61] Cuban Americans were far from the only ethnic lobbyists, but they quickly became one of the two best financed.

The Foundation-associated PAC helped finance the campaigns of Cuban Americans who promoted its hardline stance on Cuba. All Cuban American Congressmen, for example, received Cuban American PAC contributions. Not merely the three in South Florida, where the Foundation was based, but also Menéndez in New Jersey. Although Menéndez depended first and foremost on the backing of powerful local Democrats in Hudson County, New Jersey, he was the third largest recipient of Cuban American political contributions in the late 1900s. The Foundation financed Menéndez's campaigns at a time when most of its membership and leadership had become Republican and most were Florida-based because in so doing its directorship could count on him to support embargo-tightening legislation when up for vote. They even convinced him to break partisan rank and oppose President Clinton's effort in 1999 to improve US–Cuba relations through "baseball diplomacy."[62] And the following year Menéndez joined the chorus of south Florida Cuban American politicians who publicly criticized the Clinton Administration's decision to return six-year-old Elián to his father in Cuba. His Democratic affiliation notwithstanding, Menéndez never supported a Cuba-related policy that his mainly Republican Florida campaign financiers opposed.

The Foundation, through its affiliated organizations, also supported campaigns of non-Cuban Americans, in order to rally Congressional support for the legislation it favored. In 1983, it convinced Congress to allot $10 million in federal funds for Radio Martí, to beam anti-Castro messages to islanders. The main sponsor of the bill to establish federal funding for the radio project was Senator Paula Hawkins, a Florida Republican. Although not Cuban American, she was one of the top ten recipients of Cuban American campaign funding between 1979 and 2000.

Savvy lobbying, combined with campaign donations, fueled Foundation foreign policy influence even in the post-Cold War era after Cuba posed no national security threat. It effectively lobbied for several pieces of legislation. First, Congress passed a bill in 1990 for which the Foundation had lobbied, to establish federally funded TV Martí. TV Martí was designed to beam programs with visual images to complement the work of Radio Martí. Floridian Congressman Fascell, the Democrat who had overseen the NED funding that gave the Foundation its initial financial boost, along with two other key supporters of the legislation, like Hawkins, were non-Cuban American beneficiaries of substantial Cuban American campaign contributions. The Cuban government, however, had the technology to block reception of the televised programs US taxpayers funded.

Unlike Radio and TV Martí, which focused on destabilizing Castro's rule through the airwaves, the 1992 Cuban Democracy Act that the Foundation also lobbied for was designed to destabilize his rule economically, by closing embargo loopholes. The 1992 legislation prohibited foreign-based subsidiaries of US companies from trading with Cuba, banned ships that landed in Cuba from US ports for six months, called for the withholding of US aid to countries that traded with Cuba, and restricted US-to-Cuba remittances to that necessary to cover costs of Cuban travel to the US. Key supporters of the bill received Free Cuba PAC contributions. The bill was the pet project of then Representative from New Jersey, Robert Torricelli. Torricelli argued that in further crippling the Cuban economy, Castro's government would collapse "within weeks." He was the second largest recipient of Cuban American funding between 1979 and 2000, even though he had neither Sunshine State nor Cuban roots, and even though he was a Democrat. Meanwhile, Torricelli's Senate partner in promoting the bill, fellow Democrat Bob Graham of Florida, was the sixth largest recipient of Cuban American political donations during the twenty-one-year period.

The Foundation secured additional support for the embargo-tightening legislation by courting both 1992 presidential candidates with campaign contributions. George H. W. Bush was the fifth largest recipient of Cuban American political donations. Clinton received far fewer dollars, but he was very transparent in his quid pro quo. After receiving $275,000 from Cuban Americans at two Miami Foundation-associated fundraising events during his campaign, he announced that he supported the Cuban Democracy Act then pending in Congress. But Bush, taking advantage of his presidential incumbency, signed the bill already before the 1992 election.

The next anti-Castro bill that the Foundation backed, in 1996, further tightened the embargo. It laid the legal basis for US citizen rights to sue international investors over property that the Castro-led government had expropriated, to which they laid pre-revolutionary claims. The 1996 legislation, in addition, specified that such investors be denied US entry visas, and barred Washington from normalizing commercial relations with any Cuban government that included Fidel or his brother Raúl, officially then second-in-command. The so-called Cuban Liberty and Democracy Solidarity (*Libertad*) Act was informally known as the Helms–Burton Bill, after its two key sponsors, both of whom received substantial Cuban American campaign contributions either shortly before introducing the legislation or at the time Congress deliberated the bill. Dan Burton, an Indiana Republican, received $61,000 from Cuban Americans in the 1990s, and no funding before, while Republican Jesse Helms received $76,000, almost all in 1995–96, when running for reelection.

Understanding that passage of embargo-tightening measures required wider support than that of legislative sponsors, the directors of the Cuban American PAC strategically channeled funds to candidates nation-wide whose support the lobbyists sought. Lawmakers who backed the two bills typically received substantially more contributions than those who opposed it, and few recipients of Cuban American dollars voted against the bills.

The 1996 legislation was the last embargo-tightening legislation that the Foundation lobbied for before Mas Canosa died in 1997. In 2000, after his son, Jorge Mas Santos, assumed the Foundation helm, Foundation lobbyists failed to block passage of embargo exemptions allowing for the sale of food and medicines to Cuba. Agribusiness, with economic interest in accessing the

Cuba market, had lobbied for the exemption. With the US having won the Cold War, Congressional concern with being "soft on Communism" tempered.[63] Nonetheless, the Foundation remained sufficiently influential to get a requirement inserted into the legislation that the Cuban government pay cash for purchases. It presumed that the fiscally impoverished government could afford little if not bought on credit. That same year the Foundation also successfully lobbied to reverse a move in Congress to lift travel restrictions. It convinced legislators to institute a once-a-year travel cap for Cuban American family visits. I discuss US travel policy in detail in the next chapter.

During its heyday of power-brokering, the Foundation leveraged influence not merely by lobbying and contributing to political campaigns. Mas Canosa also leveraged influence by silencing Cuban Americans who challenged his authority and the policies he advocated, including fellow Exiles who, while similarly anti-Castro, disagreed over what US Cuba policy ought to be. He allowed neither US commitment to freedom of expression nor his commitment to the Foundation goals of freedom and democracy in Cuba to get in his way. After federal authorities, for example, appointed Mas Canosa to head the advisory board of TV and Radio Martí, he orchestrated the dismissal of the first director of the radio station. Although an opponent of Castro and the revolution, the director lost his job for opposing embargo-tightening, for opposing TV Martí on grounds that it violated international agreements, and for opposing Mas Canosa's domination of the government-funded media projects. With the director's removal from office, Mas Canosa could use the federally funded media projects, along with the Foundation's local radio station, to consolidate his role as the premier gatekeeping communicator on Cuban matters. And as gatekeeper he repressed challenges to both his hardline stance on Cuba and his personal authority.

Mas Canosa also maintained his gatekeeping role by vetoing a key presidential appointment. Refusing to settle for any ethnic representation whatsoever at the highest level, he blocked Clinton's appointment of Cuba-born Mario Baeza, a partner in a prestigious Manhattan law firm, to the post of Assistant Secretary of State for Inter-American Affairs. Mas Canosa called on influential Democrats whose campaigns the Foundation PAC funded to help block the nomination. Mas Canosa considered Baeza unacceptably "soft on Cuba." The clincher was Baeza's participation in a 1992 Euromoney meeting on trade and investment in Cuba, which included travel to Havana to meet with officials there. Mas Canosa, along with other hardline Exiles, opposed both business dealings with Cuba and stepping foot in the country under Castro. Baeza, like the first Radio Martí director, paid a price for overstepping the political boundaries Mas Canosa and his allies considered permissible. Baeza was removed from consideration for the influential position.

Thus, under Mas Canosa's leadership, the Foundation built on Cuban American financial success to leverage influence over US foreign policy. It astutely made use of the system of interest group politics the US political system permits. But to speak and advocate in a single hardline voice, Mas

Canosa blunted opposition from fellow co-ethnics, even from fellow anti-Castroites of his émigré cohort, when they questioned his authority and strategy for dealing with Cuba.

The Presidential Election Cycle and Exile Policy Influence between 1992 and 2004

Exiles' national level policy influence rested on vote-leveraging, as well as savvy targeting of political contributions and lobbying. They mastered "delivering" votes in exchange for favors. Especially in the post-Cold War era, presidential elections provided Exiles with an opportunity to attain ethnic concessions, to convince incumbent presidents, and not merely legislators, to champion policies they wanted. Even as Exile influence over Congress weakened, their influence over presidents, with discretionary power, remained.

In the context of US domestic politics, the political scientist, Edward Tufte, argued that economic policy varied with the presidential electoral cycle.[64] Cuban Americans prove that ethnic policy may also be tied to the presidential election cycle. Between 1992 and 2004, a Cuban American policy cycle operated. The electoral cycle did not predetermine the ethnic policy cycle, and presidential elections did not alone determine US Cuba policy.[65] But electoral considerations patterned Washington policies during the twelve-year period, in a manner heretofore not analytically denoted. Accordingly, Cuba policy cycle varied in election and non-election years, for similar reasons that Tufte showed economic policy to vary.

Tufte convincingly demonstrated that the cyclical manipulation of economic initiatives were not always economically sound. To win reelection, politicians took advantage of incumbency to implement economic reforms advantageous to their opportunistic short-term political interests which, at times, were economically inappropriate for the long term. In such instances, once reelected, they would reverse policies. Tufte added that incumbents, however, were not entirely free to make economic policy as they chose. They may be constrained by factors beyond their control, such as pressures from divided interests, and their own incompetence.

An ethnic policy cycle would be expected to differ in what it delivered from the economic policy cycle. However, it should be similarly linked to an incumbent president's effort to use discretionary powers of office to win reelection. The ethnic policy cycle would be expected to rest on a tacit "ethnic bargain," ethnic-favored policies as a quid pro quo for political support. The vote-getting bargain in the Cuban American case is mainly foreign policy focused.[66] It is premised on promotion of a hard line on Cuba, intended to isolate and destabilize the Castro-led regime to spur its collapse.

If I am correct that national-level Cuba policy between 1992 and 2004 was intricately linked with the presidential electoral cycle, government ethnic initiatives would be expected: (1) to vary in election and non-election years; (2) to be responsive in election years to concerns and wants of the ethnic electorate; and

(3) to be reversed or left unenforced in non-election years when voter-driven reforms conflicted with non-electoral based concerns of governance. Tufte, however, focused his vote-getting policy analysis too narrowly. He ignored the role lobbyists and campaign contributors may play "behind the scenes."

Although Cuban Americans account for less than 1 percent of the US population, they leveraged the import of their vote by mainly living in the largest electoral "swing state," Florida, as well as by electing "their own" to local offices, by voting in large numbers, and by prioritizing ethnic concerns when voting. The state-based winner-take-all electoral college system contributed to the importance of their vote in presidential elections. By the turn of the century Cuban Americans accounted for 8 percent of the Florida electorate, in a state commanding one-tenth of the electoral college votes.[67]

The changing partisan base of the state created a context that worked to hardline émigrés' advantage. Florida had been heavily Democratic before Republicans, under Reagan's tutelage, began to court Floridian Cuban Americans.[68] Cuban American party-switching, including by such prominent politicians as Lincoln Díaz-Balart, contributed to the state becoming contested terrain. While Cuban Americans tend to bloc-vote, in the context of a "swing state," the extent of their bloc-voting impacts on electoral outcomes.[69]

Table 3.7 summarizes embargo loosening and tightening policies that between 1992 and 2004 were implemented in presidential election and non-election years. It documents whether the policies were implemented by an incumbent and whether the incumbent who implemented the embargo

Table 3.7 Summary of US embargo tightening and loosening measures in the post-Cold War era, and whether incumbent president loses Florida in the election

Year	Personal embargo		Macro embargo		Incumbent	
	Loosening	*Tightening*	*Loosening*	*Tightening*	*Wins Fla*	*Loses Fla*
1992		x		x	x	
1994		x				
1995	x					
1996		x		x	x	
1998	x					
1999	x					
2000	[Elián][a]	x[b]	x			x[c]
2003	x[d]					
2004		x			x	

Notes:

a Elián returned to Cuba, amidst Cuban American opposition.

b Codification of travel cap, amidst congressional pressure to lift travel restrictions (but no alteration of frequency of permitted visits).

c Incumbent vice president runs for office, associated with incumbent president's Elián policy.

d Loosening of restrictions for Cuban Americans, though tightening of restrictions for other Americans.

policies won the Florida vote. The summary table shows embargo policies, in the main, to have become more restrictive in presidential election years, and less restrictive in off-election years when inconsistent with non-ethnic-based concerns of governance. My policy cycle thesis would predict such vacillation. The influence of moneyed hardliner ethnic lobbyists with votes to deliver should peak in election years.

The ethnic policy cycle began in 1992 with passage of the Cuban Democracy Act, against the backdrop of the previously described Foundation influence-peddling. George H. W. Bush supported the bill when running for reelection, despite reservations about it,[70] to curry Cuban American votes in Florida. Understanding the importance of the state to his reelection bid, he strategically signed the legislation in Miami on the eve of the election, and at the ceremony acknowledged Mas Canosa as one of the key forces behind the new law.[71] Further indicative that his stance on the bill was electoral-driven, he had previously vetoed the so-called Mack Amendment, the precursor to the 1992 legislation.

Bush had opposed the Mack initiative because of its extra-territorial claims.[72] As a former director of the CIA, he was no friend of Cuban Communism. But he blocked the bill when lobbied by big business, including by Exxon, IBM, and ITT, resentful of interference with their profiteering via other countries, and, especially, by foreign governments, such as Canada's, which resented Washington interference in their own trade dealings.[73] At the time, business and ally support mattered more to the President than placating Cuban American hardliners.

In previously vetoing the Mack Amendment Bush demonstrated that in off-election years ethnic PAC contributions did not guarantee presidential support for legislation. Florida's Senator Connie Mack, who sponsored the proposal bearing his name, had been among the key recipients of Foundation-linked PAC money.

But Bush responded to ethnic lobbyists and political contributors when running for reelection and his opponent, Clinton, announced his support for the Cuban Democracy Act then before Congress. In the context of the election Bush withdrew his opposition to embargo-tightening through extra-territorial means. Like the Mack Amendment, the Cuban Democracy Act prohibits US businesses from third-country trade with Cuba. When pressed to choose between backing business and ally interests, and courting Cuban American Florida votes when seeking reelection, the latter mattered more to him. Further indicative that his changed stance was electoral more than ideological driven, Bush at the time permitted US companies to trade with Communist China, both from the US and third countries. In the case of China, business interests got the upper hand, as they had previously, in the throes of the Cold War.

Bush's opportunism paid off. Three-fourths of Cuban Americans in Florida voted for him, enough to win the state. With US Cuba policy mattering little, however, to most of the national electorate in the post-Cold War era, his support for the Cuban Democracy Act did not suffice to win him reelection.

The 1996 election galvanized yet another ethnic policy cycle. Like Bush in 1992, Clinton four years later took advantage of incumbency to support new embargo-tightening legislation, against the backdrop of his reelection bid.[74] And following Bush's example, Clinton in an election year signed embargo-tightening legislation that he previously had opposed. He too was especially concerned with the bill's internationally unpopular extra-territorial claims.[75] Business leaders and foreign governments found the so-called Helms–Burton Bill even more offensive than the Cuban Democracy Act. They considered it an infringement of their sovereignty and trading rights, and a violation of GATT and WTO principles.

Clinton backed the Helms–Burton Bill, despite business and foreign government opposition, immediately after the Cuban downing, in February 1996, of planes flown by the exile group Brothers to the Rescue. The downing stirred émigré fury in Florida.[76] With 75 percent of Miami Cuban Americans supportive of the Helms–Burton Bill,[77] Clinton reversed his stance on the legislation in the context of the heightened anti-Castro fervor in an election year.[78] He, like Bush, signed the legislation in Florida. He timed it with the opening of the primary contest in the state,[79] and had influential Cuban Americans invited to the signing ceremony.[80] Clinton's approval of the legislation helped him garner about a third of the Cuban American Florida vote that November, insufficient to break the Republican's lock in the state on the Cuban American electoral bloc, but sufficient to win the state's electoral college votes and his presidential reelection bid in turn. A Democratic candidate had not won Florida in twenty years.

In his memoir,[81] Clinton acknowledged that his support for the bill was good election-year politics in Florida, but that it undermined whatever chance he would have in a second term of office to lift the embargo in exchange for island reforms. The Helms–Burton Bill, among its measures, restricted presidential authority to lift the embargo without Congressional approval. Clinton also acknowledged in his memoir that because he had considered Florida critical to his reelection bid, he had worked for four years to cultivate support in the state, including among Cuban Americans. Although Clinton had an interest in making improved US–Cuba bilateral relations and changes in Cuba a hallmark of his presidency, when pressed to choose, he prioritized his reelection.

Further indicative that his support for the 1996 legislation was electoral-driven, after winning a second term, he never enforced the provision of the bill that foreign governments and investors found especially egregious: the clause that gave US citizens the right to sue international investors who "trafficked" in property they owned before the revolution. My Tufte-inspired thesis accounts for Clinton's lack of follow-through once winning reelection, when concerns of state came to the fore. But the very enactment of the legislation, with its extra-territorial reach, so angered the international community that there followed a dramatic increase in country votes in the United Nations General Assembly for condemnation of the embargo. The US paid an international price even for passage of legislation never implemented.[82] What was good for winning an election proved bad for the nation's foreign relations.

The 2000 election took the ethnic political cycle to new dimensions. It did not result in significant new embargo-tightening measures. To the contrary, in 2000, prior to the election, Clinton signed into law the legislation that allowed US food sales to Cuba. Clinton supported the embargo-loosening in an election year when ineligible to run again for office.

Far more important to the 2000 ethnic electoral cycle was the controversy over whether six-year-old Elián should stay in the US or be returned to his father in Cuba. The controversy revealed the political price a presidential candidate incurred when associated with a legally justified policy of honoring parental custody rights, defiant of Exile yearnings. That year Cuban Americans helped the younger George Bush win the electoral college vote when Al Gore won the national popular vote. Florida proved decisive in determining the election outcome. Officially Bush won the state by slightly more than five hundred votes, with over 80 percent of Cuban Americans backing him.

The 2000 ethnic electoral cycle rested, above all, on Cuban American opposition to the Democratic Administration returning Elián to his father in Cuba.[83] Seventy-nine percent of Miami Cuban Americans felt that Elián should remain in the US with his relatives.[84] With the political class taking the lead, most Cuban émigrés, across cohorts, joined the crusade to "save Elián." The Cuban American National Foundation, while still the preeminent Cuban American organization, financed Elián's Florida relatives' fight for claims to the boy. It had the backing of other hardline Cuban American groups and Miami's Cuban American political class. No prominent local Cuban American politician or radio station publicly supported Elián's father's paternity claims.

Elián innocently contributed to Bush's exceptionally strong support among Cuban Americans that year. Despite the community's tendency to bloc-vote, never before had it used the ballot box in such unity in a presidential election. Cuban Americans collectively turned against Gore, Clinton's vice president. Although in an effort to curry Cuban American votes Gore very publicly broke with the President to side with the Miami relatives in their struggle to keep Elián in America, he was damned by association with the Clinton White House. Outrage with the Clinton Administration's handling of the Elián case was so strong that Gore did not dare even campaign in Cuban American neighborhoods in Miami, for fear of facing protests.[85] The Clinton Administration's confiscation of Elián at gunpoint, captured in television footage, was the clincher. That the Administration had tried to negotiate peacefully for the handover of Elián for half a year did not matter to most Miami Cuban Americans. Gore paid deeply for White House efforts to enforce international custody rights.

So enraged were Cuban Americans over Elián's fate that they defended Bush when his victory was disputed. They intimidated the local officials who were in charge of a recount, to the point of helping shut down the effort to validate the vote.[86] The Miami Cuban American Congressmen encouraged mobilization against a recount, via Radio Mambí, after having previously rallied support for the fight to keep Elián in America. No Cuban American Miami radio station supported the recount, or Elián's return to Cuba.[87]

When running for reelection in 2004, after the Elián affair had been put to rest, Bush's support among Cuban Americans in Florida dropped from 82 to 77 percent.[88] Yet, even to exact this level of support, hardliners pressured Bush for policy concessions. They were dismayed that the President had done little during his first term to further their anti-Castro cause. Accordingly, against the backdrop of the 2004 election, Republican Cuban Americans in Florida made public their disappointment with Bush for not fulfilling 2000 campaign pledges. They were angry, for one, that Bush had not revamped the Clinton Administration's "wet-foot" policy, of returning to Cuba islanders who were found at sea while attempting to emigrate without US entry permission. They were also angry that Bush, like Clinton, suspended enforcement of the Helms–Burton Bill provision that permitted Cuban Americans to sue foreign investors trafficking in property they owned before the revolution. And they were angry that Bush had loosened the so-called personal embargo, restrictions on family visitation and remittance-sending rights. They used the context of the election to press for reforms they wanted.

Paralleling the work of hardline lobbyists with political contributions to parlay, the US-born Tallahassee legislator, David Rivera, pressured Bush to institute new hardline policies. Rivera was entrenched in Exile networks, and well socialized to their views on Cuba. In the 1980s, he had worked for then Florida Senator Connie Mack, who promoted the precursor to the Cuban Democracy Act. And before becoming a state representative he also worked for the Cuban American National Foundation, and for Radio and TV Martí. Even though he had never set foot on Cuban soil, he claimed exile authenticity, owing to his family roots. Rivera publicly asserted that "every Cuban American . . . has a moral obligation to continue the cause of a free and democratic Cuba," and added, "You grow up and all your family does is talk about Cuba. Your parents, your grandparents, they instill in you a sense of pride in the homeland."[89] Rivera went so far as to announce hopes to one day be mayor of his family's hometown, in a free Cuba. While some Cuban Americans felt Rivera overstepped his entitlement boundaries in claiming rights to island public office, in making his proclamation he reinforced Exiles' commitment to reclaim their homeland.

As Republicans, Rivera and other Cuban Americans could not realistically threaten to defect to the Democrats. However, they could and did threaten both to withhold Republican financial and tactical support, including help in fundraisers, and to remain politically neutral in the upcoming election if Bush refused to respond to their requests. The Florida lawmakers were particularly incensed when the Bush Administration in 2003 repatriated twelve Cuban boatpeople found in the Florida Straits, even though it did so in compliance with US immigration policy. The state legislators, like many in the Cuban community, felt Cubans should have special immigration entitlements, including the right to enter without official permission.[90]

Although the Bush Administration never responded to all their demands, it announced new hardline measures in spring 2004. It used as rationale recommendations of a newly released report issued by the Commission for the Assistance of a Free Cuba, chaired by then Secretary of State Colin Powell. Bush announced new funding for TV Martí and for island dissidents, and a clamp-down on Cuban American rights to visit island family and send remittances to them. While the clampdown on people-to-people cross-border rights is detailed more in Chapters 4 and 6, relevant here, Bush, in the heat of his presidential reelection campaign, reversed his previous loosening of restrictions. His interventions demonstrated yet another ethnic electoral cycle, one defined by hardline Exiles. These Exiles believed that the tightening of the embargo at the people-to-people level would help bring the Castro-led regime to heel. The new measures placated demands not only of the Florida Republican state representatives, but also of Miami Cuban American municipal and county officials, the Cuban American south Florida congressional contingent, and hardline Cuban American groups, such as Mothers and Women Against Repression, the Cuban Liberty Council (CLC), and Unidad Cubana.[91]

The "ethnic bargain" under Bush included economic gains. In 2006, Congressional auditors found that tens of millions of dollars of US Agency for International Development money, ostensibly allotted to promote democracy in Cuba, had been channeled to anti-Castro groups in Miami. The auditors found that 30 percent of the agency's Cuba-related expenditures were questionable. Critics contended that the Washington aid was more about winning votes from Florida exiles than about promoting island change. Also in 2006, a federal grand jury indicted a senior TV Martí executive for accepting $100,000 in kickbacks from a broadcast company contracted to do business with the television operation.[92] Accordingly, Cuban Americans, both personally and as a group, benefited materially from supporting Bush.

The George W. Bush ethnic policy cycle operated somewhat independently of Exile influence-peddling. More Cuban American PAC money went to Democrats than to Republicans between 1998 and 2004, although Republicans were far from excluded. The PAC overseers dispersed campaign contributions to buy political influence, whatever politicians' partisan affiliations, and irrespective of their own partisan leanings. But at the polls the Cuban American electorate backed Bush in 2004, as in 2000, even if in lesser numbers. Bush's support proved strongest among Exiles, who were the most hardline. Table 3.2 shows that while in Miami most Cuban Americans registered Republican, in 2004 the rates were highest among those who emigrated before the Freedom Flights ended.

In turn, the electoral cycles, under Clinton and especially Bush, spurred high-level patronage appointments. When Clinton withdrew Baeza from consideration for a top State Department post amidst hardliner opposition, he appointed, for example, Paul Cejas of Miami, the second largest Cuban

American Democratic political contributor between 1979–2000, to serve as his ambassador to Belgium.[93] George W. Bush appointed Cuban Americans to more visible senior positions than Clinton. Bush appointed Cuban Americans to the National Security Council and to head the Department of Housing and Urban Development during his first term of office and to head the Department of Commerce during his second term. All the appointees had emigrated as children in the early years of Castro's rule.

The high-level appointments gave symbolic power to Cuban Americans in general. But Bush concomitantly called on the appointees to advance his own political agenda. He called, in particular, on Mel Martínez, his first Secretary of Housing and Urban Development, to help deliver the ethnic vote when he ran for reelection. Bush had called on Martínez to co-chair the Commission for Assistance to a Free Cuba that legitimated the 2004 embargo-tightening measures, and then supported the Cuban American's resignation, already before the release of the report, to run for Senator in Florida. Bush counted on Martínez to maximize Cuban American turnout in the battleground state, and, afterwards, to increase Republican presence in Congress. And in his second term of office Bush called on Carlos Gutiérrez, his Secretary of Commerce, to defend his Cuba policy.[94]

Partners to the ethnic electoral cycle, in essence, tried to use one another to their own advantage. At root was a quid pro quo: individual and collective ethnic gain in exchange for votes and political contributions. But Exiles set the ethnic agenda and delivered most of the votes, particularly of the foreign-born.

The Withering of Hardline Exile Hegemony and Breakdown of the Ethnic Policy Cycle

Hardline Exile political hegemony began to break down after the turn of the century. Hardliners' influence rested not merely on "delivering the vote" and political contributions, but also on preventing challenges to their point of view from gaining a voice. Once left without a charismatic leader after Mas Canosa's death, underlying contradictions, which mainly took cohort and generation form, came to the fore. Differences in perspectives on cross-border relations came to divide the émigré community both at the leadership level and within the community at large, all the while that Cuban Americans assimilated to their new country life. Political changes at the national level also came to work increasingly to hardliners' disadvantage. Business, humanitarian, and other interests opposed to the embargo asserted themselves, less deterred by accusations of being "soft on Communism" in the post-Cold War era. Even the relative importance of Exiles at the Florida polls declined, with ever more immigrants from elsewhere in Latin America as well as New Cubans taking out citizenship and voting,[95] and as ever more second-generation Cuban Americans came of voting age. These new voters were less supportive of a wall across the Straits, and ever more Exiles were dying off.

The Leadership Divide

In 2003, Exiles formed a new PAC. In the process, the Foundation and its PAC became shadows of their former selves. Within the first year of its formation the new PAC, the US-Cuba Democracy PAC, took in over half a million dollars in funds from individual contributions of $200 or more. This was nearly four times as much as the Free Cuba PAC attracted in any one year between 1998 and 2004, and double the amount the Free Cuba PAC raised in its peak money-raising year, 1984, when Reagan courted Cuban Americans. Like the Free Cuba PAC, the new PAC relied on wealthy Cuban American contributors, from families who had fled the revolution early on. In a short time the new PAC became one of the 150 largest of over five thousand PACs nationwide, and, reputedly, the largest single political contributor on a foreign policy matter.[96]

In line with its motto, "Freedom First, Then Concession," and like the Foundation through its PAC in the past, the US-Democracy PAC became the bedrock for continued advocacy of a hardline stance on US Cuba policy. The new PAC funneled contributions to help elect anti-Castro pro-embargo candidates, to defeat pro-embargo-loosening candidates, and to create an anti-Castro constituency among Congressmen who might otherwise have been indifferent on Cuban matters. It targeted funds to seventy-five congressional candidates in its first electoral cycle. At a time when Washington was improving relations with other Communist countries and was pushing for global trade liberalization, the new PAC determinedly fought to maintain and tighten barriers across the Straits.

Committed to maintaining and strengthening the Cuba embargo, the directorship of the new PAC considered its 2004 congressional mission accomplished when all but four of the candidates it supported won their electoral bids, and when in 2005 Congress reversed initiatives to ease Cuba travel and trade. Following Foundation precedent, the new PAC backed candidates across the partisan divide and beyond its contributor base, which remained mainly Floridian. New PAC recipients included twelve Congressmen who in the recent past had consistently supported embargo-loosening measures, but voted in 2005 against all amendments pending in Congress to further relax the embargo; six Congressmen who had previously waffled in their support for embargo-loosening measures, but who voted against all of the 2005 amendments; fifteen Congressmen who reversed their stance on at least one of the embargo-loosening proposals before the legislature in 2005; and nineteen just-elected legislators who voted against all the proposed amendments.[97]

Then, in 2007, the new PAC helped block an effort by the new Democratic-dominated Congress to ease restrictions on agricultural trade with Cuba. PAC recipients who opposed the embargo-loosening included Representatives who had previously voted to lift the embargo, as well as first-time legislators. In the 2007–2008 cycle, the US-Cuba Democracy PAC made $322,500 in political donations. Fifty-two of the sixty-six Democrats who voted against the proposed embargo-loosening measure, including seventeen of the twenty-two Democratic freshmen, had received PAC contributions.[98] Accordingly, the new PAC fought to keep intact an embargo that in more than forty years had failed to topple the Castro-led government. But whereas the PAC and the Foundation under Mas Canosa's sway had effectively lobbied for embargo tightening, the success of the new PAC was limited to defensively fending off Congressional embargo-loosening initiatives.

The formation of the new PAC followed, and was associated with, the break-away of influential Exiles from the Foundation to form, in 2001, the Cuban Liberty Council (CLC).[99] The CLC's stated mission, to promote liberty and democracy in Cuba, differed little from the Foundation's. Its founders intended their group to reaffirm the wall across the Straits, which the Foundation no longer defended effectively.

The split occurred at a time when the Foundation experienced leadership and financial problems.[100] Following Mas Canosa's death in 1997, his US-born son, Jorge Mas Santos, took over the organization's helm. But the son lacked his father's charisma. He also lacked legitimacy as an authentic spokesperson for those who had fled Cuba in opposition to the revolution, in that he never knew Cuba first-hand. Despite his questionable authenticity, the Foundation directorship initially supported him after his father died because, as explained to me, they felt his family name would help further their anti-Castro cause.

Institutionalization of charisma is never easy, as Max Weber explained in his famous work on the subject,[101] and Mas Santos' effort to routinize his father's charisma was no exception. What the hardline Exile activists interpreted as a personality flaw of the son in fact had structural roots, and rested on a problem not unique to him. Indicative of how Exiles revered Mas Canosa, a prominent Cuban American Miami lawyer and anti-Castro activist who emigrated in the 1960s referred to the former Foundation leader as a saint, in an interview with me. Such deification is not easily transferable. Sainthood needs to be earned, not inherited, and hardline Exiles felt the son failed to earn sainthood on his own.

The Foundation also experienced internal financial problems. In 2004, its PAC took in a mere $5,000 in contributions, following the formation of the new PAC. And coincidentally, the value of MasTec stock, the Foundation's main endowment source which Mas Canosa established, plunged. The Foundation, as a result, had to downsize its staff, close its Washington lobbying office, and shut down its radio station.

Furthermore, in 2000, the Foundation lost important battles in Washington that the break-away faction blamed on Mas Canosa's ineffective leadership. It lost the custody battle over Elián that it had financed, and it failed to avert the partial Congressional lifting of the embargo on agricultural sales to Cuba. That Elián's father had paternity rights to the motherless child, and that the Foundation and its PAC were no match for the far larger and more influential agribusiness lobby which sought access to the Cuba market, hardline Exiles refused to concede. In the words of Dennis Hayes, in charge of the Foundation's

Washington office until it closed for lack of funds, "For a long time there was no significant economic power working against the embargo. Now the mantra is 'market, market, market'."[102] Even though Congress, in the post-Cold War neoliberal spirit, had by then lifted restrictions on trade with (and investment in) Vietnam as well as China, CLC supporters would not settle for the deal that Mas Santos had successfully brokered: the prohibition of US financing for Cuba's US food purchases, which severely constrained island buying capacity.

The hardliners also broke with the Foundation over its new conciliatory turn in bilateral relations with Cuba under Castro. Mas Santos, and his US-born Foundation Executive Director, began to favor compromise and the transforming of cross-border barriers into bridges. Mas Santos went so far as to announce willingness to meet with high-level Cuban officials besides Fidel and Raúl Castro to discuss a democratic transition. He also supported a nascent dissident movement on the island, the Varela Project, premised on bringing about political reform within the contours of the island Constitution.[103] And during the 2008 presidential campaign cycle, after a speech by the then presumptive Democratic candidate Barack Obama, Mas Santos publicly supported loosening the embargo at the people-to-people level, which I detail in subsequent chapters.[104] The hardliners who formed the CLC, in contrast, continued to insist on regime change as a precondition for cross-border dealings.

Also angering hardliners, Mas Santos supported transnational cultural bridge-building permitted by US law. Already in 2001 Mas Santos, along with the US-born Miami-Dade Mayor at the time, Penelas, very publicly promoted Miami hosting the Latin American Grammys. They were pragmatic in their support. They valued the business, prestige, and publicity the gala event would bring the metropolis. Hardline Exiles, however, opposed the event because it would bring internationally acclaimed Cuban performers to the city. The Grammy organizers planned the 2001 event in Miami after the court struck down the legality of the ordinance that prohibited the county from doing business with organizations and people who were Cuba-based. Cuban cultural performers were exempt from the embargo. With the law proven not on their side, hardliners threatened to disrupt the awards ceremony. Three weeks before the scheduled event the organizing committee finally conceded to the pressure. They moved the Grammys to Los Angeles. Hardline Exiles thus won this culture battle, a battle not against Anglos, as in the case of the English Only movement two decades in the past, but against a new Cuban American generation which by then had emerged in their midst.

But the remains of the Foundation refused to concede the new, partially intra-ethnic culture war. With new determination, the Grammy organizing committee, with Foundation backing, scheduled the annual competition again in Miami two years later. Yet, also with renewed determination, hardliners threatened again to protest if island performers attended. This time they took advantage of their political capital, their ties to then Governor Jeb Bush, and his access to his brother in the White House. As a result, the State Department refused to grant travel visas to Cuban performers scheduled to partake in the awards ceremony. The show went on, with Miami hosting the Grammys without Cuban musicians in attendance. With his upcoming reelection bid on the horizon, President Bush exercised his discretionary power here too, "behind the scenes," to side with the hardliners whose financial, media, and electoral support he counted on. The electoral-linked ethnic policy cycle accordingly in 2003 also took cultural form.

The born-again conciliatory Foundation was not organizationally alone after the turn of the century in promoting cross-border bridge-building. In 2005, it joined over twenty other organizations to form Consenso Cubano, an umbrella group committed to reconciliation and to a non-violent transition in Cuba. Affiliated groups included the newly formed Cuba Study Group, comprised of influential wealthy businessmen and professionals who had emigrated as adolescents soon after Castro assumed power. While deeply committed to regime change in their homeland, the trauma of the failed effort to keep Elián in America led them to rethink their stance on Cuba. As publicly acknowledged in the group's statement of purpose, "in the aftermath of the Elián González incident" founding members realized that "policies based on strategic rather than reflexive considerations were needed," and with this in mind they were committed to "practical, proactive and consensual approaches towards Cuba policy."[105]

Thus, hardliners reconsolidated power in the early 2000s in a manner that enabled them to maintain influence through lobbying, political contributions, and votes at the polls. However, by the time of the 2008 elections their influence over national policy through personal ties declined, in that Jeb Bush no longer served as Governor and his brother was ineligible for reelection as president. Also, by 2008 the Cuban American community had become divided in their views. Both at the leadership and organizational level, hardline hegemony was challenged as never before.

The Cohort and Generational Divide

Meanwhile, an incipient political divide festered in the Cuban American community at large, with émigré cohort and generational underpinnings. New Cubans, and US-born Cubans more equivocally, favored bridge-building which hardline Exiles aggressively opposed.

Miami survey data show Cuban Americans to differ increasingly in their stance toward the embargo in general and to sales of medicine, and especially food, to Cuba in particular, as well as toward reestablishing diplomatic ties and dialogue with the Cuban government. They also differ in their views toward the personal embargo, to travel and remittance-sending, which I detail in Chapters 4 and 6. Cuban Americans differ, first and foremost, depending on when they emigrated. The New Cubans and Exiles are, on some of these issues, poles apart (see Table 3.4). On each policy issue the New Cubans most favored barrier-lifting. Most New Cubans also opposed the ban on performances by Cuban musicians that the hardliners supported.

The 1999 controversy over a concert by the island musicians, Los Van Van, reflected the incipient cohort divide that took cultural along with political form. The New Cubans wanted the concert, by a group familiar to them from their Cuba days, while hardline Exiles opposed it. From the Exiles' vantage point, the musicians represented Castro, their nemesis. Exiles wished to keep cultural icons associated with the Castro-led government away from the new city they claimed as their own. Also, Los Van Van's music had no place in the pre-revolutionary cultural repertoire Exiles brought with them to the US.

The émigré cohort divide rested more on contrasting pre-immigration experiences than on differences in years to assimilate to mainstream US views. The first post-Castro émigrés differ most in their views from non-Cuban Americans in Miami, even though they had the most years to adopt host community values. When queried in 2000, 60 percent of non-Cubans in Miami noted that they would vote, if given the opportunity, to end the trade embargo that Exiles favored.[106]

An incipient generational divide, between the US-born and the Cuba-born, is also on the rise. After the turn of the century about half of all Cuban Americans were US-born. In Miami, US-born Cuban Americans most resembled New Cubans, not their parents' generation, on foreign policy views (Table 3.4). But the basis for similarity in views of the US-born and the New Cubans differs. The views of recent arrivals were shaped by their continued commitment to island friends and family, whereas the views of the US-born were shaped by their US upbringing. They were schooled in American values of compromise and tolerance, even when at home their Exile parents socialized them to a hardline stance on Cuba under Castro.

On support for an Exile-led military invasion, the US-born, nonetheless, report themselves as intransigent as their island-born Exile parents' generation. Support for an invasion, for revenge and reclaiming Cuba, represents an unfinished mission that the first who fled the revolution have passed on to their children.[107] Thus, drawing both on their family and on US experiences, the US-born are somewhat equivocal and contradictory in their views on Cuban matters.

The disputes over policy that fueled the CLC split from the Cuban American National Foundation were at their core generation-based. Second-generation Cuban Americans dominate the faction that remained affiliated with the Foundation. They remained committed to their parents' generation battle with Castro, while influenced in strategy by the more conciliatory style of US politics rooted in their US upbringing. Although they began their political careers carrying the hardline torch, they transformed themselves into cross-border bridge-builders. Mas Santos publicly claimed himself born an Exile, but he and his second-generation allies subjected Exile views to reinterpretation after being defeated in the battle over Elián. They came to see other US-born Cuban Americans and New Cubans as potential political constituents.

Cuban American fracturing even became manifest in partisan politics, although at the time of writing more at the leadership than at the rank-and-file level. In 2004, influential Cuban Americans publicly broke with the Republican lock that Exiles helped establish in the 1980s.[108] In the run-up to the presidential election in 2004, US-born Joe García left his post as Executive Director of the Cuban American National Foundation to work for the Washington-based New Democratic Network. His job involved attracting Cuban American Democratic voters. In the new milieu, some other influential Cuban Americans also publicly challenged the Republican Party Miami hegemony. In the next presidential cycle García, along with Raúl Martínez, contested Mario and Lincoln Díaz-Balart, respectively, for the Congressional seats they held. Martínez, the long-term mayor of Hialeah, remained a Democrat from the days before Cuban Americans became entrenched in the Republican Party. The 2008 election marked the first time that the Díaz-Balarts faced a serious challenge since they were first elected to Congress, and from fellow Cuban Americans no less. The Democratic candidates sought to appeal to the Cuban American "generational gap," by focusing less on Raúl and Fidel Castro and more on easing the personal embargo that Bush tightened in 2004, as well as on domestic issues.[109] Two thirds of US-born Cuban Americans, all, by definition, US citizens and therefore eligible to vote if of age, disapproved of Bush's 2004 tightening of the personal embargo (Table 3.4).

Against the backdrop of the growing divide in views among the electorate, and the breakdown of hardliner hegemony at the leadership level, some presidential candidates spoke out for the first time, in 2008, for loosening the personal embargo. John McCain, the Republican candidate, made public his support for the continuation of Bush's policies. Of the two final Democratic contestants, Hillary Clinton echoed a similar stance, absent political change in Cuba. Barack Obama, however, announced that he would lift Bush Administration restrictions on Cuban American rights to visit their relatives in Cuba and send them remittances. Obama argued that Bush's policies left Cubans too dependent on the Castro regime and too removed from the transformative message Cuban Americans carry.[110] In the campaign for the Democratic nomination Clinton received CLC backing and its PAC support. And in the partisan election, McCain similarly relied on CLC support. In contrast, Obama, who refused PAC money, was not beholden to moneyed Cuban Americans opposed to embargo-loosening. Under the circumstances, he took the political risk of alienating the most hardline, unlikely Democratic voters no matter what his stance. At the time, one-half of registered voters, although only one-third of Exiles, favored a return to Bush's more permissive personal embargo policies in place until 2004.[111] Obama won Florida with one-third of the Cuban American vote, and within two months in office he relaxed travel restrictions.

Conclusion

As Cuban Americans assimilated into mainstream US political life, Exiles leveraged political institutions to their individual and collective advantage.

Politically influential Exiles typically were child immigrants, who formed their views on Cuba through parental and community socialization, but who also knew how to navigate their adopted country's institutional world. They leveraged US political institutions to their ethnic, cohort-based, advantage through determined and savvy leadership, organization, generous political contributions, block-voting, and interventions beyond the rights and responsibilities of offices they held. They took advantage of political opportunities that the Republican Party made available to them, while capitalizing on their demographic concentration in what came to be the largest "swing state." They succeeded, in turn, in galvanizing a hardline anti-Castro ethnic policy cycle tied to the presidential election cycle.

Hardline Exiles' ability to leverage politics, public bureaucracies, and public resources to their advantage rested on the formation of an ethnic sociopolitical field comprised of individuals and groups with social, cultural, economic, and political capital. But it rested also on the compliance that they imposed, including penalization and marginalization of those who challenged their authority and agenda. They combined democratic with non-democratic practices. Their ability to maintain discipline, however, began to break down after the turn of the century, owing to a confluence of changes that were both internal and external to the Cuban American community.

The New Cubans, who in growing numbers are making Miami their home, contributed to the erosion of hardline Exile hegemony, with little public fanfare. They quietly, covertly, and partly illegally, defied the wall across the Straits. The remainder of the book addresses their cross-border relations and their impact.

4 The Personal is Political
Bonding Across Borders

The next three chapters focus on transnational ties at the people-to-people level, the first two on homeland visits, the third on income-sharing. Together the chapters illustrate not merely how enduring, but also how transnationally consequential, pre-immigration cohort formations may be. I show that the two contrasting émigré waves—the islanders who fled the revolution early on and the post-Soviet-era arrivals—differ in their stance toward bonding across borders. Building on their pre- and anti-revolution perspectives on life, Exiles opposed such ties. For them, the personal across borders is political. They were so committed to their stance that they deployed an array of tactics, ranging from politicking at the highest levels of national policy-making to violence and intimidation in the neighborhoods where they live, to keep others from trespassing their socially constructed wall across the Straits. At the other extreme are the New Cubans. Their post-Soviet-era crisis perspective on life predisposed them to want to bond with friends and family they left behind, with whom their lives remained enmeshed.

However, people-to-people cross-border ties hinge also on the stance of states. The US and Cuban governments set parameters to the legally possible, and both governments shifted their parameters over the years, with each at times deliberately preventing or restricting what the other allowed. For this reason, transnational people-to-people ties need be understood in broader institutional context. I show below how during the Cold War the two governments blocked cross-border bonding among Cubans united by blood and a shared culture. Afterwards, the Cuban government became more permissive, while the US government became more restrictive, although Washington was more restrictive in some years than others. The seeming anomaly in Washington's post-Cold War policy, given its claimed commitment to freedom to travel and to family values, rested on, and became enmeshed in, the election-linked ethnic policy cycle defined by Exiles, that I described in the last chapter.

Amidst Exile opposition, New Cubans transformed cross-border barriers into bridges, quietly and sometimes covertly and in defiance of official regulations that stood in their way. They had such impact even though they were politically weak. Chapter 7 addresses how far-reaching the effects of their bridge-building have been, at the macro level.

Transnational ties at the people-to-people level may take different forms. They may rest on face-to-face visits, phone calls, letter-writing, and e-mail. But prior to the 1990s all modes of communication were minimal. Telephone calls were expensive, connections poor and erratic. Calls were sometimes intercepted, and perhaps more important, imagined to be, so that Cubans felt constrained in their cross-border conversations. Similarly, letter-writing was difficult. Washington and Havana required mail to be circuited through third countries, and delivery was not dependable. What could have been a quick ninety-mile mailing took approximately one month. And letter-writers, like phone-callers, felt constrained in what they communicated, fearful that state agents would read what they wrote. Internet access still was too limited by the start of the new millennium to permit regular communication. Less than 2 percent of Cubans had internet access. Typically only islanders in research positions and high-level jobs had routine access to e-mail.

In this chapter, I focus on émigré cohort homeland visits. Face-to-face contact allows for the most intimate bonding.[1] I highlight differences in émigré bonding in the pre- and post-Soviet era, in the context of government travel policies at the time. I draw on survey data, my in-depth interviews with Cuban Americans in the Union City area as well as Greater Miami, and on published data on homeland visits.

The Cold War People-to-People Wall Across the Straits, 1959–1989

Before the revolution cross-border travel hinged mainly on people's pocketbooks. Moneyed Cubans vacationed in the US, while moneyed Americans sought sun and fun on the island, then known as the "Las Vegas of the Caribbean." Cuban émigrés could freely visit their homeland, but there were few of them to visit. In contrast, for the first three decades of Castro's rule, when the Cuban ex-patriot population in the US ballooned, few émigrés made homeland trips on principle and because they faced US and Cuban government hurdles.

Official Barriers[2]

In that governments can restrict who they let out and in, cross-border bonding needs to be understood against the backdrop of both US and Cuban visitation policies. And because permitted visits could only occur by air, not by sea, the two governments had exceptional control over cross-border get-togethers.

Washington, for its part, cut off possibilities for travel after Castro announced the revolution as socialist in 1961. The embargo it then instituted was so all-encompassing as to keep family members divided by the revolution from seeing each other. By prohibiting Americans from spending dollars in Cuba, travel to the island became near impossible.

Not until the late 1970s did Washington relax its travel policy. Viewing cross-border people-to-people ties as a potential building block for improving state-to-state relations, President Carter gave a green light for two-week sojourns, and permitted the spending of dollars in Cuba so as to make trips possible. Approximately 150,000 émigrés took advantage of the travel opening.[3] Carter's well-intentioned policy backfired, however, in that it fueled the exodus of over 100,000 islanders from the port of Mariel described in Chapter 1. Stories that the visiting Exiles told of the good life in America whetted Cubans' appetite to leave. Against the backdrop of the onslaught of illegal Mariel entrants, President Reagan restricted travel rights anew.

While pursuing its own political agenda, the Cuban government reinforced the US-imposed travel wall. From the first years of Castro's rule until the bilateral negotiated travel opening under Carter, Havana officials prohibited Cuban Americans from visiting their homeland, except under extenuating circumstances. Cuban officials sought to enforce and reinforce the values of the new society-in-the-making by containing islander contact with Cubans who rejected the revolution. Thus, the Cuban government along with the US government subordinated family concerns and commitments to their respective political priorities.

Recognizing that compliance with restrictions is best when consistent with people's private wants, the Cuban government and the Communist Party also launched a symbolic crusade to drive a wedge between those who were loyal and disloyal to the revolution. The national leadership sought to convince the populace to reject, on their own, relations with friends and family who fled the revolution. Building on nationalist and new society values, the crusade rested on stigmatizing those who uprooted. Authorities referred pejoratively to those who left not only as *gusanos* (worms), as previously noted, but also as *escoria* (scum), social degenerates and outcasts, and *apatridas*, unpatriotic, for opposing the country's historical mission to bring about a more humane society freed from imperialist influence.

In that symbolic warfare might not alone convince islanders to sever ties with family who fled in a culture deeply committed to family values, Cuban officials also instituted an array of rewards and punishments to reinforce a people-to-people wall across the Straits. Reserving job promotions and Party membership for those without diasporic contact, islanders came to have political and economic incentives to keep cross-border bonding at bay.

When during the Carter presidency the Cuban leadership briefly took exception and opened its borders to émigré visits, it envisioned institutional gain. Castro hoped, for one, to divide the Cuban American community politically, to weaken hardline Exile influence.[4] Moderates favored rights to family visits, while hardliners opposed émigrés stepping foot in Cuba under Castro. The Cuban government also had new economic reason to allow diaspora trips. Visiting émigrés would infuse dollars into the island economy, which the government could appropriate to address its first hard currency debt on any scale.[5] The government profited from the charter flights, stays in the state-owned hotels which it required, meals at state-owned restaurants, the only public diners at the time, and émigré consumer goods purchases for island relatives at state stores.

However, the Mariel crisis led the Cuban government to reimpose travel restrictions, despite continued hard currency needs. It reprioritized political considerations, first to prevent "another Mariel," then to protest the Reagan Administration's funding of Exile-run Radio Martí designed to beam anti-Castro programs to the island. During the first year of radio programming Cuban officials put a plug on all visits, when also preventing emigration. They punished families separated by the Straits who wished to get together for Washington-backed Exile efforts to convince islanders through the airwaves to bring the Castro-led government to heel. When permitting visits again, they set an annual cap of 2,500, which they gradually increased to 5,000 by the end of the Soviet era.[6]

Informal Barriers

Ordinary Cubans on both sides of the Straits kept cross-border bonding at bay on their own. They did so out of conviction to the barriers their respective governments imposed, opportunism, and fear of retribution were they to defy the taboo of travel. On the US side, Exiles, building on their anti-Castro, anti-Communist mindset, developed their own informal people-to-people foreign policy. They supported what they called a personal embargo, to prevent Communist "contamination," as well as traveler infusion of dollars into a regime they despised. So committed were some self-defined exiles to a wall across the Straits that they transformed themselves into informal border police. They took it upon themselves to punish transnational trespassers. Cuban Americans who dared defy the travel taboo faced ostracism, stigma, and economic retaliation. Even travelers who conformed with US law faced such retribution. The "border police" spared neither the successful nor the humble, neither clergy nor laity. Businesspeople, priests, and ordinary people alike paid a price for defying the hardliners' disapproval of travel.

In some instances, Exiles even used violence to keep island visits at bay. In Miami, extremist hardliners, for example, bombed the bank owned by Bernardo Benes. Although no fan of Fidel, Benes, who moved to the US in 1960, headed the so-called Committee of 75, involved in what came to be known as the Dialogue, premised on reconciliation. The Dialogue paved the way for émigré homeland visits under Carter. Benes, who in collaboration with the Carter White House engaged in shuttle diplomacy, made scores of trips between the US and Cuba on the President's behalf. Hardliners, opposed to any negotiations with their island political opponents, turned on Benes.[7] Hardliners also vandalized and firebombed the Padron Cigar factory, and organized a boycott of the factory's products. They turned on the owner not merely for very publicly breaking their taboo of travel but for meeting with Fidel.[8] They also targeted airlines and travel businesses that helped make homeland visits possible. A Bay of Pigs veteran, for example, set off a bomb at the Miami airport where officially permitted flights under Carter left for Cuba. Other travel opponents planted bombs in the Florida offices both of an airline company that announced plans to initiate a charter service to the island, and an agency that booked Cuba travel.

The New Jersey/New York area, home to Havana North, also was not spared. Omega 7, the violent Miami-based clandestine group with a New Jersey affiliate,[9] set off bombs at New York's JFK Airport where a charter service also flew flights permitted under Carter to Cuba, at the Cuban and Soviet missions to the United Nations, and at agencies in the area that booked Cuba travel. And in Union City they murdered Cuba-born Eulalio José Negrín in front of his thirteen-year-old son.[10] Negrín paid with his life for breaking hardliner ranks. He too participated in the Dialogue. Even a Union City priest with whom I spoke became the target of bomb threats and church disruptions after he visited the island. The abuse was such that the archdiocese felt compelled to reassign him to a parish in a community without Cuban Americans, off Exiles' radar screen. Hardliners refused to excuse the priest for violating their taboo of travel, even though he helped Washington officials broker the release of prisoners of conscience on his trip.

Benes, Padron, Negrín, and the priest illustrate how during the Cold War not all of the Exile cohort supported the socially constructed people-to-people wall across the Straits. But the disciplinary punishment they suffered helped hardliners reinforce their rules of the permissible.

Some Cuba-born children of Exiles joined the ranks of those favoring travel rights. The diverse value-shaping experiences that they drew upon as they came of age to interpret life for themselves led them to defy their parents' generation stance. They drew on a mix of experiences distinct from that of most of their Cuban American peers. In so doing, they illustrate how politically, and not merely—as other scholars have noted—class, race, and ethnically, segmented immigrant youth experiences may be.[11] Against the backdrop of the civil rights, anti-Vietnam War, and Left-leaning movements that captivated the hearts and minds of their native-born generational contemporaries at the time, some 1960s child émigrés, when in their late adolescence, wanted to experience Cuba for themselves. Some even collectively took their elders to task. They organized and participated in the Antonio Maceo Brigade, which sponsored solidarity work trips to Cuba.[12]

Aurelio, with whom I spoke in Miami in 2001, was one of the child immigrants who participated in a Brigade trip. He had left the island in 1960 at age ten and had lived in Puerto Rico and New York before settling in Florida. Aurelio had been very influenced by the youth culture of his US contemporaries. Captivated by the "New Left," he came to sympathize with the revolution, and to advocate cross-border bridge-building. Now a successful Miami travel agent who books trips to Cuba, he reflected on how he came to defy the personal embargo his parents, and others of their generation, adamantly supported:

The civil rights and anti-Vietnam War movements led me to question a lot. They led me to question my parents and to question the situation in Cuba. For a few years I refused even to speak to my parents . . . I was among the first Cubans to return to Cuba. I went with the first Antonio Maceo Brigade. It was an emotional experience to see the country where I was born and its culture. Things that I thought were unique to me I saw to be Cuban.

While some of Aurelio's generation found the anti-Castro milieu of Miami so stifling that they moved away,[13] most of them, on the sidelines of youth movements of the time, adopted their parents' anti-Castro mindset and stance on travel for themselves. This was especially true of non-college-bound children, and young émigrés who studied in Miami, close to home.

Although the youth who participated in the solidarity trips were well received in Cuba, many adult Exiles who took advantage of the visits permitted under Carter, had island experiences that confirmed their anti-Castro views. For psychological, principled, and pragmatic reasons many Cubans resisted bonding with visiting relatives who rejected the country's radical makeover. Some of them resented that their mothers and fathers, siblings, and other kin, had put politics above family and fled, while they, captivated by the élan of the time, sided with Fidel and became children and agents of the revolution. Psychological wounds were deep. Others, loyal revolutionaries, objected politically to bonding with opponents of the social transformation, even if close kin.

The politically and economically ambitious in Cuba, in turn, came to understand that job advancement and Party membership were reserved for those without (known) diasporic contacts. Whereas in Miami informal border police boycotted and attacked cross-border trespassers' businesses, in Cuba, where the state had a near-monopoly on work opportunities, the Party intervened as economic gatekeeper. The Party rewarded the politically faithful with the best jobs. Illustrative of the price islanders paid for retaining ties with family who fled, one person I interviewed spoke of how the Union of Communist Youth refused to allow him into its ranks because of ties he maintained with "*gusanos*," and of how he suffered professionally as a result. Cognizant of the political rules of the game, the politically and economically ambitious kept covert any cross-border ties they maintained. They thereby did not publicly challenge the state-sanctioned norms of the new society in the making.

In such ways ordinary Cubans on both sides of the Straits kept cross-border ties minimal for three decades. The island-born who interpreted the key event of their time in polar opposite ways, and either emigrated or stayed in Cuba as a consequence, on their own resisted bonding with one another. Each believed in their own moral superiority. Nonetheless, those Exiles who took advantage of the Carter opening and were well received by island family, demonstrated that ties of blood meant more than lofty political principles and that social barriers could be maintained only when institutionally sustained.

The Travel Revolution: The Breakdown of Borders in the Post-Soviet Era

In the post-Soviet era the politically constructed people-to-people wall across the Straits crumbled. Unlike the Berlin Wall, though, it never entirely collapsed under the weight of border crossers. US-to-Cuba travel reached its highest levels of the Carter era, and for successive years (Figure 4.1). The number of Cuban Americans who made homeland visits is estimated to have risen from approximately 5,000 to 7,000 in 1990 to over 120,000 in 2003,[14] but then to have dipped to 57,000 in 2004, the last year for which I have been able to ascertain reasonably reliable figures.[15]

Even in Miami where the "border police" were most entrenched, the number of trip-takers rose substantially in the post-Soviet era. Florida International University found that, as of 2007, 36 percent of Cuban Americans had made homeland trips, up from 28 percent in 2000 (Table 4.1).

Visits proved but one of several ways that cross-border bonding picked up. Improved transnational telephone service facilitated family communication. While fears of "Big Brother" eavesdropping on calls never entirely disappeared, families separated by the Straits became more willing to disregard whatever surveillance remained. Improved mail service also contributed to increased communication. The 1992 Cuban Democracy Act laid the legal groundwork for a direct mail service to and from Cuba, although letter-writers often preferred to have visitors take their mail across the Straits. And for the minority of émigrés and island relatives who gained internet access beginning in the late 1990s, communication was free and fast.[16] The stepped-up communication strengthened cross-border bonding, and accordingly served as the bedrock for visits.

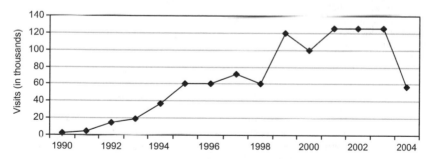

Figure 4.1 Cuban-American travel to Cuba, 1990–2004

Sources: Spadoni, "The Role of the United States in the Cuban Economy," *Cuba in Transition* (Association for the Study of the Cuban Economy, Coral Gables, Florida, August 2003), pp. 413, 414; Eckstein and Barbería 2002: 813, 814; Opening remarks by Mr. Felipe Perez Roque, Minister of Foreign Affairs of the Republic of Cuba at the III Conference on "The Nation and Emigration," May 21, 2004 (*Cuba Socialista*), in reference to all Cubans living abroad; U.S. Department of State, Commission for Assistance to a Free Cuba, 2004, Chapter 1, p. 32 (www.state.gov/documents/organization/32318.pdf); www.netforcuba. org/News-En/2006/Mar/News1059.htm.

Table 4.1 Travel and views toward travel to Cuba in 2000, 2004, and 2007, among Cuban Americans in Miami

	Year of arrival					
	1959–64	*1965–74*	*1975–84*	*1985–2000/07*	*US-born*	*Total*
Allow unrestricted travel to Cuba						
2000	39%	41%	52%	74% (1985–2000 émigrés)	58%	51%
2004	28	30	41	68 (1985–2004 émigrés)	51	46
2007	23	33	34	67 (1985–1994 émigrés) 80 (1995–2007 émigrés)	57	55
Ever traveled to Cuba						
2000	18	33	33	31	22	28
2004	23	33	37	45 (1985–2000 émigrés)	n.a.	36
2007	26	30	40	51 (1985–1994 émigrés) 40 (1995–2007 émigrés)	20	36
Still have close kin in Cuba						
2000	62	82	81	95	54	74
2004	54	76	87	95	60	78
2007	—	—	—	—	—	77
Whether current restrictions on trade, travel, and communications with Cuba personally had a major or moderate effect on interviewee and family						
2007	19	24	31	52 (1985–1994 émigrés) 61 (1995–2007 émigrés)	34	41

Source: www.fiu.edu/orgs/ipor/cuba2000; www.fiu.edu/orgs/ipor/cubapoll/YLCweb-comp.htm; and www.fiu.edu/orgs/ipor/cuba8/pollresults.html.

Note: N = 1,175 in 2000, 1,811 in 2004, and 1,000 in 2007.

Indicative of how improved communications stirred desire for face-to-face get togethers, a die-hard anti-Castroite in Union City, who emigrated in 1970 as a teenager, told me that she decided to visit island family after talking with them by phone, when phone connections improved in the early 1990s. Phone conversations reminded her that she had relatives in Cuba who cared about her. Her resistance to travel broke down in the process.

Changes in State-Level Policy Impacting on Travel in the Post-Soviet Era

The pick-up in cross-border bonding hinged partially on changes in US and especially Cuban government policies, which set parameters to the permissible. However, the Cubans who uprooted in different time periods, with different pre-immigration experiences and perspectives on life so formed, responded very differently to travel possibilities.

The Cuban Government Re-Envisions the Diaspora

The fiscal crisis resulting from the abrupt ending of Soviet aid and trade led the island authorities to desire, in desperation, dollar-infusing diaspora visitors. However, given the experience of Mariel that had followed on the heels of the Carter era visits, émigré visits were politically risky. The government's need for hard currency became so dire that it took the political risk. It allowed diaspora trip-taking on an unprecedented scale.

Officials took several initiatives to facilitate and encourage visits. They removed the cap on the number of Cuban Americans permitted to visit annually, they extended the length of time of permissible visits, and they made travel more affordable by ceasing to require visiting émigrés to stay in state-run hotels (thereby enabling hotels to concentrate on accommodating hard currency-paying tourists). Cuban authorities also reduced bureaucratic hurdles. To make visits more likely, they introduced multiple entry permits. And they retracted an earlier requirement that Cubans who emigrated illegally needed to wait five years before being allowed to visit.

High-ranking authorities also reenvisioned émigrés in a manner more conducive to cross-border bonding. Following the example of some Latin American (and other) governments at the time, the Cuban leadership reframed its portrayal of the diaspora. Officials reimagined once-outcast *apatridas* as born-again long-distance nationalists.[17] They referred to the diaspora as the Cuban community abroad,[18] part of Greater Cuba. They reclaimed those who had left, whatever personal resentment they still privately harbored toward those who rejected the revolution. The government's changed stance made for a more travel-friendly milieu. Émigrés came to feel more comfortable visiting, and islanders came to feel more comfortable hosting family who had uprooted.

Nonetheless, Cuban authorities never entirely eliminated travel barriers. They restricted visits to a few weeks, and prohibited certain individuals who were politically suspect from entry.

The Presidential Electoral Cycle and Vacillation in Washington's Travel Policy

When the Cuban government became more permissive of travel, Washington became more restrictive. Exile-driven politics, together with crises in bilateral relations, influenced official US travel policy. Despite the Cold War's end, US lawmakers refused to let Cuban Americans decide for themselves how frequently, for how long, and who on the island they could see.

Except under extenuating circumstances US regulations rarely permitted émigrés to make homeland visits more than once a year. They also could only get permission to see family, not friends. Yet, within these parameters, US presidents, both with Congressional support and independently, and across the partisan divide, varied in how restrictive they were. Even individual presidents waffled in the travel rights they honored. They manipulated the basic US right to travel, and respect for family values, with their electoral concerns. Travel rights became a key component of the election-linked Cuba policy cycle described in the last chapter and summarized in Table 3.7.

The 1992 Cuban Democracy Act, the first post-Cold War Cuba-related foreign policy legislation that President George H. W. Bush signed into law on the eve of his reelection bid, did not specifically address travel, other than to grant the Treasury Department civil penalty enforcement authority over visits. The Cuban American National Foundation that had lobbied for the Cuban Democracy Act favored a people-to-people embargo. However, legislating travel restrictions had not been their key concern at the time because the Cuban government had yet to lift its low annual cap on Cuban American visitors it let in. Meanwhile, to secure sufficient Congressional support for the passage of the bill, the Foundation had to accept a set of provisions known as Track Two, which allowed for improved cross-border people-to-people engagement through improved telephone and mail service. Émigrés who wished to communicate with island friends and family, as a result, were now able to do so more easily than in the preceding thirty years of Castro's rule.

Independent of the Cuban Democracy Act, once he was President, Bill Clinton used his discretionary power to regulate US-to-Cuba travel, sometimes stepping up while at other times loosening restrictions. In 1994, he introduced measures more restrictive than those enforced by his Republican predecessor. President Clinton limited visits to cases involving "extreme hardship," such as to see terminally ill relatives. Cuban Americans had to demonstrate "extreme humanitarian" need, and were required to obtain a special license for travel from the Treasury Department.

My ethnic electoral policy cycle thesis would predict a loosening, not tightening, of restrictions in a non-presidential election year, if non-electoral concerns might thereby better be addressed. But the 1994 crackdown needs to be understood in the context of the rafter immigration crisis that year (described in Chapter 1). While Clinton initially refused to grant entry permission to the tens of thousands of Cubans that Castro allowed to leave without US

admission permits, Exiles, who believed Cubans to be entitled to special immigration rights, turned, in outrage, on the President. Against this backdrop,
Clinton accommodated a request by Mas Canosa to tighten travel rights, in
exchange for the influential Cuban American agreeing not to oppose the
Administration's new so-called wetfoot policy, of returning to the island
Cubans found at sea trying to emigrate without entry permits, incorporated
into the 1995 immigration accord.[19] Mas Canosa pressed for the visitation
restrictions because by then the Cuban government had removed the cap on
permitted yearly visitors. As to why Clinton agreed to the clampdown on
freedom to travel, he admitted, in his memoir, that he already had his 1996
reelection bid in mind when negotiating with Mas Canosa.[20] Thus, although a
flare-up in bilateral tensions in this instance led to Presidential embargo-
tightening, Clinton's reelection ambitions shaped how he responded. Ordinary
Cuban Americans who wished see island family paid the price.

After Exile fury with the new "wetfoot" policy calmed down, Clinton, still
in an election off-year, made travel easier for those Cuban Americans who
wished to visit island family. While limiting family visits to once a year, for vaguely
defined "extreme humanitarian need," in 1995 his Administration announced
that Cuban Americans no longer needed a special license for trip-taking. They
needed only an affidavit, which airline charter companies could provide. And
with special Treasury Department authorization, they could make additional
trips. Clinton justified his changed stance politically. Visits, he argued, would
promote democracy and the free flow of ideas, a concern of state.

But, in 1996, Clinton reversed his travel policy again. First he suspended
indefinitely US-Cuba charter flights that he previously had permitted, and
shortly thereafter he signed into law the Foundation-backed Cuban Liberty
and Democratic Solidarity Act which he previously had opposed. Relevant
here, the legislation called for political changes in Cuba as a precondition for
renewal of travel rights. In a non-binding so-called sense of Congress, the law
specified that the US president was to require the Cuban government to
release political prisoners and recognize the right of association, and other
fundamental freedoms, before reinstituting general licenses for family visits.[21]
As noted in Chapter 3, Clinton supported the bill amidst Exile fury with the
Cuban government downing of planes flown by the Exile group Brothers to
the Rescue in the heat of his reelection bid, with nearly all Miami Cuban
Americans favoring the legislation. Cuban American travel rights here too
became prey to Presidential reelection opportunism.

However, once the election dust had settled, Clinton readdressed the matter
of travel rights. Respectful of the basic US right, he relaxed visit restrictions,
even though the political preconditions the 1996 legislation specified for
resumption of travel had not transpired. In 1998, when ineligible for, and
therefore unconcerned with, reelection, he reallowed US-Cuba charter flights,
and in January of the following year he both expanded the number of US
and island cities between which people could travel and eased travel license
procedures. Clinton legitimated his latest travel opening in the context of

Pope John Paul II's historic 1998 visit to Cuba. When on the island His Holiness had called for the world to open to Cuba and Cuba to the world. In justifying the travel opening, Clinton turned the Cuban Liberty and Democratic Solidarity Act rationale for restricting trip-taking on its head. Whereas the 1996 legislation called for island democratization as a prerequisite for travel liberalization, three years later Clinton reverted to his 1995 argument, that cross-border ties would foment democratization, in strengthening civil society on the island.

At the same time, Congressional momentum built up to reverse the restrictive travel stance emboldened in the Cuban Liberty and Democratic Solidarity Act, not only for Cuban Americans but for all US citizens. However, against the build-up of momentum, Exile lobbyists convinced Congress to codify into law for the first time a once-a-year travel cap in the closing months of Clinton's presidency.

George W. Bush similarly waffled in his travel policy during on and off years in the electoral cycle. After blocking moves in Congress to lift the travel ban,[22] in 2003, he put in place travel rules more permissive than Clinton's. He expanded the range of island kin Cuban Americans could visit to three degrees of genealogical remove, and ended the Clinton era requirement that visits be confined to cases of "humanitarian need."[23]

However, in the heat of his reelection bid, he, like Clinton before him, reversed his stance. This time he became more restrictive than Clinton. He reduced family visitation rights from once a year to once every three years, he narrowed the range of relatives for whom visiting permission could be attained to immediate kin, and he limited trips to two weeks, the duration previously having not been capped. He also required, anew, special Treasury Department permits for trip-taking. The 2004 regulations allowed for no humanitarian exceptions, not even to pay final respects to a dying island relative. Meanwhile, he kept Congressional moves to lift the travel ban from taking effect, through behind the scenes maneuvers.

The hardline Cuban Liberty Council (CLC), supporters of the newly formed US-Cuba Democracy PAC, had lobbied aggressively for the 2004 travel clampdown and against the Congressional lifting of travel restrictions. Other South Florida politicians also pressured Bush for a clampdown.[24] Resentful that Bush had done little to advance their anti-Castro cause during his first term in office, in return for their help in his 2000 presidential victory, outspoken Cuban American Republican politicians threatened not to fundraise and campaign for the President's reelection unless he reversed his 2003 relaxation of travel rights, as well as addressed other concerns of theirs noted in Chapter 3. In that Florida in general and Cuban Americans in particular had been central to his 2000 victory, Bush, when running for reelection, responded to their travel demands. As a backdrop and rationale for introducing new travel restrictions, Bush had used his discretionary power to form the Commission for Assistance to a Free Cuba (USDS-CAFC), which in its report called for personal embargo tightening to help hasten island regime

Table 4.2 Travel to and views toward travel to Cuba among registered and non-registered voters in Miami in 2007

	Registered	Not registered
Unrestricted travel from US to Cuba should be allowed	42%	74%
Ever traveled to Cuba	34	40
Current restrictions on trade, travel, and communications had major or moderate effect on interviewee and family	31	57

Source: www.fiu.edu/orgs/ipor/cuba8/pollresults.html.

change.[25] Indicative of how the reconstituted Cuban American National Foundation by then had been politically sidelined, it unsuccessfully argued in defense of émigré travel rights.

In responding to hardline pressures Bush undoubtedly also sensed where his votes were. Far more than non-voters, registered voters in Miami opposed unrestricted travel rights, never made a return trip, and felt personally unaffected by Bush's 2004 tightening of possibilities to visit (Table 4.2).[26] The politically active hardliners pushed for measures that for them were mainly symbolic and principled, given their views toward homeland visits. They were indifferent to the impact the policies had on Cuban Americans who wished to visit island family but had no votes to cast.

Thus, in the post-Cold War era, through 2004, presidents vacillated in how restrictive they were of homeland visitation rights, depending on whether or not their reelection took priority. They were most restrictive when campaign contributions and votes mattered most to them. In contrast, in non-election years they were more responsive to bipartisan Congressional voices that favored relaxation of travel restrictions,[27] and more respectful of US commitment to freedom of travel and family values.[28] Accordingly, in non-election years they reversed election year policies designed to win votes.

By the 2008 election cycle, however, the Democrats challenged restrictions on family visits, at the local Congressional as well as the presidential level. This marked the first time that a presidential candidate had publicly advocated embargo-loosening of any sort. In the heat of his campaign, Obama announced at a highly publicized luncheon sponsored by the Cuban American National Foundation that he would immediately allow unlimited family travel (and remittance-sending) to the island should he be elected to the highest office of the land. And indicative of how the Foundation had become a "born again" moderate organization, Mas Santos, its chief officer, explained: "We see travel as our only vehicle of changing things in Cuba. Cuban Americans are our foot soldiers."[29] His announcement coincided with the two Cuban American Democratic candidates for Congressional seats making the issue of cross-border family rights a centerpiece of their campaigns. The Democrats sought to exploit the sentiment among two-thirds of Miami Cuban Americans to end Bush-imposed restrictions implemented in 2004 at the behest of Cuban American hardliners (Table 3.4). Two months after his inauguration, Obama began to honor his promise by lifting travel restrictions.

Ordinary People's Stepped-Up Defiance of Travel Taboos

How to explain the increase in Cuban American travel, given Washington constraints and Exile opposition to cross-border bonding? Viewed from the US side of the Straits, the increase hinged not merely on the new Cuban government travel permissiveness. It rested also on diaspora changes, on the arrival of the New Cubans committed to life across borders. To a lesser extent it rested on new willingness of some Soviet-era émigrés to defy the taboo to which hardliners remained unrelentingly committed.

The New Cubans with Their New Norms and Transnational Commitments

New Cubans were the driving force behind the travel revolution. They emigrated committed to the cross-border bonding that most early émigrés opposed. The émigré cohorts, with their different island generational formations, not merely differed but conflicted in their stance toward bonding across borders. The cohort divide regarding travel was far more fundamental than the cohort culture clash and cohort contrast in macro level Cuba policy preferences I described in Chapters 2 and 3.

Indicative of the different normative perspectives of the émigrés with different pre-immigrant experiences, Florida International University found in its 2007 Miami survey that over two-thirds of New Cubans favored unrestricted travel, compared to less than a fourth of 1959 to 1964 arrivals (Table 4.1). Moreover, between 2000 and 2007, the émigrés in the US the longest became less tolerant of visits, at a time when most non-Cubans in the city believed there should be no restrictions on Cuba travel.[30] Rather than acculturate more in the intervening years to the transnationally tolerant norms of non-Cubans into whose midst they moved, the Exiles stepped up their cross-border recalcitrance. The New Cubans who agreed with the non-Cubans on views toward travel rights had also not taken on US principles of freedom to travel for themselves. Rather, their views reflected their Cuba-formed commitment to cross-border networks and norms.

Although most New Cubans approved of and coveted homeland visits, a minority did not. Some were so alienated by the hardships and lack of liberties they had experienced before uprooting that they were not interested in return trips, even if they still had family there. Manuel, a middle-aged Jewish man, who moved to Miami during the Special Period, is one such person. His minority cohort stance built on longstanding disgruntlement, dating back to the Soviet era. So opposed to the regime was he that he had tried to leave illegally on a small boat in his teens, in the 1980s. Caught by Cuban border patrol, he was sent to a labor camp for a year. But in 1993 he managed to leave legally, with a visa to study in the US.

Examples such as Manuel's aside, overall, Miami New Cubans, even more than US-born Cuban Americans, favored unrestricted travel rights. Although the second-generation immigrants were markedly more tolerant of freedom to travel to Cuba than their parents' generation, in line with their US upbringing, a substantial number of them remained influenced by their elders.

Ascribing to different norms, the cohorts, in turn, differed in their travels. While Florida International University's survey found barely more than a third of the Cuban community in Miami had ever made a homeland trip as of 2007, twice as many New Cubans as first arrivals had (Table 4.1).[31] The long-time immigrants traveled less even though they had many more years in the US to make the journey, even though they were better able to afford the cost of the trips, and even though they faced fewer institutional hurdles. Cuban authorities imposed travel restrictions only on early émigrés who were politically suspect, whereas they initially required the tens of thousands of Cubans who emigrated illegally in the 1990s to wait five years before visiting.

Exiles acted on their principles. They considered it immoral to step foot in Cuba. Their mantra was, "We will not visit. We will return." They would only return, they claimed, to a Cuba without Castro. With the revolution remaining the defining experience of their lives, they let politics stand between them and relatives who had sided with the island makeover, including when government barriers did not stand in their way.

New Cubans, in contrast, remained committed to the family they left behind and felt a moral obligation to visit them. Their morality rested on polar opposite precepts from those of Exiles. Accordingly, when asked in Florida International University's 2007 survey whether the 2004 Bush restrictions personally affected them, three times as many Miami Cubans who had emigrated since 1995 as 1959–1964 émigrés answered in the affirmative. Even though about half of the first arrivals still had close kin in Cuba, less than one-fifth of them felt deprived of rights to see them when Bush stepped up travel restrictions (Table 4.1).

With the two sets of Cuban émigrés generally living in different neighborhoods, the communities had different travel norms, as well as different class compositions. And because the first and most recent arrivals lived apart, the self-appointed border police were not routinely around the new immigrants to monitor and contest their cross-border involvements. The New Cubans live amidst a milieu so supportive of life across borders that some of them noted in conversations with me that they did not know about any opposition to travel.

Travel had such normative approval among the younger new immigrants that it made its way into Miami popular culture.[32] Cuban American singer Willy Chirino, who has a following among the younger generation, both Cuba and US-born, for example, captured the new immigrant sentiment in his lyrics about Cubans returning to the island, "*ya vienan llegando.*" To them, travel and a culture supportive of travel were mutually reinforcing.

The hardline Exile leadership that pressed for the tightening of the personal embargo accordingly spoke at best for its own émigré cohort and for those who left Cuba not long after them. But why were recent émigré views on visits not heard or represented if so different from first arrivals'? The economically humble new immigrants, as I previously noted, lacked the personal attributes most associated with political involvement in the US. And raised on the island transformed by revolution, they emigrated with little civil society experience on which to build.[33]

But recent émigrés' views were not heard also because hardline Exile leadership stood in their way. Some 1990s émigrés with whom I spoke felt silenced. When submitting editorials to the news media and when trying to speak on Miami call-in radio shows about their pro-travel stance, they were rebuffed. They believed the reason to be their opposition to Exile views.

The clash of cohort travel interests became publicly transparent for the first time when in 2004 President Bush announced his draconian clampdown on Cuban American rights to visit island relatives. The clampdown came amidst a surge in new immigrant homeland visits. In Miami, according to the Florida International University survey, the percentage of New Cubans who visited Cuba had soared from 31 to 45 between 2000 and 2004 (Table 4.1). Against this backdrop, the assault on transnational family rights to bond caused hundreds of post-Soviet-era arrivals to take to the street in protest. They picketed the offices of the Cuban American legislators whom they blamed for the new regulations.[34]

Exiles Break Rank

Although New Cubans were the main trip-takers, the percentage of 1959–1964 Exiles who defied their cohort's travel taboo increased from 18 in 2000, after some forty years in the US, to 26 seven years later. How to explain the rise in the number of Exiles who broke rank? I found their reasons to vary. Some of the early émigrés who made homeland trips were religious Catholics who were inspired by the Church's changed stance on relations with Cuba. Age-based reasons spurred others. Some elderly wanted to see their homeland still in their lifetime, while some child immigrants wished as adults to experience Cuba for themselves. Then, owing to a snowball effect, as ever more visitors returned without negative experiences, other Exiles who had been apprehensive about homeland visits got up their courage to go.

Church-inspired Visits

The Miami archdiocese, which in its opposition to the revolution had overseen Operation Peter Pan, in the 1990s reversed its decision and became a force for reconciliation and cross-border bridge-building.[35] The archdiocese, with the Catholic Relief Services taking the lead, had laid the groundwork for cross-border bridge-building already when Hurricane Lili swept Cuba in 1996. With top Miami clergy urging transnational good-will, Miami Cuban Americans donated some 100,000 pounds of food that the Catholic organization Caritas distributed in Cuba.[36] Exile generosity built on their tradition of generosity for ethnic causes they believed in.

The archdiocese used the occasion of Pope John Paul II's 1998 visit to Cuba to further cross-border religious solidarity. It circulated the replica of Cuba's patron saint, Our Lady of Charity, which I showed to be intricately associated with the socio-religious life of the Exiles reembedded in Miami, among city parishes during the run-up to the Pope's arrival; it commissioned a local church to play a carillon of the Cuban national anthem hourly from the time His Holiness stepped foot on Cuban soil until his departure four days later; and it coordinated hundreds of special masses, vigils, and processions, as expressions of solidarity with the Pope. Celebrating the Pope's visit to Cuba almost as if it were a local event, the Miami archdiocese blurred boundaries between Cuban Catholics on the two sides of the Straits. The Auxiliary Polish American Miami Bishop at the time, Thomas Wenski, went so far as to contract a cruise ship to ferry a thousand pilgrims to Havana to hear the Pope celebrate mass. Wenski had wanted Cuban Americans to show up in large numbers to demonstrate that there is "one church and that boundaries do not divide the Body of Christ," and that the Cuban people still are one people despite divisions "imposed on them against their will."[37]

For some deeply religious first-wave émigrés, the Pope's island visit proved such a key event that it led them to rethink their views on Cuba. His Holiness convinced them that stepping foot in Cuba under Castro was morally acceptable and that they should heed his call for the world to open to Cuba. Meanwhile, television coverage of the Pope's journey around the island stirred fond memories, peaked émigré homeland interest, and evoked a yearning to visit the island.

Several early émigrés with whom I spoke noted that the Pope "broke the ice." Reflecting on the impact of the Pope's visit, Pepe, a Miami lawyer opposed to Castro, spoke of how His Holiness had "conveyed the message when in Cuba that it was not only alright to help Cubans but that people had a moral obligation to do so." The religious 1969 émigré, from a prominent pre-revolutionary family, had come to feel that the best way to assist Cubans was through people-to-people contact. Another lawyer, José, who described himself to me "as conservative as they come," had for three decades adamantly supported the personal embargo. Yet he went to Cuba to see the Pope at Wenski's urging. Elisa similarly noted that she broke with her decades-old taboo of homeland visits at the time of the Pope's trip. She too was from a wealthy pre-revolution Catholic family that emigrated soon after Castro took power.

Exiles were not the only religious Cuban American Catholics to be inspired by the Church's changed stance toward cross-border ties. Jacky, an employee of a Catholic organization who emigrated during Mariel, also made her first return trip when the Pope visited. Prior to the Pope's visit she had adamantly opposed stepping foot on Cuban soil while Castro remained in power, as well as any other form of reconciliation.

Nonetheless, not all Exiles accepted the Church's new approval of cross-border bridge-building. Quite to the contrary, some hardliners, filtering anything Cuban through their anti-Castro mindset, aggressively opposed the Church's changed stance. Not only did they vilify the archdiocese's post-Hurricane Lili food drive, and threaten to kill the auxiliary bishop Augostin Román, an icon of the exile community who backed the sending of disaster relief.[38] Some also took to the streets in December 1997 to protest the Pope's impending island visit. They then went on to raise such havoc over the cruise ship contracted to ferry Cuban Americans to hear the Pope's Havana sermon that Wenski cancelled the boat.[39] The Exile-dominated Spanish-speaking radio contributed to the opposition to the cruise ship plan. The self-appointed border police accordingly deprived hundreds of religiously committed Cuban Americans of the opportunity to see the Pope and to reconnect with their homeland in a religious context. The hardliners argued that the trip-takers would legitimize Castro.

Despite the backlash, priests in some parishes proceeded after the Pope's visit to promote cross-border bridge-building. Some of them went to Cuba where they delivered services and supplies, and encouraged "adopt a parish" programs that included visits by parishioners to Cuban churches to help with repairs. Cuban American priests, in turn, invited island clergy to their parishes to celebrate mass, to perform rituals, and to preach homilies of reconciliation.[40]

Religious changes in Cuba further contributed to people-to-people bridge-building. The government and Party helped set the stage after redefining the state, in 1992, as secular, no longer as atheist, and after opening Party membership to "believers." A resurgence of religiosity among ordinary Cubans, once the state became more permissive and the crisis shattered belief in the utopian revolutionary project, helped mend relations among family members across borders who had been divided by religion as well as politics.

Thus, the Catholic Church, from the Vatican down to the parish level, and in Cuba as well as Miami, helped build an incipient bedrock for people-to-people transnational bridge-building that came to include homeland visits by some Exiles previously averse to contact with Cuba under Castro. Protestant, especially evangelical, and Jewish groups contributed to the bridge-building as well. However, they constituted a minority of the Exile exodus (although most Jews left in the first years of the country's class transformation). *Santeria* and other Afro-Cuban cults, which did attract large followings that in some instances inspired homeland trips, mainly involved New Cubans.[41]

*Nostalgia and the Desire of Elderly to Reconnect with Their Homeland
Still in Their Lifetime*

Some elderly Exiles yearned to see their homeland and island relatives still in
their lifetime, and accordingly conceded to defy the travel taboo. Giving up on
regime change any time soon, they rationalized to themselves and to others
that they broke rank only to see island relatives before they passed away. In the
1990s, Exiles became more accepting of such exceptions to the travel taboo, at
the same time that they remained morally opposed to unrestricted travel. They
rationalized that occasional trips would not erode the politically constructed
wall across the Straits or prolong Castro's reign of rule.

Elderly Exiles who had come of age in pre-revolutionary Cuba and who
opposed the island's social transformation, when taking exception to the
travel taboo, framed conversations with others about their trips in a way
that reinforced community commitment to the personal embargo. Joséfina's
experience is telling. Having emigrated in 1965 at the age of thirty-seven, the
Union City resident explained to me how she decided to go to Cuba in 1998
to see siblings she had not seen since she left thirty-five years prior. She went
reluctantly, at the urging of a sister who had made several return trips. In
Joséfina's case, her brothers, who had never left Cuba, were as anti-Castro as
she was. One of her brothers had been assassinated by "Castro's army," along
with two of his sons, and her four other brothers had served long prison
sentences for counter-revolutionary involvements. She timed her trip with the
release from prison of one of her brothers. He had served a twenty year
sentence.

Joséfina had very painful island memories that had prevented her from visiting in the past. She could neither forgive nor forget how disrespectful her
neighbors had been during the revolutionary struggle. Because of "their
ideology," she said, they refused to defend or help her family when their lives
were at risk. Her trip was such an emotional experience that even when
recounting it several years afterwards she cried. When visiting, she spent most
of her time seeing family and reliving her past, not socializing with former
neighbors. She went to church, to the cemetery to pay respect to deceased
relatives, and to the homes of kin still in Cuba.

Children of Exiles who Wished to Experience Cuba for Themselves

Some Cuban Americans who had emigrated as children at their parents' initiative, as adults wanted to connect with Cuba. While such desire had already
prompted some immigrant children to make homeland trips during the Carter
opening and to participate in the Antonio Maceo Brigade, by the 1990s more
children of Exiles, now mature adults, wished to experience the island for
themselves. I found these trip-takers to involve mainly immigrant children
who either had spent some years outside the Exile enclave, exposed to alternative perspectives and removed from community pressures, or had been

inspired by the Pope's visit. Many of my previously noted Church-inspired travelers had emigrated as children.

The immigrant children had, at best, highly selective memories of Cuba, filtered through the lenses of youth. Once reaching adulthood, some of them found living with the imagined Cuba from their childhood increasingly unsatisfactory. As adults, they wanted to know the country first-hand. Three Cuban Americans with whom I spoke are illustrative.

One, Bernardo, who left Cuba at age two in 1963, spoke to me of his generation going to Cuba out of a need "to figure things out for themselves. They ask themselves 'why am I interested in this place when I haven't ever really been there?' They return to find out what Cuba means to them, independent of what their parents told them. They go to answer the question, 'Am I really Cuban?'" He added that "without travel, without connections, the next generation of Cuban exiles won't be Cuban." Bernardo identified himself as an exile even though he was too young to remember the island first-hand or to have political reasons of his own to leave his birthplace. Rather, he had taken on his parents' interpretive frame for himself. And Bernardo had such a strong family identity with Cuba that even though emigrating as an infant, he referred to trips as "going back." He "went back" for the first time at age thirty-seven.

Marta, who also left Cuba with her family as an infant, broke the travel taboo the same year as Bernardo. She had emigrated in 1959 at less than a year old. The revolution deprived her of a parent as well as a homeland, for her father was killed in 1961 in the Exile-led Bay of Pigs invasion. Her personal loss kept her committed, as an adult, to the anti-Castro cause. She finally decided to defy the personal embargo the year of the Pope's visit. She wanted to see the Cuba of her imagination for herself. Marta's, as well as Bernardo's, families spent some years in Miami, but afterwards moved elsewhere.

Alejandra, in contrast, grew up in the Midwest, but subsequently resettled in Miami where she became a director of a private elementary school. Having left Cuba at age ten, she, unlike Bernardo and Maria, had childhood memories of island life. Her parents had sent her to live with family in Mexico in 1961, after the Bay of Pigs invasion failed in its mission to overthrow Castro. While she was not part of Father Brian Walsh's Operation Peter Pan that resettled 14,000 Cuban children without accompanying parents, her mother and father had been influenced by the hysteria of the time and preferred to send her abroad parentless than have "the Communist government . . . take her away." Ultimately her parents joined her in Mexico and took her to the US. With the traumatic experience of parental separation, she "for years . . . resisted going to Cuba." But in her dreams, she explained, "I would walk the streets of my old neighborhood." Having lived for decades imagining Cuba she decided a safe time to travel would be during the Pope's visit, even though she herself was Methodist. Her decision to visit had been personally difficult because her Miami family disapproved. "I went after my father died. I don't think I could have gone if he were still alive." The pain and fear of defying her father's principles had for years kept her from breaking his generation's travel taboo. However, after summoning her courage to break the taboo once, she made several subsequent return trips.

The University of Michigan anthropologist Ruth Behar, whose family formed part of the Jewish exodus in the initial years of the revolution, reacted similarly to Alejandra in her defiance of the travel taboo. In her words, she became "a Cuba addict." Although her father refused to say good-bye to her before her trips because he disapproved of them, the child immigrant felt "The more I went to Cuba, the more I needed to go . . . After a few months of being away . . . I started to feel an intense desire to return."[42]

Some immigrant children managed to turn family influence on its head. While Alejandra's mother and Ruth's father remained opposed to homeland visits, other immigrant children who defied the travel taboo convinced their Exile parents to accompany them on trips. My interviews suggest that mothers have been more persuaded than fathers by their children's appeal. They had more interest in reconnecting with friends and family of their past.

While US-born Cubans are not the book's focus, Florida International University surveys reveal that most in Miami respect their parents' boundary-setting. Only one fifth of US-born Cubans had ever made an island trip. The travel taboo, with some "leakage," took genealogical multi-generational form.[43]

Nonetheless, with US as well as family experiences to draw upon when of age to interpret life for themselves, some second-generation Cuban Americans willingly defied the Exiles' travel taboo. One woman with whom I spoke explained that once reaching adulthood she yearned to go to Cuba. She felt

> a need to find out what [Cuban] reality is . . . You need to find . . . where you come from . . . I go to Cuba to find out about my roots because the day my grandmother passes away in Cuba I want to know where my family lived and what they did, what the country looks like, and what the people are like . . . On top of it all, I can have a nice vacation with my family, with my culture, my roots.

She represents a second-generation Cuban American who values blood ties that bind more than politics that divide. In forming her views she built on an early childhood experience, under parental tutelage. She had visited Cuba with her mother during the Carter opening. As a result, she grew up committed to her island family, even though twenty years had elapsed between the time she first met them, as a youngster, and her second visit, as an adult at her own initiative.

Reduction of Travel Fears

Fear, on both sides of the Straits, had sustained the imaginary wall separating Cubans who differed politically but shared common blood and a common culture. Bases of fears were multiple. Fear gave the wall a social-psychological base, which, once overcome, made émigrés more willing to travel.

Self-defined exiles feared, for one, that Cuban officials would mistreat them if they visited. Their chronic portrayal of Castro as a dictator fed into such anxieties. They spoke of Castro as Hitler, the Devil, the Monster, and accordingly feared run-ins with functionaries associated with his government. Exiles who had participated in counter-revolutionary activity also worried that they would be subject to retribution were they to make a return trip. The negative experiences, memories, and suppositions of some, in turn, became the collective anxieties of many.

Exiles worried also about how ordinary Cubans would receive them. They feared hostility, resentment, and distrust. Stories that returnees during the Carter years told fed into these anxieties. Late 1970s trip-takers talked of how suspicious and dishonest they found islanders to be. Marielitos' experiences when leaving added fuel to the fire. Their neighbors and co-workers had hailed insults and thrown objects at them when leaving. While the fiery days of revolution that had pitted loyalists against turncoats had subsided in Cuba by the 1990s, earlier émigrés lived with previously formed perceptions of Cuba under Castro.

Indicative of how both personal memories and hearsay made émigrés fear visits, when Marta, who emigrated in 1960 at age twenty, got up her courage to visit thirty-four years later she carried a Bible with her at all times. The retired flight attendant was very afraid, especially of imprisonment. She visited partly to fulfill a sister's wish, a sister who had died of brain cancer in Cuba. When better received than she anticipated, Marta's visit dispelled her fears to the point that she made subsequent return trips.

There also were Miami-based fears. Cuban Americans worried for decades about rejection by their friends, neighbors, and family. They also worried of retribution at work were they to visit their homeland. Alejandra spoke about the matter. "There is not much tolerance here. They call you names and chastise you. They accuse you of being a Communist if you don't say what's mainstream, and you can get fired if they don't like what you say about Cuba or if you go to Cuba." Similarly, Rosario, a 1962 émigré who owned a bus fleet, echoed how the community contributed to trip-taking fears. Reflecting back on how strong the anti-travel pressure had been, she noted that "If you visited Cuba you received threats, and you were accused of being a Communist and pro-Castro." Fear of such epithets discouraged travel. But when émigrés who were willing to take the risks did not experience retribution upon their return, others followed their lead.

Most of all, New Cubans dispelled travel fears. Émigré cohort influence here turned topsy turvy. In place of Exiles with economic status and political clout subjecting humble new immigrants to norms they set, the collective effect of recent arrivals' trips was to allay early émigré anxieties. This was an unintended consequence of the New Cubans' continued commitment to family back home. It was not the result of a transnational political project they took on.

In the changed Miami milieu, Exiles who had mustered the courage to make homeland visits contributed to the travel contagion. They began to speak openly and joyfully about their trips, and returned with videos of their visits that they shared with family and friends. The videos humanized island life, which dispelled the hostile images Exiles had fantasized. An imagined diabolic Communist Other that had sustained the travel taboo dissipated somewhat under the circumstances. Also, in the changed milieu older émigrés perceived community criticism of trip-taking to have become more muted. Rosario, in this vein, spoke of how much the Miami mood had changed. By the 1990s, "people had become more accepting of travel," to the point that she felt she could speak openly about her trips. She had the sense that "everyone has traveled to Cuba," even though in 2000, when we spoke, only slightly more than one-fourth of Cuban Americans in Miami had ever made a return trip.[44] While some Exiles who mustered the courage to visit went only once, to close the Cuba chapter of their lives, others, with their anxieties allayed, made repeat trips.

Why Not More Visiting?

While the barriers that for over three decades had kept Cubans across borders apart broke down in the 1990s, they never disappeared. A comparison of US immigrants from over a dozen Latin American countries found only Guatemalans to have made fewer homeland trips than Cubans,[45] and among trip-takers, Cubans were least likely to visit more than once a year.[46] Cuban homeland visits were also the shortest. Eighty-four percent of Cubans reported staying less than three weeks. In contrast, 66 percent of Guayanans, who made the second briefest homestays, visited for fewer than three weeks.[47] Now that the "visiting genie" was out of the box, why did not more Cubans visit their homeland, and why did the trip-takers not visit more frequently and for longer?

Physical distance is hardly the obstacle. Cubans visit their homeland with less frequency than immigrants from Colombia, Ecuador, El Salvador, Guyana, Honduras, and Nicaragua, who have far more miles to traverse. The social distance between the US and the island was far greater than the ninety-mile stretch that physically separates the countries.

Official Obstacles

Official barriers still remain. The Cuban government continued to refuse entry rights to politically suspect émigrés, and it permitted only brief visits. Cuban immigrants' homeland visits are shorter than those of other Latin American immigrants in no small part because of island-set restrictions.

Washington regulations also kept border-crossing at bay. Cuban Americans were alone among Latin Americans in facing US restrictions on how frequently and who in their homeland they could visit. While determined travelers could covertly and illegally visit through third countries, such trip-taking is more inconvenient and costlier, and legally risky, all of which served to deter travel. The Bush Administration, in particular, stepped up arrests and fines for travel infractions.

Informal Barriers

With most émigrés not taking advantage of actual travel entitlements, state regulations alone cannot explain why Cubans bond less across borders than other Latin American immigrants. My interviews suggest that Cuban immigrants had reasons of their own for their limited travels, although the reasons differed among émigré waves.

In that recent arrivals almost without exception still have close family in Cuba, they meet Washington's minimum travel criterion. For a minority, they left their nativeland so hostile to the regime that they comfortably honor hardline Exiles' taboo of travel.

More typically, the new immigrants who have not made homeland visits, if unconstrained either by official Cuban or US travel restrictions, felt constrained by the cost of trips. The Cuban government requires entry by air, permitting charter flights only from the US. In the absence of airline competition, flights cost several hundred dollars, just to cross the Straits. And trip-takers must secure costly Cuban visas. But the costs also are normatively grounded: the gifts island family expect visiting family to bring, as I detail in the next chapter.

Among the earlier émigrés, some became indifferent to travel. They had moved on with their lives. This was especially true of immigrant children who had married non-Cubans and "fully Americanized," and accordingly had no particular yearning to connect with island family. Others had no close family left on the island to visit. Cuba was part of their history and biography, but not the world in which they lived, even in their imagination.

For others, however, politics and moral principles continued to stand in the way. Patricio, the 1970 political refugee who had fled a prison sentence he had been serving for violation of a labor law, for example, refused to make a return trip partly because he feared re-arrest for his unfinished prison term. But he added that a visit would negate his life. "It would be saying that the terrible things that happened to me really didn't occur."

And many immigrant children remained morally committed to the travel taboo out of deference to their parents. They honored their mother's and father's stance, even after they had passed away. A Cuban American judge with whom I spoke mentioned such a reason for not visiting his family homeland.

Other Exiles could not convince themselves even after the surge in trip-taking that visits would be problem-free, either in Miami or in Cuba. While one woman told me that she would not visit her nativeland because she did not want her family to suffer were something bad to happen to her on the island, other Cuban Americans continued to fear community retribution were they to defy Exiles' travel taboo. In the words of one Miami resident who fled the island soon after Castro assumed power, it is hard to "stand up to those with extreme viewpoints. People are scared to go against the exile leadership's position of boycotting the Castro government. People don't want to be accused of supporting Castro's government." And in this vein, a former Union City priest noted to me how some Exiles remained "afraid of those with a big mouth." He spoke of a man who had made three return trips. "He whispers that he is going. It's like going through the Berlin Wall. If you go, you are accused of being an agent of Cuba, a Communist, a traitor. People are fearful of these accusations."

Hardliners affirmed their boundaries to the permissible by publicly shaming some trip-takers. When the preeminent Bay of Pigs participant, Alfredo Durán, for example, defied Exiles' travel taboo in 2001 to participate in an official Cuban event commemorating the fortieth anniversary of the 1961 invasion, members of the association of veterans, in outrage, banned him from their group. In that they had purged Durán on previous occasions, the disciplinary measure was meaningless other than to remind others not to step foot in Cuba under Castro.

Still others, after breaking rank once, felt that they had accomplished their mission. Their visits allowed them to close the Cuba chapter of their lives either because they'd said their good-byes or because their trips convinced them that the revolution had destroyed the Cuba they had known and yearned for. They found Castro had destroyed their Cuba, and they came to recognize, regrettably, that there was no going back. They realized that their past could neither be resurrected nor recreated.

The fear of discovering a Cuba that was different than what they remembered kept some people from making even one return trip. Some Exiles do not want their remembered Cuba, idyllic and idealized, dispelled by an encounter with current reality. Their imagined Cuba remains pre-revolutionary based, associated with a life of privilege. A visit could demystify the Cuba to which they had remained committed in the abstract and in absentia for decades.

The memories that kept most early émigrés from trip-taking may seem very real, but memory is highly selective, not necessarily accurate, and sometimes fabricated. While perceived as personal, in Miami, memories of Cuba were collectively shared and collectively interpreted and reinterpreted, just as fears were. Exile group life sustained belief in a once-glorious Cuba, a paradise lost, and the taboo on travel helped sustain that belief. It nurtured myth-making and myth-maintenance. These were important effects the personal embargo had.

Pepe, the previously discussed prominent lawyer from a wealthy pre-revolutionary family who emigrated at age eleven in 1969, illustrates how the love of a Cuba of the imagination kept cross-border contact at bay. After more than thirty years he still had wonderful childhood memories of his school, his dog, and his spacious house in Cuba. While he used to support the personal embargo in principle, by the early years of the new millennium he no longer did. As a religious man, he was influenced by the change in the Church's stance. The Pope's visit convinced him that transnational ties would be good. Well known in the Exile community, he went public about his plans to visit his homeland. Yet, when we spoke in 2000 he acknowledged that "I just can't get myself to go ... Intellectually I want to go. Emotionally I can't." He recognized that "We need to touch, feel, and smell the place. We have built this edifice. We need to dare to go there to let go of our inhibitions. The more who come and go, the more difficult for the Cuban government to maintain control." He thinks he resisted going either because he was not ready for the final disappointment or because he feared he would fall in love with the country "as it is." Pepe demonstrates how powerful memories of the past can be in inhibiting cross-border ties in the present, even once institutional obstacles no longer stand in the way.

To retain memories of their past, real or imagined, some Exiles refused even to look at photos or videos visitors brought back from trips. Visuals of Cuba under Castro were too much for them, for fear that they might destroy the beloved Cuba of their imagination. The father of a woman in the arts, Liliana, who made several return trips, beginning in the 1990s, for example, refused not only to accompany her when she took her mother to Cuba, he refused even to look at her photographs of trips. As the daughter explained, he "had a vision of Cuba and doesn't want it to change. His family lost more wealth than my mother's. Perhaps that explains his view."

Conclusion

The lenses through which Cuba is remembered, and memory-linked views toward travel, differ among Cubans who uprooted at different times with different experiences. Recent arrivals know the Cuba of today, not of yesteryear. They live with no illusions and thus without the desire to block out the present and live in the past. For them, Cuba remembered and imagined does not stand in the way of homeland visits. Quite to the contrary. They visited to sustain commitments to island friends and family transnationalized with their move to the US. If they visited less than new immigrants from other Latin American countries, their reasons, in the main, were pragmatic: their pocketbook and government regulations.

For Exiles, lingering barriers to bonding across borders were socially constructed and politically sustained. In remaining committed to the travel taboo they could avoid confronting Cuba transformed by the revolution. Although some of them defied the wall across the Straits to which their cohort was committed, they were the exception.

How did the émigrés with commitments to different norms and perspectives react to the trips they took? This is the focus of the next chapter.

5 Cuba Through the Looking Glass

Visits only selectively broke down social barriers between Cubans across borders. Travelers who defied Exiles' travel taboo experienced their trips differently, depending on their pre-immigration views on Cuba. Such was the weight of émigrés' pasts that, at the extreme, those who came of age in pre-revolutionary Cuba and opposed the social transformation, and those who lived through the post-Soviet-era crisis, experienced their trips in contrasting ways. I found, in my in depth interviews, the first who fled the revolution to be the most negative in their reactions (see Appendix). The New Cubans, in contrast, remained so embedded in homeland life that most of them viewed trips, first and foremost, as joyful occasions to see friends and family.

The different Cubas that the émigrés experienced on visits reveals how memory, cognition, and emotions are socially contingent. Although trip-takers' pre-immigration mindsets did not always predetermine the meanings visits had, they set the parameters, shaped presuppositions, and filtered perceptions of their homeland. Exiles who had left Cuba as adults, in opposition to the revolution, when breaking their cohort's trip-taking taboo typically experienced visits as short-lived cross-border bridging affairs. Their mindset predisposed them to visit minimally and apprehensively, and to pursue little if any follow-up contact with those they saw. Their pre-revolutionary, pre-immigration perspective on Cuba inclined them to visit to renew, but not to resume, relations with islanders committed to the revolution. And they tended to rationalize their trips, to themselves and others, as personally justified exceptions to the community's taboo of cross-border ties. Their interpretive lenses, in turn, led them to politicize their reactions to trips. They found fault in, and rarely praise for, the Cuba they encountered, and they considered Castro the cause of the country's fall from grace. They did not have compassion for conditions they saw.

The New Cubans, in contrast, viewed visits as a natural part of family life. They were predisposed to bond with the loved ones they had left behind, as often as possible. They try to keep ties as seamless as physical separation permits. Values, commitments, and expectations they share with island family make for strong bonding. If recent émigrés reacted critically to conditions in Cuba when visiting, they typically did so empathically, and they attributed problems to outside causes, to the embargo in particular, because before emigrating they had been socialized to assess the country's plight that way.

Thus, visits often proved self-fulfilling prophecies. Émigrés with different pre-immigration experiences expected "different Cubas," and they encountered different Cubas as a result. Nonetheless, some who fled the revolution early on reacted to visits differently than their background predisposed them to. Again, this was most common among immigrant children who grew up with experiences not confined to the Exile world of their parents. The occasional Exile who had emigrated as an adult, who reacted more positively to visits than their background predisposed them, and who experienced Cuba differently than they had anticipated, focused on the personal: on bonding with family and finding that politics did not stand between them.

For some, the timing of visits influenced reactions to trips. Émigrés who visited Cuba during the Carter opening and since the crisis of the 1990s stepped foot in different Cubas, into Cubas where living conditions differed, where people's commitments to the revolution differed, and where people's views toward the diaspora differed. Nonetheless, there were Exiles with pre-formed mindsets so critical of Cuba under Castro that they were blinded to the changes that had transpired between the 1970s and the post-Soviet era.

The Meanings of Visits

Indicative of how émigrés experienced trips differently depending on their pre-immigration generation formation, for recent arrivals, trips helped maintain a family life still embedded in Cuba. Visits contributed to transnationalizing family life, and to revitalizing ties that bind while living apart. In contrast, for Exiles who emigrated as adults, trips sometimes allowed them to reacquaint with relatives. But especially when they had no close kin still on the island, their visits tended to be alienating experiences. For these émigrés, visits put psychological closure to the Cuba of their imagination. Among early émigrés who had left the island young, however, reactions to visits varied, depending on kinship contacts they established when visiting and on pre-trip presuppositions about Cuba. The more positively predisposed to the revolution they were before trips, and the more intimate the ties that they established on trips, the more favorable their reactions.

Exile Temporary Bridge-Building

Because the co-ethnic social circles of Cubans who fled the revolution early on opposed travel, the minority who broke rank and trespassed across the Straits typically did so in a manner that reinforced the personal embargo. They were rather secretive about their trips, they rarely reestablished close relationships that they sustained long distance after returning to the US, and when they admitted trip-taking to fellow Exiles they rationalized why they took exception to the taboo. A Union City priest captured the essence of their trips. "For the majority of the older people who visit, their experience doesn't change them. Their visits confirm their beliefs. They say the government is a disaster and they claim that 'They were right to leave.' They confirmed what they felt before."

Most Exiles with whom I spoke visited during the Carter opening. Some even made multiple trips during that period. Only one-third of them visited both in the 1970s and in the post-Soviet era, two time periods when the Cuban government permitted diaspora trips on a large scale. By the 1990s most Exiles who had previously visited had distanced themselves emotionally from island family to the point that the temptation to travel had been put to rest. Such social distancing contributed to their cohort's hardline travel stance. They could make public virtue of their private predispositions. And as their aging island relatives died off, they faced even less of a dilemma between the political and the personal, between their principles and family loyalties.

Remberto's critical reaction to trips he took is illustrative. The retired construction worker who had emigrated to Miami in 1962, at age twenty-nine, made not only one but two return trips during the Carter years, to see two brothers who had stayed in Cuba. His two other brothers who had stayed in Cuba had committed suicide. Fearful before leaving that he would be imprisoned upon touching Cuban soil, his trips upset him from start to finish. Already in the Miami airport he was bothered by co-ethnics who took it upon themselves to serve as "border police." "People mocked you for going to Cuba and they treated you unprofessionally. They made abnormal searches of your luggage and refused to treat you with respect." He also disliked how difficult it was to get permission to visit, and how when on the island "the Cuban government treated you like a third-class citizen. In Cuba there was a separate airport for Miami flights. It's ridiculous how we were treated." Once making it through the hurdles, he was taken aback by the poverty, misery, desperation, and delinquency that he witnessed. Times were so tough that he claims even his family stole things from him.

Remberto remained frozen in his memories. When we spoke more than twenty years after his visits, he presumed conditions under Castro had not changed. He complained that "in Cuba things are getting worse and worse. The CDRs [the grass-roots state organization, the Committees for the Defense of the Revolution] watch your every move. And Blacks are taking over control of the government." When asked if he was positive about anything, he asserted "nothing." "People are destroyed and there is malnutrition." Finding his two trips emotionally upsetting, he decided not to return "until Fidel is gone." Although he had quietly and covertly maintained contact with his family from the time he had emigrated until his return trips, his relations with kin who remained loyal to the revolution cooled as a result of his visits. He broke off ties with his brothers in 1980 and has had very little contact with them since.

Joséfina, who emigrated in her thirties in 1965 and settled in Union City, reacted similarly to a return trip. Coming from a family deeply opposed to the revolution, she reluctantly and apprehensively visited island relatives in 1998.

While one of her brothers, along with his son, as previously noted, had been assassinated by "Castro's army" and other brothers had served long prison terms for counter-revolutionary involvements, her family divided generationally over the revolution. Her visit helped defuse inter-generational tensions, but little more. A niece of hers, who had come of age in the idealistic early years of the new society in the making, had joined the Communist Party and supported Castro. For Joséfina, her visit helped mend wounds with the niece. The niece had become so politically committed to the revolution that she had refused even to speak to Joséfina when she telephoned from the US. Silence served to sustain barriers between them. Even in the confines of her home the niece had supported the country's leadership taboo on ties with stigmatized "*gusanos.*" The revolution had convinced her to reimagine her aunt, who had been her chaperone in the bourgeois days before the revolution, as a stigmatized Other. She accordingly cut off communication with Joséfina. A phone conversation was more than the niece would tolerate.

Joséfina's visit led them "to make peace and to forgive each other." But Joséfina, like Remberto, viewed her trip as putting closure to the Cuba part of her life. She suspected that she would never see any of her island family again. When leaving she told them "now we have seen each other. We have talked. We can die in peace." The trip did not become a springboard for subsequent cross-border bonding.

When alluding to her trip upon her return, Joséfina reinforced Exiles' normative commitment to the travel taboo. She made a point of telling people that she went only once and only to see family. She felt a need to justify her travel and affirm that she made a one-time exception to the taboo.

Another woman, Laura, who emigrated in 1959 and made a return trip around the same time as Joséfina at her daughter's urging, was so disillusioned with and alienated from the Cuba she encountered that she felt the country was not her home anymore. With no family left on the island, her trip was not an emotional homecoming. Experiencing a life lost, she had no desire to ever visit again. The trip led her to put the Cuba chapter of her life to rest. Her experience illustrates how in supporting a wall across the Straits Exiles sustained their belief in, and commitment to, an idealized Cuba that was no longer existent. Their moral stance had important social and political consequences. It helped them keep alive their opposition to Castro and the regime that they associated with him.

A few of the early émigrés with whom I spoke, however, had positive experiences that led them, upon their return to the US, to no longer support the personal embargo. For different reasons, trip-taking in these instances also eroded commitment to the anti-Castro cause that for decades Exiles had championed. Visits broke down barriers that the travel taboo had served to keep intact. Marta, who emigrated in 1960 at age twenty, was one such person. Although so fearful on her first trip back, in 1994, that she carried a Bible with her at all times, she happily found that people on the island were very friendly. She bonded with island family and former friends whom she found "very noble and very caring," so much so that she made four additional trips during the following two years. She did not even let Washington's once-a-year cap stand in her way.

A fervently anti-Castro man who had resisted contact with Cuba for decades had a similar experience to Marta. He broke the personal embargo he had imposed on himself and visited around the turn of the century. He, too, enjoyed the visit so much that he immediately planned another trip. Both he and Marta responded so positively to their trips because they met up with old acquaintances in new clothes. They encountered friends and family whose views on the revolution had been shattered by the crisis of the 1990s. Their pre-immigration anti-revolutionary mindsets were not so entrenched as to keep them from recognizing how the values of Cubans with whom they previously disagreed had changed.

Yet, family who divided over the revolution at times had become so estranged that get-togethers, in their words, were experienced as "encounters." One man described his entire life as "reencounters and separation between family." He was eighteen in 1962 when his parents, opposed to the revolution, packed up and left. As a "child of the revolution" he chose to stay. Although he had missed his family deeply, he had minimal contact with them because he felt it to be risky. His mother died some twenty-five years after emigrating, before he had a chance to see her again. His father, whom he finally saw after thirty years of separation, reentered his life as a disabled, elderly man confined to a wheelchair. Two years later he met two of his sisters. He met one of them for the first time, as she had not yet been born when his parents left. The other, a teenager when his family fled, was a middle-aged woman when they remet. When they got together politics no longer stood between them. Ties of blood bound them. So captivated was he by his "reencounters" that the once-committed revolutionary decided to leave Cuba and reunite with his family in the US. For him, visits ended his estrangement from his "*gusano*" family that separation had sustained for decades. While his wife accompanied him, in a repeat of his own personal history, his children stayed behind. With politics not standing between them, though, he did not break off ties with them, as he had with his parents when they emigrated.

On balance, Exiles who remained committed to their pre-immigration generational battle with Fidel thus were correct to oppose cross-border travel, though not necessarily for the moral reasons they claimed. In many instances, for these émigrés defiance of the travel taboo ended their support for the personal embargo and their belief in the idealized, imagined Cuba the taboo had helped sustain. Exile border trespassers came to realize that history had destroyed "their" Cuba. And for some, trips led them to realize that presumed differences between family who had divided over the revolution were unfounded, and to stop believing, in turn, that politics should keep them apart. In honoring the travel taboo, Exiles could continue to live in their past.

New Immigrant Bonding

Recent immigrants made more return trips and they visited with shorter time lapses between trips than Exiles because they remained enmeshed in island life and wanted it so. The very émigrés who knew Castro's Cuba best were most sympathetic to bonding with people there, with their visits reinforcing their homeland ties.

The Cuba that most new immigrants' lives remained enmeshed in was apolitical. This too may seem surprising since they and their island family grew up in a Communist regime that Cold War analysts portrayed as highly politicized.[1] The 1990s crisis had led Cubans, whether or not they emigrated, to narrow their concerns to the personal and pragmatic. At the same time they remained deeply Cuban in their identity. Their sense of belonging remained island-rooted, which they affirmed on visits.

Their sense of belonging was family-embedded, also defying Cold War conceptions of Communist regimes. Critics of the revolution, from the days of Operation Peter Pan shortly after Castro assumed power to the movement four decades later to keep six-year-old Elián in the US, misrepresented the impact the revolution had on kinship commitments. Recent émigrés viewed visits as a way to reaffirm family ties reconfigured across borders with their uprooting. In this vein, a Miami travel agent noted that most of her customers are poor, recent arrivals. Within a few months after arriving they come to her office for travel information. "They constantly make plans . . . to see family in Cuba with whom they want to spend time. They want to stay involved in the lives of friends and family back home." She contrasted their attitude with that of the older immigrants, who are less interested in visiting people they left behind. The Cubans who fled the revolution early on, while not anti-family, set country boundaries to the family with whom they bonded.

Some long-time Miami residents recognize the different meanings the immigrant waves attach to visits. The previously noted businessperson who relocated in the US already during the Batista era noted that his gardener, who came around 1990, "simply makes money and goes. Trips are a routine part of his life." The gardener travels to Cuba approximately every two months, not letting Washington's travel regulations get in his way. He travels through third countries to evade US restrictions. Similarly, Alejandra, the school director whose parents sent her abroad after the failed Bay of Pigs invasion, contrasted how differently her generation and recent émigrés viewed visits. Her manicurist, who moved to Miami in the post-Soviet era, goes frequently to see her grandmother in Cuba. "Their ties are incredible," she explained.

New arrivals are so enmeshed in life back home that they plan trips to coincide with birthdays, holidays, and other family festivities. In the years when Washington only permitted visits for family emergencies, their claimed emergencies peaked during holiday season. Trips permit shared celebration of events families value that, in turn, reinforce and renew kinship solidarity in new transnationalized form. The landscaper, for example, makes a point of visiting on holidays. And Laurencio, the Cuban-trained doctor who moved to Miami in 1999 after winning an immigration lottery exit visa, within a year planned a return visit, timed with his son's birthday.

For travel agents who book Cuba trips, Christmas is their busiest season. Christmas trips testify to how ordinary Cubans shared norms informally across borders that defied officially sanctioned norms. Castro had not acknowledged the day commemorating Christ's birthday as a national holiday until the Pope's 1998 visit. However, before then families had privately continued pre-revolutionary customs, which included get-togethers on Christmas and the Day of the Kings in early January. The commemorations retained social if not religious significance to them.

For the New Cubans trips were so enmeshed in family life that they were not experienced as "encounters" and not politicized. In this vein, Eduardo, a man from a pre-revolutionary upper-class family who worked as a manager in a state enterprise until he emigrated in 1992, for example, noted that the rafters who escaped to Miami around the time he did not only "return more often [than earlier émigrés] but they face less shock from their families when they go. The bonding comes more naturally because . . . the expectations of family on both sides of the Straits have become more realistic." He contrasted the situation among families recently transnationalized with return visits by earlier émigrés in years past. "I remember the first time one of my relatives arrived from the US. It was an aunt from Miami who came in 1979." She visited when Eduardo still lived in Cuba. "I had millions of questions. I kept looking at my aunt and comparing her with the people I knew who had stayed in Cuba." The new immigrants experience no comparable estrangement. For them, physical separation typically involves no social distancing.

New Cuban visits have an economic base. As poor as most recent immigrants are, their families in Cuba depend on them financially. Their trips are associated with income sharing in cash and kind. As detailed in the next chapter, many recent arrivals moved to the US with the intent to help island kin. Orlandina, who moved to New Jersey in 1991 where she works as housekeeper, is illustrative. She visits Cuba every two years, although she wishes that she could afford to go more frequently. When she came to the US she left her children behind. But in moving she saw herself as assisting, not abandoning, them. Economic necessity drove her to mother transnationally. As she explained, "I would return . . . more often if I could. The only thing holding me back is the cost of trips." Even if she visits infrequently, however, she feels very involved in family life back home. She phones home weekly and sends packages whenever she can. Transnational mothering is common among other new immigrants as well.[2]

Exile Cohort Children: Bonding, Bridging, and Breaking Away

Children of the first families to flee the revolution varied more than their parents' generation in their reactions to trips. With few, if any, first-hand memories of Cuba before their families fled, trips often challenged their preconceptions. They often were shocked by the Cuba onto which they stepped foot.

Some immigrant children who visited Cuba as adults happily built bridges, but little more. This was especially true of returnees who no longer had relatives on the island. Bernardo, who left Cuba as a three-year-old in 1963, is a case in point. Thirty-five years later he made a return trip with his mother, who was from a very wealthy pre-revolutionary family. The two of them officially went on a family visit, to conform with the only exception to the travel embargo Washington permitted. However, they no longer had family on the island, or so they thought. When in Cuba his mother discovered two cousins. For her, the trip provided a chance "to reconnect with places, and people still there," as well as to have "closure" with her native land. For him, his first trip enabled him to see all the places he had heard about when growing up. Much to his surprise, he felt estranged from the Cuba he experienced. His first trip, as well as two subsequent trips he took in a professional capacity, led him to feel "unCuban," different from Cubans who stayed on the island. The estrangement ultimately led him to distance himself from the Cuba he had imagined his entire life and with which he had identified in his thoughts. Without close kin still in Cuba with whom to bond, and without bonding emotionally with his distant relatives, he lost interest in visiting again.

Bernardo's conception of Cuba prior to his trips had been entirely imagined, based on no previous first-hand island memories. Because his parents had raised him to believe in their remembered Cuba, he viewed Cuba through their lenses and he expected he would experience the Cuba that they had, which the revolution proved to relegate to history.

As a result of his visits Bernardo came to feel more American and Spanish and less Cuban. The Spanish identity that came to the fore rested neither linearly in his family's lived experiences nor territorially in his own lived world. His grandparents, not he or his mother or father, grew up in Spain. His "regression" involved repressing his more immediate and direct Cuban heritage. At the same time, in identifying as American he moved forward in time, to where he and his parents settled after Cuba. His Cuba experience, filtered through lenses acquired through his parents, was so alienating as to lead him to repress his Cuban heritage and highlight both his family's earlier and later heritage. He had multiple identities to draw upon, and his island trips put his Cuban identity to rest.

Despite detaching himself emotionally and culturally from Cuba, Bernardo became a cross-border bridge-building advocate. He felt that all Cuban Americans should visit Cuba. Once you have a chance to "see people you haven't seen in a long time you can begin to rebuild those bonds." Unlike hardliners of his parents' generation, he felt that "reconnecting and rebuilding needs to occur."

Other Exile children, however, had travel experiences that triggered greater bonding. This was true for Liliana, who had left Cuba in 1959 when she was one years old. Because her father had been an officer in Batista's army, her family was quick to leave when Castro took power. With no first-hand memories, she was a *de facto* second-generation immigrant like Bernardo. As an adult, she first visited Cuba in 1997, in a professional capacity. She was so taken by her experience that she subsequently returned multiple times, and not merely on work-related missions. She recounts:

> I was blown away on my first visit . . . I cried every night because it was the first time I felt at home. It was similar to when Jews go back to Israel and experience their roots. There were Cubans talking with their hands! And I knew their accent! I felt completely at home. As a result, I began to change. I experienced a sense of homecoming. My sister who left at six and went back with me (on a subsequent trip) at age forty-five felt the same.

Although Liliana no longer had blood relatives on the island, on her first visit she met her godmother whom she came to treat as family.

In visiting, Liliana felt that she had found her roots for the first time. She thought that even though she did not agree with Castro, she felt she would have stayed in Cuba had she been old enough to make the decision for herself. She sensed a one-ness with people on the island. Liliana, as well as the sister she alluded to, had spent many years away from Miami. Liliana thinks that made them open to experiencing their visits so positively.

Similarly, Alejandra, the director of the Miami private school who emigrated in 1961 at age ten, and who had lived many years in the Midwest, was deeply moved by her first return trip, in 1998. After finally getting the courage to return, she started to visit about three times per year. Whenever she returns, she visits her distant island relatives—second and third cousins. She sees them more frequently than many of her Miami kin because she finds bonding with them to be more meaningful, even though they live farther apart, even though get-togethers are harder to arrange, and even though her island relatives are of greater genealogical remove. And even though face-to-face contact with island relatives is intermittent, she envisions the ties as ongoing and as a reason to visit whenever possible.

For Alejandra, bonding with island family rested on an emotional breakthrough that led her, like Liliana, to become a "born-again Cuban." Their visits led them to see Cubans on the two sides of the Straits as cut of the same cloth. They came to identify with people who until then they had envisioned, pejoratively, as Communist "Others." For them, trips shattered support for the wall across the Straits, and the negative conception of Cubans under Castro the wall sustained.

Other children who emigrated in the 1960s viewed Cuba and Cubans through more political lenses. However, even perceived political differences with island family did not necessarily stand in the way of cross-border bonding. Rosario, the bus fleet owner who emigrated with her family at age eight, first went back to Cuba during the Carter opening, and later returned four add-itional times. Despite reservations about the revolution, she did not let that poison her relations with family who remained loyal to Fidel. "I love my Cuban family and nothing can change the way I feel towards them," said she. "The warmth of my family was as if I had never left Cuba, as if they lived with me all the time." She added,

> In Cuba I have relationships with people who don't think the way my father did about the revolution . . . I saw my godfather, for example, who was pro-Castro . . . Politics didn't matter. He still loved me . . . We dis-agree but we respect each other. He has his point of view and I have mine.

Possibly because she left Cuba as a child and first returned as a late teenager when on the verge of interpreting life for herself, she was more open than older Exiles not to let politics stand in the way of blood ties.

Rosario's emotional bonding rubbed off on her US-born daughter, who as a child she took with her on homeland trips. Her daughter's early memories had a long-lasting impact, so much so that when she visited twenty years later on her own as an adult she reacted similarly to the new immigrants for whom cross-border bonding is second nature. Even though two decades had elapsed between her first and second trip, she yearned to be with island family. Her trips in her youth had broken the ice. They led her to be committed emotion-ally to family that knew no borders. In her words,

> The worst part of traveling is having to leave Cuba . . . In those few days with your family you get so attached to them . . . not only my family but also their neighbors. Everyone is so lovable . . . The most difficult part is having to say goodbye to people that you really wish you wouldn't have to say goodbye to . . . Everyone wants to wait until the last moment to say goodbye because they know that they might not be able to see you again. You don't know when you'll be able to come back, to share another meal with them . . . to be with them.

Like Alejandra, Rosario's daughter envisions relations with island family to be ongoing, even though she never knows when she will reunite with them face-to-face.

Dario, who had moved to New Jersey as a teenager in 1967, was as con-scious as Rosario of political differences between him and his family who stayed in Cuba. But both he and his island relatives were pleasantly surprised by a get-together, so much so that he became inspired to make another return trip. He and his family took delight in how open-minded they found each other to be. For them, trips became a base of bonding.

Other immigrant children who in growing up had been influenced by the progressive movements in the US in the 1960s, and who accordingly were positively predisposed to the revolution before visiting, bonded with island family on trips. This was true of Aurelio. His first trip back, in the 1970s, had been "an emotional experience, to see the country where I was born and its culture. Things that I thought were unique to me I saw to be Cuban." Aurelio travels frequently to Cuba and looks forward when visiting to get-togethers with island relatives. "I see them whenever I go. [My relatives] talk with passion and love. They worry about how we are doing." He finds that people in Cuba "have a greater sense of family than here, even toward family who left." Although he tried, he never convinced his parents to make a return trip. His parents show disinterest in the island family who show interest in them. Whereas his parents put politics above family, the same was not true of his island relatives.

Aurelio, Liliana, Alejandra, and Rosario, all children of self-defined exiles, emotionally identified with the Cuba that they experienced when they broke their parents' generation travel taboo. The four of them had relatives still on the island whom they bonded with. Bonding with island relatives led them to claim and reclaim their Cuban roots and identity. Three of the four had spent some of their formative years away from Miami, where they were exposed to other-than-the-exile points of view. They could filter their island visits through an interpretative frame that was broader in range and less fixed in formation than that of the émigrés confined to Miami.

Cuba Through Different Lenses

Cuban immigrants with different island generational formations filtered island life on visits through contrasting cognitive lenses, and when they saw similar Cubas they interpreted what they saw differently. Their reactions to trips typically proved to be self-fulfilling prophecies. They perceived Cuba according to their preconceptions. Exiles experienced Cuba negatively and blamed the problems they observed on Castro. Recent arrivals, in contrast, were more empathic about suffering they saw. They tended to view Cuba through lenses similar to those of islanders, having experienced the crisis of the 1990s together, and those lenses were not red-tinted Marxist-Leninist. Beneath the veneer of Communist continuity were people who had become non-ideological and pragmatic. The children of Exiles who as adults visited Cuba varied most in how they perceived Cuba, just as they varied most in the bonding their travels induced. They viewed visits through prisms that drew on the broadest repertoire of lived experiences.

Exiles' Black Cuba, of Castro's Making

Many Exiles reconfirmed on visits why they despised the regime. Their mind-sets predisposed them to find fault in and no praise for island life. Their interpretive lenses filtered out any good in the Cuba they associated with Castro. Their remembered vision of an idyllic island colored how they saw the country. Consciously or not, they saw what they were looking for.

Joséfina, whose family suffered deeply for its opposition to the revolution, for example, filtered her one return visit in 1998 through her determinedly anti-Castro mindset. She was horrified by what she saw. She found Cuba under Castro to be filled with "misery and disaster." For example, she noted the lack of transportation in her provincial home town of Matanzas. She was shocked to find people there mainly relying on bicycles to get around. So too was she shocked by her family's impoverishment. She found it painful to see how her relatives lived. She nonetheless managed to react positively to encounters with government officials. Anticipating the worst, she was surprised by how professionally they treated her.

Laura, in turn, who was so put off by the country she experienced on her one return trip forty years after uprooting that she turned her back forever on the island, had viewed her trip through nostalgic, rose-colored pre-revolutionary lenses. Viewed in this manner, she felt she returned to paradise lost. Her mindset kept her from seeing anything familiar or likable. The Cuba she remembered was idyllic. Whatever injustice fueled the revolution was not part of her remembered past or interpretive frame. To her surprise and dismay, she found no basis for her memories in today's Cuba. She filtered her trip through memories of a Cuba she missed and longed to recreate. Nostalgia often leaves people without an anchor by which to relive their past, and Laura was no exception. Nowhere could she find the only Cuba she was prepared to relate to. Her mindset both kept her from finding anything good in Cuba that could be attributed to the revolution, and from relating to a Cuba that was different from the one she remembered. Although the Cuba she remembered had long been relegated to the dustbin of history, it had lived in her imagination until her return trip. For decades in self-imposed exile she fondly recalled a life that for her was full of pleasure and privilege. In the transformed Cuba, she could not reconstruct that life. With her trip demystifying her imagined Cuba, she sadly realized that there was no going back in time, and therefore no reason to physically go back again.

The dark lenses through which the first émigrés viewed Cuba under Castro did not keep some who made multiple return trips from seeing the country in different shades of gray on different visits. The changes they picked up on typically, however, reconfirmed their anti-Castro, anti-regime bias. Having emigrated in his twenties in 1964, Eduardo, a Union City businessman, for example, visited both in the late 1970s and again in the 1990s. He was shocked by the country's downturn in the interim. He was shocked by the increase in prostitution and alcoholism, the deterioration of the work ethic, and people's deepened distrust. He felt that "everyone was on nerve pills . . . So many years of struggle and yet so little to show for it." He wondered where were all the benefits from the years of Soviet subsidies. "You don't see them." He also felt that the health of the population had deteriorated. "People lack medicines." He was critical of and without compassion for those who were suffering.

Another woman, who also emigrated in the 1960s, echoed Eduardo's shock about the country's deterioration in the time between her homeland trips. She too visited Cuba in the late 1970s and again in the 1990s. When visiting in the post-Soviet era she found that "everyone was stealing to survive. People's values deteriorated so much that their concept of work changed." Her one delight was the rise in religious tolerance, although this implicitly was a criticism of the revolution. Cuban authorities who had stigmatized and discriminated against believers for decades had become more tolerant in the 1990s, as religion muted discontent with the bad economic times.

Visiting Exiles, ironically, did not attribute the island's downturn to the embargo that they supported on the supposition that it would contribute to regime collapse. They personalized the cause of the misery they homed in on. They blamed it on Castro, and in so doing attributed greater importance to the ruler than he deserved. Castro had not alone remade Cuba.

Exiles who emigrated as adults, if positive about their visits, focused on the personal. They were impressed with people they met.

New Immigrant Empathy and Attribution of Problems to US Cuba Policy

Recent immigrants who had themselves experienced crisis-ridden Cuba, and whose lives became transnationally embedded upon moving to the US, were sensitive to the problems islanders faced in their everyday lives. Their defining island experience before uprooting shaped how they viewed their homeland on visits.

Their life before uprooting shaped how they interpreted island problems. Some continued to envision Cuba through pre-immigration government-formed lenses. Cuban authorities blamed the economic downturn on the US blockade, the *bloqueo*. To blame the Soviet Union, which had disappeared from the world stage, would have been self-defeating for the country's leadership. It would suggest the Cuban regime's own potential fallibility, since it was built on similar economic and political precepts. So too would it have been self-defeating to blame the island woes on domestic problems rooted in the socialist transformation.

A nationwide island poll Gallup conducted in 1994 found most Cubans accepted the official story, that US sanctions were the source of island woes.[3] Several of the islanders who emigrated amidst the crisis with whom I spoke took the interpretation with them. The Union City housekeeper, Orlandina, who emigrated in 1991, and who made several return trips, for example, noted with dismay that "The economic situation in Cuba worsened since I left. Because of the blockade and other problems, my family is experiencing tremendous difficulties." Even her discourse was revealing. While Orlandina, along with other New Cubans, spoke of a blockade, the first who fled the revolution talked of an embargo. A blockade implies a deliberate externally imposed wall, whereas an embargo implies a morally sanctioned cut-off of ties. The new immigrant lingo derives from their Cuba days, from internalization of the official story. Thus, even when recent arrivals saw suffering on visits, they perceived its causes differently than did Exiles.

Orlandina added a religious filter to her interpretation of Cuba's plight. An evangelical convert, she attributed island disarray to the country having "turned away from God," as well as to the "*bloqueo*." Orlandina's perceptions reveal how some recent immigrants piled on interpretive frames acquired in the new country to views brought from their homeland.

Whether religious or not, recent émigrés were distraught about the unrelenting hardships they perceived their relatives faced. But their demoralization included compassion and empathy without political spin. Thus, Orlandina added with dismay that "Every time I return to Cuba my heart breaks. It is very difficult to witness the suffering and poverty. Cuba has regressed and it doesn't seem to get better." Her family was always poor, but their situation had worsened in the 1990s. And Eduardo, who emigrated in 1992, was so demoralized by the stories he heard from trip-takers that he was uncertain whether he would ever visit. He was not politically opposed to visiting Cuba, but most people he knew returned from trips depressed. "Even people who left a short time ago are shocked by what they encountered in Cuba." Unlike early émigrés, neither Orlandina nor Eduardo blamed the economic downturn on Castro.

Variability in Views Among Children of Exiles

Although Exiles raised their children to loath the revolution, their progeny, when visiting Cuba as adults, viewed island conditions through a spectrum of lenses. Some saw Cuba negatively, affirming their parents' generation's beliefs, while others were more accepting of the Cuba they met up with.

At one extreme was Julia, a computer programmer, who made one return trip in 1996, twenty-five years after she emigrated as a thirteen-year-old. She was critical of almost everything. "It was like walking into a museum where nothing was repaired. That Hitler monster! When he is gone it could be wonderful, but there's been forty years of decay. Even the spirit of the people has been damaged. For generations they've been unable to express themselves." She was so demoralized that she did not dare visit the mansion where her mother lived before the revolution.

Julia found Cuba to be even worse than she anticipated:

> I imagined that the country would be somewhat decayed, . . . [but] I had no idea that it would look like it had been bombed. Buildings had collapsed. There was rubble all over the place . . . It was like Beirut. All I did was cry when I first arrived. Havana is a beautiful city but it is in ruins . . . Everything was much worse than I had expected . . . Cuba is . . . a giant prison. Even if you are not in jail you can't go anywhere or do what you want. Everything is going backwards. There are people still using horse-drawn carts. It's like the stone-age. Going to Cuba is like going back in time.

Her trip more than confirmed her preconceptions, and she interpreted the Cuba she experienced through a politicized prism.

Changes that positively impressed Julia were not accomplishments of the revolution. Rather, she took pleasure in the growing disillusion with the revolution. She approvingly noted, for example, that "change is taking place in Cuba. Compared to when I was young, many more people are against the regime and more critical of it." Having left Cuba in 1970, Julia had experienced Cuba in the 1960s, when criticism of the revolution was taboo. People then either were committed to and optimistic about the new society in the making, or reluctant to express their misgivings.

While Julia's trip confirmed her disdain for what she interpreted as the Cuba of Castro's making, she remained a committed Cuban. She viewed her trip through nationalist and not merely political-ideological lenses. Her nationalist lenses were Exile-defined. She was outraged that Cuban authorities treated her as a foreigner and outsider. Although born there,

> I'm called a foreigner in my own country . . . You have to travel with permission from the government and you are limited in how long you can stay. I think this is very insulting . . . Cuba requires Cuban Americans to travel under a Cuban passport, with an entry permit, like a visa. It is ironic that we have to request a visa to return to our own country.

Julia wanted rights, not obligations, in Cuba.

Julia distinguished her sense of national identity from that of Cubans who had never left. She was dismayed to find people "hardened and distrustful, so imbibed with stupid nationalism they couldn't see through it." Julia differentiated loyalty to the nation from loyalty to the state, and criticized islanders who fused the two. Upon moving to the US she had become a long-distance nationalist, committed to an imagined nation that in the concrete no longer existed.[4] Julia thus could not find the Cuba that she looked for.

Iris, a professional writer and editor who emigrated at age seven shortly after Castro assumed power and settled in Union City with her mother and father, also viewed Cuba through her parents' generation lenses. On four trips to Cuba as an advanced teenager between 1978 and 1980 she was taken aback by regime repression. She also found that people were distrustful of her, even her island family. Her cousin, a doctor, suspected her to be a spy for the US government. Before visiting, Iris had questioned whether her mother had made the right decision to take her to America. But after visiting, she was convinced that her mother had been correct. Following her 1980 trip, she said, "I decided consciously and intellectually to exile myself from Cuba." She illustrates how "being an exile" may be a state of mind, an acquirable state of mind, not necessarily grounded in first-hand political persecution.

Iris admitted that she felt schizophrenic about her reaction to Cuba. She connected emotionally with her home country and family there, but felt that what she witnessed was very wrong. For example "the apartheid tourist industry and the *diplo* dollar stores" (as dollar stores used to be called before the 1990s, when they were officially accessible only to foreign dignitaries, broadly defined). Iris's outrage peaked on what came to be her last trip. The psychological terror she experienced then caused her to decide never to return again as long as Castro was in power. That trip coincided with the Mariel crisis. She witnessed *actos de repudio*, acts by ordinary Cubans who turned, at Party instigation, on their neighbors and co-workers who at the time were seeking refuge in America. Angering her all the more, on her last trip a functionary confiscated her passport and refused to return it to her for two weeks. She was livid, and made to feel insecure. Each trip further reaffirmed her image of Cuba as repressive, which she blamed on Castro. Her last trip was the clincher. "Castro is the source of the cancer in Cuba. If he dies . . . we will still have to deal with the cancer's metastasis." He destroyed "civil society and civic consciousness. Fidel has replaced the nation with a system centered around himself. Fidelism versus nationalism. The Cuban family, the basic unit of social cohesion, even this has been torn apart."

Two decades after visiting, Iris remained frozen in her views of Cuba. She was frozen in views of Cuba under Castro, not the pre-revolutionary Cuba her parents' generation remembered. Yet, she filtered her trips through the anti-Castro mindset that she acquired from her parents. While most of her parents' generation who refused to step foot in Castro's Cuba had visions of a regime that was more imagined than real, Iris, as a result of visiting, confirmed the basis for Exile antipathy to the revolution. That Cuba could have improved in any way under Castro was not within her frame of comprehension.

Viviana, who also emigrated in the 1960s in her youth, similarly viewed return trips through her parents' generation's lenses. She visited Cuba not only during the Carter years but again twenty years later. Her father, a wealthy pre-revolutionary accountant, had owned seven houses in Santiago de Cuba, all of which the government expropriated, one of which it transformed into a clinic that offered free health care unavailable before the revolution. Despite the new social service provisioning that she observed first-hand on return trips, she was highly critical of the Cuba she returned to, especially after her trip in the post-Soviet era. Echoing Exiles' reactions, she found working and living conditions, values, and social relations to have deteriorated. She was especially shocked by how suspicious people had become of one another. Her island family had become fearful of their neighbors, and not because their politics differed. They worried that neighbors would steal money and gifts that visiting relatives brought. "Everyone stole to survive, and values deteriorated to the point that people's concept of work changed." She sensed work to have lost meaning. She also was surprised by the new dollarization of economic life, which she felt put most Cubans at a disadvantage since "they weren't paid in dollars and weren't allowed to purchase dollars easily for transactions." She also was shocked that the new economy of scarcity had turned hygienic essentials, such as toilet paper, into luxuries. For the first couple of days when visiting she did not want to touch anything, appalled by the lack of hygiene. As conditions in Cuba in crisis deteriorated, her island relatives had grown critical of the revolution, and Viviana easily piled their disillusion onto her preconceived negative impressions.

Viviana was shocked by other changes as well, which reflected badly on the government. She was especially shocked by emergent new inequities in the post-Soviet era. She found tremendous socio-economic differences among neighborhoods. The new tourism and foreign businesses that the government welcomed in the post-Soviet era improved life in rich neighborhoods while poor neighborhoods suffered from neglect.

However, Viviana was not so blinded that she saw only changes for the worse. She was impressed by new religious tolerance, tolerance she attributed to the Pope's visit. She also felt that relations with the diaspora had taken a turn for the better. She had been taken aback in the 1970s by how distrustful islanders were of visiting exiles, a distrust she blamed on Party and CDR stigmatization of Cubans who left. She sensed islanders at the time were scared to be overly friendly with visitors from the US for fear of stirring the ire of local officials. When she returned in the late 1990s, though, she found that even government officials treated her nicely. She was cynical, though, as to why. "Everyone was looking for a tip." By the late 1990s she, in essence, sensed a build-up of transnational trust but breakdown of local trust. Her frame of mind left her critical of the regime at the same time that the changes she perceived suggested a withering away of state influence, to her liking.

Marta, the infant immigrant who never forgot or forgave the Castro-led government for killing her father in the Bay of Pigs invasion, also viewed Cuba on a visit through a critical frame of mind. Her views were reaffirmed when Cuban authorities denied her more than one visitation visa. Yet, her one trip convinced her that the country had changed since her parents' days and that it would never again be the island that they had known and loved. Exiles and their children who honored the personal embargo shielded themselves from such a realization. Having taken on her parents' interpretive frame of Cuba, she idealized life before Castro, a life "known" through tales her mother told, which were filtered through well-to-do pre-revolutionary lenses. With no close family left in Cuba to bond with, she returned to the US convinced that Castro had ruined the country.

At the other extreme was Aurelio. Although of roughly the same age and émigré cohort as Viviana, and although, like Viviana, he returned to Cuba for the first time in the late 1970s, he viewed his visit through very different lenses. He was impressed with Cuba, with its education and healthcare systems and with how self-confident children there were "compared to us in the exile community." And when he returned twenty years later he was impressed by people's resilience and how they "sustained the system despite hardships." He acknowledged a need for change but felt that it was happening. "There is no way back. And if there were less US pressure, the changes would be a lot faster."

Aurelio viewed Cuba initially not through the Exile lenses learned from his parents, but through, as previously noted, the New Left perspective he took on in the US from non-Cuban peers. Acknowledging that on his first trip he had been idealistic in his views toward the revolution, he believed himself now to be more realistic. The lenses through which he viewed Cuba shifted figuratively from red to a paler, more translucent gray-pink. By the start of the new millennium he saw Cuba to be more complex, though still partly positive. He did not "revert" to the unreconstructed anti-Castro mindset of his parents' generation.

The former Union City priest who had negotiated the release of political prisoners between 1978 and 1980 was also impressed with the changes he observed on his return trips. He had left Cuba in 1961 at age sixteen. While on reflecting back he admitted that "perhaps deep down I wanted everything in Cuba to be wrong and bad and that I was right to have left, I was impressed to see improvements in many areas, in housing, health, and education—and throughout the island. There were doctors for the first time in the country-side." He last visited Cuba in 1980, before the 1990s crisis caused havoc even in social service provisioning and the government commissioned many medics to overseas missions to generate hard currency which depleted the domestic supply (described in Chapter 7).

Between Julia, Iris, Viviana, and Marta, on the one hand, and Aurelio and the priest, on the other, were others of their age and émigré wave who saw Cuba with greater nuance. They found both praise and fault in the Cuba they encountered. Minimally, they were not so blinded as to be oblivious to changes that had transpired between visits. Rosario, for example, who visited Cuba five times between the late 1970s and late 1990s, never became frozen in earlier negative impressions. While she did not become as positive in her perceptions as Aurelio, her bonding with family on trips sensitized her to island changes in the interim that she liked. She found that the government had become much less controlling. On her first trip "everyone was very careful to always carry their identity card. Police were constantly checking people's identification. People were very scared, the situation tense." In the 1990s, she sensed that fear had subsided. She was impressed that Cubans felt comfortable listening to Cuban American music openly in public places. American influence could be felt. And having taken a video camera with her, she was pleasantly surprised how free she was to record whatever she wanted.

Her US-born daughter who accompanied her on trips found that visits deepened her understanding and appreciation of both the US and Cuba. Conditions she experienced on the island led her to feel lucky to live in America, but simultaneously to value the quality of islanders' social relationships. Viewing Cuba through different lenses than, for example, Viviana, she did not perceive distrust. "When you go to Cuba you see the solidarity among friends as well as family." In contrast, she noted, "People in the US only think about themselves and their own needs. In Cuba, people are struggling, but they are more loving and warm, more concerned about each other." She differentiated between social and economic life, and was positive about the former.

Dario, who, as previously noted, emigrated at age thirteen in 1967 and now works for the Homeland Security Administration, in turn, was impressed on recent visits by "many Cubas." He found that most people there were interested in dialogue. "People my age and younger . . . had an open mind and were open to discussion." The change he focused on was change he considered to be for the better. He noticed much more anti-government feeling in 1999 than when he visited sixteen years earlier. People had become more openly critical. At the same time, he was surprised by how little had changed economically. "Those who were poor remained poor and no one questioned it."

Closer to Aurelio's end of the spectrum were Alejandra and Liliana who had spent time in the US outside Miami, removed from the Exile milieu. Unlike Aurelio, though, they had never experienced the 1960s American youth movement, and accordingly never viewed Cuba through comparable Left-leaning lenses. While raised to resent the revolution, the two women filtered trips through frames focusing on the personal, and they were deeply moved by the Cuba they experienced. Alejandra, the school director, for example, found Cubans to be "so resilient. Life is frustrating but the people try to put on their best. Their education and cultural awareness is impressive." Alejandra added that she "feels so free there."

Having emigrated at age ten in 1961, Alejandra had selective childhood memories of Cuba that proved more imagined than real. But when visiting she accepted the Cuba that differed from her preconceptions. "In my dreams I would walk the streets." The Cuba she (re)discovered "was almost surreal." Remembering Cuba through lenses of a child, "Things were much smaller than I had remembered and trees had grown."

But child immigrants were not alone in remembering pre-revolutionary Cuba through rose-colored magnifying lenses. Exiles who left the island as adults also magnified their paradise lost. Without reality checks, absence had not merely made the heart grow fonder, but life lost bigger and better. In the book *In Cuba I Was a German Shepherd* the novelist Ana Menéndez captures how self-defined exiles exaggerated and glorified their past. In the book's title story a mixed breed dog, Juanito, who sought refuge in Miami, meets and proposes marriage to a white female poodle with whom he imagines he could have gorgeous puppies. The poodle rebuffs Juanito, saying she is a refined breed of considerable class and he a short insignificant mutt. Juanito retorts, "Here in America, I may be a short, insignificant mutt, but in Cuba I was a German shepherd."

Liliana, in turn, noted that "people have a hard time, but they also have a sense of life." She found Cuba "very different than the Miami image," the image her family conveyed to her as a child. She grew up thinking "that Cuba was like Eastern Europe—gray and fearful. But I found it *gorgeous*." The contrast with Joséfina, whose anti-Castro pre-immigration mindset led her to find the island filled with "misery and disaster," and with Julia, who found Cuba filled with "forty years of decay," is striking.

In viewing island life through personalized lenses Alejandra and Liliana resembled the New Cubans. However, the two women's lenses were new, transformed from old, and acquired very differently than those of recent émigrés. And their shift in lenses made for greater emotional spin. For both Alejandra and Liliana visits involved a break with their past and a break with their parents.

Even some children of the first émigrés who did not become "born again Cubans" came to understand island life as transformed by the revolution more from a Cuban than an exclusively Exile perspective as a result of visits. Bernardo, who as previously noted, emigrated as a child soon after the revolution and returned with his mother, thirty-five years later, for example, had mixed reactions to the country he witnessed, and reactions that were different than he anticipated. On the one hand, he noted, that "when you look beyond the destruction you can see what life was like for your parents . . . Even if the country is torn apart, and buildings are in ruins and the countryside ravaged, Cuba still is a beautiful country. It has so much natural beauty." He added that to his surprise, "everything looked abandoned, in need of repair. The exiles themselves abandoned the country. They just got up and left. It was the right decision at the time. That we stayed away so long is another story." Although having left Cuba as an infant, Bernardo here acknowledges his identity as an exile, and the Exile interpretative frame he took on for himself. But Bernardo also admitted that he was more impressed with people on the island than his conservative upbringing had led him to anticipate. Because of stories he heard growing up, he expected people to be tired and depressed. Instead, he, like Alejandra, was impressed with people on the island, with their resilience and ability to have a stable family life in the face of very hard times.

Even for Bernardo who came to feel "un-Cuban" in Cuba, he returned to the US critical of the Cuban American leadership and Washington's Cuba policy. His trips left him more grounded in what he considered the reality of the Cuba of today. "I now know," he said, "what it is like to live there and . . . what people are going through." His visits shaped his views, for example, toward the "Elián saga." They led him to feel that politicians on both sides of the Straits used the boy to advance their own political agendas, and that cross-border family relations were dysfunctional. Had he not visited Cuba he probably would have reacted differently, he felt. "I would have thought that returning Elián to Cuba would have been terribly tragic. Now I know that his life in Cuba won't be so bad." His trips gave him a perspective "that blended both sides of the story."

Yet, when immigrant children had positive perceptions of Cuba transformed by revolution their views were not so fixed as to be irreversible. Having grown up with a critical mindset, they could easily bring that mindset back to the fore. Those who "reverted" to earlier, critical interpretive lenses had unpleasant island experiences. One Cuban American, who, inspired by the New Left, had made her first trip back in the 1970s as a participant in a solidarity group, became more conservative as she aged and outspokenly critical of the revolution. She became so critically outspoken that the Cuban government stopped granting her entry visas, which further affirmed her aversion to the regime.

From People-to-People to Organization-Based Transnational Ties

While most travelers experienced Cuba at the individual and family level, in the post-Soviet era some travelers were so moved by visits that upon their return they became involved in groups that contributed to bases of cross-border bridge-building. Their ability to do so, however, was severely constrained by both US and Cuban regulations. Organizational involvements took a variety of forms, and they varied among émigré waves. I illustrate ways that people with whom I spoke were inspired by trips to become, upon their return to the US, involved in groups engaged with Cuba.

Cultural

Some émigrés with whom I spoke were so moved by visits that they took it upon themselves to initiate cultural ventures with cross-border reach. I found children of Exiles who visited Cuba as adults most apt to do so.

Liliana is a case in point. Building on her professional background in the arts, she co-founded a non-governmental organization in the US to support the arts in Cuba. Her first return trip to the country that she had left at age one in 1959 so transformed her into a "born again Cuban" that she wanted to do something to help islanders. The group she co-founded collected donations of dance shoes and outfits, music sheets, paint supplies, and the like, for Cubans. It also raised funds in the US for island non-political cultural projects, the only cross-border projects that were allowed under the embargo.

Alejandra, the school director who also emigrated as a youngster in the early years of the revolution, was similarly so "turned on" by her first return trip in 1998 that she decided to make documentaries portraying life in Cuba for commercial distribution in the US. While Liliana sought to improve cultural life in Cuba, Alejandra wanted to make island culture accessible to Americans who did not know Cuba first-hand. Alejandra wanted to highlight positive aspects of the revolution, especially in education and healthcare, so that the American people could see that "not everyone in Cuba lives in concentration camps." Alejandra's professional quality videos visually humanized life in Cuba to US viewers, demystifying the "diabolic Other" that for decades had helped sustain the personal embargo. She formed a non-profit group that oversaw the production and distribution of her videos, and when on the island she elicited the help of Cubans for her video projects.

Social and Athletic

One trip-taker with whom I spoke, Natalio, informally organized a cross-border athletic "league." It built up good-will and bonding at the people-to-people level. Natalio, the former high school teacher who emigrated to Miami in 1981 where he became a small businessman, never broke off ties with Cuba where his father, daughter, and ex-wife still live. He made nine return trips to see them. Feeling good about earlier visits, in 1997 he decided to organize an annual informal softball tournament in his Old Havana neighborhood. Local players competed against a visiting émigré team he put together. While at first involving only adults, he later added youth teams. With the Miami teams getting together during the year to practice and to fundraise for equipment and uniforms for their Havana counterparts, the sports exchange strengthened community on both sides of, as well as across, the Straits.

Natalio's initiative was popular and successful because he built on Cubans' passion for baseball, a sport Americans brought to Cuba before the revolution.[5] But his initiative was popular also because he did not politicize the competition. Cubans he involved on the two sides of the Straits responded much more positively to the cross-border competition that he organized than had Exiles to the so-called baseball diplomacy that President Clinton and Castro sponsored in 1999. Trying to serve as athletic gatekeepers, hardline Exiles had first tried to prevent the games the two governments permitted, and after failing to do so protested at and politicized the play-off in Baltimore (see Chapter 3).

The Cuban and Cuban American teams that Natalio informally organized, which built on shared bi-national sports enthusiasm, were modest in scale compared to the state-to-state brokered games. But in building bridges they were more effective.

Religious

Religious groups engage in the most extensive, routine, and organized cross-border bridge-building.[6] Protestants, Jews, and Afro-Cuban sects,[7] along with Catholics, proselytize and promote religious-based activity on the island. Their involvements mushroomed after the Cuban government became more permissive of religion in the 1990s.

The transnational religious activity varies, however, among émigré waves. Catholic, Jewish, and long-established Protestant denominations mainly involve Exiles, while evangelical Protestants mainly involve the New Cubans.

Elisa and José, from families that emigrated soon after the revolution, demonstrate how Catholic Church-based visits inspired some to involve themselves subsequently not only in religious but also in secular civic bridge-building groups. They were so moved by their visits that upon returning to Miami they became active in new groups with cross-border reach, and made subsequent trips to Cuba in conjunction with the groups. José, who emigrated with his family soon after Castro assumed power and who described himself as deeply conservative, returned to Cuba for the first time in 1998. He went to hear one of the Pope's masses. Emotionally moved, he made a second trip soon thereafter with Catholic Charities Miami, and he reinvigorated a conservative international lay organization with close ties to the Vatican in which his family had been active before the revolution. The group in Cuba had become moribund once most of its anti-Castro members fled the country, and it was not revitalized in Miami until José took the initiative after his first return trip. Revitalized, the group began to send money and medical supplies to Cuba, and it sponsored island parish-level social service projects. As he noted, such formal involvements were more typical of his émigré wave than of New Cubans.

Inspired as well by her trip during the Pope's visit, Elisa, in turn, became a cross-border bridge-building activist upon her return to Miami. Through non-religious as well as religious groups she went on to travel to Cuba multiple times, and inspired others to follow her example.

Some religiously based cross-border involvements that visits inspired were more modest in scale. For example, a Hialeah woman who left Cuba in the early 1980s and first returned as a representative of a Catholic group during the Pope's trip, was also so moved by her visit that she maintained contact with Cuban Catholic counterparts once back in the US. Inspired by her visit, she even contemplated returning to Cuba to do missionary work.

But not all religious-based visits became springboards for subsequent cross-border organizational involvements. When émigrés filtered their stays through lenses that confirmed their negative preconceptions, upon returning to the US some "reverted" to honoring the travel taboo they had defied. This happened especially to self-defined exiles who had no island family with whom to bond and who found their formal contacts alienating. Marcela's experience is illustrative. Having emigrated in the early 1960s at age ten, she went to Cuba twice in the early 1990s as a representative of a Presbyterian group. Her Presbyterian contingent met with the Party official in charge of religious affairs to try to expedite setting up a church-sponsored social service agency on the island. With no family left in Cuba, she focused on her social and religious mission and was unhappy with what she experienced. "They were bunkers of Hitler, unfriendly. I know our conversations were recorded." She had such an alienating experience that she decided never again to go to Cuba under Castro or even to complete the Presbyterian initiative. Her trips confirmed her antipathy to the revolution and to Castro, learned from her parents as a child.

Evangelical groups that mainly involve New Cubans far overshadow such established Protestant denominations in their cross-border reach. Evangelicals use homeland visits to proselytize. Some also bring resources from their US congregations to sister congregations on the island.

The Jewish community in Cuba, in contrast, is a fraction of what it once was. Most island Jews left in the first years of the revolution, with the exodus of the well-to-do. But beginning in the 1990s, as the Cuban government became more tolerant of religion, and the US as well as Cuban government more permissive of trip-taking by religious groups, Cuban American Jews, known as Jubas for their coupled identity as Cubans and Jews, through their visits revitalized the island Jewish community that their families had abandoned. Some also became cross-border Jewish-based bridge-builders. They helped island Jews rediscover their religious heritage, and helped them materially. Through the Joint Distribution Committee, Cuban American Jews restored island synagogues, sent pharmaceuticals, and coordinated visits by doctors who tend to people with medical needs on their trips.[8] Ramón, a retired computer programmer who emigrated to Miami during Castro's first years of rule, for example, belongs to a Jewish group that collects clothing, medicines, and eyeglasses for the small remaining island Jewish community. He routinely travels to Cuba with donations, and takes advantage of his visits to bond with Jewish people there. The personal relationships he established serve as a bedrock for repeat trips.

Political

Explicitly political people-to-people cross-border activity is limited, and, at times, covert and illegal, because the Cuban government screens which émigrés it lets in and what they can do. Cuban officials viewed the overtly political as the most subversive cross-border activity, as possible seeds of regime transformation.

Exiles accounted for most of the politically engaged, with their political agenda worked out in advance. Some of them focused on promoting cross-border dialogue and reconciliation, others on explicitly promoting island political change.

Some new, small pro-democracy anti-Castro groups, committed to bridge-building, reconciliation, and dialogue, were formed in the 1990s. The Committee for Cuban Democracy was one. Most of its members had left Cuba in the 1960s in their youth. Perceiving the embargo as counter-productive, they cultivated ties with island dissidents who shared their views. They also favored rights to family visits, perceiving the family as a fundamental building block of society. However, limited in resources and number, the group never became a major political player in Miami and Washington, much less in Cuba.

There also are some Cuban Americans who, inspired by their visits, took it upon themselves, as individuals, to promote political bridge-building. In this vein, the previously noted businessman who emigrated before the revolution decided after a trip to Cuba in the early 1990s to try to promote dialogue between politicians on the two sides of the Straits. On subsequent trips he scheduled meetings with middle-level officials whom he found "understood the need for change" and whom he found more politically accommodating than their US counterparts. He went on to foster bridge-building through a Cuban American group affiliated to the Democratic Party to which he belonged. An initial trip, not politically motivated, inspired his subsequent cross-border political involvements.

Conclusion

In sum, the émigrés who defied the politically constructed wall across the Straits that most Exiles defended even when both US and Cuban authorities permitted homeland trips, typically experienced their visits through interpretative frames that they assumed before emigrating. Consequently, the first who fled the revolution were negative and political in how they viewed their trips, while the New Cubans were apolitical, family-focused, and empathic. For émigrés of both waves, trips tended to be self-fulfilling prophecies. They experienced the country the way they expected to. Child immigrants were the most varied in their reactions to trips, differing depending on the range of influences to which they had been exposed by the time that they were old enough to interpret life for themselves. Children of Exiles who viewed visits most positively had almost without exception spent some of their youth away from Exile influence.

And while for most travelers visits were an individual and family affair, for some, they became a building block for cross-border organizational involvement. The cohort lenses through which émigrés filtered visits here also came into play, influencing the type of activity in which they engaged. However, all organizationally grounded bridge-builders faced institutional obstacles that truncated and set parameters to their transnational activity. Of far greater consequence in impact have been the people-to-people transnational economic ties that the crisis of the 1990s unleashed, which mainly involve the humble New Cubans. The next chapters address these ties and their impact.

6 Transforming Transnational Ties into Economic Worth

Cubans' transnational ties came to have economic worth as émigrés generously shared their new country earnings with family members they had left behind. Although remittance-sending rarely occurred during the Soviet era, the annual infusion of diaspora dollars surged from an estimated $50 million in 1990 to over a billion dollars at the start of the new millennium (see Table 6.1),[1] with the US believed to account for 80–90 percent of all remittances that islanders received.[2]

The survey research firm, Bendixen and Associates, found in their survey of one thousand Cuban Americans in 2005 that over half of those living in Miami, and 41 percent nationwide, shared earnings with people in their homeland, and over half of the remitters shared earnings with two or more islanders.[3] Moreover, once transnational income-sharing took off, it quickly became routinized. Eighty-six percent of the US remittance-senders noted that they sent money home at least twice yearly, one-third of them said they sent money monthly.[4] Meanwhile, from the Cuban side of the Straits, two-thirds of a small sample, of 175 non-randomly selected people, reported the same year that they had received remittances five to eight times annually from persons abroad.[5]

Cubans are far from the only immigrants to send remittances to their homeland. Remittances to Latin America quadrupled in the 1990s, and by 2007 totaled $66.5 billion.[6] Although Cuba's post-1990 rate of increase was five times greater than the regional average, its 1990 base was lower than that of most other countries in the region.

How to explain Cuban immigrants belatedly joining the regional bandwagon, and infusing dollars into a socialist economy where the government for years had made dollar possession illegal? Although I show ordinary Cubans on the two sides of the Straits to have brought about the change, remittance-sending remained partially contextually contingent. First delineating how during the Soviet era both the US and Cuban governments, and ordinary Cubans on the two sides of the Straits, kept remittance flows at bay, I show, afterwards, how Washington and Exiles remained the key obstacles. US remittance policy became embedded in the Exile-backed presidential election cycle, in tandem with travel policy. But I proceed to show that despite the obstacles, with the arrival of New Cubans, new islander yearning for remittances, the development

Table 6.1 Remittance-sending to Cuba, the Dominican Republic, and El Salvador

	Cuba	Dominican Republic	El Salvador
(a) Millions of dollars			
1980	—	183	11
1985	—	242	126
1990	50	315	322
1995	537	794	1,061
1999	800	1,519	1,374
2000	1,030	1,800	1,800
2005	800[a]	2,700	2,800
(b) Average annual dollar remittance per Cuban, Dominican, and Salvadoran immigrant in the US in:			
1980	—	1,083	116
1990	67	882	681
1999	848	2,237	1,805
2005	844	3,885	2,498
(c) Average annual dollar remittance per home country resident in:			
1990	5	45	64
1995	48[b]	99	177
2000	92	176	292
2005	71	251	404
(d) Annual amount of total remittances as a percent of GDP			
1990	.5[c]	5	6
1999	5	15	17
2005	3	13	18

Sources: Central Banks for Dominican Republic and El Salvador (as compiled by Manuel Orozco, personal communication, and analyzed in his "Globalization and Migration," 2001); ECLAC 2000; USBC, *Statistical Abstract of the US 1992*, p. 42 and *2000*, p. 48; World Bank, *World Tables 1995*, p. 249; UNFPA 1990, p. 35; EIU, *CCR* February 2001, p. 22 and November 2006, p. 5; WB, *WDI 2001*, pp. 12, 44, 362, *2006* and *2007* (web.worldbank.org and web.worldbank.org/WBSITE/external/datastatistics); WB, *WDR 1997*, pp. 220, 248 and *2002*, p. 232; *New York Times* April 17, 2003: 6; Spadoni 2003, p. 420; Orozco 2007; ONE 2001, p. 2; Inter-American Dialogue 2004; Inter-American Development Bank 2007, p. 5; Migration Policy Institute, *MPI Data Hub* (www.migrationinformation.org/datahub/countrydata/data.cfm).

Notes:
a Personal communication, Manuel Orozco.
b Based on mid-1995 population estimate, Manuel Orozco.
c Mid-1991.

of new island norms that provide a bedrock for desire for dollars, the emergence of new transnationally grounded businesses, and new informal reward for income-sharing, remittance-sending surged. I show, though, that the changes did not suffice to induce immigrants from Cuba to remit as much as immigrants from a number of other Latin America countries, including from the Dominican Republic and El Salvador, with roughly similar-sized homeland populations. For Cubans, constraining forces remain.

In this chapter I draw on my interviews in Cuba as well as in the US and on US and Cuba survey and statistical data, official documents, and secondary sources.

Barriers to the Formation of Transnational Ties of Material Worth During the Era of "Soviet Solidarity," 1959–89

Cuban Americans remitted little to island family between 1959 and 1989 not because of lack of money. They shared less with people in their homeland than many other Caribbean and Central American émigrés even though they were wealthier.[7] Government policies, community norms, and informal social pressures kept remittance-sending low. The very forces that minimized cross-border sociability also restrained cross-border income-sharing.

Institutional Barriers

Both the US and Cuban governments restricted cross-border income-sharing during the Cold War. As they prioritized their own institutional, ideological, and political concerns, they kept émigrés from sharing their new country earnings with the family they had left behind.

Because transnational remittance-sending at the time had been minimal, Washington did not set up any specific legislation to regulate it when instituting the embargo. At the same time, Washington provided no legally sanctioned means whereby Cuban immigrants could send money to family still in Cuba.[8]

President Carter was the only Cold War President to lift barriers to diaspora cross-border income-sharing. His administration permitted Cuban Americans to remit up to $500 quarterly to their island family, and an additional $500 to cover emigration costs. It also made package-sending easier. President Reagan, however, reined in Carter's options.[9]

The Cuban government, in turn, gave islanders little reason to covet remittances. During the Soviet era it kept dollar possession and most private economic activity that dollars might finance illegal, except when permitting émigré visits under Carter. The Cuban government also discouraged islanders from coveting a materialist lifestyle that remittances might allow, as well as from maintaining ties with émigrés who might share some of their new country earnings.

The Party, along with the government, relied on more than the law to keep transnational people-to-people economic ties at bay. They set norms and manipulated job access in ways that discouraged islanders from such ties. Islanders were to emulate the revolutionary "new man" that Che Guevara symbolized and morally called for. The ideal revolutionary, as noted in Chapter 1, was non-materialist, selfless, and committed to the good of society, not personal gain. Membership in the selective Party, as well as job promotions, hinged on revealing no markers of diasporic ties. Although the country's leadership never completely prevented Cubans from receiving money and goods from family who emigrated, it offered no positive and numerous negative incentives for such acquisitions.

Informal Barriers

During the Cold War most Cubans on both sides of the Straits complied with their respective government's regulations. While Chapters 2 and 3 described how Exiles helped each other economically, their economic solidarity stopped at the border.

Hardline Exiles had, from their vantage point, many principled reasons for not sharing their new country earnings, even as they shared in the American Dream. They did not want to infuse money into their homeland economy under a government they despised. They accordingly favored a people-to-people economic embargo along with the social wall across the Straits.

Early émigrés were more willing to send presents in-kind. But because few of them made homeland trips except in the Carter years, they had to rely on the mail for gift-giving, without confidence that their island family would receive what they sent. The most hardline in their midst, moreover, opposed gift-giving in kind as well as cash, and used violent means to enforce their stance. Sometimes they placed explosives in mailings. This gave island officials a pretext to confiscate packages, which further disinclined émigrés from mailing gifts. Juan Enrique, who as a child of the revolution had stayed in Cuba when his parents left in 1962, for example, told me how his mother occasionally sent him packages. But she stopped after she heard that someone in Miami had put a bomb into one of her mailings.

Ordinary islanders gave Exiles added reason not to send remittances, in-kind as well as cash. Those who internalized the values of the revolution or who feared the negative consequences of demonstrating material markers of diaspora ties discouraged their family from gift-giving. Imported gifts took on a negative symbolic value in the new society in formation. In this vein, Pavel, a Party-member cinematographer, remembers receiving packages from his family who left in 1960. "When the packages started arriving . . . I remember thinking, 'Who do they think we are?' They sent packages with the most basic items, such as Colgate toothpaste and brand-name shampoo. I was outraged by their lack of understanding . . . We didn't fight a revolution for Colgate toothpaste! We fought for more important rights."

Materialism fell out of favor in the 1960s when officials aggressively pushed to create "the new man" and to transition rapidly to an egalitarian communist society concerned with the collective good and not private gain.[10] Captivated by the revolutionary élan, Cubans resented "*gusanos*" who defied and sabotaged the moral, anti-materialist precepts of the new society in the making. Thus, for such loyal revolutionaries as Pavel, transnational gift-giving soured transnational social ties that political differences independently wore thin.

Co-workers and neighbors, meanwhile, convinced Cubans who were not won over by the state-sanctioned norms of the new society that they should conceal any gifts received from abroad. They informally served as moral police on the Cuban side of the Straits. "You didn't want to show that you had clothing from abroad or signs of American influence," a Catholic agency employee recounted. She added that people who received gifts "were very careful when and where they used them." They worried that their neighbors who were Party and mass organization activists might report them.[11]

In a similar vein, the 1967 émigré, Dario, who works for the Department of Homeland Security, remembers that when he visited Cuba in 1983 his cousin showed him a closet filled with packages his mother had sent from the US. The cousin pleaded with Dario to tell his mother to stop sending clothing because he and his family "don't want them and can't wear them." As a university professor, he could not dress in American apparel, in that the dress code at the time was anti-American. Were he to have worn the clothing, he would have aroused suspicion and gotten in trouble. Because Cubans recognized US clothes when they saw them, and because the embargo kept out US goods, an imported wardrobe revealed ties with Cubans who rejected the revolution. Signs of such ties could jeopardize careers.

Dario's cousin's experience illustrates how Cubans who wished to succeed in the state socialist hierarchy needed to be non-materialist and un-American in their presentation of self. In stashing gifts away, the cousin treated the material goods as artifacts, relics of a lifestyle that had fallen out of favor with the revolution. That he held on to the artifacts rather than discard them suggests an ambivalence on his part.

Public conformity served to reinforce the norms of the new society, regardless of islanders' private yearnings. The impersonal manner in which family in the diaspora sometimes sent packages, or envelopes with money, had a comparable effect. Islanders were miffed when items arrived without letters. Émigrés often omitted notes because they did not want their island relatives to get into trouble. However considerate their motives, they violated islander gift-giving norms embedded in Cuban culture. How one gave gifts became contentious and drove a further wedge between families on the two sides of the Straits. Meanwhile, impersonal gift-giving kept cross-border material-sharing from strengthening transnational solidarity.[12] Thus, Pavel, the cinematographer, also complained that his aunts in the US "never sent personal letters telling us about their lives or asking us about ours." He could not help but question their motives. "Did they want to impress me with how much better off they were in Miami?" For similar reasons he resented a cousin who never wrote. "He just sent money. I was appalled."

While informal and formal constraints kept material transfers at bay, some families who reconfigured across borders defied the norms of the new society. Not internalizing the new norms, they coveted gifts from overseas kin and evaded barriers that stood in their way. They did so quietly and covertly, without public fanfare. One woman with whom I spoke had an aunt who emigrated before the revolution who "always helped our family. She used to send gifts, though now (since the 1990s) she sends money." Emigrating before Castro took power and therefore not caught up in the revolutionary struggle and opposition to it, the aunt never accepted the Exile hardline. Similarly, a man admitted that since 1974 his family had received help from family who had moved to Spain. Even under Franco, Spain never prohibited ties with socialist Cuba.

Most islanders, in sum, shied away from transnational ties of material worth not merely because institutional barriers stood in the way. They resisted such ties also because they believed in the revolution and the norms it instilled, because they felt informal pressure to comply with the anti-materialist norms of the new society even if they personally coveted gifts, and because they feared the consequences of the material demonstration of diasporic ties. The situation changed dramatically, though, when émigrés loaded with gifts visited in large numbers during the Carter years. Carter's temporary lifting of the travel embargo did more to induce islanders to question anti-materialist revolutionary precepts than Washington's state-level embargo.

The Transformation of Cross-Border Ties into Material Worth: The Cuban Crisis of the 1990s

Barriers to people-to-people cross-border material sharing broke down more when the Soviet Union's demise fueled a subsistence crisis. The crisis led islanders to put revolutionary principles, professional and political ambitions, and private fears of diasporic ties aside and turn to family abroad for help. Barriers initially broke down informally, covertly, and illegally, but then, on the Cuban side, formally as well. Nonetheless, state barriers remained, on the US, but also the Cuban, side of the Straits, which influenced how much émigrés remitted, for what, and how. Also, for remittances to be forthcoming, Cubans in the diaspora needed to become willing income-sharers.

Changes in Cuba

As the economy slipped into a deep recession that the Cuban government euphemistically referred to as the Special Period in Peacetime, islanders reenvisioned overseas family as a potential economic asset. They ceased to see transnational ties as a liability. With the crisis leaving them unable to survive on rationed offerings that remained affordably priced but insufficient in quantity, they turned to the diaspora for dollars to finance black market purchases that became essential for sheer survival. Prices for goods in the black market became unaffordable on official earnings. Thus, in desperation, Cubans tried to convince family abroad to by-pass state regulations that stood in the way and to defy Exile opposition to remittance-sending.

The new obsession with survival immediately led Cubans to reimagine the diaspora. As Jesús, a child psychiatrist in Havana, noted:

During the moments of most extreme hardship in the Special Period it was really remarkable . . . People couldn't eat . . . There was a feeling of desperation and a striking feeling of being rescued by those abroad . . . A flood of "rescue packages" suddenly arrived in the neighborhoods . . . People received money and packages, including from people they had never previously met. This is when there was a sudden change in perceptions of and relations with family abroad.

Even though he was a Party activist, he was emotionally moved by the outpouring of generosity. His Miami relatives, including young cousins whom he had never met, "went out of their way to be generous and express their solidarity." The crisis led him, like many other once-committed revolutionaries, to rethink not only their views toward those who emigrated but also their views toward material support from them.

Cubans typically took the lead in convincing family abroad to income-share. For many, this was not psychologically easy. In reaching out to overseas relatives they implicitly acknowledged both the failure of the revolution to meet their most basic needs, and the wisdom of those who left. Pedro, a city planner, echoed the view of many islanders at the time. He spoke of how "many families who had cut contact with their relatives had to swallow their pride and initiate contact . . . It was the only way to survive the crisis."

Lourdes even turned to assistance from a previously estranged relative. The timing of the crisis could not have been worse for her. Just when the economy was sinking into deep recession she, with a six-year-old child, divorced her adulterous alcoholic husband. To make matters worse, she had quit her job to take care of her sick aunt and uncle. The money she made informally as a masseuse was not enough to support her family. She managed only because her relationship with her mother in Miami improved in the context of the crisis. Her mother began to send medicines and clothing, as well as money. Lourdes' feelings towards her mother suddenly changed, even though deep down she remained resentful that her mother had abandoned her when she joined the Mariel exodus. New material bonding with her mother masked unhealed psychological wounds.

If Cubans in crisis did not find it easy to reach out to relatives whom they had previously rejected, their wonderful sense of humor made coping somewhat easier. Islanders jokingly redefined gift-giving *gusanos* as *mariposas*, worms transformed into butterflies. And they joked of having *fe*, the Spanish word for faith, but short for *familia en el exterior*, family abroad. With the crisis, of course, transnational kinship ties were no laughing matter. The alternative for many in the first years after Soviet aid and trade ended was near-starvation.

Islanders differed, however, in their success at transforming diaspora ties into economic worth. Having family abroad was no guarantee that help would be forthcoming. Some Cubans who put former political differences aside faced relatives abroad who remained deeply opposed to the revolution and unwilling either to forgive or forget. They refused to send any money, or they helped only sparingly so that their island kin could cover their most basic subsistence needs. As Cubans under Castro broke with the norms of the revolution, many Exiles remained entrenched in their pre- and anti-revolution mindset that put politics above family.

Relations among some families divided by the revolution were so damaged that Cubans could not call on them even when they were in dire need. Mercedes, a divorced journalist who at age fifteen found herself unexpectedly living with her grandmother, is a case in point. As a teenager, she was captivated by the utopian movement to build a new, just society. But her mother, like Lourdes' mother, fled to Miami. She left "without a good-bye." "Initially my mother and I corresponded by letter, but there was so much conflict between us. She was very critical of the revolution, and her letters attacked everything I believed in and worked for." Mercedes added that her mother

> was more concerned about her political beliefs than about how I felt. She gave me no emotional support. I became bitter and aggressive. Finally, her letters became so painful that I asked her to stop writing. I said "It would be better not to write because the day the Americans invaded we would be on opposite sides killing each other . . . [W]e would never agree." We never wrote to each other again. I don't know if my mother is dead or alive. We have not spoken in over thirty years.

Although desperate for assistance, Mercedes felt it would be hypocritical to start looking for her mother

When islanders emigrated individually in the post-Soviet era they often left as part of what they called "a family project." Families strategized to send their most employable family members abroad, young adults, on the assumption that those leaving, unlike in the past, would maintain homeland ties and income-share. Cubans accordingly cultivated the creation of new diasporic ties. They did not merely rely on ties of old. Bendixen and Associates' surveys show island parents to be the main beneficiaries of the new transnational income-sharing.[13] Parental favoritism points to a new transnationally embedded inter-generational normative commitment.

Beginning in the Special Period, Cubans also took temporary work abroad to become, in essence, their own source of remittances. When attaining such work they tried to save their earnings to use upon their return home. Similarly, Cubans who attended professional conferences abroad pocketed as much of their per diem allowances and stipends that they received as possible, for homeland use. These Cubans often shared some of their foreign earnings with island family, at times extracting favors in return. One unmarried woman social scientist told me of how in exchange for hard currency earned abroad that she shared with a male relative, he helped her with household repairs.

Although the new impetus for the formation of transnational ties of economic worth came from ordinary Cubans, amidst the crisis the government became more tolerant of the cross-border income-sharing and even initiated reforms to make remittance-sending more likely. The initiatives, and reasons for the state's changed stance, are detailed in the following chapter. Relevant here, the changes removed obstacles to, and tacitly encouraged, family income transfers.

Changes in the US

While Cubans and the Cuban government came to look more favorably on the diaspora and its dollars, Washington lawmakers, with Exile backing, did not respond in kind. Quite to the contrary, they became more obstructive. Presidents, however, vacillated in the barriers they set, responding most to hardline Exile wishes when running for reelection, with their eyes on the Florida electoral prize. They modified their remittance policy in tandem with their travel policy, the two key components of what became known as the personal embargo.

US remittance restrictions were designed to limit Cuban government access to hard currency. In that Cuba depended almost exclusively on hard currency in the post-Soviet era for trade, investment, and foreign loan repayments, as detailed in the next chapter, hardline Exiles reasoned that without access to diaspora dollars the Castro-led regime might collapse.

Responding to Exile lobbying on the eve of his reelection bid, President George H. W. Bush accepted a proviso in the Cuban Democracy Act that he signed into law to restrict remittance-sending. It specified that remittances to Cuba be limited to financing travel to the United States. The restrictions were to remain in effect until the US President determined, and reported to Congress, that the Cuban government had instituted democratic reforms and moved toward establishing a free market economic system.[14]

Clinton introduced new restrictions, never having recognized, upon taking office, the Cuban Democracy Act ban on income transfers other than to finance immigration. And in 1994 he prohibited the sending of gift parcels as well as cash, except on a case-by-case basis for island family faced with extreme humanitarian emergencies. Then, the Cuban Liberty and Democratic Solidarity Act which he signed into law in 1996 specified, in a so-called sense of Congress, that the Cuban government permit the "unfettered operation of small businesses" before the US reinstate general licenses for sending of family remittances to Cuba.

The same election considerations, combined with bilateral crises, that led to tightening both the embargo and visitation rights, explain why Clinton clamped down on remittance sending prerogatives in 1994 and 1996. While preoccupied with reelection, in 1994 he faced the so-called rafter crisis, and in 1996 the Cuban shooting down of planes flown by the Exile group Brothers to the Rescue.

After 1996, however, when ineligible for reelection, Clinton lifted remittance along with travel restrictions, as my Cuban American policy cycle thesis would predict. In 1998, he reinstated the right of Cuban Americans to remit up to $300 quarterly to island family, even though the economic changes in Cuba that were specified as prerequisite in the Cuban Liberty and Democratic Solidarity Act had not transpired. He argued, contrary to the stated logic in the 1996 legislation, that cross-border people-to-people economic, along with social, ties might improve state-to-state relations. Then, in January 1999, he relaxed remittance-sending rights even further, in announcing that all US citizens, whether or not they had close family on the island, could send up to $1,200 in remittances annually (except to high-level Cuban officials).

In 2003, an off-election year, George W. Bush, Clinton's Republican successor, made remittance policy even more permissive. Deploying his discretionary power, his administration announced that travelers could take with them on visits up to $3,000, above and beyond the $300 they could send quarterly from the US. However, when running for reelection, Bush became far more restrictive than Clinton, in his remittance as in his visits policy. Bush lowered the amount of remittances trip-takers could carry with them on visits to $300, and he narrowed the range of islanders with whom Cuban Americans could income-share to the same immediate kin to whom he had restricted visitation rights that year. The income-transfer cap allowed Cuban émigrés to remit one-third to one-half the amount the average Latin American immigrant at the time shared with their family in their homeland.[15]

In 2004, Bush also clamped down on Cuban American rights to gift-give in-kind.[16] His administration capped the weight of luggage travelers could take on trips to forty-four pounds. Previously there had been no cap, with the average estimated weight of traveler luggage sixty pounds. The Bush administration also curtailed the range of goods permissible to be mailed, capped the value of sendable goods, and restricted packages, along with income transfers, to immediate family. Cuban Americans could only send food, radios, batteries, vitamins, medicines, and medical equipment, with a monthly value no greater than $200. They could not send clothing, seeds (for growing food to meet subsistence needs), and personal hygiene items, which were previously permissible.[17]

The tightening of remittance restrictions, along with travel restrictions, contributed to an estimated 20 percent drop-off in cross-border income transfers the first year Bush's 2004 regulations came into effect (see Table 6.1). In that many Cuban émigrés had relied on trip-taking for income-sharing, Bush's travel crackdown contributed to the decline in income-sharing.

When clamping down on remittance-sending rights Bush responded to Exile pressures, in the middle of his reelection bid. He, like Clinton before him, subordinated family values to electoral opportunism. He sought to placate outspoken hardline Cuban American personal embargo proponents that he counted on to deliver the Florida vote.

Thus, between 1992 and 2004, on the US side of the Straits, remittance policy, like visits policy, became embroiled in electoral politics to the point of becoming a component of the foreign policy cycles hardline Exiles pressed for.

But Bush tightened the personal embargo in 2004, against the backdrop of nearly half of registered Cuban American voters sending remittances to island relatives.[18] It was against this backdrop that Obama, in his 2008 Presidential bid, broke with precedent and promised, if elected, to lift the personal embargo on remittances along with travel restrictions.

Who Remits and For What?

Who Remits?

Diaspora generosity surged, until 2004, against the backdrop of Washington obstacles, Cuban American leadership opposition, and a tradition of minimal if any cross-border income-sharing partly because some Exiles had a change of heart when their island family faced near-famine, but mainly because of changing diaspora demographics. The New Cubans, who increased in number by approximately twenty thousand a year since the 1994 and 1995 US-Cuban immigration accords went into effect, moved abroad commited to transnational income-sharing. Their views toward economic generosity were shaped by the island crisis that they experienced before uprooting.

Florida International University's surveys of Miami Cuban Americans in 2004 and again three years later found that two and one-half times as many of the New Cubans as 1959-to-1964 émigrés had sent remittances at least once (see Table 6.2). More new immigrants than Soviet-era arrivals sent remittances even though they had far fewer years in the US in which to income-share, just as they were more likely to have made homeland trips. They also sent more money. In 2003, New Cubans were nearly four times as likely as the first émigrés who fled the revolution to send $1,000 or more. They sent more even though, overall, as noted in Chapter 2, they were far poorer.

Table 6.2 Percentage of Cuban Americans in Miami who sent remittances in 2004 and 2007 (2007 in parentheses)

| | *Year of arrival* | | | | | |
	1959–64	*1965–74*	*1975–84*	*1985+*	*US-born*	*Total*
Sent money to relatives	31 (31)	44 (45)	53 (51)	75 (1985–94:76) (1995–2007: 77)	52 (47)	54 (58)
Interviewee or family sent money in 2003	20	24	35	50	29	34
Sent over $1,000 in 2003	3	4	5	11	11	7

Source: FIU-IPOR, *FIU/Cuba Poll* 2004 and 2007 (www.fiu.edu/orgs/ipor/cuba2004/years.htm; www.fiu.edu/orgs/ipor/cuba8/pollresults.html).

Note: N = 1,811 in 2004 and 1,000 in 2007.

The survey by Bendixen and Associates in 2005 found, nationwide, and not merely in Miami, the poor, recent immigrants to be the most generous.[19] The firm's interviews point to an inverse correlation between income earned, as well as length of time in the US, and income shared. Three-fourths of the remittance-senders the firm interviewed had moved to the US since 1990. The richest émigrés, who left in the 1960s, accounted for only 5 percent of the remitters.

Bendixen and Associates also found in 2005 that immigrants who bonded most with island families were most apt to income-share. Eighty-eight percent of remittance-senders communicated by phone at least monthly with the person to whom they sent money.[20] Face-to-face visits, though less frequent than phone-calling, also came with income-sharing. Rare was the visitor who arrived empty-handed, without gifts in cash, kind, or both. Cross-border social and economic ties, in essence, were mutually reinforcing.

The Velazquez Institute, in turn, found that among over eight hundred Cuban Americans surveyed in Florida in summer 2004, views toward remittance-sending hinged on when émigrés had moved to the US and at what age.[21] The oldest Cuban Americans, whose generational formation rested on opposition to the revolution, were most likely to embrace Bush's 2004 people-to-people embargo tightening.

My survey of Cuban émigrés in Union City and Miami further confirms émigré cohort contrasts in remittance-sending (see Appendix). Nearly all post-Mariel arrivals, but only half of Exiles, income-shared. The New Cubans I interviewed also shared more on average: three times as many of them as the first who fled the revolution remitted more than $1,200 annually, the US government's legal maximum.

Recent arrivals have many of the personal attributes found in general to predispose immigrants to send remittances. Worldwide, studies show remittance-sending to be correlated with motivation for emigration, time lapse since emigration, kin still in homeland, country-of-origin language retention, frequency of homeland visits, and migrant income.[22] The archetypal international remittance sender is a recent immigrant who moved abroad to improve his or her economic lot, and who has family in the home country with whom he or she can linguistically communicate and with whom he or she bonds face-to-face.

Yet, Cuban émigré generosity can only partly be explained by such personal attributes. Most Exiles after forty years in the US still speak Spanish with family (Table 2.4), and they typically remit less than the poorer New Cubans.

Instead, the Cuban émigré experience demonstrates that cross-border income-sharing cannot be explained solely at the individual level. Individual attributes that influence transnational generosity need to be understood in a broader social context. Díaz-Briquets and Pérez-López explain the Cuban anomaly politically: refugees remit less than economic immigrants.[23] They correctly highlight that the first Cuban émigrés were not politically predisposed to cross-border income-share. But Díaz-Briquets and Pérez-López fail to recognize that it was Cuban émigrés' *interpretation* of themselves as refugees, as exiles and exiled, collectively as well as individually, that explains why they rarely sent remittances. The authors fail also to denote, and explain why, post-1990s émigrés, with their distinctive homeland experiences, tend to interpret their reason for uprooting differently than earlier arrivals, and accordingly subscribe to norms conducive to cross-border income-sharing.

While most of the self-defined exiles conformed with their émigré cohort's normative commitment to the people-to-people economic embargo, some who still had close relatives in Cuba at the time of the island crisis covertly defied what they publicly professed. They did not practice what they preached. Publicly, they reinforced Exile opposition to income transfers that helped the Castro-led government access hard currency. Privately though, they helped island family in need. They wanted other émigrés to do what they would not. Illustrative of this, in December 2001, the television program, *Sixty Minutes*, featured a well-known Miami radio talk show host who used the airwaves to attack remittance-sending. The producer of the program segment had learned that the radio commentator had sent money to island family. When she asked him in front of the television camera to explain the contradiction between his words and deeds, he retorted, "But he's my brother!" He felt exempt from the standards he set for others. Similarly, a journalist whom I interviewed in Union City the same year wrote about her opposition to remittance-sending, but she confessed to me that she sent money to her sister. In her words, she sent enough so that her sister would "not die." When personally forced to choose between political principles and filial loyalty, the latter mattered more to both media personalities.

Remittances for What?

For what purposes did émigrés income-share? Some usages defied preexisting island mores, and both US and Cuban regulations.

Remittance senders almost without exception saw themselves as helping island family purchase essentials. Bendixen and Associates, in their large national survey,[24] and I in my smaller Miami and Union City surveys (see Appendix), found this to be true. Remittance-senders intended their funds mainly to feed their island family. I found other intended purposes of remittances to be, in declining order of importance, for health needs, consumer goods purchases, home improvements, and small-scale business ventures.

Émigrés also remitted goods in-kind. They sent packages from the US and brought gifts on visits. I found medicines, together with eyeglasses and dentures, to be, by far, their main in-kind presents. Less frequently they gave clothing and items usable for small entrepreneurial ventures. It is important to note that I conducted my interviews with rank-and-file Cuban Americans before Bush's 2004 crackdown on package-sending rights and the weight of luggage travelers could take to Cuba.

Estimates in Cuba concur that around the turn of the century, cash remittances mainly financed family consumption.[25] Islanders resembled most Latin American remittance recipients in their usage of income transfers.[26]

The reliance on remittances for basic food, as well as for health needs, reflects a remarkable turn of events on the Cuban side of the Straits. The revolution in principle and for three decades in practice had guaranteed islanders an affordable if minimal diet and free health care. Usage of remittances for these purposes accordingly reflected a breakdown in state cradle-to-grave provisioning, a centerpiece of the country's socialist makeover. As of around 2004, more Cubans than Latin Americans in eight other countries used remittances to help address basic family needs.[27]

Only a few immigrants whom I interviewed, as noted in the Appendix, targeted funds for investment, and half of those investing upgraded their housing. While the Cuban government guaranteed that no person paid more than 10 percent of his or her earnings on housing, and while 86 percent of Cubans in the early 2000s lived in housing they owned,[28] over the years the quality of living quarters had fallen into severe disrepair. With dollars islanders could finance renovations, mainly with black market purchases, or finance house-swaps informally and extra-legally to upgrade where they lived. And with improved housing some Cubans converted their quarters into money-making businesses. They rented out rooms, converted their homes into bed-and-breakfasts patronized by tourists, and set up small restaurants.[29]

The few émigrés who targeted remittances for other investments provided cash or supplies for small family undertakings. Some ventures took on cross-border dimensions, as described below. But both the US and Cuban governments obstructed such investments, which could, if profit-making, reduce islander economic dependence on family abroad. The US embargo prohibited Americans from investing in Cuba, while the island government required private ventures to be owner-operated, to employ only family members, and to pay very steep (and regressive) taxes, which, combined, obstructed capital accumulation. And Havana authorities only allowed certain types of private activity, with the parameters of the permissible changing over the years.

Whether for consumption or investment, Cubans relied on remittances to supplement earnings from state sector jobs, the real value of which plunged in the post-Soviet era. Although officially the peso and dollar remained on par, the black market exchange rate soared to 130 pesos to the dollar in 1993. The peso subsequently recuperated some, but not all, of its former value. Goods the government distributed through the ration system remained affordable, but rationing came to cover no more than one-third to one-half of family needs.

The rank-and-file Cubans I interviewed reveal how important remittances had become to everyday life in the post-Soviet era. Nearly 70 percent of the over 80 percent who had family living abroad received remittances. Of the non-recipients, three of them had no need. They did well on their own in the new economy. One, Stefan, was a successful employee of a joint venture. He had a car, a beautiful home, a cell phone, and a computer, thanks to job perks and money he received "under the table" supplementing his meager official salary. The other two were fortunate to have good and well-located housing that they could convert into businesses to capitalize on the new tourism: one opened a very successful restaurant, the other opened a bed-and-breakfast. The others who received no remittances would have liked the material support. With one exception, their family had left in the early years of Castro's rule or during Mariel, and the interviewees had broken off ties with them beyond repair, owing to their opposing stance on the revolution. They, as a result, did not expect overseas family to income-share. But the brother of the one exception, a chef, had emigrated two years before we spoke, after a "marriage of convenience" to a foreigner which enabled him to leave the country. Reflecting how Cubans in the post-Soviet economy expected those who uprooted to income-share, the chef suspected that his brother sent money to their mother and that she hoarded it. He was deeply resentful as well as suspicious, and managed only because he illicitly took food home from work to feed his family.

Miamization of Cuban Norms

When possible, people came to use remittances for more than basic needs, as cross-border bonding transformed island norms and values. Cubans began to embrace openly the material lifestyle that the United States epitomized and their overseas relatives personified. They no longer needed to seek refuge abroad to be acquisitive. Cubans embraced the imported lifestyle to the point that the previous stigma of it disappeared. Dollars (and Cuban convertible currency) earned informally and at times illegally through tourism, black marketeering, and some state jobs, also contributed to the cultural transformation, but only remittance recipients were enmeshed in ongoing transnational ties that had such an effect.

I found that it did not take islanders long in the post-Soviet era to covet diaspora dollars for more than subsistence. Cubans came to welcome not just Colgate toothpaste that such "good revolutionaries" as Pavel, the cinematographer, had found so repugnant when deeply committed to the revolution in its early years, but soap, shampoo, detergent, and then electric fans, televisions, VCRs, prestige-label clothing and shoes, and other luxury items. By the early 2000s Cuban awareness of US brandnames had become among the highest in any non-English-speaking country.[30] Visiting émigrés, with their gifts and US-attained values, and US movies (including those seen on videos and DVDs visiting émigrés brought), contributed to the US-inspired consumerism. Remaining residues of "Che" Guevara's utopian vision of the "new man" joined the Soviet Union in the dustbin of history. Cubans ceased to consider materialist consumption as socially unacceptable. As a result, differences in lifestyle between families on the two sides of the Straits came to hinge increasingly on differences in purchasing power than on life perspectives. The economic crisis that led Cubans to reimagine the diaspora led them, in turn, to take on diaspora values.

So much did the taboo on American-style consumerism break down that Cubans proudly flaunted materialism in their everyday life. Island teenagers coveted comparable items to their US counterparts, Nikes, iPods, and the like.

Goods that in the heyday of revolutionary enthusiasm had symbolically served as sources of stigma and condemnation now came to carry cachet. "The Miami Cuban culture promotes lycra (spandex), puffy hair, lots of make-up, and gold," bemused a state enterprise employee to me when we spoke in 2002. With remittances from a sister who left in 1980 and from another who left in 1998, he painted his house, fenced it in, and furnished it with a TV, VCR, CD player, stereo, computer, wireless phone, and beautiful artwork. "Class distinctions have become more noticeable," he noted. He added that there is now a "new class . . . a disjunction . . . Many of those who (recently) migrated and their island families are lower class with limited education. But they have access to a lifestyle that is inaccessible to the professional class loyal to the revolution." The new consumerism, he correctly observed, came to hinge more on diaspora ties than on stature in the Cuban socialist hierarchy.

This man's home renovations revealed a new desire not merely to be materialist but conspicuously so. While families used to fix up the interior of their homes when economically possible, they left exteriors untouched. Commenting on the change, Pedro, the city planner, complained to me that "Now people put up fences and paint the outsides [of their homes]. They want to show that they are living better than their neighbors. They're into conspicuous consumption . . . It used to be taboo to show that you lived better than others."

Indicative of how enthusiastically acquisitive islanders had become, a sixty-year-old Havana woman proudly paraded around her neighborhood showing off a new Transcard she attained. The card permitted her to purchase goods at no personal cost. She boasted how she could spend hundreds of dollars with the card that her daughter, who emigrated after marrying an American in the late 1990s, had paid for.

Further contributing to the breakdown of the austere norms that the revolution initially inculcated was the rise of a new managerial class associated with firms involving foreign capital permitted in the post-Soviet era. They enjoyed a lifestyle that most islanders did not, including most remittance recipients. This "new class," which Stefan epitomized, drives imported cars, conspicuously walks around with cell phones, and employs gardeners, housekeepers, babysitters, and drivers, the sort of household help nearly obliterated with the class transformation in the early years of Castro's rule.

Popular culture partly made a parody of the materialist norms of the new Cuba. The film *Paradise under the Stars* captured the decadence of the materialistic turn, as a Havana taxidriver noted to me. The film depicts an immigrant who returns from Spain during a funeral. The driver commented on how "The Cubans were so excited about the gifts that they forgot about the funeral!"

Transnationalization of the Cuban American Community Economic Base

New Cuban transnational economic ties fueled and were fueled by economic changes in Miami as well. Entrepreneurial Cuban Americans, especially in such municipalities of Miami-Dade County as Hialeah where many New Cubans live, capitalized on and contributed to the new island consumerism.

For three decades the exile community was mainly inwardly oriented economically, as immigrants not only built up the ethnic enclave economy described in Chapter 2, but scorned dealings with Cuba under Castro. Cuba-oriented businesses risked community ostracism and boycott. In the words of a Miami businessman with whom I spoke, "If you didn't comply with the 'politically correct' way, they hurt your business. They called your customers and pestered you on the phone."

During the Soviet era, retribution for defying the community-sanctioned taboo on business with Cuba at times took a violent turn. Both the experiences of a previously noted Miami travel agent that booked flights, and the air charter company that transported people from the US to Cuba, testify to this. One of the main Cuban American travel agents for years felt the need to move around Miami with a bodyguard. Hardline Exiles referred to him as a Communist, which, while a badge of honor in Cuba, was a source of stigma in Miami. That the man himself fled the revolution early on did not matter to the critics. The stigmatization, as well as the violence, reinforced Exile boundaries of the economically permissible.

Perceptions of retribution lingered on after the Cold War, and constrained the economically ambitious in old Cuban American neighborhoods. But in new immigrant communities, Exiles who took it upon themselves to serve as "moral police," became ineffective. Recent arrivals, enmeshed in ties across borders, approvingly patronized neighborhood businesses with transnational reach.[31] Previously exclusively enclave-oriented businesses, including some that were Exile-owned, began in the 1990s to target the island market as well.

One new business that provided a bedrock for remittance-sending rested entirely on transnational trust. So-called *mulas* (mules), a name borrowed from the drug trade, made a business of carrying money and goods from the US to the island. Numbering possibly in the thousands, they were known through word-of-mouth.[32] Their businesses rested on their reputation, and on networks extending from émigré neighborhoods to customs officials to distributors in Cuba.

Many US-based *mulas* were self-employed. Around the turn of the twenty-first century they typically traveled to Cuba twice monthly, some through third countries so as to evade US travel and remittance restrictions. A number of them co-partnered with family on the island who helped deliver diaspora-sent gifts, both in cash and kind, to designated island recipients. Other *mulas* were hired by travel agencies that diversified their offerings to capitalize on the new demand for delivery services in the 1990s. Travel agency *mula* employees tended to be paid in-kind, with a plane ticket that allowed them to visit island family at no personal cost.

Some émigrés, though far fewer, set up informal "mini-banks." Four of the émigrés whom I interviewed reported making use of them to send money to island family. The "bankers" take deposits from co-ethnics whose island kin can withdraw the money almost immediately from island "bank" partners. Such "banks" had operated already in years past but in smaller numbers: when transnational ties were minimal, tense, and normatively taboo. Willy, the journalist who emigrated in 1994, for example, remembers a mini-bank that his father covertly and illegally operated in their provincial hometown in the early 1970s. His father, together with family who left for Miami in the early years of Castro's rule, ran a makeshift transnational financial venture. Émigrés put dollars into a bank account that Willy's relatives in the US set up. His father, upon receipt of telephone confirmation of deposits, distributed in pesos the money for whom the deposits were intended. His father thereby attained dollar savings in Miami that he later drew upon, and he profited from the differential between the official and unofficial dollar–peso exchange rate at the time. He paid island recipients at the less favorable official exchange rate. His father thereby accumulated capital outside the country, a rare occurrence in Cuba under Castro. His ability to do so hinged on personal ties and trust, which he, along with his Exile relatives, cultivated despite the then-countervailing pressures. Willy knew of at least three other transnational mini-banks that had operated in the provincial city where he had lived.

The long-standing mini-banks reveal that some Cubans who were divided by the revolution not only maintained ties when social pressures to sever them were strongest, but capitalized on them, and in ways that defied the embargo. Unlike *mulas*, the "bankers" required no travel to function.

In the post-Soviet era, *mulas* and "bankers" *created* niches for their informal, covert, and often illegal services by pricing their services somewhat below rates charged by formal remittance transfer businesses, by not insisting on compliance with US remittance-sending regulations with which formal transfer businesses had to comply, and by building on transnational ties and trust. *Mulas* and mini-bankers asked no regulatory questions.

Formal wire transfer businesses, in contrast, catered to Cuban Americans who wished to comply with US regulations and who believed the regulated businesses to be more dependable. Since they faced little competition in the Cuban market, these companies charged more to send money to Cuba than to other Caribbean and Central American countries,[33] and they kept the transfer costs to Cuba high when rates to other countries dropped.[34]

Around the turn of the century officially approved remittance companies transferred an estimated 25 to 40 percent of the money Cuban émigrés shared with island family. Most émigrés, the New Cubans above all, preferred to take the money with them when visiting, to ask friends and family who took trips to deliver money for them, or to rely on the informal couriers and, to a lesser extent, informal mini-banks. Ironically, Cubans received more money informally than Latin American remittance recipients in less regulated market economies in the region. However, under other names in other countries the equivalents of *mulas* also responded to the demand among new immigrants for informal cross-border transport of goods in cash and kind.[35]

Washington, more than Havana in the post-Soviet era, imposed remittance restrictions that had the unintended effect of driving monetary transfers underground. Many remitters, as well as recipients, favored bypassing regulations that left a paper trail and that restricted who could income-share, with whom, and how extensively.

Bush's 2004 remittance and travel clamp-down, however, drove a wedge into the informal transfer mechanisms. Bendixen and Associates found that 83 percent of the Cuban Americans they surveyed in 2005 reported relying on formal transfer agencies. The cut-back both in travel rights, to once every three years and to see only immediate family, and in the amount of money permissible to take on trips from $3,000 to $300, drastically reduced the frequency as well as the scale of cash-carrying émigré travel by both ordinary Cuban Americans and by *mulas*.[36]

Other informal businesses premised on cross-border ties and trust continued relatively immune to the new US regulations. In my interviews with émigrés I learned of a few such transnational ventures. An island-trained doctor, for example, who emigrated in the late 1990s without credentials to practice in the US, set up an "informal 1–800-Flowers for Cuba" business. Cuban Americans in Miami pay him for funeral arrangements for island family. The doctor-turned-businessman works with an island-based network to deliver food as well as flowers for island funerals. Another example involves a *mula* who diversified her offerings to include cross-border food delivery. With money collected from Miami clients the *mula* mobilizes her family in Cuba to purchase food from farmers that they deliver to persons the Cuban American customers designate.

Stores in Cuban American neighborhoods also came to cater to the Cuban alongside the local market. Pharmacies and shipping companies offer island delivery services. While some of these cross-border businesses pre-date the 1990s, their island reach expanded dramatically in scale and scope in the new immigrant era. Large stores that sell inexpensive merchandise, including in bulk, in addition, have come to target the Cuban market. Some of them advertise that they have "todo para Cuba," everything for Cuba. Prior to the new immigrant era such advertising might have prompted business boycotts by irate Exiles. The businesses, with new immigrants increasingly in their midst, began to consider it in their economic interest to encourage purchases for islanders.

Indicative of how stepped-up cross-border bonding fueled transnational retail trade, an owner of one of Hialeah's main mega-discount stores acknowledged in 2000 that most of the $1.2 million worth of goods he sold yearly ended up on the island.[37] With savvy business acumen, the store owner, a 1967 émigré, targeted the new immigrants whom he calculated wanted cheap items not merely for themselves but for their family in Cuba. He posted big welcoming signs outside his store when the 1994 rafters arrived. Cognizant that new immigrants do not make homeland visits empty-handed, the store owner, no friend of Fidel but prioritizing profits over politics, offered what he called "*gusano* bags" free of charge to clientele who spent $100 or more. His name for the bags jokingly played on the stigmatized name Cuban officials ascribed to the small pieces of luggage they permitted "*gusanos*" to take with them when they fled the revolution early on. The storeowners' bags were intended, however, to carry goods to, not from, Cuba.

So common did gift-bearing visits become that storeowners provided scales where customers could weigh merchandise, so as to comply with airline luggage-weight restrictions. And because of the luggage constraints, the Hialeah storeowner who offered the "*gusano* bags" astutely featured light-weight items that Cubans covet, such as cosmetics and mosquito netting.

Islanders, in turn, sometimes made profits from items that visiting relatives brought with them. They sold goods on the black market, especially items brought in bulk. And some Cubans established informal and typically illegal money-making rental businesses with goods émigrés brought. For example, islanders set up mini "Blockbusters," with videos and DVDs visiting relatives gave them. In these instances Cubans, in effect, turned themselves into emissaries of US storeowners, in the belly of the state-directed socialist economy.

Not all US businesses fueling island consumerism were Cuban American-owned. This was especially true of the multinational wire service companies. Cuban American storeowners, however, who housed wire services facilities in their stores, co-profited. Customers would likely buy goods once in the stores.

In sum, neither Cuban nor US government regulations blocked cross-border economic activity. Nonetheless, official policies kept much of the business informal and limited to the transfer of cash and consumer goods. Most of the retail trade, though, was based on items no longer manufactured in the US. The owner of the Hialeah discount store spoke on this point. He noted with irony that much of his business rested on selling goods manufactured in Communist China for consumption in Communist Cuba.

Symbolic Pay-Off of Generosity: The Transnationalization and Transformation of Social Status in Cuba

Whilst transfers of money and goods move almost entirely in one direction, from the US to Cuba, they impact on bases of stratification that straddle the Straits, involving mainly the New Cubans. With nothing material to offer émigrés in return for their generosity, islander remittance recipients reciprocate in-kind, symbolically. Valuing what is reciprocated, for the New Cubans, material sacrifice generates its own reward. The reciprocity, in turn, encourages them to continue to income-share. My interviews with Cubans on both sides of the Straits suggest several ways that generosity is symbolically rewarded, although appreciated mainly only by post-soviet era arrivals.

Remittance-sending in the post-Soviet era, for one, raised migrant home-land social standing, and in a manner that turned the 1959-to-1989 cross-border status schema on its head. Islanders began to reenvision émigrés, who previously had been pejoratively portrayed as worms and scum, as heroes. Jesús, the child psychiatrist, understood the situation well. "Once you leave Cuba (now)," he noted, ". . . you no longer are viewed as an exile, as a *gusano*, but as an outsider with an almost superhero aura. Even your family now sees you differently." Cubans who previously denigrated their compatriots who uprooted, as authorities had taught them to do, began to reimagine those abroad in a favorable light. The shift came during the crisis. The new stature was a reward for cross-border income-sharing.

Islanders, in turn, came to treat émigrés with new respect. Several Cuban Americans with whom I spoke felt the change. In this vein, a woman recounted to me how she experienced "almost a civil war" on the part of neighbors and co-workers when her family fled in the 1960s, and how she had eggs thrown at her when she attempted to flee from Mariel in 1980. But she marveled about how islander attitudes toward her changed in the 1990s. In 1980, she had been stigmatized as scum, subjected to repudiations by neigh-bors and co-workers, and treated like a criminal. She had been a victim of *actos de repudios*, the repudiation acts the Party encouraged against those who sought then to leave. Finally attaining permission to emigrate in the late 1980s, when she visited during the Special Period the same people who had turned on her in the past treated her, she felt, "like a *señora*," with dignity. Another woman who managed to leave from Mariel, and who returned yearly in the 1990s with thousands of dollars and gifts for island family, also came to feel like a distinguished guest on visits. In honor of one of her trips her family painted their house. And even Jesús, who never permanently emigrated but who took temporary work in Europe, felt more respected since working abroad.

Émigrés also experienced new deference. When visiting, some émigrés enjoyed privileges that were normally reserved for top island officials. One man recounted how he received special treatment when he made return trips to see his father. When he went to a taxi stand to get transportation in the provincial city where his father lived, he could go to the front of the line once he let it be known that he was from "*la comunidad*," the Miami Cuban community. Such preferential treatment began during the Special Period, when islanders, in need, reenvisioned the diaspora.

Income-sharing émigrés also gained new authority in Cuba. An unemployed Cuban woman, estranged from her mother who abandoned her when joining the Mariel exodus, for example, reenvisioned her mother in the 1990s as "the matriarch." The change came when her mother became her family's principal breadwinner.

New transnationally embedded authority is also patriarchal, and sometimes extends to relations that previously ended in divorce. Thus, Laurencio, the island-trained doctor who works as a factory laborer in Hialeah, feels more appreciated by his former wife's family than when he lived in Cuba, even though since moving he had become professionally *déclassé*. He noted that despite the break-up of the marriage, his influence over his ex-wife's household had increased since he emigrated. "Although I'm not living on the island, I have decision-making power both in my own and my former wife's household. My ex-wife doesn't work because of the money I send." He felt that the money he sends gives him authority over his wife's household that the divorce had truncated before he emigrated.

The very act of emigrating became so status-enhancing in the transnationalized context that how those who uprooted made a living mattered little. Pedro, the city planner, in this vein mentioned with dismay that Cubans now see those living abroad as superior regardless of their source of income. "They could be trash collectors! Cubans feel they are part of the elite." Similarly, a professional couple in Cuba who earned a combined monthly peso income equivalent to $30 from their public sector jobs, relied on a lump sum of $200 visiting relatives left them to buy such basic foods as cooking oil and milk for their children. The man disconcertedly noted that, "It's ironic. I'm better educated and I have a better career than my visiting relatives. Yet, I have to recognize that I couldn't survive without them. They are perceived by Cuban society and by my family as being members of a superior class, and we treat them that way."

Comparable status is not bestowed on Cubans engaged in similar low-skilled work on the island or on émigrés within the communities where they resettled. The status is embedded specifically in the cross-border context. Low-skilled work did not itself gain stature. Rather, the relevance of work, in the minds of people back home, became irrelevant. Migrant generosity and demeanor on visits mattered more.

Émigrés are so concerned with home-country status expectations that they sometimes behave in ways that are disingenuous, to validate and reinforce stature associated with their move abroad. "Some may be in debt, with mortgages and car payments, but they come here and act as if they are wealthy and without problems," Pavel, the cinematographer explained. An émigré concurred. "You feel you must even dress and act a certain way when you come back, flaunting prosperity. Society and your family need to see that you can succeed and are in a superior position to them because you migrated." For such reasons some émigrés even rent jewelry for visits to impress islanders.

Émigrés' new status comes with costs, linked to new islander expectations of them. They feel the need both to stay abroad and to continue to share earnings. Jesús, the child psychiatrist, spoke to the matter. "Return migration isn't possible because family, neighborhood, and society [now] don't accept that you want to come back." Having taken temporary work abroad, he felt "permanently exiled," a status he, unlike the first who fled the revolution, did not consider a badge of honor. He sensed that his network of friends and co-workers, as well as family, would consider him an economic failure and remiss in his moral economic commitment to them were he to return permanently. The social pressure was such that he even felt it would be difficult to return to his job in Havana's premier pediatric hospital and reintegrate professionally. Informal social dynamics now pressure islanders to go and remain abroad, in order to income-share. Some émigrés, as a result, feel unwelcome at home, not, as before, for leaving, but for returning.

The new cross-border material-symbolic exchanges, and bases of stratification to which they gave rise, are not entirely voluntarily sustained, as Jesús' experience conveys. Transnational income-sharing has come to be seen as a duty. Reflecting on his new-felt moral obligation, Jesús noted that, "It is very difficult for those who leave now, as the pressure on you is tremendous . . . There is a strong implicit social contract between a migrant and his family," a "contract" that, in his view, was "almost a religion. You are pressured to succeed and solve all your family's problems. You need to visit to fulfill an obligation to your family."

A "social contract" implies that there are negative sanctions if a commitment goes unfulfilled. To avoid the pain of shame, immigrants face added incentive to income-share. When Jesús, for example, returned without money from temporary work he took in Europe, his siblings and parents did not question him. He passed on to them gifts of clothing that his European friends had given him. In contrast, his friends and neighbors turned their backs on him when he had nothing for them. Some of his friends were even angered when he tried to explain how difficult it was to live abroad. Jesús' experience reveals that while Washington in most post-Soviet era years only allowed income transfers to family, islanders without remittance-sending kin abroad expected friends who went abroad to help them.

Thus, whereas in the peak years of revolutionary zeal, gift-giving was frowned upon, in the new normative milieu and new economy non-gift-giving came to be a source of scorn. In this vein, Jesús experienced a very different reaction to gift-giving than Dario's cousin, the university professor who in the pre-crisis years had hid clothing from his family in the US in his closet in order to avoid revealing material markers of diaspora ties. Jesús' experience differed also from Pavel's who in the early revolutionary years had criticized his family in the US for sending such basics as Colgate toothpaste. Jesús faced humiliation for lack of gift-giving.

Marcel Mauss perceptively addressed non-voluntary aspects of gift-giving.[38] His analysis is relevant for understanding the build-up of benefit-generating transnational ties among New Cubans across the Straits, although his work did not focus on immigration. Mauss argued both that a gift is its own reward, for gift-givers benefit in turn, and that there is no free gift. A person who gives materially induces social obligation, including repayment with a counter-gift. Mauss argued that the reward may be symbolic, the period for repayment may be unspecified, and the items exchanged need not be of equal value. Indeed, he noted that unequal exchanges contribute to and reinforce honor, prestige, and authority. The very act of gift-giving may be prestige-generating, and cement a set of mutual commitments. Underlying the formation of benefit-generating transnational social ties among Cubans spanning the Straits were such gift-giving dynamics.[39] The cross-border reciprocal exchanges of remittances and symbolic reward unified the parties involved in ways that geographic separation might otherwise have worn thin. The reciprocity also increased the likelihood that subsequent transnational material sharing would be forthcoming.

The symbolic rewards islanders had to offer appealed mainly only to the New Cuban immigrants. Recent arrivals appreciated the status conferred, which they did not enjoy in their adopted homeland and often did not enjoy before uprooting. Many of the earlier émigrés who left the island in opposition to the social transformation, in contrast, reject the social system in which island symbolic reward is embedded. Although there are exceptions, most Exiles feel little if any obligation, incentive, or desire to income-share.[40] One exception I know is Silvia, who emigrated young, with her family in 1960, and who after her first homeland visit became committed to cross-border bridge-building. She has cousins in Cuba to whom she determinedly brings videos and other gifts on visits. Meanwhile, for most Exiles, by the 1990s their everyday lives had become US focused and US enmeshed, with the economically successful enjoying status in their adopted country. They had no need to turn to their homeland for social recognition. Accordingly, moral commitment and the rewards that sustain cross-border income-sharing tend to be cohort specific.

In sum, changes both at the macro and individual level, in institutional practices and in norms, and in Cuba as well as the US, all contributed to the surge in remittance-sending in the post-Soviet era. The US and Cuban governments continued to obstruct and set contours to remittance-sending, in some years more than others. However, the Cuban government in particular, did so less after than during the Cold War. Meanwhile, their control over remittance flows weakened, as Cubans wanted family abroad to income-share more, and the diaspora became more committed to sharing new country earnings. New technology eased transnational income transfers, but only because of new cross-border norms and networks did émigrés make use of it.

Limits to Émigré Cross-Border Generosity: The Cuban Diaspora in Comparative Perspective

While changes on both sides of the Straits created the bedrock on which transnational bonding took on economic worth, in comparison to many other Latinos, Cuban immigrants remain less generous. At the turn of the century Cuban immigrants in the US remitted monthly, on average, less than $100, while the typical Latin American immigrant remitted $250.[41]

Comparisons with Dominicans and Salvadorans are revealing (Table 6.1). Immigrants from the two countries in the region, for reasons that I note in the Introduction, help highlight unique and more generalizable features of the Cuban diaspora and Cuban transnationalism. In 1990, before the arrival of New Cubans, the average Dominican and Salvadoran in the US remitted ten

or more times as much as Cuban immigrants. While the differential subsequently diminished, as of the early 2000s, immigrants from the two other
countries reportedly remitted more than twice as much per capita as Cuban
Americans, and in 2005 they still remitted some three to four times as much.
Moreover, in 2005 the average Dominican and Salvadoran home country resident received, respectively, over three to nearly six times more remittances
than the average Cuban on the island, but down from nine and more than
twelve times as much in 1990.

How to explain why Cuban immigrants remain, on average, less generous,
despite the surge in Cuban émigré remittance-sending in the post-Soviet era?
The answer rests on more than differences in the size of the respective diasporas.
Indeed, Cubans substantially outnumbered Dominicans and Salvadorans in
the US until the early 2000s (Table 6.3).

Of greater import, the institutional milieu in the US encouraged Dominicans
and Salvadorans to remit more than Cubans. Cubans faced unique government obstacles. They alone faced a people-to-people embargo that limited
how much and to whom they could remit and the frequency of permissible
visits conducive to income-sharing. And they alone were subject to a general
embargo that prohibited remittances for investment, as well as the formation
of the transnationally embedded hometown associations that Dominicans
and especially Salvadorans (and other immigrants) established. Hometown
associations encourage collective, along with individual, remittance-sending.[42]
Cuban Americans' closest approximation to hometown associations, affiliates
of the umbrella group Cuban Municipalities in Exile, as described in Chapter 2,
were dominated by early émigrés opposed to cross-border bridge-building.[43]

Moreover, the leadership stance toward remittance-sending and toward
cross-border ties conducive to remittance-sending among Cuban Americans
on the one hand, and Dominican and Salvadoran leadership on the other
hand, differed. Most influential Cuban Americans opposed transnational
monetary flows that Salvadoran and Dominican diaspora leaders supported,
especially before the breakdown of hardline hegemony around the time of the
2008 election.

Meanwhile, more rank-and-file Salvadorans and Dominicans than Cubans,
overall, were predisposed toward cross-border income-sharing. Although
Salvadorans in the US include many refugees from their home country's 1980s
civil war, the politically displaced upon resettling were committed to helping
family they left behind.[44] They demonstrate that refugees are not inherently
antagonistic to transnational income-sharing.[45] The first Cubans, who like
Salvadorans, envisioned themselves uprooting for political reasons, unlike
Salvadorans, developed a morality antagonistic to remittance sending. The
New Cubans, predisposed to income-sharing, remain a minority of the Cuban
population in the US (Table 1.3).

And in terms of the respective homeland governments, Cuba's created
conditions least conducive to income transfers. The Cuban government,
alone, restricted the longevity of diaspora visits, curtailing the cross-border

Table 6.3 Immigration to the US from Cuba, the Dominican Republic, and El Salvador

	Cuba	Dominican Republic	El Salvador
(a) Annual legal immigration from			
1980	15,100	17,245	6,101
1985	20,300	23,787	10,156
1990	10,645	42,195	80,173
1995	17,937	38,512	11,744
2000	18,960	17,465	22,543
2005	36,261	27,504	21,350
2006	45,614	38,069	31,783
(b) Total foreign-born population by place of birth			
1980	608,000	169,000	94,000
1990	751,000	357,000	473,000
2000	952,000	692,000	765,000
2005	948,000	695,000	1,121,000
2006	982,000	811,000	1,091,000
(c) US foreign-born Cuban, Dominican, and Salvadoran populations as % of home country population			
1990	7	5	9
2000	9	8	13
2005	8	7	16
2006	9	8	16

Sources: USDJ-INS, *INS 1998*, p. 27; USDHS *2005 Yearbook of Immigration Statistics*; USBC, *Statistical Abstract of the United States 1984*, p. 92, *1987*, p. 11, *1992*, p. 42 and *2000*, pp. 10, 48, 822; PRB 1991; World Bank, *World Development Indicators 2001*, p. 362, *2006* and *2007* (web.worldbank.org and web.worldbank.org/WBSITE/external/datastatistics); World Bank, *World Development Report 2002*, p. 232; United States Department of Commerce, United States Census Bureau 2001, p. 12; Migration Policy Institute, *MPI Data Hub* (www.migrationinformation.org/datahub/countrydata/data.cfm); Table 1.1 in this book.

bonding conducive to the build-up of social ties of economic worth. And the Cuban government, alone among the three governments, restricted private economic activity which could draw on remittances.

Such conditions, in combination, contributed to Dominican immigrants especially, and Salvadoran immigrants secondarily, being more engaged with their home country than Cuban immigrants.[46] This was true at the institutional, community, and individual level.

Addendum: Transnational Social Capital Formation

The Cuban experience suggests a previously unanalyzed form of social capital, transnationally rooted. This addendum briefly contrasts characteristics and correlates of social capital transnationally embedded with those of social capital described by others as embedded in a single country. I do so for the interested reader.

Coleman and Bourdieu first conceptualized social capital.[47] They defined it as benefits obtained through personal ties governed by norms of reciprocity. Sources of social capital include shared values, enforceable trust, and bounded solidarity.[48] Basing their analyses on domestic dynamics in the US and in Western Europe, they added that social and other forms of capital, namely economic, human (education and skill), cultural, and symbolic, are mutually reinforcing and potentially interchangeable and fungible. Granovetter contributed to the understanding of social capital build-up, in his work on the US, in arguing that those with a broad range of "weak social ties" were better able than those with fewer but stronger social ties to cultivate benefit-generating relations.[49]

Analysts of immigration and transnationalism who address matters of social capital have transported the concept developed in the context of rich countries to the poorer countries of the world. They presume that social capital dynamics operate similarly in all countries and across borders. In the context of Latin America-to-US immigration, Massey et al.,[50] for example, elucidated how variations in quality and quantity of social capital influenced immigrant adaptation, such as job attainment. In subsequent work he and collaborators addressed the economic impact in the home country of such cross-border ties.[51] Portes, Haller, and Guarnizo,[52] in turn, have pointed to the emergence of transnational entrepreneurs who build their businesses on contacts across borders, suggesting accumulation of economic capital transnationally based to be social capital contingent. And Levitt,[53] building on research among Dominicans in their homeland and in the US, argued that social capital is fungible with other forms of capital across borders, as Coleman and Bourdieu argued to be true within well-to-do countries. Levitt claims that individuals who start out with more social as well as human and financial capital, that is, with more contacts along with more education and money, are more likely to succeed across borders, and that forms of capital are transferable from the immigrant community to the home village.

These and other scholars, however, do not address how and why transnationally embedded social capital may differ in form and effect from nationally embedded social capital, and why it is a form of capital that is likely to build up especially among poor people across borders. Drawing on the Cuban experience, I summarize conditions that appear conducive to the build-up of transnational social capital and its distinctive characteristics and correlates.

To begin with, the Cuban experience suggests that cross-border ties are not inherently benefit-generating, and that norms of reciprocity, bounded solidarity, and trust may take form where they were previously non-existent. But even when conditions are suitable, immigrants must be convinced to share assets they might, in principle, prefer to hoard. Humble immigrants, in particular, might rather retain all their meager earnings to best improve their lot in their new land. The typical Latin American working in the US in the first years of the new millennium remitted about a seventh of the meager $20,000 they earned.[54]

Transnational family-based social capital is a form of social capital that by definition is embedded in relations among people who are located across borders. It is a form of social capital in so far as it is premised on bounded relations of trust that provide benefits to the parties involved. But the Cuban experience reveals that for ties across borders to become benefit-generating, parties across borders must have goods or services, material or non-material, that the other wants and cannot otherwise fully attain. Aspiring remittance recipients do best when they reciprocate in kind, when they offer symbolic reward for gifts of economic worth to people appreciative of such reward.

The Cuban experience, in turn, suggests that transnationally grounded social capital may best build on "strong social ties." It also tends to be bundled differently, and to be less fungible with other forms of capital, than Coleman, Bourdieu, and Levitt suggest. Transnational social capital formation hinges on an exchange of immigrant economic *decapitalization* for symbolic capital. Conversely, immigrants who maximize their own economic capitalization, by hoarding their earnings, may experience symbolic and social decapitalization. Disgruntled non-immigrants may stigmatize and disrespect such émigrés.

Bourdieu noted that symbolic capital entails deference and obedience.[55] In the Cuban case I showed symbolic capital to include respect, esteem, prestige, and authority, in addition to deference. It rested, however, on immigrant valuation of the homeland people who bestowed the symbolic recognition. Recent, but not earlier, immigrants from Cuba appreciate such recognition.

Yet, even when remittance-senders and recipients perceive themselves as gaining from the exchange of economic for symbolic capital, cross-border benefit-sharing is not necessarily voluntarily sustained. It is involuntarily sustained when migrants who might prefer to return home feel pressure from non-migrants to stay abroad and share earnings, and when they feel pressure to share more than they prefer.

The relationship between forms of capital is also distinctive in the transnational context in that the build-up of potential economic capital, in the form of remittances, is not necessarily correlated with human capital accumulation, at least not in the early stages of cross-border social capital formation. Poorly educated immigrants may earn more abroad than better educated people in their homeland because they access a better-paying labor market. And non-migrant remittance recipients, in turn, may attain earnings that are unrelated to their education and skills, owing to the generosity of their transnational ties. Human capital takes on different meaning across than within country borders. Further reflecting a distinctive clustering of social with other forms of capital in the transnationalized context, low-skilled work that is devalued both in the new country of settlement and in the country of origin may gain value in the transnationalized context when income earned is shared. More accurately, work itself may lose value other than the material sharing it enables.

The Cuban case also points to how institutional and normative milieus shape transnational social capital build-up. Because social ties are shaped by the context in which they are embedded, the more hospitable to bonding and income-sharing the milieu is, the more benefit-generating ties are likely to be. But the institutionally and normatively relevant milieu is not necessarily only that which is preexistent. Hospitable conditions may be created and expanded by interested parties, as they were among Cubans on both sides of the Straits in the post-Soviet era.

In turn, in the US context, Coleman argued that the breakdown of the traditional nuclear space-based family had negative social consequences in contributing to social disintegration and normative breakdown.[56] However, the break-up of the space-based nuclear family as some members emigrate does not inherently result in what Coleman called low social capital. In the process of transnationalization, Cuban intra-family dynamics often change but do not necessarily become dysfunctional. As young adults are the most employable abroad, when they emigrate, they garner new remittance-related stature, authority, and respect, including vis-à-vis their elders. Non-migrants' desire for remittances induces bonding that physical separation might otherwise wear thin. And in that siblings, aunts and uncles, grandparents, and even more distant relatives, may be material beneficiaries of transnational social ties, the Cuban experience suggests that extended family relations may even be strengthened with the territorial transnationalization of families. Physical separation, of course, is not without emotional costs to separated kin, and transnational social relations may be strained rather than strengthened should remittances not be forthcoming or be less than expected.

Yet, the Cuban case also suggests that domestic social ties may break down as transnational ties build up. Cubans viewed remittances as a limited good. While sharing of migrant dollars often brought struggling island relatives together, at times the desire for remittances strengthened cross-border solidarities while simultaneously weakening island kinship bonds. Competition for overseas remittances may make kin in the homeland distrustful of one another and competitive for the loyalty of relatives abroad. This was seen on occasion among Cubans with whom I spoke. Also, when relatives abroad have access to assets that domestic kin do not, local family members may come to value relations with family in the diaspora more than with kin in their midst. The Cuban experience demonstrates that bonding domestically and transnationally are not necessarily complementary and cumulative. Family-based transnational ties, and transnational social capital in turn, may build up while nationally based social ties fracture.

Finally, in the process of transnationalization, the significance of social ties may change. They may become benefit-generating in ways that they were not when based in a single country. In this vein, New Cuban immigrants felt an imperative to help relatives they left behind "because they were family." Before moving abroad they often felt no such compunction and rarely income-shared.

7 Dollarization and its Discontents

Homeland Impact of Diaspora Generosity

Focusing on remittances from the Cuban side of the Straits and at the macro level, this chapter demonstrates that the Cuban government came to have its own reasons not merely for tolerating, but also for encouraging, transnational income transfers. Yet, from its vantage point, diaspora dollars were a double-edged sword. While providing much-needed hard currency, they simultaneously eroded state command of the economy and precepts on which the revolution originally had been premised. The humble, politically marginalized New Cubans who were committed to cross-border income-sharing will accordingly be shown to have changed Cuba more than the Exiles who for decades tried to undermine the regime.

The transnational impact remittances have hinges on the social context in which they are embedded. States constitute an important part of that context. They, in principle, have the capacity to control cross-border income transfers, to appropriate money for themselves, and to regulate usages the recipients make of remittances. This chapter, based on published primary and secondary sources, demonstrates that the Cuban government is no exception. However, states are never entirely free to determine the scale of remittances or their uses. Ordinary people can informally and illegally defy state policies that stand in their way. The Cuban populace as well will be shown to be no exception, despite subjugation to a seemingly strong, autocratic state.

In the aggregate, remittances may generate consequences that neither the generous income-sharing friends and family abroad nor their homeland recipients and homeland government intend, want, or fully understand. They may transform societal norms, values, and practices. They may also create new tensions and societal contradictions as governments, on the one hand, and remittance recipients, on the other, each wish to maximize diaspora dollars and determine their usage for themselves. Also, new tensions may arise as the people without transnational ties of economic worth lack the same material possibilities as remittance recipients. These outcomes will also be shown to be true in Cuba.

Cuban Government Efforts to Reintegrate into the Market-Based Global Economy

The Cuban government's stance toward remittances must be understood against the backdrop of its desperate need to reintegrate into the market-based global economy once Soviet aid and trade abruptly ended. The timing of the dissolution of the Soviet empire could not have been worse for Cuba. During the entire period of incorporation into the Soviet bloc the country had not been as dependent on the superpower and its allies for trade as it was in the last years before the fall of the Berlin Wall. Trade with countries that were in the bloc at the time of its collapse accounted for over 85 percent of island commerce. Just fifteen years earlier, the bloc had accounted for as little as 52 percent of island imports and exports.[1]

So traumatic was the impact of the bloc's collapse that, within four years, former member countries' share of island trade plunged to 22 percent, while the total value of trade fell to about one-fourth the 1989 level.[2] With trade having accounted for about half of the island's gross national product, the cut-off of exports and imports played a key role in the economy's contraction by over 30 percent between 1989 and 1993.[3]

The government had no option but to reintegrate into the hard currency-based world economy that had shaped island developments before the revolution.[4] Yet, in the post-Soviet era it had to fend for itself without the aid, trade, and investment advantages the US had provided before the revolution. Making matters worse, it faced new US obstacles to its global market reintegration, at a time when ordinary Cubans wished to increase commercial relations more with the US than with any other country.[5] I briefly summarize the difficulties, which provide the backdrop for understanding the shift in Havana authorities' stance toward remittances in the post-Soviet era. Comparisons with the Dominican Republic and El Salvador, summarized in Table 7.1, highlight Cuba's difficulties. As noted, despite differences, the two countries provide interesting bases of comparison. The Dominican Republic is an island economy that offers economic opportunities of roughly comparable scale to Cuba, but it is market-based and not constrained by a US embargo with extra-territorial reach. In the case of El Salvador, Washington contained island economic options during its civil war in the 1980s. However, afterwards, the US extended opportunities to the Central American country that it continued to deny Cuba, at the same time that Salvadorans who fled the country's tumult set in motion the remittance-sending diaspora described in the last chapter. Of the three countries, Cuba, alone, instituted a socialist political economy.

When Cuba set about reintegrating into the hard currency-based international economy it was weighed down by debts it had accumulated during the Soviet era. The debts were to non-US Western creditors, as well as to the Soviet Union. As of 1989, the country had the second highest ratio of hard currency debt to hard currency export earnings in Latin America, and by 2005 its 1989 hard currency debt had doubled.[6] Its debt in 2005 was more than

Table 7.1 Macroeconomic performance, foreign debt, and government sources of hard currency in Cuba, the Dominican Republic, and El Salvador in select years

	Cuba	Dominican Republic	El Salvador
(1) GDP ($ US billions, current)			
2001	27.5[a]	21.6	13.8
2002	28.4[a]	21.6	14.3
2003	29.9[a]	16.3	15.0
2004	31.1[a]	18.5	15.8
2005	36.1[a]	29.1	17.0
2006	41.7[a]	30.6	18.3
(2) GDP per capita			
2001	2,500	2,180	2,040
2002	2,582	2,260	2,080
2003	2,718	1,970	2,190
2004	2,909	1,920	2,330
2005	3,223[a]	2,300	2,450
2006	3,723[a]	2,850	2,540
(3) Foreign debt (US billions)			
2001	10.9	3.3	2.9[b]
2002	10.9	3.8	3.4[b]
2003	11.3	4.2	4.8[b]
2004	13.8[a]	5.1	5.3[b]
2005	14.5[a]	6.1[b]	5.5[b]
2007	17.2[a]	—	—
(4) AID (net official development assistance or official aid)			
(a) millions of dollars			
1994	47	60	305
1999	58	195	183
2000	44	56	180
2005	88	77	199
(b) aid per capita (dollars)			
1994	4	8	55
1999	5	23	30
2000	4	8	29
2005	8	8	29
(5) DIRECT FOREIGN INVESTMENT (millions of dollars)			
1990	54.0[c]	133	2
1999	178.2	1,338	231
2000	399.9/448	953	173
2004[d]	100[d]	645	466
2005	—	1,000	517
(6) EXPORTS (US millions)			
1990	5,100	2,170	582
1995	1,507	765	998
2000	1,630	5,200	1,164
2005	2,726[a]	5,818	3,586
2007	3,734	—	—

(*Continued overleaf*)

Table 7.1 Continued

	Cuba	Dominican Republic	El Salvador
(7) TOURISM			
(a) in-bound tourists (thousands)			
1990	327	1,305	194
1995	1,100	1,552	—
1999	1,561	2,649	658
2000	1,952	—	—
2005	2,261	3,691	1,154
(b) tourist receipts (millions $)			
1990	243	900	18
1999	1,714	2,524	211
2000	1,948	—	—
2004/05	2,100ᶜ	3,508	543

Sources: World Bank, *World Development Indicators 2001*, pp. 210, 340, 348, 356, *2006* (http://devdata.worldbank.org/data-query), and *2007* "Quick Query" (www.web. worldbank. org/WBSITE/external/datastatistics); Euromonitor, *World Economic Factbook 1989/1999* (London: Euromonitor, 1998), p. 143; EIU, *CCR* May 2001, p. 20, August 2001, pp. 28, 30 and August 2006, pp. 5, 28, 29; EIU, *CCP 1997–1998*, p. 36 and *1998–1999*, p. 35; EIU, *Cuba Monthly Review* September 2008, p. 20; World Bank, *World Development Report 1997*, pp. 218, 242; World Bank, *World Tables*, p. 77; *Cuba Transition Project* (http://ctp.iccas.miami.edu (Issue 15, June 2005)); www.latinbusinesschronicle.com/ statistics and www.latinbusinesschronicle.com/statistics/reports/070306/tourism.htm; Pérez Villanueva 2004, p. 173; *CIA World Fact Book* (El Salvador, Dominican Republic) (www.enotes.com/world-fact-book).

Notes:
a estimate.
b long-term debt dod.
c 1993.
d In 2001 the government last released information on foreign investment (EIU, *CCR* August 2006: 29).
e 2004.

twice that accumulated by the Dominican Republic and El Salvador. Compounding the gravity of Cuba's fiscal situation, foreign banks had cut the country off from new credit lines ever since the government suspended loan repayments in 1986. Additionally, Russia took over Soviet debt claims, and demanded that Cuba repay what it allegedly owed in hard currency. In 2006, Russia argued this debt stood at $20 billion,[7] although at the time of writing, Cuba had yet to agree on the size of the debt or on repayment terms. Fortunately for Cuba, China and Venezuela offered new credit lines.

Cuba, meanwhile, accessed little foreign aid to offset what Soviets had provided. Comparisons with El Salvador, and with the Dominican Republic in the 1990s, reveal how little concessionary bilateral and multilateral aid Cuba received when most in need.[8] Washington blocked Cuba both from its own bilateral funding and from multilateral sources over which it had strong influence.

The increasingly important European Union (EU) only minimally came to Cuba's rescue. It blocked the country from receiving non-emergency humanitarian aid and barred Cuba from the Cotonou Agreement, an EU trade and aid pact with developing countries. It also demanded political reform as a precondition for assistance. Particularly notable, Cuba's former Communist ally, the Czech Republic, took a leading role in convincing the EU to deprive the island of aid.[9] The post-Communist Czech government, deeply committed to market democracy and dismissive of its past, like Russia immediately following the Soviet Union's dissolution, showed no residue of good will toward its former ally. Finally, in 2005, under the influence of Spain's socialist government, the EU somewhat softened its stance toward Cuba. However, negligible new aid came Cuba's way as a consequence.

Foreign private investment, in principle, could provide an alternative source of development capital, including producing hard currency-generating exports, revenue that could be drawn upon to repay foreign loans (and thereby also qualify for new loans) and to cover the costs of imports essential for expanding the economy. Although the government under Castro had rejected such capital for three decades on nationalist and ideological principle,[10] faced with an economic crisis after the Soviet Union disappeared from the world stage such moral precepts became yet another luxury it no longer could afford. To attract overseas investors, however ambivalently, it guaranteed property rights in a revised Constitution and it issued a new investment code. In the new context the investment stock rose from 54 to 1931 million pesos between 1993 and 2000.[11] Yet, in the latter year, Cuba still attracted far less foreign investment than the Dominican Republic, although more than El Salvador. The US embargo, and its tightening in the 1990s in response to Exile lobbying and PAC contributions, kept Cuba from accessing US and certain other capital.[12] Cuba managed to attract some non-US investment, especially in mining, energy, and infrastructure. However, small foreign investors met with such unfavorable business conditions that in 2002 more than half of the seven hundred joint ventures and cooperative production undertakings that involved foreign private investors, in partnership with the Cuban state, operated at a loss. Many of them closed, and foreign investment dropped off.[13]

Exports could serve as an alternative source of development capital, as well as hard currency for foreign dealings. By 2000, Cuba's export earnings, however, stood at less than one-third their 1990 level. During the same decade, Dominican export earnings, half Cuba's in 1990, had surged to over three times Cuba's. Although Cuba still generated more export earnings than El Salvador at the turn of the century, Salvadoran exports doubled in the 1990s while Cuba's nosedived. And while Cuba's export earnings picked up in the first years of the new millennium, they remained around half the 1990 level, and by then El Salvador as well as the Dominican Republic were exporting more.

In the export domain as well, Washington contributed to island economic woes. On top of the embargo that had prohibited US purchases of Cuban goods since the early years of the revolution, the Cuban Democracy Act constricted Cuba's export market by giving third countries a disincentive to trade with Cuba. The 1992 legislation, as noted in Chapter 3, banned boats that docked on the island from accessing US ports for six months and specified that aid be withheld to any country that traded with Cuba. At the same time, Washington expanded Dominican and Salvadoran options, first through the Caribbean Basin Initiative and then through the Central American Free Trade Agreement (CAFTA). In that Washington during the same years extended "most favored nation status" to Communist China and resumed trade relations with Communist Vietnam,[14] anti-Communist moral principles did not drive US–Cuba trade policy. Rather, the Exile politicking described in Chapter 3 led to the exceptionalism of US foreign policy toward Cuba. Business, behind the economic opening to the two Asian Communist countries, had less interest in the smaller Cuban market, although, as also noted in Chapter 3, agro-business successfully lobbied in 2000 for a partial, one-way trade opening with Cuba, for exports of US farm products.

The collapse of Cuba's sugar trade stood at the heart of the island's dramatic drop-off in export earnings. Although sugar had accounted for approximately three-fourths of island trade earnings for most of the twentieth century, by 2005, sugar generated only 5 percent of the island's dramatically reduced export revenue. Low sugar prices on the world market and new total dependence on the open world market for sales (in which only 10 percent of all sugar is traded), plus a plunge in production from over eight million tons in the last years of the Soviet alliance to only somewhat more than a million tons, contributed to the drop-off in earnings.[15]

Nickel sales partially offset the drop-off in sugar revenue. However, the sector did not provide an engine of growth that served as an alternative to sugar. Meanwhile, government efforts to develop non-traditional exports paid off little. It set up free trade zones to try to attract investors for the labor-intensive low-skilled manufacturing that had been relocating from richer countries with high labor costs to poorer, low-cost labor countries since the late 1980s. But this initiative never attracted much foreign investment. By 2000, the value of such manufacturing, along with other non-traditional exports, stood at half their level when Soviet trade ended.[16] That same year, such manufacturing generated half of Dominican and Salvadoran export earnings.[17] Dominican and Salvadoran preferential access to the US market made those two countries more attractive to businesses investing in off-shore production. At the same time, Washington's removal of trade barriers attracted foreign investors to off-shore production in Communist China and Vietnam.

Cuba was much more successful in developing hard currency-generating services. Primary among them was tourism. Although Castro had mothballed tourism when he first assumed power, the sector became very important in the 1990s, to the point that until 2005, it was the country's main source of foreign exchange.[18] Castro had initially reined in tourism because of its association with the decadence of the Old Order that the revolution sought to reverse. But when in dire need of hard currency, the government restored its former niche in the international tourist market. With state agencies contracting most of the tourism, the government was able to access foreign currency the travelers spent. So successful was the Cuban government that by 2005 the surge in tourist earnings had offset the plunge in export earnings (Table 7.1).[19] The Cuban tourist industry boomed despite Washington's continued ban on US-to-Cuba tourism and on US investment in the sector. The US accounts for most Caribbean vacationers.[20]

Even more impressively, the Cuban government parlayed the revolution's impressive human capital development into a foreign exchange-generating resource. Neither the Dominican nor Salvadoran (or other Latin American) governments sponsored comparable initiatives. As of 2005, exports of human services purportedly generated $4.6 billion.[21] And the following year they accounted for nearly half of island hard currency earnings, twice the amount tourism generated.[22] Cuba's most ambitious labor contracts involved health care and educational provisioning to Left-leaning Hugo Chávez's Venezuela, in oil-for-social assistance swaps.[23] A newly formed state-owned entity that negotiated overseas contracts acquired the earnings, while paying the cadre sent abroad primarily in pesos.[24] In comparison with other Latin American countries, Cuba was well positioned to send teachers and health care providers abroad. Cuba had the best student/teacher and best doctor per capita ratios in the region.[25]

From the state's vantage point, international service contracting avoided the negative features associated with tourism. Development of the tourist infrastructure itself required scarce hard currency. Also, tourism fueled informal, illegal, and unsavory domestic economic activity (e.g. prostitution), and private economic activity (e.g. restaurants, room rentals) that eroded government authority and control over the economy.

Yet, the prioritization of overseas human service provisioning was not problem-free. For one, the Bush administration tried to sabotage the provisioning. It encouraged defections by Cuban doctors on overseas missions, by publicizing that they could qualify for US immigration visas. Secondly, the exporting of skilled cadre also entailed domestic social costs. As the government sent about one-third of its doctors on overseas assignments, island health care services deteriorated. And Cuba was limited in the number of foreign countries able and willing to pay for the services.

The economic restructuring, nonetheless, helped the per capita national product rebound by 2006 to the level when the Soviet era ended.[26] But hard currency revenue remained insufficient to pay off the foreign debts to qualify for new Western credit lines, and to cover the costs of imports that would allow the economy to forge significantly beyond the level of the Soviet era. And government hard currency-generating strategies created, as well as addressed, problems.

Government Facilitation of Diaspora Dollar-Sending: Convergence of State and Ordinary Cubans' Interests

When desperate for hard currency the government initiated measures also to encourage islanders to turn to their family abroad for dollars. In doing so, however, the revolution took yet another U-turn.

During his first two decades of rule, Castro had kept cross-border people-to-people income transfers minimal not merely by containing islander ties with compatriots who rejected the revolution (except for the brief period under the Carter administration), but also by prohibiting use of dollars. The government subjected dollar-holders to incarceration for up to three years and to 500 peso fines. Recipients of cash transfers from abroad had to convert foreign currency into pesos. Since there were few commercial goods available to buy at the time, people had little incentive to bypass and defy state regulations. Thus, even though the Carter era visits infused dollars into the economy, curtailment of most visits and transnational ties after the Mariel crisis contributed to the diaspora infusing only $50 million the year the Soviet bloc broke up (Table 6.1).[27]

But when the post-Soviet-era economic downturn made reliance on peso earnings nearly impossible, islanders refused to let government restrictions stand in their way. After taking the lead in seeking diaspora dollars, from family abroad, the government soon initiated reforms to encourage greater remittance-sending. Reforms made dollar use legal and gave islanders a new reason to covet remittances. The combination of new state initiatives and increased islander desire for dollars contributed to the surge in remittance inflows to over a billion dollars by the first years of the new millennium. In a ten-year period diaspora generosity brought in $3 billion more than foreign investors.[28]

Most important, the government legalized dollar possession in 1993. Islanders could, as a consequence, use foreign currency in their everyday lives. No longer fearful of state dollar confiscation and retribution for foreign currency possession, people's desire for dollars picked up and family abroad became less apprehensive about income-sharing.

The government went on to expand dollar-based consumer and savings possibilities, further inducing islanders to want their family abroad to send remittances. It expanded consumer options by allowing islanders to patronize state-linked dollar stores that it previously had reserved for diplomats, visiting émigrés, and other foreigners. It also expanded the number of such stores and their stock. Various state enterprises, including CIMEX, TRD-Caribe (affiliated with the Ministry of the Revolutionary Armed Forces), Cubalse, and Caracol, instituted dollar chain stores that ordinary Cubans could patronize. As of 2003 there were three hundred state dollar retail outlets in Havana, and one thousand nationwide.[29] Stores offered basic foods, but also such non-durables as freezers, fans, furniture, televisions, and more. Among the offerings were items the government had removed from peso retail outlets at the start of the economic crisis, when it concentrated its much-depleted fiscal resources on subsistence needs.

The government also set up new currency exchange outlets, CADECAs (*Cajas de Cambio*), throughout the country. At the CADECAs islanders could easily and legally exchange money from abroad into domestic currency for economic activity that remained peso based.

The government, in turn, expanded the banking system to allow for dollar deposits. Dollar recipients thereby had a safe place to keep foreign currency that they did not use immediately for consumption, and could earn interest on their deposits.

At the end of the 1990s, the state even became an agent of transnational hard currency transfers. State-owned enterprises entered the remittance business, partnering with international money transfer companies such as Western Union and El Español.[30] The government thereby facilitated émigré money-wiring which islanders could access in a secure, quick manner.

Islanders benefited from the new state initiatives. Remittance recipients' material living standards improved. They could legally supplement state rations, and they could attain non-durables on a scale not previously possible in Cuba under Castro. Indicative of the pick-up in consumption, sales at state-run stores increased 2.3-fold in the late 1990s.[31] And between 1998 and 2003, sales rose from $870 million to more than $1.3 billion.[32] Anyone with dollars could patronize the stores, but remittances came to account for an estimated 80 percent of the foreign currency islanders accessed.[33]

At the same time, the government benefited from the reforms. It could access the dollars that the diaspora generously shared with island relatives through purchases at the dollar stores. The very name of the dollar stores, Tiendas de Recuperación de Divisas (TRDs), Shops for the Recovery of Hard Currency, highlighted a key function of the newly permitted consumerism. In 2003, islanders spent, according to estimates, 75–80 percent of the remittances they received in purchases at the stores.[34] Thus, while store purchases allowed dollar-holders to upgrade their living standard, most money flowed into state channels. Meanwhile, purchases at the state dollar stores increased demand for domestically produced goods, thereby stimulating economic growth. Approximately half the items sold at TRDs came to be of local origin.[35]

The government was also able to access hard currency through the money-wiring it permitted. It imposed a tax on the service provisioning. In the early 2000s, the government annually took in over $100 million in wire service fees.

In addition, the government could direct savings deposits in a manner that, in principle, stimulated the economy. State-run banks drew on deposits to make loans to state enterprises, and profited from interest charges.[36]

Furthermore, the reforms enabled the government to strengthen the legal over the illegal economy. In allowing the dollar to be used as domestic legal tender (until 2004) and in encouraging foreign exchange conversion through official channels at the CADECAs, the government reined in the black market in dollars.[37] And, the dollar stores, also in principle, could rein in the black market consumption that had mushroomed amidst the crisis.

The government set the CADECA exchange rate at a level that was more favorable to dollar holders than it ideally might have liked. Although the official exchange rate remained one peso to the dollar, at the CADECAs the government honored the higher informal "street" exchange rate. While giving dollar holders the monetary upper hand, the government gave ordinary Cubans reasons to exchange foreign for domestic money in a manner it could access. Moreover, a range of government initiatives served to drive down the dollar-for-peso informal exchange rate from over 130 to 21 pesos to the dollar between 1993 and 2000. The government thereby also restored much, though far from all, of the value the peso had commanded in the Soviet era.

From the state's vantage point, the restoration of the peso's worth had political pay-off in turn. Once subsistence became more affordable and less precarious, pent-up social tensions defused somewhat.[38]

State-Benefiting at Senders' and Recipients' Expense

While islanders took the lead in securing diaspora dollars, the government increasingly exploited the generosity of Cubans abroad at recipients' expense. State and dollar-holder interests came to conflict as well as overlap.

The government, for one, profited from sales at the TRDs.[39] It taxed profits of, and held dividends (*aportes*) in, the state-run stores. While it continued to heavily subsidize the prices of basic goods allotted through the ration system, these items, as previously noted, addressed only about one-third to one-half of household minimal monthly needs. The goods sold at the new state dollar stores, in contrast to those rationed, were highly priced. Authorities justified what they claimed as an ideal mark-up, 240 percent above cost, on equity grounds:[40] a tax on consumers to fund programs for dollarless islanders. They claimed the mark-up would allow for distributive justice, for dollarless islanders to benefit from remittances they themselves could not attain. The government accessed most of the mark-up in that the TRDs were expected to turn over 230 percent of charges. The TRDs could retain the other 10 percent.[41] Cubans without access to hard currency could benefit from the *de facto* consumer tax to the extent that the government allotted the revenue to their advantage. However, there was no institutional guarantee.

Second, the government established a market for state enterprise products at the TRDs. High fees charged for transnational package-sending and for visitors' excess baggage (and Washington's lowering of the permissible weight of luggage in 2004) created a people-to-people based cross-border tariff wall that cut Cubans off from alternative better quality, less expensive émigré-provided imports. The percentage of sales at dollar stores domestically produced rose from 18 in 1995 to 55 in 2001.[42] Cuban economists referred to the domestically produced hard currency-generating goods as "exports within the borders."

By periodically raising prices at the TRDs the government increasingly advanced its economic interests at consumers' expense. Price hikes in 2002 contributed to an 8 percent inflation in consumer prices,[43] and those in 2004 raised consumer costs, on average, an additional 15 percent.[44] Notably, officials advanced a different rationale for the 2004 price jolts than for the 240 percent retail mark-up previously claimed as ideal. They claimed the 2004 price hikes were intended to compensate for the anticipated drop-off in remittance inflows that Bush's tightening of the personal embargo that year would have. Thus, as islanders received fewer dollars, the government reduced the purchasing power of the dollars they received.

Castro rallied patriotism to deflect anger at the price hikes. Portraying Bush as the culprit for restricting travel and remittance-sending, Castro mobilized huge demonstrations to protest what he claimed to be a new US national security threat.[45] But not fooled by the mask of patriotism, islander anger with the abrupt and steep rise in living costs led the government to partially retract the price hikes. It lowered prices of the least expensive items, the goods those with few dollars could afford. However, it did not restore prices to their previous levels.

Even after the price adjustments, real disposable income lagged behind economic growth.[46] With the price hikes in the hard currency sector the leading source of the rise in living costs, the state benefited more than remittance (and other hard currency) receivers from the macro economic improvements.

The government also profited substantially from money-wiring. Its regulations left islanders with less of every diaspora dollar wired to Cuba than to Mexico, Central America, and elsewhere in the Caribbean.[47] In 2006, international money transfer companies charged about nineteen cents for every dollar remitted to Cuba, whereas the average transaction cost to the other countries by then had dropped to about 6 cents per remitted dollar.[48] Government enterprises that partnered with international transfer agencies split service charges.

Then, when the government ruled in late 2004 that Cubans could no longer use dollars as domestic currency, its profiteering at remittance recipients' expense took on a new dimension. It required hard currency trade-in for so-called CUCs (Cuban Convertible Pesos), promissory notes with dollar value on the island. The state could thereby access dollars which until then had circulated informally in the economy, estimated at around $300 million in 2004.[49] In charging a 10 percent service fee for the currency conversion,[50] dollar recipients were thereby doubly taxed at a steep rate, through both forced currency conversion and state store purchases, and triply if they received their money wired from abroad. Remittance recipients were left with less and the state with more of every dollar the diaspora shared.

In that the government introduced no surcharge on non-dollar hard currency conversion, Cubans dependent on income transfers from the US, where nearly 90 percent of the diaspora live, bore most of the brunt of the dollar crackdown. The government imposed the dollar charges to offset new transaction costs the Bush administration imposed on third country banks that dealt with Cuba's dollars.[51]

The government went on to alter the exchange rate in a manner disadvantageous to dollar-holders. In 2005, it lowered the dollar/peso exchange rate from 26 to 22 pesos (after the informal exchange rate had risen from 21 pesos to the dollar in 2000), and the hard currency/convertible peso exchange rate from 1:1 to 1:0.93.[52] The readjusted exchange rates resulted in islanders receiving less local currency for dollars they turned in. Island authorities claimed the readjusted rates improved the value of the peso, to the benefit of the peso-dependent population.[53] While true, the politically justified changed exchange rates were also beneficial to the government, in that it could thereby release less local currency for every dollar remittees turned in (while reducing the overvalued dollar).

The state also profited from temporary overseas work it permitted islanders to contract privately in the post-Soviet era, when islanders, in effect, became their own source of remittances.[54] It permitted Cubans for the first time to leave the country, for just short of a year, without losing their jobs and other rights. As islanders took advantage of the opportunity to earn hard currency abroad, state agencies benefited from exit fees. Some Cubans worked abroad in agreement with their ministries of employment, in which case they were obligated to remit a portion of their contracted earnings to their ministries. In 2008, the Ministry of Higher Education, Health, and Culture, for example, demanded their employees share 50, 50, and 30 percent of contracted overseas earnings respectively.[55]

The government, in addition, introduced new taxes on the self-employed, whose entrepreneurial ventures often made use of remittances from family abroad.[56] The tax was designed to increase state revenue, including in hard currency, while reducing the earnings of the self-employed.

Government-Incurred Remittance Costs

Remittances may appear to be a cost-free source of state revenue, but they proved to be a mixed blessing from the state's vantage point. They caused as well as addressed problems. The problems they generated were social, political, cultural, and normative, as well as economic. These impacts were largely unintended, and not considered by the diaspora who generously shared a portion of their earnings. Hardline Exiles were correct in their claims that remittance-sending helped the Castro-led government keep afloat. However, they did not recognize how remittances simultaneously eroded state legitimacy, state political and moral authority, state control over the economy and society, and the moral precepts on which the revolution had been premised. Remittances alone did not cause these consequences, but they were an important contributing factor. They had ripple effects in diverse institutional domains.

Economic Costs

The mainly remittance-based informal dollarization of the economy, first, undermined state sector productivity and the delivery of services that were central to the government's socialist source of legitimacy. With few state jobs paying more than the equivalent of $20 per month, far less than the average amount remittance recipients received without any work effort whatsoever, the incentive to labor in peso-paying state jobs withered. In the new economy earnings hinged more on who you knew abroad than on hard work, skill, and merit. Under the circumstances, labor motivation remained highest in those peso-paying state jobs that provided informal and often illegal access to dollars (and CUCs), and to goods that could be pilfered for family consumption and black marketeering.

Growing disillusion with peso-paying jobs, in turn, contributed to a domestic, along with overseas, brain drain. Professionals left state jobs for low-skilled work in tourism. Working in tourism became the main alternative to remittances for securing hard currency. Salaries in tourism were not higher than at other state jobs, but employees in the sector could informally access tips and hard currency in other ways. People also left state jobs to run small, private tourism-related ventures, such as bed-and-breakfasts and small restaurants, known as *paladares*.[57] Some room renters earned more in a day than state sector employees earned in a month. And Cubans who catered to the new tourist demand for prostitution could earn more in an hour than at a state job in a month. The gravitation to tourism thus left the government with a deteriorating return on its investment in schooling, along with social problems. While no publicly available data exists on the scale of the domestic brain drain, it is perceived to be so pervasive that Cubans refer to the occupational shift as the "inverted pyramid," to capture the devalued return to education in the new economy.[58] Along with perceptions of an "inverted pyramid," city dwellers in Cuba were much less likely than elsewhere in Latin America, on average,[59] to believe people in their country can get ahead by working hard, to be satisfied with their work, and to feel that they can achieve at work what they do best.[60]

The cash-strapped government also initiated some costly worker-incentive reforms, both in hard currency and in pesos, to stimulate state sector productivity and to convince labor to toil in priority state sector jobs. The reforms included labor costs that governments in market economies need not assume. State enterprises in key sectors began to feed, clothe, and house their workers,[61] to offer performance bonuses, and to pay employees a portion of their salary in hard currency (and then in convertible pesos with domestic dollar worth). Bonuses at the turn of the century amounted to one to seven times the monthly base-wages in pesos.[62] These bonuses cost the state $228 million in scarce hard currency, which amounted to one-fourth to one-third of total estimated remittance intake at the time (and a higher percentage, according to the most conservative Cuban remittance estimates). The government also raised base-pay earnings to motivate labor, at additional fiscal costs to the state.

In 2005, for example, it more than doubled the minimum wage, which cost nearly 1,800 million pesos.[63]

The government singled out doctors, teachers, and police for wage gains, in 1999 and again in 2005.[64] Doctors and teachers were central to the provisioning of the cradle-to-grave benefits associated with the revolution. They also were essential for fulfillment of international service contracts. In turn, the government considered police so important as crime surged that it set their salaries equivalent to those of doctors, and increased in number the police force in Havana.[65]

The purchasing power of the peso had so declined that the government also increased pension and welfare payments in 2005, at the cost of approximately 1,200 million pesos,[66] and expanded subsidized offerings through the ration system. These measures benefited the peso-dependent populace whose living standards had dramatically deteriorated, especially relative to those of dollar-holders. In hoping thereby to reduce peso-dependent resentment towards remittance recipients, the added fiscal expenditures were to have political pay-off.

The government, meanwhile, faced resistance from dollar-holders to various of its dollar-attaining strategies, which cut into its ability to profit from diaspora generosity. First, dollar-holders were sparing in the money they traded in. Cubans are estimated to have exchanged at CADECAs only about $10 million in 1996 and $20 million four years later,[67] in years when remittances possibly totaled, respectively, about one-half and one billion dollars (Table 6.1). Also, the Cuban diaspora, as noted in the preceding chapter, made only limited use of the wired services from which the government earned revenue (especially before Bush's 2004 crackdown on travel rights went into effect). Compared to immigrants from other Caribbean and Central American countries, and Mexico, those from Cuba wired less of the money they remitted. Then, when the government introduced taxes on the self-employed who drew on remittances for their ventures, the number registering as self-employed declined 23 per cent within four years.[68] The tax drove private activity underground, if not out of existence. Furthermore, few islanders deposited dollars in the state bank system. In 1998, for example, they deposited only $50 million.[69] With dollar holders, in contrast, spending $870 million that year at dollar stores, and over a billion in the first years of the new millennium, the government found itself needing to rely primarily on a consumer-based strategy to access Cuban hard currency and to stimulate economic growth.

The Breakdown of the Moral Order

Remittances directly and indirectly fueled black market and other illicit activity. This eroded state moral authority, as well as state control over the economy. The state's near-monopoly of permissible dollar (and dollar-equivalent) based commerce had the unintended effect of fueling black market sales, on a scale rarely found in market economies where most transactions take place through legal private venues. Because anyone who priced goods below dollar store prices created a market for their goods, the government's consumer-based strategy to appropriate hard currency induced both illicit trade and theft of items from state jobs to vend privately.

Dollars gained informally also fueled an illicit housing market that both undermined government control over housing access and fueled additional illicit activity. A bustling underground market in homes and apartments in Havana gave rise to illegal agents and speculators, sales scams,[70] and theft of building supplies from state enterprises to sell on the black market. Remittance-recipients were the main Cubans who could afford the illicit dealing.

Illustrative of the scale of off-the-books housing activity, and of the ineffective government efforts to rein it in, in 2000, the government confiscated more than 2,000 illegally obtained homes in Havana and it revoked the room rental licenses of home owners who either renovated their quarters or rented rooms in hard currency without authorization. Fines exceeded $1 million.[71] Addressing symptoms, but not the underlying source of the problem, four years later it clamped down again on illegal housing deals.[72] While the government remained officially committed to providing everyone with shelter that cost no more than 10 percent of family earnings, and to allotting housing on the basis of need and "revolutionary attitude," islanders with hard currency could evade the requirement of political obeisance as prerequisite for housing. They also could sabotage the state's commitment to distribute housing justly.[73]

By the first years of the new millennium, crime, pilfering, and corruption in general had become so rampant that Castro announced that they could destroy the revolution.[74] Against this backdrop the government and Party launched new initiatives to try to halt the wrong-doing. They tried to reinvigorate the largely defunct state-linked block organizations, the Committees for the Defense of the Revolution, to fight the breakdown of law and order at the neighborhood level.[75] And they launched the so called Battle of Ideas to try to get the populace to recommit to moral precepts of the revolution.

Ineffective in themselves, the government simultaneously resorted to "law and order" initiatives. In 2001, the government established a Ministry of Audit and Control,[76] and in the next few years it sacked state employees not only for their own illegal dealings but for failing to prevent theft by subordinates.[77] Then, in 2007, the Ministry of Labor stepped up penalties for bureaucrats found guilty of corruption and pilfering.[78]

Castro considered crime so pervasive that he turned to economics and social work students to serve as moral police. Unlike in the first years of the revolution when Castro turned to youth to serve as agents of a utopian socialist project, in the post-Soviet era the government called on them to fight a dystopia of crime and corruption. Economics students helped conduct state enterprise audits, which uncovered rampant pilfering.[79] And authorities assigned young social workers to take over servicing Havana petrol stations from corrupt employees who illicitly sold gas in hard currency for private gain.

Crimes and misdemeanors, nonetheless, continued because officials left the root cause of infractions unaddressed: islander yearnings for improved living standards, and inadequate means to attain them through legally sanctioned means.

Cuba was not alone in experiencing a breakdown in law and order at the time. Theft, pilfering, looting, gang activity, kidnappings and killings surged across Latin America as neoliberal reforms drove living costs up and many people's earnings down.[80] But Cuba was alone in the extent that crime eroded state control of an economy and a state socialist project. Islander desire for hard currency (and, after 2004, for CUCs) fueled the normative, social, and economic breakdown.

The Erosion of Revolutionary Precepts

The influx of remittances, in turn, eroded precepts of the revolution. The government became part of its own problem. The consumer strategy that the government promoted to induce remittance-sending in a manner it could access, served to encourage individualism and acquisitiveness over its initial emphasis on collectivity, equality, and on moral over material values. For this reason, the government was ambivalent in its stance toward remittances. The Communist Party Central Committee, for example, spoke of how ideologically contaminating dollars were.[81]

Unequal islander access to remittances undermined egalitarian precepts of the revolution. Claes Brundenius estimated the Gini coefficient, a measure for assessing inequity in income distribution, to have worsened between 1986 and 1999, from 0.22 to 0.41.[82] And Jorge Mario Sánchez-Egozcue estimated that in the early 2000s remittance recipients earned between two hundred and eight thousand times more than the average monthly wage.[83]

The impact remittances had on income distribution differed in Cuba from market economies in the region. In the other countries, where income inequality ranks among the worst in the world, remittances received by the poorer population reduced income differentials.[84] In contrast, in Cuba where the revolution, through land, wage, and welfare reforms, had dramatically reduced historical inequities, remittances countered this trend by widening the income spread.

The new income inequality had a range of ramifications. It resulted, for one, in new dietary inequality. Almost all islanders could afford the portion of their diet that rations continued to cover. But they could not equally afford food needs that rationing left unfulfilled. Prices at private farmer markets that had been permitted since 1994, and at state stores, cost ten to one hundred times as much as their price-regulated equivalents.[85] Prices at newly instituted state-run markets were somewhat lower, but the selection of goods was inferior. Remittance recipients consequently enjoyed dietary options unavailable to those dependent on the peso.

Remittances also exacerbated the racial inequities that the revolution had reduced. The diaspora on whose generosity islanders depend is, as noted in

Chapter 1, overwhelmingly White. Because non-Whites, overall, benefited under Castro, few of them emigrated. Few dark-skinned thus have family abroad to whom they can now turn for remittances. This puts them at a decided disadvantage in the new informal transnationally grounded dollarized economy.[86] New race-based inequality is thus an unintended consequence of earlier revolutionary race-based gains.

The ramifications of unequal race-based access to remittances are multiple. Mark Sawyer quotes a Cuban woman named Yolanda in his book on race and the revolution that discusses the matter. Yolanda notes:

> Blacks have fewer relatives in Miami. We do not get remittances . . . [I]f you get remittances you can start a business, have nice things . . . Some jobs cost money if you want them . . . [And] without dollars, it is hard to get medicine, clothes, an apartment, and good food. It is especially hard to find a nice place to live.

Making matters worse, the dark-skinned also face the most difficulty accessing jobs in tourism, people's main alternative means to access hard currency. Those without hard currency fill the ranks of Cuba's new poor.

Indicative of the new race-based remittance divide, a study found in the 1996–2002 period that approximately 10 percent of Blacks and only slightly more mixed-blood *mestizos*, but 40 percent of Whites, received remittances.[87] And De la Fuente estimates that the average annual per capita remittance earnings of non-Whites to be half that of Whites.[88] At the same time, the non-Whites who in small numbers emigrated over the years and who send home remittances are contributing to new income disparities in Cuba among non-Whites, between those with and without dollar access. Emergent race inequalities thus are not resulting in a return to the pre-revolution racial status quo ante.

The new remittance-linked income inequality also reverses the early revolution commitment to reducing rural–urban historical disparities. In the first decade of the revolution the government promoted "a maximum of ruralism, a minimum of urbanism."[89] The rhetoric reflected an effort to reduce the country's centuries-old urban bias. But fast-forwarding to the post-Soviet era, Havana, with 20 percent of the island's population, received approximately 60 percent of remittances.[90] More émigrés lived in Havana than elsewhere before uprooting.

Dollar-linked differences in lifestyles, in turn, compounded tensions tied to poor living conditions. The peso-dependent populace resented their absolute, along with their relative, deprivation. Labor union and public forums revealed the resentment.[91] Worker dissatisfaction, according to one study, rose from 27 to 41 percent between 1989 and 1999.[92] And when the economy improved in the first years of the new millennium the peso-dependent population resented that their living standards remained stagnant. Castro pleaded for patience. Workers in whose name the revolution had been made were embittered.

Cubans with dollar access have not, however, solidified into a new privileged class. With Cubans differing markedly in the amount of remittances they receive, they are themselves economically divided. And the government restricts, as noted, private dollar-based capital accumulation among all hard currency recipients.

Thus, the New Cubans who defied hardliner efforts to block people-to-people transnational social and economic ties set in motion changes that contributed to a transformation of island socialism as Cubans for decades knew it. State moral and economic authority eroded, and new tensions evolved in the society at large and in state–society relations. At the same time, the state exploited the generosity of the mainly humble new immigrants who were morally committed to their family in their homeland. While the government's overseas human service contracts did not cause comparable domestic consequences, by the time they became an important alternative source of hard currency revenue, ordinary Cubans had vested interests in continued access to remittances. For this reason, contradictions inherent in diaspora generosity continued.

The Politics of the Quiet Transformation

Dollarization eroded the socialist economy without concomitantly ushering in a democratic-market transition. No significant transition occurred even with the shift in rule from Fidel to his brother, Raúl, temporarily in 2006 and permanently two years later. Since an analysis of island politics is beyond the diaspora's homeland impact, which is my focus, I will only briefly address how the government and ruling Communist Party responded politically to their worst crisis since 1959.

A Shift in Ideological Base of Legitimation: From Marxist-Leninism to Nationalism and Patriotism

Recognizing Marxism-Leninism had lost appeal as survival became people's primary preoccupation, and as former country allies discredited its legitimacy, Fidel quickly shifted to a focus on nationalism and patriotism to muster loyalty and legitimacy.

Heroic leaders of Cuba's lengthy nineteenth-century struggle for national independence were used to justify the present. The government staged events to coincide with dates important in the political calendar of the past, but not May 20, which it continued to associate with what it called the pseudo-republic and which Exiles honored as their own day of homeland patriotic affirmation. While the revolution all along had been framed in a historical context, in a manner that gave the Cuban socialist transformation a nationalist bent, in the post-Soviet era the past became a key political prop.

Patriotism similarly served as a powerful political prop. Castro quite remarkably transformed symbolically the most significant public protest under his rule into a patriotic cause. On August 5, 1995, the one-year anniversary of the large Havana protest of between one to two thousand protestors, precipitated by severe food scarcities, Castro claimed the event a "great revolutionary victory." He further reframed the symbolism of a day that might have become a base for resistance on which an anti-regime movement might have built by organizing a "Cuba Vive" manifestation, involving half a million islanders. In Poland, for example, Solidarity kept the spirit of struggle alive that ultimately ushered in a market-based democracy by repeatedly mobilizing yearly in memory of a labor uprising that the government had repressed.

Castro most successfully rallied patriotism in a regime-legitimating manner in response to the Cuban Americans who mobilized to prevent the return of Elián to his father in Cuba after his mother had died at sea. Castro made the custody battle a nationalist crusade.

Castro also turned national elections into patriotic plebiscites, into a "show of unity." If we are to believe official reports, even at the peak of the crisis, only 20 percent of voters refused to support a "united vote," for the entire slate of official candidates. And playing to patriotism, in the late 1990s the populace was told to view their vote as a "rejection of the Helms [–Burton] Bill."

The Institutional Make-Over

In the post-Soviet era no state institution changed more than the military. Its initial build-up had been linked to the Cold War Soviet regime. Although the government continued to consider itself besieged by the "colossus of the North," without Soviet aid and diminished fiscal resources, it dramatically downsized the armed forces and withdrew from overseas military projects. At the same time, it reinvented the military. The military assumed a new importance in the economy. Military recruits were assigned to "beans, not bullets," to help address the food crisis, while top brass took command of key government ministries. Then, as the government lost control over corruption, crime, and misdemeanors, the military took on anti-graft duty.[93] And when Raúl assumed the reins of government after Fidel became ill, the long-term Minister of Defense became head of state with the backing of loyal armed forces.[94]

The Communist Party also underwent changes. It became more inclusive. Most notably, it opened its ranks to religious believers. So too did it internally democratize somewhat. For the first time members gained the right to elect committee cadre by direct secret vote. In addition, the Party took new initiatives to rid its ranks of corruption. Members who had abused their positions, who were derelict in their duties, and who deviated from what the leadership defined as the limits of the permissible were purged. The "clean-ups" contributed to Party "purification." However, the frequency of cadre replacements pointed to endemic problems not solvable through personnel changes.

The administrative apparatus, in addition, underwent change that suggested new responsiveness to ordinary people's concerns. The Constitution, revised in 1992, granted the electorate the right for the first time to directly elect Provincial and National Assembly representatives. And the government initiated district-based Popular Councils with full-time administrators to address neighborhood concerns. Castro initiated the Popular Councils at the time of *glasnost*, the Soviet Union's political opening that became the bedrock for the East European transition to market democracies. He called for the reform no doubt to stave off a possible contagion effect of the collapse of East European Communism across the Atlantic. However, with meager fiscal resources local administrators could do little. They mainly depended on creative local initiatives.[95]

Meanwhile, the top leadership oversaw periodic shakeups in the commanding heights of key government institutions. By replacing many of the old with young cadre, the generation that matured amidst the post-Soviet-era crisis gained representation at the highest levels of governance. Although the replacements were not free to use formal power as their generation might so choose, they gained a political voice and assumed a formal stake in the political system.

At the same time, the mass associations that had organized ordinary Cubans on a territorial and functional interest-group basis since the early years of Castro's rule, lost vitality in the 1990s. While ossifying and not adapting to the populace's changed needs and concerns, they also became ineffective instruments of state control.

Selective Recourse to Repression

Unable to rely on the Party, mass organizations, the system of governance and administration, and ideology to maintain moral order and control, the top leadership periodically reverted to repression. At times it rallied Rapid Response Brigades, goon-type squads, to quell neighborhood dissidence. And at times it removed reformers from their jobs. Especially notable, in 1996, Raúl Castro, then officially second-in-command, orchestrated the reassignment of prominent intellectuals in the Party-affiliated Centro de Estudios sobre América to other employment. Those ousted had advocated market reforms and participatory democracy, though not a change in governance.

The government periodically also arrested and imprisoned dissidents, while continuing to deny them access to the media through which they could disseminate their ideas. The government cracked down particularly on dissidents with ties to the US government. The most massive crackdown occurred in 2003. Nonetheless, dissidents remained active, albeit under state watch. Meanwhile, the arts enjoyed greater latitude of expression than in the past.

Ironically, the Cuban American leadership contributed to fragmentation in the island dissident movement. Moderate and hardline Miami groups allied with, and financially supported, different opponents of the island regime. Moderates, for example, associated with the reinvented Cuban American National Foundation backed Osvaldo Paya's Varela Project for electoral law reform, amnesty for political prisoners, freedom of expression, and the right to own small businesses. The hardline CLC, in contrast, refused to support Payá because he focused on change within the contours of the Cuban political system. Instead, it supported Marta Beatriz Roque, and provided her with tens of thousands of dollars.[96] On May 20, 2005, the day Cubans commemorated national independence before Castro assumed power, Roque held a well-publicized Assembly to Promote Civil Society that some hundred delegates representing many small dissident groups attended. In selecting May 20 she built on the pre-revolution base of national identity, which Exiles honored. But indicative of the divide within the dissident movement, with different US Cuban American allies, when Roque tried to organize a national congress of independent librarians in October 2006, even Cuba's independent librarians' organization refused to participate.

Transition in Leadership and Basis of Rule

Meanwhile, Fidel's ability to rely on his charisma to maintain legitimacy wore thin. Charismatic authority rests on ongoing proof of worth, which became difficult once the economy went into deep recession and his health deteriorated. Fidel's own self-presentation changed under the circumstances. A purely charismatic leader stands outside the routine obligations of family life and this-worldly involvement, and for nearly four decades he was no exception. Yet, in a turnabout, Fidel used the occasion of his eightieth birthday, while recuperating from intestinal surgery, to warn his people that they should prepare for difficult news.[97] Allowing himself to be photographed while recuperating, he wore a red, white, and blue Adidas warm-up suit, not his usual military fatigues. The warm-up suit, in the colors of the Cuban flag, conveyed a patriotic twist to his recuperation.

Then, when Raúl officially took over the helm of government, the country faced the problem of transition from charismatic rule. No doubt because he was cognizant of the difficulty, Raúl promoted a Party-guided collective leadership in which he delegated responsibilities. "The only substitute for Fidel can be the Communist Party of Cuba," he asserted.[98] Concomitantly, Raúl acknowledged that he would not deliver speeches like his brother, a master orator in his heyday. Raúl, moreover, was known as a family man, more mundane in his concerns and commitments than Fidel.[99] Raúl accordingly let island people know that his rule would rely on a different base of legitimation.

Ordinary Cubans' views and expectations eased the leadership transition. While not envisioning their government to be democratic, they appreciated its social welfare provisioning, even amidst cutbacks. Thus, the thousand adults that Gallup polled in September 2006, in Havana and Santiago de Cuba, were divided in approval of the country's leadership.[100] Compared to city-dwellers in twenty other Latin American countries that Gallup surveyed, fewer in Cuba were satisfied with freedom in their everyday lives. But 98 percent of the Cubans believed education to be accessible to anyone who wanted to study, regardless of income, and 78 per cent of them were satisfied with their country's education system. The average percentage who felt similarly in the other countries was 52 and 59, respectively. And more than twice as many of the Cubans as other Latin Americans believed their country's university system to be superior to those of others. Cubans similarly praised government-provided health care, and did so far more than did the other Latin Americans. Cubans' positive assessment extended to treatment of their children. Nearly all Cubans interviewed felt that their children had the opportunity to learn and grow on an everyday basis and that their children were treated with dignity and respect. Two to three times as many Cubans as other Latin Americans had such positive assessments of conditions for their children. The post-Soviet-era crisis did not shatter Cuban confidence in their government's commitment to cradle-to-grave support, including for the next generation, their country's future.

The government and Party restructuring, containment of opposition, and selective use of repression, against the backdrop of appreciation of state social welfare provisioning, led few Cubans to turn to politics to bring about change. Under the circumstances, disgruntled islanders complained among themselves, turned to religion for solace, or sought exit over voice,[101] namely, they envisioned their future to rest on emigration more than change at home.

Those who leave in the years to come will join the ranks of the humble New Cubans already abroad, who, through bonding across borders, have unwittingly set in motion a transformation of socialism in Cuba. Together they will relegate Exiles—who have shared in the American economic and political Dream, while supportive of a wall across the Straits—increasingly to the sidelines of Cuban history.

8 Reenvisioning Immigration

I have shown the US adaptation of Cubans who uprooted at different times to vary, in ways partially rooted in, and theoretically explained in terms of, their pre-immigration past. Existing theories of immigrant adaptation leave this important aspect of the adaptation of the foreign-born unaddressed. Below I briefly summarize differences in how Cuban immigrant waves adapted in the US and enmeshed themselves in homeland ties that bear the imprint of their variant pre-immigrant pasts. I then highlight the theoretical implications of the case study and their likely relevance for an improved understanding of other immigrant group experiences. I conclude the chapter by addressing how US Cuba policy might be improved upon to meet the range of Cuban immigrant wants, along with US national concerns.

In Sum: The Lives Cuban Émigrés Lead

In many respects Cubans followed the path of earlier immigrants, and excelled at doing so. Many have been "model immigrants." They have shared in the American Dream. They have also assimilated and even acculturated. They have become political and community leaders and active participants in associational life. And what has proven good for them has proven good for America. They helped transform Miami into a multicultural, economically buoyant city with hemispheric reach, pivotal to US interests in an era of globalization and a post-9/11 world when improved relations with other peoples and cultures are essential.

Yet, not all Cuba-born have shared in the Dream. A minority have lived amidst the Other America, and contributed to its Hispanic base. They have lived in poverty, resisted acculturation, and not partaken in the rights and obligations of citizenship. And not all who have shared in the Dream have done so entirely through legitimate means. The success of some rested on corruption, crime, and abuse of public office.

I showed different adaptations of the Cuba-born to be contingent on when they uprooted. The first-generation immigrants who opposed Cuba's radical social transformation, filtered through pre-revolution lenses, and, at the other extreme, those who not only grew up in a Cuba transformed by revolution but also experienced the trauma caused by the ending of Soviet aid and trade and the delegitimation of Soviet bloc Communism, differ markedly in their US adaptation and homeland views and involvements. Their different adaptations and stances toward Cuba were shaped by their different pre-immigration pasts. While the weight of immigrants' pasts hinged partly on their age at immigration, age assumed different meaning among the émigré waves.

The 1980s Marielitos experienced a Cuba transformed by revolution far more than Exiles did. However, they tended to interpret it through lenses formed before the revolution, and accordingly shared views on life with those who preceded them abroad. Many Marielitos had opposed the country's radical makeover, but had previously been unable to leave or stayed because they anticipated Castro's rule to be brief. Still others initially sided with the new government, but in becoming disillusioned "reverted" to their pre-revolutionary mindset. The younger of the émigré wave, who did not know the Old Order first-hand, tended to filter their lived world through lenses of their elders, learned at home. Yet, having lived through the revolution, they understood its complexities, and as a result were more accepting of cross-border ties than the first who fled the revolution.

With opposition to the revolution their key life-forming experience, the first post-Castro arrivals viewed themselves in their new land as exiles and exiled, sometimes justifiably, sometimes not. In either case, though, their definition of self proved real in its consequences. Remaining committed to winning the war with Castro that they lost when living in Cuba, they were transnationally engaged, but with an idealized, imagined Cuba. Most of them refused to deal with their homeland under Castro's tutelage in the concrete. The émigré cohorts so differed in their perspectives that if they visited their homeland they filtered life there differently. Exiles were most critical. The Cuba they encountered proved a self-fulfilling prophecy. Their idealized Cuba was nowhere to be found.

The émigré cohorts had their natural home in different social classes and class cultures, all the while that each cohort was socio-economically diverse. Differences in social class backgrounds contributed to diversity in immigrant experience, at the same time that social class had different meaning to émigrés who grew up before and after the revolution.

Émigrés' pre-immigration pasts retained meaning in part because many of them settled in close proximity, worked and socialized together, and married "their own." Their pasts retained meaning also because they imbued life in their new land with their own shade of meaning. This was especially true of Exiles. They established their own civic associational life and calendar of rituals in their new land that reinforced their identity and concerns.

Exiles attached such symbolic and social significance to Little Havana in Miami and to Union City in New Jersey that they, and to a lesser extent subsequent arrivals, returned there "to be Cuban" even when they lived and worked elsewhere and the communities no longer were majority Cuban. In Miami, Exiles also staked out claims to the greater metropolitan area.

Along with embedding sites with their own shade of meaning, they intervened to keep the city "uncontaminated" by the Castro regime. They established themselves as Cuban gatekeepers, and imposed their views on others in their midst.

While Cubans left their imprint in both Union City and Miami, their imprint differed in the two settings. Context mattered. Miami offered more economic opportunities for enrichment, and settlers there, who already came from Cuba with more economically useful assets, had better local labor market opportunities. Because Union City was much smaller, and because Cuban Americans came to be a demographic minority there, the politically ambitious were more pressed to compromise, and to pursue inter-ethnic alliances, than in Miami. Increasingly Cuban Americans in Miami accessed positions of political power and influence, while in Union City they began to be replaced by others as of the early years of the new millennium. However, a few who built on a local Cuban American political base in Union City, and in neighboring West New York, attained higher office. Also, because Union City was much smaller, the Cubans who settled there became more enmeshed in the non-Cuban midst in which they lived. Union City offered less so-called institutional completeness, multiple settings that brought Cuban Americans, and mainly only Cuban Americans, together. And because Union City, unlike Greater Miami, was without posh neighborhoods, the economically successful moved away. The New Jersey settlement, as a result, maintained a working-class culture and it never built up a wealthy economic base, while Miami diversified economically. Thus, in Miami, Exiles were better able to develop assets and leverage local for national influence. At the same time, New Cubans had more impact in Miami because there, unlike in Union City, they had the force of numbers.

Yet, in neither Union City nor Miami did the Cuba-born entirely live in a homeland-transplanted past. They concomitantly assimilated and acculturated to their adopted country, and established bases for new pan-Hispanic identity.

Children of Exiles, whether born in the US or Cuba, were influenced by their elders. Some, as a consequence, even perceived themselves as exiles, premised on an imagined Cuba that they never knew or remembered first-hand. First-generation values in such instances took multi-generational hold. Yet, US-born and immigrant children who spent some of their formative years away from the Exiles' social world, and who therefore had more varied experiences to draw on, were less hardline, more eclectic in their views, and more open to reflection, compromise, and change in views. Age at immigration and location of residence accordingly contributed to certain diversity in cohort views and involvements.

All the while that Exiles recreated Miami and Union City in their own image, and socialized their progeny to their conservative anti-Castro life perspective, conditions in Cuba changed so dramatically as to alter islanders' views and values. The crisis that the demise of Soviet bloc aid and trade brought about shattered lingering utopian beliefs in the country's socialist project. And many youth who came of age amidst the crisis questioned, and were alienated from, the official revolutionary project. Islanders in the new milieu came to view life pragmatically, through the prism of family concerns.

The New Cubans who moved to the US brought this new mindset with them. While beginning to assimilate and acculturate to their adopted country, and wanting their children to do the same, they retained ties with friends and family whom they left behind. They embedded their lives across borders, in relations that rewarded income-sharing with respect, prestige, and stature. Meanwhile, their transnational ties infused new materialist norms in Cuba, decreased islander economic dependence on the state, eroded Cuban state control of the economy and society, introduced new income inequities, and undermined the socialist basis of stratification premised on performance in the state-run economy. The New Cubans accordingly did more to transform island socialism than the wealthier and politically influential Exiles who had tried for decades to unravel the revolution. New Cubans' impact was an unintended consequence of their family morality transnationalized with their move abroad.

The Cuban government, with its own hard currency needs in the post-Soviet era, implemented measures to facilitate diaspora cross-border family income-sharing. It thereby contributed to setting in motion the very dynamics that eroded its institutional base and moral underpinnings. And as it instituted measures enabling it to access ever more of every dollar the diaspora generously remitted, ordinary Cubans bore the costs.

Hardline Exiles kept New Cubans bridge-building commitment off the political radar screen by intimidating and silencing challengers to their point of view, by monopolizing the media, by monopolizing, together with their US-born children, positions of power held by Cuban Americans, by interest group politicking, and by bloc-voting. Even though they accounted for less than 1 percent of the US population, they so effectively leveraged votes and political contributions as to put in place a presidential election-linked ethnic policy cycle between 1992 and 2004, centered on embargo-tightening. But the policies attained in the name of all Cuban Americans promoted Exile interests while undercutting those of the New Cubans.

Although on the political sidelines, I showed New Cubans, nonetheless, to defy institutional and normative barriers that stood in the way of their cross-border bonding. In so doing they contributed to a quiet erosion of hardliner hegemony. Further fueling the erosion of hardliner hegemony was a growing split within the Cuban American leadership ranks, partly generation based. Some influential Cuban Americans began to engage in new thinking about Cuba and about cross-border relations, against the backdrop of the failure of hardline policies to bring the Castro-led regime to an end. The failed Cuban American effort to convince Washington and the American people to let six-year-old Elián González stay in the US, rather than be returned to his father in Cuba after his mother died at sea, proved a view-changing event for some who fled the revolution early on when young, as well as for some US-born. In defeat, they shifted from cross-border barrier supporters to cross-border bridge-builders. Cuban Americans, as a result, no longer spoke in a single voice. By the 2008 election cycle, hardline hegemony was challenged to the point that Democratic candidates for the first time became bridge-building proponents. This transpired both in the South Florida Congressional and presidential contests.

As enduring as pre-immigration formed views remained, even after the battle to "save Elián," I showed the Cuban émigré experience also to be shaped by the broader political, cultural, and economic context in which immigrants' new country lives took hold, with contextual conditions changing over the years. The first émigrés benefited from Washington's Cold War anti-Communist geopolitical agenda at the time of their arrival. They received unique rights and benefits, which aided their new country adaptation. Lingering benefits that post-Soviet-era arrivals receive result mainly from the political clout the pioneering wave built up. The émigré waves also faced different cultural milieus and economic opportunities. Exiles contributed to these changes, although they never were the only force at play. Winning a culture war with Anglos into whose midst they moved, Exiles transformed Miami into a Spanish-speaking and Hispanic-friendly city that made later arrivals' adaptation easier and different. The first émigrés also impacted on job options for later arrivals, first through their formation of an ethnic enclave economy and then through contributing to the formation of a local economy with hemispheric reach. At the same time, Exiles failed to prevent an informal transnationalization of the local economy that spanned the Straits in the New Cuban era. Also impacting on job options, global economic restructuring since the 1970s eliminated industrial and expanded service sector jobs. Émigrés accordingly faced different economic prospects depending on when they arrived.

The context impacting on émigrés' new country adaptation, and especially on their cross-border involvements, included changes in Cuba. In Cuba, norms and practices, and needs and wants, changed at both the state and societal level.

Yet, émigrés of the different waves responded differently to the macro changes in Cuba as well as the US. Their different responses reflected enduring cross-border effects of their pre-immigration cohort formations.

Theoretical Implications

The Cuban experience reveals that immigrant adaptation may involve new country assimilation and acculturation and transnational engagement, as the assimilation and transnational paradigms respectively capture. However, neither frame of analysis accounts for how and why immigrants' pasts weigh in varied ways on both their new country adaptation and cross-border involvements, and with what consequences. My historically grounded émigré cohort thesis addresses the lacunae.

Building on Mannheim's understanding of how long-lasting late-adolescent views, based on lived experiences, may be, I argued that immigrants may take their life perspectives so formed with them when they move across borders. Generational experiences with long-lasting impact may be differently interpreted depending on social class, race, gender, and the like. A Mannheimian frame of analysis thereby helps explain why Cubans initially divided deeply over the revolution, with many of those opposed to it uprooting. It also helps explain why the self-defined exile cohort continued to oppose the revolution from their adopted country, even as they assimilated in the new country. They continued committed to ideas formed in their pre-immigration past.

With generation formations historically contingent, a Mannheimian frame of analysis gives reason to expect foreign-born who uproot at different times with different pre-immigration experiences to view life differently, and accordingly adapt differently to their new country and relate differently to their homeland. Differences in the views and involvements among first-generation Exiles and New Cubans are theoretically explained in terms of their different pre-immigration lived worlds.

Imbuing life in their new country with their own shade of meaning, Exiles remained committed to an imagined Cuba, in the absence of homeland ties. And the Exiles who defied their cohort's taboo of travel, encountering a Cuba different from that which their cohort idealized in their imagination, contributed to a breakdown in homeland commitment. Neither the assimilation nor the transnational paradigm can explain these dynamics. The transnational paradigm, in particular, would anticipate cross-border trip-taking to deepen, not to detach, ties.

Since late adolescence serves as the key time when folk interpret life for themselves, a Mannheimian frame of analysis gives reason to expect greater variability in life perspectives among child immigrants than among their parents' generation. Young immigrants have new country experiences, along with old country experiences and views learned at home, to draw on as they interpret life for themselves. This explains the greater diversity of perspectives among children of Exiles than among their parents' generation.

By the same token, Mannheim provides the basis for anticipating, and understanding how and why, each age-group does not necessarily interpret life uniquely. Age-groups may identify with and take on the views of others. In Mannheimian language, they may "attach themselves" to another age-based cohort, especially when they perceive, correctly or not, their experiences to be similar. This proved partially true of Marielitos, vis-à-vis Exiles. Neither the assimilation nor transnational paradigm account for the historical and contextual meanings age assumes.

Building on Mannheim, Ryder gave reason to expect that such traumatic experiences as revolutions and economic crises may lead people to rethink previously formed life perspectives. This helps explain why Cubans who experienced the deep recession that ensued when Soviet aid and trade ended came to share a common life perspective, different from that of Exiles, whether or not they emigrated, and became disillusioned with the revolution even when previously committed to it.

Ryder added that generations are not necessarily equally free to express their views and do not necessarily have the same capacities to organize to advance their own concerns. The powerful may impose their views on others. They can determine what is normatively acceptable, and penalize non-conformity. Generational dynamics accordingly are contingent on the broader social and cultural context in which they are embedded, and on how power and influence are exercised. Power is undertheorized in both the assimilation and transnational frames of analysis.

In the context of immigration, the Mannheimian frame of analysis, in modification, also provides an explanation for why émigré cohorts with different human, social, and economic assets, different commitments, priorities, and determination, and different capacities to organize and impose their views and ways on others, differ in influence in their new milieu. Exiles' cultural and political influence is thereby explained. Yet, the politically, economically, and organizationally weak may resist the views and ways of the more powerful, including informally and covertly, with the cumulative effect being potentially substantial. This occurred among the New Cubans. They contributed not only to an erosion of Exile hegemony within the Miami Cuban American community but also to an erosion of Cuban government authority, as they quietly evaded the personal embargo Exiles promoted. An émigré cohort analysis helps explain conditions under which this may occur, and why.

With adaptation shaped, but not predetermined, by life before uprooting, immigrants may adjust to their new land in ways that do not entirely reproduce their past, all the while that they do not necessarily accept without modification ways where they resettle. Drawing on distinctive pasts, and responding to distinctive new country conditions depending on when and where they resettled, the foreign-born may forge new identities, new cultural practices, and new mixes of new and old country ways. Neither the assimilation nor the transnational thesis provide theoretical explanation for conditions under which such newly imagined identities and practices take hold. My historically and contextually grounded frame of analysis, in contrast, provided explanation.

In sum, I show the utility of a historically grounded émigré cohort thesis to address aspects of first-generation immigrant adaptation that both the assimilation and the transnational theses leave unaddressed. In combination, they can deepen our understanding of how and why immigrants may differ in their new country adaptation and homeland engagement, even when of the same home country origins and even when living for similar numbers of years in their adopted country. My book helps document and explain the long-term cross-border imprint immigrants' pasts may have.

How Unique is the Cuban Immigrant Experience?

How useful is my historically grounded cohort thesis for an improved understanding of other immigrant group experiences? The utility naturally awaits in-depth historical analyses of other foreign-origin groups.

For the time being, my limited comparisons of cross-border involvements of Cuban immigrants on the one hand, and Dominican, Salvadoran, and, to a lesser extent, other Latin American immigrants on the other hand, addressed in the book suggest the Cuban diasporic experience to be exceptionally conditioned by politics at the people-to-people as well as state level. At the same time, the Dominican and Salvadoran comparisons suggest homeland crises to induce not merely increased emigration but to alter "who emigrates" and their homeland commitments. For immigrants of all three countries the move to the US did not in itself give rise to cross-border involvements, to transnational norms, and to practices in both the homeland and new land conducive to immigrant transnational income-sharing. In the Dominican and Salvadoran cases, like the Cuban one, homeland traumas spurred changed life views that gave rise to new transnational generational formations.

Salvadoran and Dominican comparisons also highlight certain Cuban émigré "exceptionalism." While US and Cuban government policies impacted on who emigrated, on new country receptivity and adaptation, and on homeland ties, only Cuban émigrés who uprooted in response to their homeland's economic crisis shared much in common with the so-called new immigrants from the Dominican Republic and El Salvador, (and from other Latin American countries). There is reason to believe that the Exiles, with their pre- and anti-revolution generational formations,[1] in contrast, are more representative of émigrés from countries that underwent major societal makeovers which they opposed. Even so, such politically motivated émigrés would be expected to build on their distinctive pasts in somewhat distinctive ways.

In this vein, the Cuban-Salvadoran comparison suggests the prosaic, that not all refugees are alike. I showed Salvadoran refugees to take it upon themselves very quickly to help family in their homeland, in ways neither earlier non-refugee Salvadoran émigrés nor the first who fled the Cuban revolution did. The Salvadoran civil war, and the dislocations it generated, left the Central Americans economically devastated. Salvadorans who fled the civil war viewed their homeland through their lived experience before uprooting, through lenses of family needs and family commitments. Cubans and Salvadorans who similarly uprooted for political reasons thus interpreted their homeland experiences differently, and in ways that differently impacted on their new country adaptation and especially their transnational engagement. Meanwhile, because Salvadorans who emigrated before the civil war had very different experiences than those who experienced the strife, they related very differently to their homeland from their new land. The early émigrés have been focused far more on the US and less on El Salvador. My historically contextualized understanding of homeland generational formations and their new country embedding helps account both for Salvadoran-Cuban refugee (exile) and Salvadoran émigré wave adaptation differences.

There is reason to believe, in turn, that a historically grounded cohort analysis can help explain how and why diverse waves of immigrants from other countries that experienced social revolutions adapted differently upon uprooting.

For example, it provides an analytic frame to account for the different US adaptation and transnational involvements of diverse waves of first-generation immigrants from Vietnam,[2] China,[3] and Poland.[4] Differences are partly traceable to distinctive pre-immigration experiences.[5]

A historically grounded generational analysis may also help explain why today's children of so-called new immigrants are adapting differently in the US than did children of immigrants in the past, and in ways other theories leave unaddressed. Kasinitz, Mollenkopf and Waters, for example, point to differences between second-generation Italians who came in the first half of the twentieth century and US-born Dominicans who uprooted more recently.[6] The authors presume that the differences are traceable to changes in the US in the interim. While partially true, in that context matters, they do not examine how differences in pre-immigration family experiences may also be at play.

What Should be Done?

In the case specifically of Cuban immigrants, how might Washington improve its policies to address simultaneously yearnings of Cuban immigrants and its own institutional concerns? This book has shown that US policy addresses interests of first, but not recent, émigrés.

Washington should first and foremost revise its so-called personal embargo policy. In that Washington grants legal immigrants from other countries freedom to travel to their homeland at the frequency they choose and allows them to decide for themselves how much of their income they share and with whom in their homeland, it should extend the same rights to Cuban immigrants. Washington would thereby not only stop intruding in matters that are typically considered private, but would also simultaneously advance its own institutional interests. Cuban émigrés who visit with material goods and US values serve, in effect, as unofficial US ambassadors.

US remittance-sending restrictions, moreover, fuel immigration pressures by constricting islander homeland economic options. They also contribute to continued islander economic dependence on the Cuban state. Both of these outcomes are contrary to US strategic interests. While beyond the focus of the book, Washington's state-level embargo also exacerbates these conditions, both by not allowing Cuban Americans, as well as other Americans, to invest in private economic ventures on the island and by limiting US trade. Island poverty that US policy exacerbates does not necessarily fuel domestic pressure for change, as embargo supporters have presumed.

There also are US domestic reasons why the travel, along with the macro level, embargo should be lifted. For one, important sectors of the US business community, across the partisan divide, oppose restrictions on their trade with, investment in, and travel to Cuba. They see the embargo as antithetical to their economic interests. Two, the embargo is at odds both with the neoliberal policies that Washington in general promotes and with its policies in place vis-à-vis other Communist countries. Chinese and Vietnamese immigrants are not subject to a personal embargo or to homeland investment and trade restrictions. Three, Cuba poses no geopolitical national security threat since the Soviet Union's demise. Finally, the continuation of the embargo is disrespectful of the wants of most Americans, as reflected in public opinion polls. At the start of the new millennium, over 86 percent of Americans nationwide favored the right of US companies to sell food and medicine to Cuba and two-thirds thought that the embargo was ineffective. Close to 60 percent of those surveyed said the embargo should be ended.[7]

Congress and Presidents have allowed themselves to become captive to the special interests of the cohort of Cuba-born who fled the revolution early on. With rare exception, these Cuban immigrants do not know their homeland in the post-Soviet era first-hand. National policy-makers should not let political contributions by a minority of wealthy, well-organized, hardline émigrés lead them to turn their backs on the US's founding principles and business interests, and the preferences of most Americans.

If US national policy-makers want change in Cuba, if they want policy consistency, and if they want to advance the principles on which the country is premised, the personal embargo should be ended. Ironically, in responding to hardliners, US policy-makers are ignoring the yearnings of the very Cuban émigrés who have proven themselves to be agents of island transformation.

Appendix
Field Research

In this Appendix, I summarize my fieldwork sources of data, first in the US, then in Cuba.

A. Survey of Rank-and-File Cuban Americans in Greater Miami and the Union City, New Jersey Area

I interviewed 104 rank-and-file persons in the two communities who emigrated since 1959. Because of the limited size of my sample, I only differentiate, below, between respondents who emigrated in the 1959–1979 period and since. Responses to in-depth questions appear in the text of the book, not in the Appendix.

Summary of findings by year-of-emigration (percent, unless otherwise indicated)

		1959–1979	1980–2002	Total
1.	When emigrated	68	32	100
2.	Age of emigration			
	0–5	6	0	4
	6–21	72	24	57
	22–65	23	70	38
	66+	0	6	2
3.	Occupation in Cuba			
	Upper class [includes professionals]	55	48	50
	Middle class	27	36	33
	Working class	9	0	3
	Homemaker	9	0	3
	Informal work	0	16	11
4.	US occupation			
	Upper class	67	29	56
	Middle class	26	36	29
	Working class	4	7	5
	Homemaker	3	4	3
	Unskilled	0	18	5
	Unemployed	0	7	2

(*Continued overleaf*)

	1959–1979	*1980–2002*	*Total*
5. Education			
High school or less	11	15	12
Some college	5	8	6
College+	84	77	82
6. Where educated			
Cuba	32	91	50
US	13	3	10
Both	56	6	40
7. Total number trips to Cuba since 1990			
Never	61	63	70
1	13	12	11
2–5	20	20	19
6+	6	4	0
8. Impact of trip			
Unfazed	34	63	41
Positive	28	19	25
Negative	15	6	13
Mixed	23	13	21
9. Reason emigrated			
Political	100	32	77
Economic	0	42	14
Both	0	19	6
Family	0	6	2
10. Amount money send			
None	42	4	29
Sends, amount unspecified	38	36	37
$1,200 or less	11	29	17
More than $1,200	9	32	17
11. Purpose of remittances (raw numbers, not percentages, among those specifying purpose; some providing money for multiple usages)			
Basic needs, make life easier			
Consumer goods	17	20	37
Medicine	6	2	8
Housing	1	3	4
Business	1	3	4
Migration	3	0	3
Debt payment	0	1	1
12. Frequency of remittances			
Never	51	6	37
Less than 4 times a year	26	17	23
4 or more times a year	23	78	40
13. How send money to Cuba (raw numbers, not percentages)			
Informal business	5	12	17

	1959–1979	*1980–2003*	*Total*
Formal business	8	4	12
Personally brought (or by friend, family)	12	5	17
14. Send gifts in-kind (raw numbers, not percentages)			
Sends, gift unspecified	5	4	9
Clothes	4	3	7
Medicine (includes glasses, dentures)	45	14	59
For business	2	2	4
House-related items	0	1	1
15. Where live			
New Jersey	45	21	37
Florida	55	79	63
16. Where born			
US	2	0	2
Havana	30	41	33
Cuba, not Havana	41	53	45
Cuba, unspecified	26	6	20
17. Race			
White	97	91	96
Black, mulatto	3	8	4
18. Religion			
Catholic	82	46	71
Protestant	13	29	18
Other	5	25	11
19. Friends who are Cuban American			
Few, less than half	28	17	22
About half	22	0	11
Most	50	83	67
20. Family in Cuba			
None	21	3	15
Distant	44	9	33
Close	35	88	53
21. Contact besides visiting			
None	45	0	33
Yes	55	100	67
22. Islander visitors			
None	28	69	42
1+	72	31	58
23. Gender			
Male	65	59	63
Female	35	41	37
24. How respondent self-identifies			
Cuban	26	96	54
Hybrid (Cuban American, Cuban & American)	61	4	38

(*Continued overleaf*)

	1959–1979	*1980–2002*	*Total*
American	8	0	5
Hispanic	3	0	2
Other	3	0	2
25. Marital status			
Never married	6	17	10
Married/widowed	73	47	63
Divorced/remarried	21	37	27

B. Template for Interviews with Key Informants/ Community and Institutional Leaders

I modified each interview to make it relevant to the person with whom I spoke. But a basic set of issues on which I focused included:

1. biography of individual (where born, age emigrated, age, career history, family socioeconomic history);
   if Cuba-born, whether made return trips (when, frequency, reactions), send remittances (to whom, since when, amount; in cash and kind); groups to which belong
2. history of organization he/she leads: when founded; how, when, and why it changed over the years
3. activities in which the organization engages;
4. group membership and leadership: percent who are Cuban American; of those who are Cuban American, what percent emigrated in different time periods and percent foreign-born
5. ties to other groups: which, for what, when
6. revenue: source of funding; fundraising activities
7. institutional ties with Cuba: for what and when; views toward such ties; how ties changed over the years
8. ethnic identity, ethnicity of personal social networks
9. views on key events, e.g. Elián, the Pope's visit to Cuba, Latin Grammys
10. impressions of the Cuban American community

    a. how it changed over the years economically, politically, socially, and culturally (when, why)—in general, and with respect to transnational relations (e.g. visits, remittances);

    b. which Cubans, if any, have left, when, why, and to where

    c. what are the key business, professional, cultural, and other Cuban American groups and how have they changed over the years

    d. émigré waves:
       (1) main differences between them (in background, views toward remittances and visits, group involvements, key concerns);

(2) relations between émigré waves and how, when, and why they changed over the years

11. how the city has changed over the years

    a. role of Cuban Americans in those changes
    b. relations between Cuban Americans and other local race/ethnic groups

12. suggestions of other people to contact: influential people in different institutional domains; people knowledgeable about Cuban Americans

13. US Cuba policy: views toward it (and community views toward it), extent community complies

The thirty-five key informants/institutional and community leaders whom I interviewed in the Union City area included activists in eleven social and cultural groups, five religious leaders, eleven influential politicians, three business people, four persons associated with the media, and one travel agent. In Miami, forty-three interviewees included seven persons associated with social groups, six religious leaders, fifteen politicians, three business people, eight persons associated with the media, two travel agents, and two income transfer agencies. Politicians included a former Senator and mayor, incumbent mayors and commissioners, and state representatives, plus groups with stated political missions. I also interviewed five persons associated with government agencies, namely the Immigration and Naturalization Service (INS)/Department of Homeland Security, the State Department, and the Treasury Department.

C. Cuba Interviews

In Cuba, as in the US, I targeted two sets of people for interviews: key informants, with expertise relevant to my study, and ordinary people. All interviews took place in Havana.

Twenty-six persons were interviewed as key informants. They included employees associated with state agencies, persons in the remittance business and in banking, affiliates of non-governmental organizations, including religious organizations, and economists, sociologists, and other scholars knowledgeable about and affiliated with institutions concerned with immigration, remittances, family visits, the diaspora, US and Cuba bi-lateral relations, and the state of the Cuban economy and society. These persons were interviewed, in an open-ended fashion, about a range of topics depending on their field of expertise. Topics included immigration patterns; the backgrounds of émigrés; cross-border ties, family visits, and remittances (including uses and effects), and how they changed over the years; how Cuba changed in the Special Period; religious activity and the impact of the Pope's 1998 visit to Cuba; US and Cuba policies and how, when, and why they changed; transnational institutional involvements; the "Elián crisis;" private economic activity, how it changed during the Special Period, and the role of remittances in financing the activity; employment patterns, economic life, social and cultural conditions, and changes in the post-Soviet era. Some people were interviewed multiple times. People I knew from previous trips to Cuba served as initial contacts. Each person interviewed was asked for the names of other relevant people to talk with.

Twenty-eight rank-and-file Cubans were, in turn, interviewed. I began here too with people I previously knew, each of whom was asked for other contacts. In addition, people I met in diverse settings also were interviewed. The goal was to sample a range of people, on the basis of race, age, gender, and occupation, in order to be able to assess similarities and differences in how people coped with the Special Period and were enmeshed in diasporic ties. Still other individuals were targeted because they operated small business ventures, such as room rentals and small restaurants, so as to learn how, if at all, remittances served as a source of initial start-up capital. These Cubans were asked similar questions as the experts, but about their specific personal experiences. That is, they were asked about family they had who emigrated; when they emigrated, and frequency and forms of contact (e.g. visits, telephone conversations, letter-writing) with them; how their relations with people abroad changed in the post-Soviet era; whether they received remittances, since when, and uses made of them; how their lives changed in the post-Soviet era; the type of work they do, both formal and informal; and their views toward immigration. Since the interviews were open-ended, many other topics were addressed as well.

Notes

Introduction

1. *USBC, 2006 American Community Survey.*
2. Huntington 2004.
3. Puerto Ricans outnumber Cubans. However, they are, by birth, US citizens.
4. For more information about the survey and methodology see Eckstein and Barbería 2002.

1 Immigrants and the Weight of Their Past

1. Mesa-Lago 2000 and 2004; Leogrande and Thomas 2002.
2. Eckstein 1994/2003. See Mesa-Lago 2000 and 2004 for an alternative interpretation of shifts in policy emphasis in different periods under Castro.
3. See Pedraza 2007, in particular, for a discussion of émigré political life before uprooting.
4. Aguila Trujillo 2001. I focus on Cubans who emigrated directly from Cuba to the US. However, some Cubans unable to attain US entry visas when wishing to emigrate, first settled elsewhere. From there they subsequently moved to the US. Beginning under President Reagan, the Exile formed Cuban American National Foundation oversaw the move to the US of more than ten thousand Cubans from other countries (Haney and Vanderbush 2005: 44–45).
5. Between 1930 and 1950 only about 35,000 Cubans emigrated, mainly to the US. Aja Díaz 2006: 61.
6. For a summary of US immigration trends, and theories to explain it, see Bean and Stevens 2003, and references therein.
7. In the post-Soviet era the Cuban government, for example, required doctors to work five years before they could qualify for exit visas, so that it could recoup a return to its investment in medics' training. Doctors' interest in emigrating picked up when the value of their peso earnings declined to the point that they became, in the lifestyle they could afford, *déclassé*.
8. Washington's global admit policy had such biases, especially before the 1965 immigration reform eliminated national quotas. See Skrentny 2002.
9. Masud-Piloto 1996: 52. The US State and Justice Departments developed a visa waiver policy that Engstrom (1997) describes as a most dramatic example of bending immigration policy to meet a US foreign policy objective. By 1962, the US had issued approximately four hundred thousand visa waivers for Cuban nationals.
10. Torres 2003.
11. Masud-Piloto 1996: xxiv.

12. Ibid.: 68; Engstrom 1997: 29.
13. Masud-Piloto 1996: 135.
14. See Masud-Piloto 1996; Henken 2005; Ackerman and Clark 1995.
15. The Mariel opening followed some ten thousand Cubans storming the Peruvian Embassy, hoping to leave, and the *balsero* opening followed a protest by one to two thousand Havana residents distraught with the subsistence crisis following the Soviet pull-out. When forced to choose, the government favored exit over protest for change at home.
16. Typically there has been an inverse correlation between cutbacks in legal emigration options and illegal departures. During the 1982 and 1993 period around 7,600 Cubans entered without official US entry permission, over 6,670 of them between 1991 and 1993. Castro 2002: 9.
17. For a general discussion of Cuban immigration and US Cuba entry policy during the Castro era, see Masud-Piloto 1996.
18. The lottery gave priority to Cubans with work experience, education, and family reunification. On the lottery, see Castro 2002: 8–9.
19. In 2002, for example, Cubans accounted for the admission of about 24,900 of 26,800 North American "refugee and asylee adjustments" (USDHS 2003).
20. Figure 1.1 includes only legal entrants. Except in the years when Castro permitted Cubans to leave without US entry permission, more Dominicans and Salvadorans than Cubans probably emigrated illegally.
21. USDHS 2003: 19, 33 and 2006: 10.
22. For other delineations of Cuban émigré waves see, for example, García 1996, Pedraza 1985, 1996, 2007, and Amaro and Portes 1972.
23. An important exception were Cubans who had emigrated to work in the tobacco industry in Florida (Ingalls and Pérez 2003). These Cubans left their homeland with very different lived experiences, as laborers, than most Cubans who emigrated in the first years under Castro's rule.
24. Del Toro 2003.
25. Reputedly, when Batista threatened to build a highway through the club's golf course for "national security purposes," the club relented and permitted him membership. Louis Pérez shared this Havana lore with me, without knowledge of its veracity.
26. Amaro and Portes 1972.
27. I do not agree with Pedraza's (2007) uniform delineation of the Cuban diaspora as refugee-based. The label is most applicable to the first who fled the revolution, although not even to most of them (e.g. see Amaro and Portes 1972). I address the matter in more detail in Chapter 8. On differences between refugees and immigrants, see Kunz 1973, 1981.
28. Eire 2003: 309.
29. Eire 2003: 51.
30. Eire 2003: 158, 266.
31. Pérez 1999.
32. Eire 2003: 71.
33. Del Toro 2003: 27, 111.
34. Gimbel 1998: 30.
35. See Krull and Kobayashi (forthcoming) for a discussion of women brought up in pre-revolutionary Cuba who never emigrated despite their opposition to the social transformation.
36. For more detail on these émigrés, see Amaro and Portes 1972.
37. Zeitlin 1970.
38. On pre-revolution political generations, see also Aguilar-León 1972.
39. Huberman and Sweezy 1969: 118.
40. Engstrom 1997: 16.

41. Eire 2003.
42. Cited in Pedraza 2007: 73.
43. Fagen 1969; Wald 1978.
44. Fagen 1969; Bunck 1994.
45. Domínguez 1978.
46. According to Florida International University's 2004 survey, about half of the émigrés who uprooted during the first two decades of Castro's rule believed the main reason Cubans leave to be lack of freedom. Approximately another fourth believed the main reasons to be a combination of economic and political. In my survey a higher percentage noted emigration to be politically driven.
47. Pérez 1992.
48. Benglesdorf 1994; Roman 1999; Harnecker 1980.
49. Ojito 2005: 113.
50. Arenas 1993: 278.
51. Arenas 1993: 284, 288.
52. García 1996: 65.
53. See also Castro 2002: 7; Rodríguez Chavez 1992: 84; Bach, Bach and Triplett 1981.
54. García 1996: 63; Arenas 1993.
55. Ojito 2005.
56. Ojito 2005: 132.
57. Ojito 2005: 132.
58. See also García 1996: 72. Feeling a moral commitment, Miami Cuban Americans, however, raised over $2 million to help the new arrivals meet immediate needs. They also tried to help newcomers find jobs. García 1996: 72.
59. See the *Miami Herald* series of articles commemorating the twenty-fifth anniversary of the Mariel exodus in April 2005.
60. I discuss the "rectification campaign" and the underlying institutional, in contrast to professed ideological, rationale for the policy shift, in Eckstein 1994/2003: Chapter 3.
61. Hernández 2005.
62. Domínguez 2005: 164.
63. My discussion of youth who came of age during the Special Period draws on the work of Maria Isabel Domínguez 2005.
64. Fernández 2000.
65. On illegal emigration in the post-Soviet era, see Rodríguez Chávez 1996.
66. This framing of emigration is consistent with the "new economics of labor migration," which points to the decision to uproot as resting on collective family and household, if not also community, efforts to overcome homeland difficulty in accessing capital and credit. See Stark and Bloom 1985.
67. To leave legally Cubans had to pay fees to the government roughly triple the average annual state salary, which in the post-Soviet era no longer covered minimum subsistence needs. In addition, they had to pay plane fees costing hundreds of dollars. Legally sanctioned emigration thus became an option mainly only for islanders who could supplement their state salaries with black market earnings or who had relatives abroad willing to absorb the costs. After 1995, when US and Cuban authorities agreed to collaborate in returning to the island Cubans found at sea seeking to emigrate without official permission, speedboat escapes became preferred for illegal entrants. The speed of the trips minimized detection at sea. But speedboat transport cost about $8,000 to $10,000 around the turn of the century, thirty times the average islander's official yearly earnings. Thus, islanders became even more dependent on family abroad to cover illegal rather than legal emigration costs.

68. Once Washington routinized admission, with bilateral accords signed in 1994 and 1995, it established a skill bias to immigrant entrants. It gave preference to people with skills, as well as to family reunification. At the same time, though, the Cuban government contained a "brain drain" by restricting professionals to whom it granted exit permits. In the post-Soviet era Cuban authorities even sparingly authorized travel visas to doctors, because the health cadre who were denied emigration visas turned to travel to international conferences as an emigration strategy.

69. Few agriculturalists qualified for Washington's family reunification and skill-based admit preference system. But new government initiatives in Cuba in the 1990s may also have inclined certain agriculturalists to stay. The government transformed state farms into cooperatives and it established private markets where farmers could sell surplus they produced beyond their obligations to the state at market prices determined by supply and demand.

70. For a discussion among Cuban scholars about why Cubans emigrate, including about the island's culture of immigration, see Hernández et al. 2002.

71. Symmes 2008: 324–25.

72. Scott 1985. Scott considers resistance by those who are dominated as a weapon of the weak.

2 Immigrant Imprint in America

1. Alba and Nee 2003, Waters and Jiménez 2005, and Bean and Stevens 2003 provide excellent syntheses of the vast literature on assimilation and immigrant incorporation in the new immigrant era. Earlier analyses include Alba 1990, Lieberson 1985, Waters 1990, and Gans 1992. Gordon 1964 delineates different aspects of assimilation, and conditions under which they are likely to transpire.

2. Rumbaut 2004.

3. See, for example, Alba and Nee 2003 and Waters and Jimenez 2005.

4. Waters and Jimenez 2005, Alba and Nee 2003.

5. See, for example, Portes and Zhou 1993, Portes and Rumbaut 2001, Waldinger and Feliciano 2004. The term segmented assimilation has been used to capture such differential adaptation. If foreign-born assimilate into lower class groups, they may take on those groups values, and limit their economic prospects in turn.

6. See Wilson and Portes 1980 for the original conceptualization of the enclave thesis. For a more recent analysis by Portes of enclave dynamics that explores its different impact on different émigré waves, see Portes and Shafer 2007.

7. See, for example, Sanders and Nee 1992, Light and Karageorgis 1994, and Waldinger 1994.

8. Waldinger 1994.

9. The literature on people-to-people transnationalism is also already too vast to cite. Some examples include Glick Schiller, Basch, and Szanton-Blanc 1992; Schiller and Fouron 2001; Robert Smith 2006; Guarnizo 1997, 1998; Levitt 2001; Portes, Guarnizo and Landolt 1999; Portes, Haller and Guarnizo 2002; Kyle 2000; Massey, Durand, and Golding 1994; and Smith 2006. For review essays and collections of essays, see Kivisto 2001, *Global Networks* 1 no. 3 (July 2001), and *International Migration Review* 37 no. 3 (Fall 2003). These works can be consulted for additional references.

10. Levitt and Glick Schiller 2004.

11. Mannheim 1952.

12. Ryder 1965.

13. Scott 1985, 1990.

14. Anderson 2006.
15. Island-born immigrants typically refer to themselves as Cuban. Immigrant children are more likely to self-identify as Cuban American. I typically refer to the foreign-born as they would, except when usage of the term "Cuban" confuses people on the island with immigrants.
16. Erlick 1970.
17. Data personally obtained from the Department of Homeland Security in 2007.
18. *New York Times* February 21, 2008: C11.
19. This is a remarkable degree of concentration. There are more than 4,000 counties in the US, and less than 1 percent of all Americans are of Cuban origin. Boswell 2002: ii, 3, 25. See also www.epodunk.com/ancestry/Cuban *New York Times* April 11, 2000: B-1; Boswell 2002: 27, 28; *Miami Herald* September 17, 2001 cited in www.miami.com/herald September 20, 2001.
20. Data personally obtained from the Department of Homeland Security.
21. http://www.miami.com/mld/miamiherald/5907411.htm.
22. Cubans were joined by Puerto Ricans, Nicaraguans, and Colombians, and in smaller numbers by Mexicans, Central Americans other-than-Nicaraguans, and others from the Caribbean (Boswell et al. 2002: 13, 14, 17, 21; United States Census Bureau State and County QuickFacts, Miami-Dade County, Florida http://quickfacts.census.gov/qfd/states/12025.htm). Latin Americans were lured by the city Cubans remade, at the same time that deteriorating conditions in their home countries induced them to uproot. Not only revolutions, but civil wars, natural disasters, deteriorating economic conditions, and stepped up crime and insecurity, led rich and poor alike to follow the Cuban example and make Miami their home.
23. García 1996: 74–75.
24. The metropolitan area encompasses almost the entire county of Miami-Dade. It includes over two dozen municipalities that range substantially in size.
25. www.epodunk.com/ancestry/cuban; Boswell 2002: 3.
26. Cuban immigrants are exceptional in their geographic concentration, as distinct from, in Massey's 1985 words, their spatial assimilation.
27. When drawing here and elsewhere in the book on FIU-IPOR surveys, I cite the survey institute's émigré cohort classification. Most in the Institute's 1959–1964, 1965–1974, 1975–1984, and 1985–2004 (and its distinction in 2007 between 1985–1994 and 1995–2007) émigré cohorts correspond, respectively, to the Golden Exiles, Freedom Flighters, Marielitos, and New Cubans. Few Cubans emigrated from the time the Freedom Flights ended until the Mariel exodus, and afterwards, until the *balsero* (rafters) exodus following the break-up of the Soviet Union. While the 1959–1964 émigrés form the core of the Exile cohort, many who left until the Freedom Flights ended shared with them a similar pre-revolution generation formation.
28. *Miami Herald* April 24, 2002 www.miami.com/mld/miamiherald/news/locl/3315360.htm.
29. Portes and Shafer 2007: 167.
30. Other Latin American immigrants similarly tend to interact and identify mainly with their own country-of-origin group, rather than with *Latinos/Latinas* of diverse national origins. DeSipio 1996: 177.
31. García 1996: 74; Portes and Stepick 1993: 175.
32. García 1996: 114.
33. Portes and Stepick 1993: 161, 175.
34. García 1996: 74, 210. According to the group US English, in 2008, Florida was one of thirty states with English laws (www.us-english.org).
35. Unless otherwise indicated, my information on language draws on FIU-IPOR 2004, summarized in Table 3.4.

36. Higham 2002.
37. Portes and Stepick 1993: 41–42, 46.
38. Bean and Stevens (2003: 169–70) imply that the Cuban American perceptions reflect a shift in the new immigrant era. The continual influx of immigration from non-English language countries, especially from Spanish-speaking countries, may increase the perceived benefits of language maintenance and bilingualism. On the impact of continued immigrant group influx on the adaptation of immigrants, see also Waters and Jiménez 2005.
39. Cubans are not alone among Hispanics, nationwide as well as in Miami, in increasing their command of English over the years. This is especially true inter-generationally (www.pewhispanic.org/site/docs/pdf; Alba 2006).
40. Putnam 2000.
41. Tweed 1997.
42. García 1996: 99.
43. García 1996: 95.
44. Goffman (1974) speaks to the more general role such boundary-setting may have.
45. FIU-IPOR 2000.
46. García 1996: 197.
47. Portes and Stepick 1993: 138.
48. Suro 1998: 176.
49. topics.nytimes.com/top/references/timestopics/people/c/celia_cruz.
50. Reflecting the political lenses through which Cubans of the two sides of the revolutionary struggle viewed the Queen of Salsa, island authorities considered Celia Cruz a traitor to their cause. They tried to remove her from islanders' collective memory by banning her music after she defected, and they barely made public mention of her death. The two sets of Cubans, on their respective sides of the Straits, attributed opposing symbolism to the star singer.
51. I describe a sampling of social, cultural, and economic groups in this chapter. Chapter 3 focuses on political groups. Exiles, however, imbue even nominally non-political groups with their own shade of meaning. Unless otherwise indicated, I base my discussion of groups on information from interviews that Anne Fernández and I conducted. Anne wrote an excellent undergraduate term paper in 2001 at Harvard based on her research. I also draw on printed information obtained from organizations whose leaders I interviewed, including from their websites. I supplement this data with material from secondary sources. Some groups have chapters both in Miami and Union City. This is especially true of the political groups, such as Alpha 66, an ex-political prisoners' group, el Movimiento 30 de Noviembre, and the Cuban American National Foundation. Typically the Miami groups take the lead. There are a few specifically women's, though not feminist, groups.
52. FIU-IPOR 2004.
53. Philanthropy impacts on relations among donors. Research in the US shows that gala fundraising events strengthen social ties among the well-to-do (Ostrower 1995).
54. Didion 1987: 52–53.
55. The 1966 Cuban Adjustment Act entitled Cuban émigrés to residency status after one year and citizenship five years later, plus Medicare, Medicaid, and welfare.
56. A famous US example of a health-based service organization that reinvented itself rather than face demise was the March of Dimes after the discovery and dissemination of the vaccine that cured polio. On the March of Dimes, see Sills 1957.

57. www.ligacontraelcancer.org.
58. This information comes from www.ligacontraelcancer.org, plus an interview I conducted. I could not identify the ethnicity of two members of the Board of Directors.
59. Also indicative of how "Anglos" had their own organizational world, the Miami Chapter of the Junior League, a prominent women's group, one of nearly three hundred affiliated Leagues worldwide, had no more than four Hispanics on its seventeen-person board of directors in 2004–2005 and a membership that was approximately 80 percent non-Hispanic White. And no more than four of the eighty presidents of the association since the formation of the Miami Chapter were Cuban or other Hispanics (inferred from surnames). www.juniorleagueofmiami.com.
60. Anne Fernández quotes the assessment by a member.
61. The equity members, who lived in the island's condominium complex, included international and national glitterati who made Miami a winter home.
62. García 1996: 91.
63. Suro 1998: 169.
64. Symmes 2008: 330.
65. Pérez 2001: 103. Pérez notes how exceptional it is for one-fifth of the children of an immigrant group to attend private schools, especially schools the group itself establishes and administers. The schools were bilingual.
66. Cited by Anne Fernández.
67. Suro 1998: 170.
68. Symmes 2008.
69. See Portes 2005: 201 for a listing of groups affiliated with the two umbrella associations in Miami.
70. García 1996: 92.
71. Orozco et al. 2005; Menjivar 2000; Burgess 2004; Levitt 2001.
72. García 1996: 92–93.
73. García 1996: 93–94.
74. Estimates by Anne Fernández.
75. The Cuban American who served as publisher of the *Miami Herald* in the early 2000s was US-born, with one Cuba-born parent.
76. In publicly retaining their ethnic commitment, Cuban Americans admitted into the highest Miami circles differed from minorities tapped to serve in the national "power elite." At the national level, ethnic identity gets downplayed (Domhoff 1967).
77. The group, GRASP (Guantanamo Refugee Assistance Services Program), run by women, aimed to help rafters learn to apply for work and social assistance, acquire command of English, validate professional credentials, and adopt ethical standards (e.g. not to rely on bribes). After receiving initial funding from the United Way, GRASP secured nearly half a million dollars of federal funds channeled through county offices. While providing rafters with support not made available to other new immigrants, GRASP was especially concerned with preventing a repeat of the nativistic backlash the Mariel arrivals had unleashed.
78. The IPUMS sample of the census is not available specifically for Union City.
79. The 2004 American Community Survey, found, for example, the Cuban population in the US to have a higher level of education and home ownership, as well as a higher median household income, than other Hispanics. That year the median household income for Cubans was $38,000, compared to $36,000 for other Hispanics and $48,000 for non-Hispanic Whites. However, the median income for US-born Cubans, at $50,000, exceeded that of non-Hispanic Whites. Cited in Pew Hispanic Center 2006.

80. Díaz-Briquets and Pérez-López 2003: 12, 15; Portes and Shafer 2007: 165.
81. However, his island living costs had been far less, for he, like all Cubans, paid no more than 10 percent of his income on housing and nothing for health care, and food he received through the ration system cost little.
82. In the near future émigrés' technical training may decline, for in the post-Soviet era the younger generation have no access on any scale to subsidized overseas training. Many Cubans studied in the Soviet Union before it broke up.
83. Studies of the relationship between self-employment and income among immigrants differ in their findings. Some find a positive correlation (e.g. Wilson and Portes 1980; Light 1984; Waldinger 1986; Portes and Zhou 1996). Others find no positive correlation (e.g. Bates 1994).
84. Portes and Shafer 2007: 171.
85. Díaz-Briquets 1985; Portes and Stepick 1993: 133.
86. Boswell 2002: 35.
87. Similarly, by the turn of the century the embroidery business for which Union City had been famous, and which had employed many Exiles in their early years in the US, had moved overseas where labor was cheaper. It thus was not a possible source of employment for New Cubans when they arrived.
88. I focus on personal income. However, Pérez 1986 correctly notes that Cubans benefited financially from women working, from *family* earnings. The median household income among Cubans was higher than among other Latin American immigrants, but lower than among some Asian immigrant groups, such as Chinese. See Portes and Rumbaut 2001: 74.
89. Controlling for years in the US, only in 1990 did another émigré cohort, that of the 1970s, include more high-income earners.
90. There was one exception. In 2000 among the over-40 year-olds the percentage of self-employed was highest among 1970 arrivals.
91. See Pedraza 1985: 4–52; Portes and Stepick 1993: 46.
92. García 1996: 69.
93. Dideon 1987: 90; Grenier and Stepick 1992: 11.
94. Portes and Stepick 1993: 46.
95. The SBA does not categorize Hispanics by country of origin.
96. Portes and Stepick 1993: 132–40.
97. Although the focus here is on Miami, in the years when Union City was predominately Cuban more than 90 percent of the businesses on Bergenline Avenue were owned by island-born. *New York Times* February 21, 2008: C11.
98. Portes and Stepick 1993: 133.
99. Sassen 2006.
100. www.co.miami-dade.fl.us/portofmiami/cargo_facts.htm; Kanter 1995: 285.
101. Grenier and Stepick 1992: 2.
102. Kanter 1995: 284, 303.
103. Michael Harrington 1981 spoke of "the Other American," unable to share in the American Dream. Writing at a time of low immigration, Harrington noted the Other American to include elderly and unskilled, and victims of labor-displacing technological innovations.
104. The poverty rate among Cuban American elderly is more than triple the rate among non-Hispanic Whites. And the poverty rate is higher among island than US-born Cuban Americans. Pew Hispanic Center 2006.
105. Pew Hispanic Center 2006.
106. See, for example, Wilson and Portes 1980; Portes and Bach 1985; and Portes and Shafer 2007.
107. Huntington 2004.

108. Other analysts, focusing on other immigrant groups and other labor markets, question the very concept of an enclave economy separate from the broader labor market. Or they qualify the conditions under which ethnic economies work to the advantage of members, in terms of employment access and, especially, employee, along with employer, earnings. See Logan et al. 1994; Waldinger 1993; Bean and Stevens 2003; Sanders and Nee 1992. The Koreans, like the Cubans, formed an ethnic economy.
109. Pew Hispanic Center 2006.
110. The one exception was among forty to sixty-four year-olds in 1980.
111. Non-Cuban Americans, of course, may also exploit Cuban (along with other Latin American) immigrants in Miami.

3 Immigrant Politics: For Whom and for What?

1. In similar fashion during the last large immigration wave, in mayor cities White Anglo-Saxon Protestants left politics to the foreign born, to Irish in particular, as they concentrated on making money.
2. Verba *et al.* 1995.
3. While this chapter focuses on Miami, Cuban Americans, both island and US-born, also dominated Union City politics. However, by 2007, their representation in city governance was on the decline, following their dramatic demographic drop-off. In 2007, one Commissioner was Cuban American and another was half Cuban American, half Puerto Rican. The others were Dominican, Ecuadorian, and "Anglo." And in neighboring West New York the same year, which by then had a slightly larger Cuban population than Union City, only one Commissioner, along with the mayor, were Cuban American. Embedded in a multi-ethnic local political milieu, Cuban American politicians in the two New Jersey communities played by more inter-ethnic coalition-building politics than in Miami-Dade County.
4. Cubans have a higher citizenship rate than other Latin American immigrants. However, Asian immigrants also have a high citizenship rate.
5. Citizenship rates in Miami remained lower than nationally even though Cuban American leaders in the "Second Havana" promoted naturalization to garner political power locally and to influence Washington foreign policy (DeSipio 1996: 153). The Miami rates were lower even among Cuban Americans of voting age. It would appear that Cuban Americans who dispersed were more predisposed to politically assimilate than those who settled where ethnic attachments were strongest.
6. Cuban émigrés are not the only Latin American origin with high voter registration rates. The same is true of Dominican immigrants. In contrast, rates are lower among Mexican immigrants. DeSipio 1996: 156.
7. Robert Dahl 2005 argued already decades ago that immigrant groups became more focused on class than ethnic concerns once upwardly mobile economically.
8. *Miami Herald* September 4, 2000: 1.
9. Moreno and Warren 1995; Hill and Moreno 2002.
10. Dario Moreno estimated in 2005 that 60 percent of the Cuban American state legislators were island-born. Personal communication December 2005.
11. Mario and Lincoln's grandfather had served as mayor of his hometown and as a Congressman, and their father served as majority leader in the House of Representatives in Batista's government.
12. Nordlinger 2003.
13. *New York Times* March 8, 2006: 16. In an irony of history, Lincoln's and

Mario's aunt, Rafael's sister, briefly was wife to Fidel. But that did not keep the Díaz-Balarts from turning politically on the Cuban head of state.

14. Guerra 2007: 11.
15. FIU-IPOR conducted its 2004 survey before Bush clamped down on Cuban American rights to visit and send remittances to island family.
16. Moreno and Rae 1992.
17. www.galegoup.com/free_resources/chh/bio/lehtinen_i.htm.
18. Table 3.3 shows fewer registered voters to favor a US military intervention, probably because they have more faith in "their own." Cuban Americans blame the failure of the Exile-led Bay of Pigs invasion on President Kennedy's refusal to provide troops and other military backing.
19. While accepting US policy, only 28 percent of registered voters favored an expansion of agricultural trade to Cuba beyond its current level.
20. Brito et al. 2005.
21. Moreno 1997.
22. *New York Times* June 20, 1998: 8.
23. Date 1998.
24. The Florida Medical Association refused to tolerate exam exemption. The Association argued that patients' healthcare would be at risk. *St. Petersburg Times* May 21, 2000, www.sptimes.com/News/052100/Perspective/End_the_favoritism.shtml).
25. *New York Times* March 28, 1999: 36. Similarly, constituents judged politicians associated with political machines a century ago, during the previous period of large-scale immigration, more by the goods and services they delivered than by compliance with the law. Mayor Curley in Boston, for example, remained notoriously popular despite imprisonment for breaking the law.
26. *New York Times* March 28, 1999: 36 and November 1, 1991: 14.
27. An incident that captured the attention of the media and the Miami popular imagination involved him showing up unannounced late at night at the home of a retiree who had sent him a caustic letter.
28. His city manager and a city commissioner, for example, were convicted of taking bribes from city contractors.
29. People known as ballot brokers had become common. They paid or manipulated voters to give them signed, blank absentee ballots that could then be cast for any candidate. *New York Times* November 12, 1997: 20; Alberto Russi, a 92-year-old political boss in Little Havana in the late 1990s was charged with possession of more than one hundred absentee ballots and found guilty of four counts of voter fraud, while Suárez and his staff were found to have tampered with nearly five thousand absentee ballots. www.thegully.com/essays/a. . ./00113miami_vote_fraud.htm.
30. *New York Times* June 20, 1998: 8.
31. www.campaignwatch.org/semdti.htm. Despite leaving office in disgrace, Suárez in 2001 ran again for mayor. He was, however, defeated.
32. Moreno and Warren 1995. Indicative of the Cuban American base that the Republican Party built up beginning in the 1980s, all Cuban Americans in the Miami-Dade County delegation to Congress were Republican, whereas none of the other Representatives were. And at the state level, the Republican Party chose a Cuban American for its chief officer in 1998.
33. His wife claimed that he hurled a terracotta tea container at her during a marital dispute that bruised her head.
34. *Miami Herald*, cited in http://familyinjustice.com/local/miami_mayor_carollo.html.
35. More than a dozen officers were indicted on federal charges that they planted evidence and lied to cover up their role in several shootings.

36. In 2006 Díaz, however, was found guilty of a conflict-of-interest real estate deal involving some fellow city officials. www.miamisunpost.com/newsb04120708.htm.
37. Brito et al. 2005.
38. http://findlaw.com/ap/o/623/11–15. Key developers associated with Díaz's "Miami 21," the name of his urban renewal undertaking, included Democrats, such as big-time Florida developer Jorge Pérez, of the Related Group, and Paul Cejas, the large Democratic contributor who Clinton appointed ambassador to Belgium. They involved not only Republicans. Non-Hispanic national developers also won major local contracts.
39. The "Miami miracle" was racist in its effect, if not in intent. Victims of the condo development and rise in housing costs banded together to form a civic group, Miami Neighborhoods United, but to little avail.
40. *New York Times* May 20, 1998: 8.
41. The Latin Builders Association (LBA), the largest Hispanic construction association, powerful lobbying organization, and local campaign contributor, for example, led a demagogic campaign against an ordinance whereby commissioners were to demand two-thirds approval for some zoning changes. The measure was designed to control reckless building in the county. Builders in general, and the LBA in particular, developed unsavory reputations, as a president of the LBA publicly acknowledged (*Miami New Times* www.miaminewtimes.com/issues/1995–07–20/feature.html).
42. *New York Times* May 20, 1998: 8.
43. *New York Times* June 20, 1998: 8.
44. African Americans' resentment of Cuban Americans prompted protest not only when Exiles tried to ban Mandela from speaking in Miami, as previously noted, but also after the arrival of Marielitos whom they felt received job preference. African Americans protested on three other occasions in the 1980s. Suro 1998: 175.
45. Portes and Stepick 1993: 46.
46. Their politicking helped keep the domestic price of sugar substantially above the world market price at a time when Washington promoted free trade. They also fought Florida environmentalists concerned with their business activity eroding the fragile Everglades ecosystem. The Fanjuls managed never to invest heavily in clean farming methods and alternative energy. Furthermore, they lobbied, with others in the sugar industry, for extending the deadline of the Everglades clean-up, in conformity with the Clean Water Act, from 2006 to 2016. *New York Times* July 31, 2008: 14, 16.
47. One brother, a life-long Democrat, served as co-chair of Clinton's 1992 Florida presidential campaign, while another, who identified with the Republicans, was a member of "Team 100," the select group who donated more than $100,000 to the 1988 George H. Bush presidential campaign. The Republican brother served as vice chairman of the Bush-Quayle finance committee (www.opensecrets.org/pubs/cubarcport/players.asp).
48. www.canfnet.org.
49. Black and Black 2002.
50. Fonzi 1993: 46–48, 57.
51. *New York Times* July 13, 1982: 1.
52. Fonzi 1993: 11; Haney and Vanderbush 2005: 43–44.
53. Fonzi 1993: 37.
54. *New York Times* June 20, 1998: 8.
55. "CANF Members and Directors through 1994," Cuban Information Archives Document 0239 http://cuban-exile.com/doc_226–250/doc0239.html; Tamayo 2002.

56. Unless otherwise indicated, my discussion of Cuban American PACs draws on the multitude of superb data prepared by the Center for Responsive Politics and available at their website www.opensecrets.org, including in separate files at ubsl/cubareport.asp, pubs/cubareport/appendix.asp, and pubs/cubareport/legislation.asp). PAC contributions accounted for 19 percent of all Cuban American political donations between 1979 and 2000, with the Foundation the only Cuban American PAC of significance during these years. Cuban American political contributions totaled $8.8 million in the twenty-one-year period, and accounted for nearly half of Florida's Hispanic campaign contributions. Florida ranked first, nationwide, in money raised by Hispanic PACs.
57. *New York Times* June 20, 1998: 8.
58. Franklin 1993.
59. Although Florida based, the Foundation established chapters in Union City and in Puerto Rico. The New Jersey branch coordinated New York area activity for the organization.
60. Smith 2000.
61. Other ethnic lobbyists, such as Armenians, Lebanese, Greeks, and Italians, raised less than $200,000 in the 1990s.
62. The "baseball diplomacy" involved an exchange of games between Cuban All-Stars and the Baltimore Orioles, in Cuba and the US, to promote cross-border good-will. After failing to prevent the games, Menéndez helped organize opposition at the US stadium site, in Baltimore. He helped arrange for a large bus caravan to transport protesters from the New York-New Jersey area to the Baltimore game, where they were joined by a smaller contingent from more distant Miami. Exiles associated with the Cuban American National Foundation, an important contributor to his political campaigns, orchestrated the effort to obstruct the play-offs.
63. Schoultz 2009.
64. Tufte 1978.
65. Antipathy to Communism influenced US policy during the Cold War, and continued to do so after its end. However, in the post-Cold War era it cannot account for vacillations in how hardline US policy was, all the while that Cuba remained Communist. It also cannot explain why US policy-makers tightened the Cuba, while lifting the China and Vietnam, embargoes. Anti-Communism helped legitimate policies that I show to be grounded in domestic politics. Moreover, some lawmakers opposed embargo-tightening while remaining ideologically anti-Communist.
66. Presidents, as part of the "bargain," also appointed prominent Cuban Americans to key administrative posts. This was especially true of President George W. Bush.
67. www.cubanet.org/CNews/y03/ago03/15e4.htm.
68. Black and Black 2002. When Chair of the Dade County Republican Party in 1984, Jeb Bush worked successfully to make his party the Cuban émigrés' natural political home. Under his sway, between 1979 and 1988 the percentage of Republicans among registered party members in the county spiraled from 39 to 68 percent (Finnegan 2004: 74).
69. Additional evidence that Cuban American Florida bloc voting results, in no small part, from Republican success at courting once-Democrats and not from an inherent conservatism of Cuban Americans, is suggested by Cuban Americans more likely to vote Democratic outside of than in Florida (DeSipio 1996: 29). Overall, though, Cuban Americans are more likely than Mexican Americans and Puerto Ricans to be Republican.
70. Morley and McGillion 2002: 45–46.

71. Schoultz 2009: Chapter 12.
72. In the mid-1970s the Republican Ford administration granted US subsidiaries the right to trade with Cuba through third countries.
73. Eckstein 1994/2003: 282, fn 33; Morley and McGillion 2002: 43, 49.
74. Cuban American lobbyists failed, however, to block Washington from implementing the component of the 1995 US–Cuba bilateral accord that specifies return to Cuba of islanders found at sea trying to make their way across the Florida Straits without US entry permission. On this matter, see Domínguez 2006. Yet, as I note, Mas Canosa convinced Clinton to tighten the personal embargo in exchange for his not opposing the change in immigration policy.
75. Morley and McGillion 2002: 52–113.
76. The Brothers to the Rescue planes that the Cuban government shot down were, at the time, over international waters, very close to Cuba's. On previous missions the Exile group had intruded upon Cuban airspace to leaflet islanders to oppose Castro's government. Before firing, the Cuban government had issued warnings to the pilots to leave.
77. FIU-IPOR 1997.
78. The White House inserted a presidential waiver for the controversial Title III that entitled US nationals to sue foreign investors who trafficked in confiscated property that they had owned before the revolution. At the same time, the bill also codified the embargo, previously subject to presidential discretion.
79. Morley and McGillion: 2002: 105.
80. Schoultz 2009: Chapter 13.
81. Clinton 2004: 701, 727.
82. The percentage of countries that condemned US Cuba economic sanctions rose from 33 in 1992 to 73 after the Helms–Burton Bill went into effect, and then to 88 in 2001. Domínguez 2008: 206.
83. While the Elián affair trumped all other concerns, hardliners were unhappy with Clinton's slight lifting of restrictions on money transfers and travel following the Pope's 1998 visit to the island, with his permitting sales and donations of medicines to Cuba, with his promotion of the baseball diplomacy, with his collaboration with the Cuban government on antinarcotics matters, and with his "wetfoot" policy, of returning to Cuba islanders found at sea attempting to emigrate illegally. *New York Times* July 7, 1999: 1.
84. FIU-IPOR 2000.
85. Flores et al. 2008.
86. Finnegan 2004: 70.
87. Francisco Aruca ran two well-known, more liberal radio programs, one in Spanish, the other in English. However, he did not own the media station that aired the programs. The Committee for Cuban Democracy also ran a centrist radio program.
88. Flores et al. 2008.
89. Joe Crankshaw, "Florida lawmakers are battling Castro," http://canf.org/2004/&in/noticias%cuba_2004-feb.
90. www.cubancentral.com/article.asp?ID=97.
91. San Martín 2003.
92. *Miami Herald* November 17, 2006/www.miami.com/mld/miamiherald/16042431.htm.
93. www.opensecrets.org.
94. Bush also made Gutiérrez co-chair of a second Commission for Assistance to a Free Cuba.
95. By 2008 Cubans made up only about 45 percent of Florida's Hispanic registered voters, down from 75 percent in 2000. *New York Times* June 1, 2008 (www.nytimes.com/2008/06/01/us/01florida.html).

96. Unless otherwise indicated, information on the US-Cuba Democracy PAC, as well as on the Cuban Liberty Council (CLC), comes from their respective websites (www.uscubapac.com/nav.html and www.cubalibertycouncil.org), and from my own interviews with leadership of the CLC and the Cuban American National Foundation.

97. Latin American Working Group November 2005, as cited in *La Alborada* (Cuba American Alliance Education Fund November 15, 2005).

98. Swanson 2007.

99. The US-Cuba Democracy PAC raised money not merely from Cuban Americans who broke with the Foundation but also from some who remained associated with it. The donors who gave to the new PAC while maintaining their Foundation affiliation valued the PAC mission independent of intra-ethnic organizational in-fighting.

100. The 2001 split-off was not the first fissure within the Foundation, but it was the most far-reaching in impact, and it was the first to take generational form. Previously, for example, Frank Calzón broke with the Foundation and formed his own anti-Castro organization, Freedom House. After Calzón's split-off the Foundation flourished. The basis of Calzón's break-off rested more on a power play, and opposition to Mas Canosa's demagogic centralization of power, than to differences over strategy or organization objectives.

101. See Eisenstadt 1968.

102. Tamayo 2002.

103. Elliott and Valle 2003; Inter-American Dialogue 2007.

104. www.nytimes.com/2008/06/01/us/01florida.htm.

105. www.cubastudygroup.org.

106. FIU-IPOR 2000.

107. Support for an exile-led invasion even rose, from 60 to 71 percent, between 2004 and 2007 (Table 3.4). Support increased in the three-year interim among all cohorts as well as generations.

108. Finnegan 2004.

109. www.politico.com/news/stories/0408/9754.html.

110. www.msnbc.msn.com/id/20369459.

111. FIU-IPOR 2007.

4 The Personal is Political: Bonding Across Borders

1. The chapter does not address the fewer Cuba-to-US visits. No publicly available information exists on US visiting, although in 2000 an estimated 38,000 Cubans made family-related visits to the US. www.cubasocialista.cu/texto/csiroque040521.htm. Washington restricted visitors for fear that they would overstay their visas and use the opportunity to emigrate.

2. I refer the interested reader to consult my more detailed discussion of US and Cuba government visits policies, and their institutional underpinnings, in Eckstein 2009 and in Eckstein and Barberia 2002.

3. Eckstein and Barberia 2002: 814.

4. García 1996: 51. Moderates, who had been invited to participate in what Cuban authorities called The Dialogue, in 1978, pushed for visitation rights that hardliners opposed. At that juncture hardliners had not yet solidified their political dominance (see Forment 1989).

5. Cuba had accessed Western loans after world market sugar prices surged in the mid-1970s. Following a downturn in the sugar market, the government was left without sufficient hard currency from exports to pay money owed to overseas lenders. See Eckstein 1980.

6. In 1989, Marazul, the main travel agency booking Cuba trips, sent 5,000 Cuban Americans on visits (www.marazul.com/history).
7. Levine 2002.
8. García 1996: 49.
9. Omega 7 targeted Cuban officials and individuals, organizations, and businesses that dealt with or allegedly supported the Castro-led government. Omega 7 attacks included bombings, shootings, and assassinations. Many of its members were veterans of the Bay of Pigs invasion trained in demolition, intelligence, and commando techniques. In Union City Exile businessmen allegedly clandestinely funded Omega 7 and other hardline anti-Castro groups. Militants established a network through which they collected "taxes" from the Exile community. They then distributed funds to the groups they supported. According to a FBI report, businessmen provided an estimated $100,000 to such groups (http://cuban-exile.com/doc_001–025/doc0011.html).
10. Didion 1987: 100–101; García 1996: 50.
11. Portes and Zhou 1993.
12. Members of the Arieto group, including the editors of an arts and politics magazine with that name, organized the trip. One member of the first brigade, Carlos Muñiz, was assassinated in Puerto Rico in early 1979.
13. Dideon 1987: 119.
14. See also Eckstein and Barberia 2002: 813.
15. The Government Accountability Office (USGAO 2007: 31–33) concluded that data is too unreliable to assess the number of trip-takers in 2005 and 2006. All Cuban Americans who obtained special travel licenses did not necessarily make use of them; some may have traveled under general or group licenses, and others may have traveled without permission via third countries. Indicative of the range of estimates for 2005, the International Trade Commission estimated that about 171,000 US travelers entered Cuba, mainly Cuban Americans visiting family, while the US Treasury Department reported issuing about 26,000 travel licenses and the Department of Homeland Security reported 90,000 passengers traveling directly from the US to Cuba. Spadoni, in a personal communication with me, estimated, based on the USITC data, that approximately 136,800 Cuban Americans visited Cuba in 2005.
16. In 2008, Cuba was estimated to have a fixed line penetration of 10 percent and some 200,000 computers connected to the Internet, among a population of nearly 11.5 million inhabitants. Mello Veiga 2008.
17. Fouron and Glick-Schiller (2002) describe the Haitian diaspora as long-distance nationalists.
18. Officials had portrayed the diaspora as the Cuban community abroad very briefly at the time of the Carter era visits, to encourage islanders to accept émigrés whom they had previously been told to shun. But with the Mariel exodus, the country's leadership galvanized loyal revolutionaries to turn on those opting to join the diaspora.
19. Since 1966, Washington had extended immigration rights to such Cubans, in conjunction with the Cuban Adjustment Act.
20. Clinton (2004: 615) told Gabriel García Márquez, whom he met at the home of Bill and Rose Styron when vacationing on Martha's Vineyard, to tell Castro that he "has already cost me one election (for the Arkansas governorship, in 2000). He can't have two." The renowned Latin American author was a personal friend of Castro.
21. www.usinfo.state.gov/usa/laws/majorlaw/h927_enr.htm, sec. 112
22. LeoGrande 2008: 23.
23. The Bush Administration, however, clamped down on other-than-family travel, such as by education groups, which Clinton had permitted.

24. The Cuban American South Florida Congressional and state legislature contingent, and municipal and county officials, along with such hardline groups as Mothers and Women Against Repression and Unidad Cubana, also put pressure on Bush to tighten the personal embargo.
25. The report, as well as one issued in 2006, also called for pro-democracy and civil-society building in Cuba, to further island regime change. Anti-Castro Miami groups benefited materially from the Bush Administration initiative. Thus, tens of millions of dollars of US Agency for International Development money, ostensibly allotted to promote democracy in Cuba, were channeled to Florida-based groups. USGAO 2006: especially Table 9, p. 50.
26. Survey after the election, in 2007.
27. Schoultz 2009: Chapter 13 and LeoGrande 2008: 36–44. Bush, however, refused to concede to Congressional interest in lifting the travel ban altogether.
28. Noteworthy is that Bush loosened the personal embargo even though, following 9/11, he singled Cuba out as part of the "axis of evil."
29. "Democrats See Cuba Travel Limits as a Campaign Issue in Florida," *New York Times* June 1, 2008 (www.nytimes.com/2008/06/01/us/01florida),
30. See also FIU-IPOR 2000.
31. A higher percentage of the 1959–1964 émigrés whom I interviewed made homeland trips (see Appendix), no doubt because I purposely sought individuals who had made, and not only who had resisted, island visits.
32. A survey by the Velasquez Institute (2004) found younger and not merely recent immigrants to look favorably on homeland visits. The youngest immigrants would be those who experienced Cuba transformed by the post-Soviet-era crisis.
33. The 1990s crisis, however, contributed to Cubans developing their own collective as well as individual solutions to their newfound problems. On embryonic social activity independent of the state, see essays in the book edited by Tulchin et al. (2005) and by Dilla Alfonso et al. 1994.
34. *Wall Street Journal* September 20, 2004: 4.
35. Before the 1990s some clergy individually took on cross-border missions. However, community opposition then made such efforts difficult and the archdiocese neither promoted nor supported the endeavors.
36. Catholic Relief Services delivered over $20 million worth of supplies to Cuba between 1993 and 2001, after Hurricane Michelle in 2001, as well as after Hurricane Lili in 1996.
www.reliefweb.int/w/rwb.nsf/0/19cc5cd4a1123b6985256afe0054fbe4).
Following Hurricane Michelle Church World Service, the relief arm of the Protestant National Council of Churches, also funneled resources to Cuba.
37. www.us.net/cuban/cuban%20affairs/ca1998/bishops98–1.htm.
38. Hardliners not only discouraged donations, but wrote anti-Castro slogans on cans and containers. Castro refused marked items, donations he interpreted were motivated by politics, not compassion.
39. Wenski instead chartered a plane for a day that transported some one hundred eighty clergy and laity to Cuba for the Pope's Havana mass.
40. Mahler and Hansing 2005.
41. Although Bush initially exempted religious travelers from his clamp-down on travel in 2004, because the number of émigrés who used the religious loophole for visits soared, he quickly clamped down on this basis of visits as well.
42. Behar 2007: 17.
43. When Washington most restricted travel, fewer US-born than Cuba-born qualified for personal embargo exceptions.
44. FIU-IPOR 2000.

45. Orozco et al. 2005: 16. Nationalities of other immigrants surveyed included Colombians, Ecuadorians, Salvadorans, Guatemalans, Guyanese, Hondurans, Mexicans, Nicaraguans, Dominicans, Bolivians, and Jamaicans. The illegal status of many Guatemalans may explain why they made fewest homeland trips. Illegal immigrants run the risk of reentry problems following homeland visits.
46. Orozco et al. 2005: 16.
47. Ecuadorians and Salvadorans, however, were more likely than Cubans or Guyanese to stay less than a week.

5 Cuba Through the Looking Glass

1. See, for example, Linz 1975.
2. See, for example, Parrenas.
3. www.marxmail.org/facts/cuba_gallup.htm.
4. On the nation as an imagined political community capable of transplantation, see Anderson 2006.
5. See Pérez 1999: 255–78; González Echevarria 1999.
6. See Crahan and Armony 2008.
7. Cuban sects, such as *Santería*, for example, sponsored hard currency generating programs for immigrant induction that typically involved New Cubans.
8. Behar 2007.

6 Transforming Transnational Ties into Economic Worth

1. Both because the inflow of remittances is hard to monitor and because the Cuban government considers them politically controversial, the exact amount of money the diaspora sends remains unknown. Remittance estimates include hard currency Cubans themselves earn abroad which they bring back when returning to the island. For a discussion of the range of remittance estimates, and estimating difficulties, see Spadoni 2004.
2. Spadoni 2003.
3. Bendixen and Associates 2005: 11, 12.
4. Bendixen and Associates 2005: 12.
5. Orozco 2005.
6. IDB-MIF 2004, 2008; Inter-American Dialogue May 2007, p. 7.
7. Pew Hispanic Center 2006; Table 6.1; Inter-American Dialogue 2007; Orozco 2005; Burgess 2008.
8. For a more detailed discussion of shifts in US remittance policy, see Eckstein 2009.
9. Barberia 2004: 390–91; USDS-BWHA 2004.
10. Eckstein 1994/2003: Chapter 2.
11. In Eckstein 1994/2003 I argue that the government had institutional economic and not merely ideological reasons for promoting non-materialist values in the 1960s. It could thereby devote more revenue to investment.
12. Bourdieu 1986: 253 argues that a personalizing of gifts is essential for material sharing to induce a build-up of social capital, benefiting-generating social ties.
13. Bendixen and Associates 2005: 16.
14. www.state.gov/www/regions/wha/cuba/democ_act_1992.html.
15. *Economist* February 23, 2002: 42; *New York Times* July 14, 2003: 16 and May 1, 2008: 17.
16. EIU, *CCR* August 2004: 15.

17. http//lexingtoninstitute.org/932.shtml; EIU, *CCR* August 2004: 15; www.cubanfamilyrights.org.
18. www.fiu.edu/orgs/ipor/cuba8/pollresults.html.
19. Bendixen and Associates 2005.
20. Bendixen and Associates 2005: 17.
21. Velazquez Institute 2004.
22. See, for example, Russell 1986; Díaz-Briquets and Pérez-López 1997: 423; Rumbaut 2002.
23. Díaz-Briquets and Pérez-López 1997.
24. Bendixen and Associates 2005: 19.
25. According to an *Economist* report (October 23, 2001: 23), 96 percent of Cuban remittances financed family consumption.
26. Massey et al. 1998; Economist Intelligence Unit, *Latin American Country Briefing*, October 23, 2001.
27. Orozco et al. 2005: 34.
28. EIU, *CCR* November 2005: 20.
29. Room renters often operated on both sides of the law. They reported some rental earnings and meal charges, to appear law-abiding, while withholding information on all their activity to limit tax fees.
30. *New York Times* Section 3 May 26, 2002: 4.
31. Portes, Guarnizo and Landolt (1999) refer to such persons as transnational entrepreneurs.
32. Orozco 2004.
33. Orozco 2002a, 2004. In 2004 there were one hundred twenty-six registered remittance forwarders, ninety of them in Florida, the most important of which were Western Union and El Español. Barberia 2004: 395.
34. Also, because official transfers required affidavits, more staff work was required. Inter-American Dialogue 2007.
35. In 2000, nearly three-fourths of the funds Mexicans received in remittances from the US were sent electronically. The percentage was so high largely because the Mexican government made a concerted effort to lower sending costs.
36. Bendixen and Associates surveyed Cuban Americans nationwide, and not merely in Miami and Union City (and neighboring West New York). Outside these cities Cuban Americans typically lack access to *mulas* and other informal transfer businesses. The firm's survey base, thus, no doubt contributes to the high reporting of reliance on formal transfer mechanisms.
37. www.miamiherald.com August 10, 2000: 3.
38. Mauss 1967.
39. For example, Fouron and Glick Schiller 2002: 187; Itzigsohn et al. 1999; Menjívar 2000: 100; Landolt, Autler, and Baires 1999; and Lessinger 1995, note that immigrants from Haiti, the Dominican Republic, El Salvador, and India, respectively, feel an obligation to send remittances. Dominican and Salvadoran remittance-sending picked up dramatically following drastic economic downturns in the respective immigrants' home countries. The crises changed expectations, with immigrants coming to feel an obligation to send remittances to relatives they left behind to an extent they previously had not.
40. When they help island family, they more typically do so in kind than cash. The government cannot thereby access income shared.
41. *New York Times* January 14, 2003: 16; *Economist* February 23, 2002: 42.
42. Burgess 2009; Orozco 2002b; Levitt 2001; Menjívar 2000; Hamilton and Chinchilla 2001: 208–15. An estimated 8 percent of Salvadoran, and 9 percent of Mexican immigrants, belong to hometown associations. However, many more donate collective remittances (Burgess 2009). On Latin

American immigrant hometown associations more generally, see Orozco et al. 2005: 26–30, 55.

43. Some *municipio* groups, however, sent medicines and clothing to needy people in their hometowns, and a few sent funds for construction and renovations (García 1996: 92).

44. Two-thirds of the thirty-six Salvadorans in California who Menjívar (2000), for example, interviewed felt financially responsible for someone in El Salvador.

45. I here take issue with Díaz-Briquets and Pérez-López 1997.

46. Orozco et al. 2005: 56.

47. Coleman 1988, 1993 and Bourdieu 1986.

48. Social ties are central to social capital formation in so far as they are influenced by expectations. I refer to social capital as an individual/family asset, although the term has also been applied to organizations, communities, and nations (cf. Putnam 2000). Portes 2000 addresses the importance of bounded solidarity to social capital formation. For an extensive theoretical discussion of social capital as a form of capital, see Lin 2001.

49. Granovetter 1974.

50. Massey et al. 1987.

51. Massey et al. 1998.

52. Portes, Haller, and Guarnizo 2002.

53. Levitt 2001: 62, 200.

54. *Economist* February 23, 2002: 42; *New York Times* July 14, 2003: 16.

55. Bourdieu 1977. For a discussion of Bourdieu's conception of symbolic capital, see Swartz 1997.

56. In the context of the US, Hao 1994, as well as Coleman 1993, argued that single-headed households had such negative effects. In Cuba, crime rates spiraled in the post-Soviet era, but mainly because of the deep economic recession that the cut-off in Soviet bloc aid and trade caused, and the breakdown of previous social controls under the circumstances

7 Dollarization and its Discontents: Homeland Impact of Diaspora Generosity

1. LeoGrande and Thomas 2002: 334.

2. LeoGrande and Thomas 2002: 330.

3. ECLA 2000; Pérez Villanueva 2004.

4. Wallerstein 1974 and 1979.

5. Gallup Organization 2006. Forty-four percent of the thousand Havana and Santiago de Cuba residents Gallup surveyed said they wished to improve relations with the US. The two next most frequently mentioned countries with which they favored improved relations were China (17 percent) and Venezuela (15 percent).

6. Eckstein 1980 and 1994/2003: 247 and Table 7.1.

7. EIU, *CCR* August 2006: 29. Russia pressed for repayment of loans for such projects as a nuclear facility that the Soviet Union left unfinished, for imports never delivered, and for debt incurred in a defunct currency that had no agreed-upon hard currency value.

8. For a summary of Soviet aid, see LeoGrande and Thomas 2002.

9. EIU, *CCR* May 2005: 7.

10. Cuba instituted a foreign investment law in 1982, but negotiated few deals before the 1990s.

11. Pérez-López 2004: 151.

12. See pp. 109–110 for more details on the 1992 Cuba Democracy Act and the 1996 Cuba Liberty and Democratic Solidarity Act.
13. Cooperative production agreements involved a foreign investor who provided machinery, credits, and supplies in exchange for a share of profit or a product, while the company remained 100 percent Cuban-owned. Brundenius 2003: 6. Making matters worse, foreign investors repatriated more money than they brought in. Ritter 2004: 8, 9.
14. Mexico, in turn, benefited from the North American Free Trade Agreement (NAFTA).
15. In part, it became less economically rational for the government to invest in sugar production after both the price it received for sugar sales fell to around one-third what the Soviet bloc had paid and production costs rose (especially when Soviet oil subsidies stopped).
16. Eckstein 2003: fn 11, p. 305; Sánchez-Egozcue 2003.
17. World Bank, *WDI 2001*, 210.
18. Pérez Mok and García 2000; Monreal 2004; Brundenius 2003; EIU, *CCR* August 2001: 25. Aside from directly generating hard currency, tourism stimulated import substitution, particularly of light industrial goods. Reflecting this effect, imports dropped from accounting for approximately 88 percent of the goods and services tourism consumed in 1990 to 31 percent in 2001, all the while that tourism expanded. Monreal (2004) refers to tourism-induced domestic manufacturing in hard currency as "exports within the borders" and as export-substitution. On tourism, see also Pérez Mok and García, 2000: 5; EIU, *CCR* August 2001: 28.
19. While most hotels were 100 percent Cuban-owned, they were foreign-managed.
20. Washington also tried to pressure third countries not to invest in island tourism. The Jamaica-operated Super Club, for example, pulled out of Cuba after being warned by the US State Department that it was violating US law by trafficking in confiscated property (EIU, *CCR* August 2004: 24).
21. EIU, *CCR* November 2006: 27.
22. Sánchez-Egozcue 2007: 7.
23. In the early 2000s Cuba had more than thirty-one thousand health professionals working in seventy-one countries (Sánchez-Egozcue 2007: 17). The largest contingent worked in Venezuela, but seven hundred went to Bolivia after the election of Evo Morales to the presidency, financed by Venezuela under Hugo Chávez (EIU, *CCR* November 2006: 27). Venezuela also financed the commissioning of Cuban doctors to a number of other Latin American countries, and treatment of Latin American patients in Cuba (e.g. free eye surgery for four thousand Panamanians in 2006) (*Boston Globe* April 16, 2007: 3). Venezuela, in essence, contracted Cuba to provide aid, capitalizing on Cuba's comparative advantage in social service provisioning. There is no publicly available information documenting how much the Cuban government made from the overseas contracts. On Cuban overseas contracts, see Feinsilver 1993 and 2007. In 2005, the government founded Servicios Medicos Cubanos under the Council of State specifically to contract overseas medical missions.
24. The Cuban government paid overseas workers small hard currency supplements.
25. Eckstein 2003: 249, 250, and references therein.
26. EIU, *CCR* November 2006: 21.
27. See Barberia 2004 for a more detailed discussion of the government's shifting remittance regulations.
28. Barberia 2004: 387.

29. USDS-CAFC 2004: 35.
30. Cuban Americans with Internet access, in addition, acquired a new web based way to transfer money, cash2Cuba, that charged a lower commission rate than the wire services. Based in Canada, the service provides registered Cuban recipients with a card with which to make cash withdrawals. The remitter sends money that the island recipient withdraws in cash at banks or official exchange agencies, using a special Cuban corporation, CIMEX (which also operates dollar stores), debit-type card.
31. Spadoni 2003.
32. EIU, *CCR* August 2001: 20 and *CCR* June 2000:19; Barberia 2004: 372–73.
33. Spadoni 2003. Most of the other hard currency islanders accessed came from a combination of informal and illegal activity linked to tourism and black marketeering, and from convertible currency (or hard currency worth) supplements to state sector peso earnings allotted to motivate labor.
34. USDS-CAFC 2004: 35. See also Spadoni 2003. In that these State Department figures became justification for President Bush's clampdown on remittance-sending rights in 2004, the estimates may be exaggerated.
35. See Monreal 1999 and 2004.
36. Barberia 2004: 370.
37. García Molina 2005: 32.
38. The opening of private and then state-run markets, and the break-up of state farms, further reduced tensions by stimulating production that helped bring prices down.
39. Different state institutions operate the dollar stores, but they are expected to turn over hard currency revenue to the central government.
40. This means an item that cost $100 to produce or import, would carry a 140 percent tax and sell for $240.
41. Interview with a Cuban economist in 2002.
42. Barberia 2004: 375.
43. EIU, *CCR* February 2003: 9.
44. EIU, *CCR* August 2004: 19.
45. EIU, *CCR* August 2004: 9, 11.
46. EIU, *CCR* November 2005: 9.
47. IDB MIF 2004, Orozco 2002, USDS CAFC 2004.
48. Inter-American Dialogue 2007.
49. EIU, *CCR* November 2004: 18.
50. The government exempted the exchange of other foreign currencies for convertible local currency from the surcharge. This encouraged remittance-sending in other-than-dollars, for example, in Canadian dollars and euros. In the other hard currencies the government avoided transaction costs which US authorities in 2004 imposed on third-country banks that exchanged Cuba's dollars.
51. Within half a year after Havana authorities introduced the taxation on dollar conversion they reduced the share of hard currency remittances in US dollars from 90 to 30 percent (EIU, *CCR* August 2005: 22). On the advantages and disadvantages of dollarization versus euroization, from the Cuban government's vantage point, see Rose and Yanes Faya 2004.
52. EIU, *CCR* May 2005: 10.
53. While justified politically, the government had economic reasons to adjust the exchange rate.
54. Participants in state-contracted, state revenue-generating overseas missions also earned hard currency. Julie Feinsilver estimated that doctors on overseas missions in the early 2000s received as much as $183 per month from the

Cuban government and $250–375 from host countries. Personal communication. See also Feinsilver 2007.

55. Cubans who earned money above and beyond the contract could retain the income for themselves. Until 2007 employees of the Ministry of Higher Education were required to turn in 75 percent of their overseas earnings.
56. The self-employed were not, however, exclusively dependent on cash and materials provided by family abroad. Islanders also made use of black market sources of revenue and supplies, and goods stolen from state jobs.
57. Henken 2000.
58. Uriarte 2008: 286.
59. Gallup Organization 2006. The Gallup Cuba data is based on interviews with one thousand Cubans in Havana and Santiago de Cuba.
60. EIU, *CCR* August 2004: 14. Despite mounting resentment, in 2006 three-fourths of the Cubans that Gallup interviewed expressed confidence in the state health care (as well as education) system. Almost without exception they felt the social services to be universally accessible. This is more than twice the percentage who, on average, felt that way in cities in twenty other countries Gallup surveyed in the region. And two and one-half as many residents of Havana and Santiago as residents in the other cities said their country received the best quality education. Media.gallup.com/worldpoll/pdf/TFCuba022207.pdf.
61. Workers received debit cards usable only at designated stores. In this manner the government addressed consumer demand while minimizing the circulation of money that could fuel the black market.
62. UCTEC March 17, 2002: 12.
63. EIU, *CCR* August 2005: 21.
64. *Economist* October 23, 1999: 37; EIU, *CCR* February 2001: 19 and August 2001: 22; World Bank, *WDI* 2001: 48.
65. Anderson 2006: 50.
66. EIU, *CCR* August 2005: 20, 221.
67. Barberia 2004: 370.
68. EIU, *CCR* May 2001: 18.
69. See EIU, *CCR* August 2001: 20 and *CCR* June 2000: 19. Low interest rates, of 0.5 percent annually, for depositors of more than $200 gave the populace little incentive to bank.
70. *New York Times* January 28, 2008, p. 1.
71. EIU, *CCR* May 2001: 19.
72. EIU, *CCR* May 2001: 10, *CCR* August 2004: 20, *CCR* November 2005: 20.
73. EIU, *CCR* November 2005: 20.
74. On rent-seeking, corruption, theft, and employer bribery to access jobs offering illicit money-making opportunities, see Díaz-Briquets and Pérez-Lopez 2006; Eckstein 2000 and 2003b: 236.
75. EIU, *CCR* August 2001: 13; EIU, *CCR* August 2006: 20.
76. See EIU, *CCR* August 2004: 11 and August 2005: 15 and November 2005: 13.
77. EIU, *CCR* August 2006: 20.
78. EIU, *CCR* November 2006: 15.
79. *Economist* June 17, 2006: 43.
80. Portes and Roberts 2005.
81. LeoGrande and Thomas 2002: 352.
82. Brundenius 2002.
83. Sánchez-Egozcue 2007: 6.
84. Evidence from other Latin American countries suggests that initially

remittances do not improve income distribution because the poorest people cannot afford the costs of immigration. With time, as opportunity costs diminish and low-income people can take advantage of transnational networks, remittances improve the distribution of income in homeland countries. See Koechlin and Leon 2006.

85. On costs of food in different markets, and on nutrition and targeting of state resources affecting dietary intake, see Togores and García 2004.

86. See de la Fuente 1998. With few kin in the diaspora to qualify for family reunification-based US entry, non-Whites were more likely than Whites to make use of the lottery Washington introduced in the mid-1990s. Aguirre and Bonilla 2002.

87. Espina Prieto and Rodríguez Ruiz 2006: 47. On race and remittances, see also de la Fuente 1998 and 2008.

88. De la Fuente 2008: 320.

89. Eckstein 1994/2003: Chapter 6.

90. US-Cuba Trade and Economic Council (UCTEC), "Economic Eye on Cuba" (March 17, 2002), p. 12; http://www.cubatrade.org. On regional inequality in remittance receipts, see also Espina Prieto and Rodríguez Ruiz 2006: 47.

91. EIU, *CCR* November 2000: 18.

92. EIU, *CCR* February 2001: 11.

93. EIU, *CCR* August 2006: 2.

94. The greatest internal challenge within the military ranks to Raúl's authority resulted in the execution of General Arnaldo Ochoa Sánchez in 1989, officially for crimes against the state.

95. Dilla 2004: 38–42 and Dilla 2002; Dilla et al. 1997; Davalos 2000.

96. www.cnn.com/2005/world/americas/05/20/cuba.rally.

97. Anita Snow, AP, August 13, 2006.

98. *Boston Globe* January 21, 2007: 13.

99. When Fidel ceded power in the summer of 2006, he gave Carlos Lage, who oversaw the post-Soviet era economic transition, José Ramón Balaguer, the health minister, José Ramón Machado Ventura, the long-time Party leader, Esteben Lazo, the country's most powerful Black leader, and Francisco Soberon, the central bank president, responsibility for aspects of his legacy. *Boston Globe* January 21, 2007: 13.

100. Gallup Organization 2006.

101. Albert Hirshman 1970 coined the phrase.

8 Reenvisioning Immigration

1. While recognizing differences among Cuban émigré waves, Pedraza 2007, in contrast, implies all Cuba-born to be refugees. The 1966 Cuban Adjustment Act defines Cuban émigrés as *refugees*. This categorization is Cold War-based. It does not, in most instances, reflect the conditions under which most post-Soviet era émigrés left their homeland. Even US post-Cold War Cuban admission policy is premised on an immigration, not a refugee, accord.

2. The first Vietnam War immigrants, for example, adapted better to the US than subsequent arrivals. Their different adaptation has roots in their different pre-immigration experiences, and the age at which experienced. See Shapiro et al. 1999; Shelley 2001.

3. Philip Kuhn 2008; Pieke et al. 2004.

4. Erdmans 1998.

5. Erdmans 1998 shows a different pattern among Polish immigrant generations than I have documented among Cubans, traced to distinctive Polish lived

experiences before uprooting. For example, earlier first-generation Polish émigrés came primarily for economic reasons and they were mainly poor peasants, whereas more recent Polish émigrés mainly came for political reasons and were better off economically. With varied backgrounds, they have adapted differently to the US and have related differently to their homeland.

6. Kasinitz, Mollenkopf and Waters 2004: 399–402.
7. FIU-IPOR 2000.

Bibliography

Ackerman, Holly and Juan Clark. 1995. *The Cuban Balseros: Voyage of Uncertainty.* Miami, FL: Cuban American National Council.

Aguilar-León, Luís. 1972. *Cuba: Conciencia y Revolución.* Miami, FL: Ediciones Universal.

Aguilar Trujillo and José Alejandro. 2001. "Las remesas desde exterior," in *Cuba. Investigación Económica.* Havana: Instituto Nacional de Investigaciones Económicas, 71–104.

Aguirre, Benigno and Eduardo Bonilla Silva. 2002. "Does Race Matter Among Cuban Immigrants? An Analysis of the Racial Characteristics of Recent Cuban Immigrants." *Journal of Latin American Studies* 32, no. 2 (May): 311–24.

Aja Díaz, Antonio. 2006. *Tendencia de la Emigración desde Cuba a Inicios del Siglo XXI.* Havana: Centro de Estudios de Migraciones Internacionales (CEMI), Universidad de la Habana.

Alba, Richard. 1990. *Ethnic Identity: The Transformation of White America.* New Haven, CT: Yale University Press.

———. 2006. "Mexican Americans and the American Dream." *Perspectives on Politics* 4, no. 2 (June): 289–96.

Alba, Richard, Douglas Massey, and Ruben Rumbaut. 1999. *The Immigration Experience for Families and Children.* Washington, DC: American Sociological Association.

Alba, Richard and Victor Nee. 2003. *Remaking the American Mainstream.* Cambridge, MA: Harvard University Press.

Amaro, Nelson and Alejandro Portes. 1972. "Una sociología del exilio: Situación de los grupos cubanos en los Estados Unidos." *Aportes* 23 (January): 6–24.

Anderson, Benedict. 2006. *Imagined Communities: Reflections on the Origin and Spread of Nationalism.* London: Verso.

Anderson, Jon Lee. 2006. "Castro's Last Battle: Can the Revolution Outlive Its Leader?" *The New Yorker* (July 31): 46–55.

Arenas, Reinaldo. 1993. *Before Night Falls.* New York: Viking.

Bach, R., J. Bach, and T. Triplett. 1981. "The Flotilla 'Entrants': Latest and Most Controversial." *Cuban Studies* 11: 29–48.

Banco Central de Cuba. 2000. *Informe Económico 2000.* Havana: Banco Central.

Barberia, Lorena. 2004. "Remittances to Cuba: An Evaluation of Cuban and U.S. Government Policy Measures." Pp. 353–412 in Jorge Domínguez, Omar Everleny Pérez Villanueva, and Lorena Barberia (eds.), *The Cuban Economy at the Start of the Twenty-First Century.* Cambridge, MA: Harvard University Press.

Bates, Timothy. 1994. "Social Resources Generated by Group Support Networks May Not Be Beneficial to Asian Immigrant-Owned Small Businesses." *Social Forces* 72, no. 3: 671–90.

Bean, Frank and Gillian Stevens. 2003. *America's Newcomers and the Dynamics of Diversity*. New York: Russell Sage Foundation.

Behar, Ruth. 2007. *An Island Called Home: Returning to Cuba*. New Brunswick, NJ: Rutgers University Press.

Bendixen and Associates. 2005. "Remittances to Cuba from the United States." Washington, DC May 25, 2005. www.bendixenandassociates.com.

Bengelsdorf, Carollee. 1994. *The Problem of Democracy in Cuba*. New York: Oxford University Press.

Black, Earl and Merle Black. 2002. *The Rise of Southern Republicans*. Cambridge, MA: Belknap Press of Harvard University Press.

Borjas, G. J. 1986. "The Self-Employment Experience of Immigrants." *Journal of Human Resources* 21: 485–506.

———. 1990. *Friends or Strangers: The Impact of Immigrants on the US Economy*. New York: Basic Books.

Boswell, Thomas. 2002. *A Demographic Profile of Cuban Americans*. Miami, FL: Cuban American National Council.

Bourdieu, Pierre. 1977. *Outline of a Theory of Practice*. Cambridge: Cambridge University Press.

———. 1986. "The Forms of Capital." Pp. 241–58 in J. G. Richardson (ed.), *Handbook of Theory and Research for the Sociology of Education*. New York: Greenwood Press.

———. 1992. "The Logic of Fields." Pp. 94–114 in P. Bourdieu and L. Wacquant (eds.), *An Invitation to Reflexive Sociology*. Chicago: University of Chicago Press.

Brito, Vanessa et al. 2005. "Manny Diaz and the Miami Renaissance." Unpublished paper.

Brundenius, Claes. 2002. "Whither the Cuban Economy After Recovery? The Reform Process, Upgrading Strategies and the Question of Transition." *Journal of Latin American Studies* 34, part 2 (May): 365–96.

———. 2003. "Tourism as an Engine of Growth: Reflections on Cuba's New Development Strategy." Paper presented at the LASA Congress, Dallas (March).

Bunck, Julie Marie. 1994. *Fidel Castro and the Quest for a Revolutionary Culture in Cuba*. University Park, PA: Pennsylvania State University Press.

Burgess, Katrina. 2005. "Migrant Philanthropy and Local Governance in Mexico." Pp. 99–155 in Barbara Merz (ed.), *New Patterns for Mexico: Observations on Remittances, Philanthropic Giving, and Equitable Development*. Cambridge, MA: Harvard University Press.

———. 2009. "Neoliberal Reform and Migrant Remittances: Symptom or Solution?" Pp 177–95 in John Burdick, Philip Oxhorn, and Kenneth Roberts (eds.), *Beyond Neoliberalism in Latin America?* London: Palgrave.

Castro, Max. 2002. "The New Cuban Immigration in Context." *The North-South Agenda* 58, October. Miami: North-South Center, University of Miami.

——— and Thomas Boswell. 2002. *The Dominican Diaspora Revisited: Dominicans and Dominican-Americans in a New Century*. Miami: North-South Center, University of Miami.

Central Intelligence Agency (CIA). n.d. *CIA World Fact Book (El Salvador, Dominican Republic)*. www.enotes.com/world-fact-book.

Chun, Sung-Chang and Guillermo Grenier. 2004. "Anti-Castro Political Ideology among Cuban Americans in the Miami Area: Cohort and Generational Differences." *Latino Research* 2, no. 1 (November): 1–9.

Clinton, Bill. 2004. *My Life*. New York: Alfred A. Knopf.

Coleman, James S. 1988. "Social Capital in the Creation of Human Capital." *American Journal of Sociology*. Vol. 94, Supplement. 95–120.

———. 1993. "The Rational Reconstruction of Society." *American Sociological Review* 58 (February): 1–15.

Comisión Económica para América Latina y el Caribe (CEPAL). 2004. *Política social y reformas estructurales: Cuba a principios del siglo XXI*, coordinated by Elena Álvarez and Jorge Mattar. United Nations and Havana: CEPAL and the United Nations Development Program, and the Instituto Nacional de Investigaciones Económicas de Cuba.

Comité Estatal de Estadísticas (CEE). 1991. *Anuario Estadístico de Cuba 1989*. Havana: CEE.

Commission for Assistance to a Free Cuba (CAFC). 2004. *Report to the President*. May. Colin Powell, Secretary of State, Chairman.

Corbett, Ben. 2004. *This Is Cuba: An Outlaw Culture Survives*. Cambridge, MA: Westview Press/Perseus Books Group.

Crahan, Margaret and Ariel Armony. 2007. "Rethinking Religion and Civil Society in Cuba." Pp. 139–63 in Bert Hoffman and Laurence Whitehead (eds.), *Debating Cuban Exceptionalism*. New York: Palgrave Macmillan.

Cue, Lourdes, Kevin Hill, and Dario Moreno. 2001. "Racial and Partisan Voting in a Tri-Ethnic City: The 1996 Dade County Mayoral Election." *Journal of Urban Affairs* (Fall): 291–307.

Dahl, Robert Alan. 2005. *Who Governs? Democracy and Power in an American City*. New Haven, CT: Yale University Press.

Date, Shirish. 1998. "Lobbyists Wine and Dine Florida Lawmakers." *Palm Beach Post*. www.campaignfinance.org/tracker/summer98/2date.html.

Davalos, Roberto. 2000. *Desarrollo local y descentralización en el contexto urbana*. Havana: University of Havana.

De la Fuente, Alejandro. 1998. "Recreating Racism: Race and Discrimination in Cuba's Special Period." *Georgetown University Cuba Briefing Paper Series*. Washington: Georgetown University, 18.

———. 2008. "Recreating Racism: Race and Discrimination in Cuba's Special Period." Pp. 316–25 in Brenner, Philip, Marguerite Rose Jiménez, John Kirk, and William LeoGrande. *A Contemporary Cuba Reader: Reinventing the Revolution*. Lanham, MD: Rowman and Littlefield.

Del Toro González, Carlos. 2003. *La Alta Burguesía Cubana 1920–1958*. Havana: Editorial de Ciencias Sociales.

DeSipio, Louis. 1996. *Counting on the Latino Vote: Latino as a New Electorate*. Charlottesville: University of Virginia Press.

Díaz-Briquets, Sergio and Jorge Pérez López. 1981. "Cuba: The Demography of Revolution." *Population Bulletin* 36 (April). 2–41.

———. 1997. "Refugee Remittances: Conceptual Issues and the Cuban and Nicaraguan Experiences." *International Migration Review* 31, no. 2 (Spring): 411–37.

———. 2003. *The Role of the Cuban-American Community in the Cuban Transition*. Miami, FL: Institute for Cuban and Cuban-American Studies, University of Miami.

———. 2006. *Corruption in Cuba: Castro and Beyond*. Austin: University of Texas Press.

Didion, Joan. 1987. *Miami*. New York: Simon and Schuster.

Dilla Alfonso, Haroldo (ed.). 2002. *Los recursos de la gobernabilidad en la Cuenca del Caribe*. Caracas: Nueva Sociedad.

———. 2004. "Larval Actors, Uncertain Scenarios, and Cryptic Scripts: Where is Cuban Society Headed?" Pp. 35–50 in Joseph Tulchin et al., *Changes in Cuban Society since the Nineties*. Washington, DC: Woodrow Wilson Center, Report on the Americas.

——— et al. 1994. *Participación popular y desarrollo en los municipios cubanos*. Caracas: Fondo Editorial Tropykos.

——— et al. 1997. *Movimientos barriales en Cuba*. San Salvador: Fundes.

DiMaggio, Paul and Walter Powell. 1983. "The Iron Cage Revisited: Institutional Isomorphism and Collective Rationality in Organizational Fields." *American Sociological Review* 48: 147–60.

Domhoff, G. William. 1967. *Who Rules America?* Englewood Cliffs, NJ: Prentice Hall.

Domínguez, Jorge. 1978. *Cuba: Order and Revolution*. Cambridge, MA: Harvard University Press.

———. 1990. "The Cuban Armed Forces, the Party and Society in Wartime and During Rectification (1986–1988)." Pp. 45–62 in Richard Gillespie (ed.), *Cuba After Thirty Years: Rectification and the Revolution*. London: Routledge.

———. 2004. "Cuba's Economic Transition: Successes, Deficiencies, and Challenges." Pp. 17–48 in Jorge Domínguez, Omar Everleny Pérez Villanueva, and Lorena Barberia (eds.), *The Cuban Economy at the Start of the Twenty-First Century*. Cambridge, MA: David Rockefeller Center for Latin American Studies, Harvard University.

———. 2006. "Latinos and US Foreign Policy." *Working Paper Series* 06–05. Cambridge, MA: Weatherhead Center for International Affairs, Harvard University.

———. 2008. "Cuba and the *Pax Americana*." Pp. 203–11 in Philip Brenner, Marguerite Rose Jiménez, John Kirk, and William LeoGrande (eds.), *A Contemporary Cuba Reader: Reinventing the Revolution*. Lanham, MD: Rowman & Littlefield.

Domínguez, Maria Isabel. 2005. "Cuban Youth: Aspirations, Social Perceptions, and Identity." Pp. 155–70 in Tulchin et al., *Changes in Cuban Society since the Nineties*. Washington, DC: Woodrow Wilson International Center for Scholars, Latin American Program.

Duany, Jorge. 1994. *Quisqueya on the Hudson: The Transnational Identity of Dominicans in Washington Heights*. New York: Dominican Research Monographs, CUNY Dominican Studies Institute.

Dunn, Marvin and Alex Stepick III. 1992. "Blacks in Miami." In Guillermo Grenier and Alex Stepick (eds.), *Miami Now! Immigration, Ethnicity, and Social Change*. Gainesville: University Press of Florida.

Durand, Jorge, Emilio Parrado, and Douglas Massey. 1996. "Migradollars and

Development: A Reconsideration of the Mexican Case." *International Migration Review* 30, no. 22: 423–44.

Durkheim, Emile. 1964. *Rules of Sociological Method*. New York: Free Press.

Eckstein, Susan. 1980. "Capitalist Constraints on Cuban Socialist Development." *Comparative Politics* (April): 253–74.

———. 1994/2003. *Back from the Future: Cuba under Castro*. Princeton, NJ: Princeton University Press (1994) and New York: Routledge (2003).

———. 2000. "Resistance and Reform: Power to the People?," *DRCLAS News* (Winter). Cambridge, MA: David Rockefeller Center for Latin American Studies, Harvard University.

———. 2003. "Diasporas and Dollars: Transnational Ties and the Transformation of Post-Soviet Era Cuba." Cambridge: Massachusetts Institute of Technology, Center for International Studies. http://web.mit.edu/cis/www/migration.

———. 2004a. "On Deconstructing Immigrant Generations: Cohorts and the Cuban Émigré Experience." Working Paper 97. San Diego: University of California at San Diego, Center for Comparative International Studies (May) (http://www.ccis-ucsd.org/publications/working_papers.htm)

———. 2004b. "Dollarization and its Discontents: How People Are Remaking Cuba in the Post-Soviet Era." *Comparative Politics* (Spring): 313–30.

———. 2009. "The Personal is Political: The Cuban Ethnic Electoral Policy Cycle." *Latin American Politics and Society* (Spring).

——— and Lorena Barberia. 2002. "Grounding Immigrant Generations in History: Cuban Americans and Their Transnational Ties." *International Migration Review* 36, no. 3 (Fall): 799–837.

Economic Commission on Latin America and the Caribbean (ECLAC, Comisión Económica para América Latina y el Caribe) of the United Nations. 2000. *La Economía Cubana*. Mexico, DF: Fondo de Cultura Económico.

Economist Intelligence Unit (EIU). 2002. *Country Forecast. Latin American Regional Overview*. London: EIU, March.

———. *Cuba Country Reports (CCR)*. 1990–2008. London: EIU.

———. *Cuba: Country Profile (CCP)*. 1990–2008. London: EIU.

Eire, Carlos. 2003. *Waiting for Snow in Havana: Confessions of a Cuban Boy*. New York: Free Press.

Eisenstadt, S. (ed.). 1968. *Max Weber: On Charisma and Institution Building*. Chicago: University of Chicago Press.

———. 1956. *From Generation to Generation: Age Group and Social Structure*. Glencoe, IL: The Free Press.

Elliott, Andera and Elaine del Valle. 2003. "Mas Santos Makes Offer to Talk with Cuba Leaders." *Miami Herald* (January 31). www.cubanet.org/CNews/y03/jan03/31e3.htm.

Engstrom, David. 1997. *Presidential Decision-Making Adrift: The Carter Administration and the Mariel Boatlift*. Lanham, MD: Rowman and Littlefield.

Erdmans, Mary Patrice. 1998. *Opposite Poles: Immigrants and Ethnics in Polish Chicago, 1976–1990*. University Park: Pennsylvania State University Press.

Erlick June. 1970. "First Week in a New Land, A Time of Worry and Hope." *Jersey Journal* November 30: 1.

Espina Prieto, Rodrigo and Pablo Rodríguez Ruiz. 2006. "Raza y desigualdad en la Cuba actual." *Temas* no. 45 (January–March): 44–54.

Euromonitor. 1998. *World Economic Factbook 1989/1999*. London: Euromonitor.

Fagen, Richard. 1969. *The Transformation of Political Culture in Cuba*. Stanford, CA: Stanford University Press.

Fagen, Richard, R. Brody, and T. O'Leary. 1968. *Cubans in Exile: Disaffection and the Revolution*. Stanford, CA: Stanford University Press.

Feinsilver, Julie. 1993. *Healing the Masses: Cuban Health Politics at Home and Abroad*. Berkeley: University of California Press.

————. 2007. "La diplomacia medica cubana: cuando la izquierda lo ha hecho bien." *Foreign Affairs en Español* (October–December) (and 2007 "Cuban Medical Diplomacy: When the Left Has Got It Right," www.coha.org).

Fernández, Damián. 2000. *Cuba and the Politics of Passion*. Austin: University of Texas Press.

Finnegan, William. 2004. "The Political Scene: Castro's Shadow." *New Yorker* May 19. Pp. 70–78.

Flores, Juan, Jessica Lavariega Monforti, and David Moreno. 2006. "Manny Diaz and the Miami Renaissance." Paper delivered at the Western Political Science Association Meeting (March), Albuquerque, New Mexico.

Flores, Juan, Maria Ilcheva, and Dario Moreno. 2008. "Hispanic Vote in Florida. 2004 Election." In Rudy de la Garza, David Leal, and Louis DeSipio (eds.), *Latinos in the 2004 Election*. Boulder, CO: Westview Press.

Florida International University (FIU), Institute for Public Opinion Research (IPOR), 1997, 2000, 2004, 2007. *FIU/Cuba Poll*. http://www.fiu.edu/orgs/ipor/cubapoll.

Fonzi, Gaeton. 1993. "Who is Jorge Mas Canosa?" *Esquire* (January): 86–89, 119–22.

————. 2003. "Jorge Who?," *Cuban Information Archives* Document 0063, 2003. http://cuban-exile.com/doc_051-075/doc0063.html

Forment, Carlos. 1989. "Political Practice and the Rise of an Ethnic Enclave." *Theory & Society* 18: 47–81.

Fouron, Georges and Nina Glick-Schiller. 2002. "The Generation of Identity: Redefining the Second-Generation within a Transnational Social Field." Pp. 168–210 in Peggy Levitt and Mary Waters (eds.), *The Changing Face of Home: The Transnational Lives of the Second-Generation*. New York: Russell Sage Foundation.

Franklin, Jane. 1993. "The Cuba Obsession." *The Progressive* (July). http://ourworld.compuserve.com/homepages/JBfranklins/canf.htm

Gallup Organization. 2006. "Gallup Organization's Cuba ThinkForum." *Gallup World Poll*. Princeton, NJ: Gallup Organization (media.gallup.com/worldpoll/PDF/TFCuba022207.pdf).

Gans, Herbert. 1992. "Comment: Ethnic Invention and Acculturation, A Bumpy-Line Approach." *Journal of American Ethnic History* (Fall): 43–51.

————. "Toward a Reconciliation of 'Assimilation' and 'Pluralism': The Interplay of Acculturation and Ethnic Retention." Pp. 161–71 in Charles Hirschman, Josh DeWind, and Philip Kasinitz (eds.), *The Handbook of International Migration*. New York: Russell Sage Foundation.

García, Maria Cristina. 1996. *Havana USA: Cuban Exiles and Cuban Americans in South Florida, 1959–1994*. Berkeley: University of California Press.

García Molina, Jesús. 2005. "La economía cubana desde el siglo XVI al XX: del colonialismo al socialismo con Mercado." *Estudios y Perspectivas*, vol. 28: 1–54. México: Naciones Unidas, CEPAL.

Georges, Eugenia. 1990. *The Making of a Transnational Community: Migration, Development and Cultural Change in the Dominican Republic.* New York: Columbia University Press.

Gimbel, Wendy. 1998. *Havana Dreams: A Story of Cuba.* New York: A. A. Knopf.

Glaser, Barney and Anselm Strauss. 1967. *The Discovery of Grounded Theory: Strategies for Qualitative Research.* New York: Aldine de Gruyter.

Glazer, Nathan and Daniel Moynihan. 1963. *Beyond the Melting Pot: The Negroes, Puerto Ricans, Jews, Italians, and Irish of New York City.* Cambridge, MA: MIT Press.

Glick Schiller, Nina, Linda Basch, and Christina Szanton-Blanc (eds.). 1992. *Towards a Transnational Perspective on Migration: Race, Class, Ethnicity, and Nationalism Reconsidered.* New York: New York Academy of Sciences.

———. 1994. *Nations Unbound: Transnational Projects, Postcolonial Predicaments and Deterritorialized Nation-States.* Basel, Switzerland: Gordon and Breach.

Glick Schiller, Nina and Georges Fouron. 2001. *Georges Woke Up Laughing: Long Distance Nationalism and the Search for Home.* Durham, NC: Duke University Press.

Goffman, Erving. 1974. *Frame Analysis.* New York: Harper and Row.

———. 1986. *Stigma: Notes on the Management of Spoiled Identity.* New York: Simon and Schuster.

Goldring, Luin. 1998. "The Power of Status in Transnational Social Spaces." Pp. 165–95 in L. Guarnizo and M. Smith (eds.), *Transnationalism from Below.* New Brunswick, NJ: Transaction Press.

González, Echevarria. 1999. *The Pride of Havana: A History of Cuban Baseball.* New York: Oxford University Press.

Gordon, Milton. 1964. *Assimilation in American Life: The Role of Race, Religion, and National Origins.* New York: Oxford University Press.

Graham, Pamela. 1997. "Reimagining the Nation and Defining the District: Dominican Migration and Transnational Politics." Pp. 91–126 in Patricia Pessar (ed.), *Caribbean Circuits: New Directions in the Study of Caribbean Migration.* Staten Island, New York: Center for Migration Studies.

Granovetter, Mark. 1974. *Getting a Job.* Cambridge, MA: Harvard University Press.

Grasmuck, Sherri and Patricia Pessar. 1996. "Dominicans in the United States: First- and Second-Generation Settlement." Pp. 280–92 in Silvia Pedraza and Ruben Rumbaut (eds.), *Origins and Destinies: Immigration, Race, and Ethnicity in America.* Belmont, MA: Wadsworth Publishing.

Grenier, Guillermo and Alex Stepick. 1992. *Miami Now! Immigration, Ethnicity, and Social Change.* Gainesville: University Presses of Florida.

Grenier, Guillermo and Lisandro Pérez. 2003. *The Legacy of Exile: Cubans in the United States.* Boston: Allyn and Bacon.

Grosfoguel, Ramon. 1994. "World Cities in the Caribbean: The Rise of Miami and San Juan." *Review* 17, no. 3 (Summer): 351–81.

Guarnizo, Luis. 1997. "The Rise of Transnational Social Formations: Mexican and Dominican State Responses to Transnational Migration. *Identities* 4: 281–322.

Guerra, Lillian. 2007. "Elían González and the 'Real Cuba' of Miami: Visions of Identity, Exceptionality, and Divinity." *Cuban Studies* 38: 1–25.

Gutiérrez, David. 1995. *Walls and Mirrors: Mexican Americans, Mexican Immigrants, and the Politics of Ethnicity.* Berkeley: University of California Press.

Ha, Ruyet The. 2002. *Vietnamese Refugees 1975–2000: Factors and Reinforcements of Their Economic Self-Sufficiency.* Doctoral dissertation, Department of Public Administration, School of Public Affairs and Health Administration, University of La Verne, La Verne, California.

Hamilton, Nora and Norma Chinchilla. 2001. *Seeking Community in a Global City: Guatemalans and Salvadorans in Los Angeles.* Philadelphia, PA: Temple University Press.

Haney, Patrick and Walt Vanderbush. 2005. *The Cuban Embargo: The Domestic Politics of an American Foreign Policy.* Pittsburgh, PA: University of Pittsburgh Press.

Hao, L. 1994. *Kin Support, Welfare, and Out-of-Wedlock Mothers.* New York: Garland.

Harnecker, Marta. 1980. *Cuba: Dictatorship or Democracy?* Westport, CT: Lawrence Hill.

Harrington, Michael. 1981. *The Other America: Poverty in the US.* New York: Penguin.

Helton, John. 2004. "Democrats, GOP Assess Latino Impact." www.cnn.cm/ 2004/allpolitics/03/08/latino.vote

Henken, Ted. 2002. "Condemned to Informality: Cuba's Experiments with Self-Employment during the Special Period (The Case of the 'Bed and Breakfasts')." *Cuban Studies* 33: 1–39.

———. 2005. "*Balseros, boteros,* and *el bombo*: Immigration to the US since 1994 and the Persistence of Special Treatment." *Latino Studies* 3: 393–416.

———. 2008. "*Vale* Todo." Pp. 166–76 in Philip Brenner et al. (eds.), *A Contemporary Cuba Reader: Reinventing the Revolution.* Lanham, MD: Rowman and Littlefield.

Hernández, Rafael. 2005. "Mirror of Patience: Notes on Cuban Studies, Social Sciences, and Contemporary Thought." Pp. 139–54 in Joseph Tulchin et al., *Changes in Cuban Society Since the Nineties.* Washington, DC: Woodrow Wilson International Center for Scholars.

Hernández, Rafael et al. 2002. "Por qué emigran los cubanos? Causas y azares." *Temas* 31: 73–91.

Higham, John. 1992/2002. *Strangers in the Land: Patterns of American Nativism, 1860–1925.* New Brunswick, NJ: Rutgers University Press.

Hill, Kevin and Dario Moreno. 2002. "A Community or a Crowd: Racial, Ethnic, and Regional Bloc Voting: The Florida House of Representatives 1989–98." *Politics and Policy* (March).

———. 2008. "Politics and the Challenge of Ethnicity." Pp. 80–101 in J. Edwin Benton (ed.), *Government and Politics in Florida.* Gainesville: University Press of Florida.

Hirschman, Albert. 1970. *Exit, Voice, and Loyalty: Responses to the Decline in Firms, Organizations, and States.* Cambridge, MA: Harvard University Press.

Huberman, Leo and Paul Sweezy. 1969. *Socialism in Cuba.* New York: Monthly Review.

Human Rights Watch (HRW). "Cuba's Restrictions on Travel." http://hrw.org/ reports/2005/cuba1005/2.htm.

Huntington, Samuel. 2004. *Who Are We? The Challenges to America's National Identity.* New York: Simon and Schuster.

Ingalls, Robert and Louis Pérez. 2003. *Tampa Cigar Workers.* Gainesville: University Press of Florida.

Inter-American Development Bank (IDB), Multilateral Investment Fund (MIF). 2004. "Sending Money Home." (May). http://idbdocs.iadb.org/wsdocs/getdocument.

———. 2008. "Remittances to Latin America and the Caribbean 2007." http://idbdocs.iadb.org/mif/remesas_map.

Inter-American Dialogue. 2007. "Making the Most of Family Remittances." thedialogue.org/PublicationFiles/family_remittances.pdf.

Itzigsohn, José et al. 1999. "Mapping Dominican Transnationalism: Narrow and Broad Transnational Practices." *Ethnic and Racial Studies* 24, no. 4 (July): 549–77.

Kalberg, Stephen. 1994. *Max Weber's Comparative Historical Sociology.* Chicago: University of Chicago Press.

Kanter, Rosabeth Moss. 1995. *World Class: Thriving Locally in the Global Economy.* New York: Simon & Schuster.

Kasinitz, Philip, John Mollenkopf, and Mary Waters (eds.). 2004. *Becoming New Yorkers: Ethnographies of the New Second-Generation.* New York: Russell Sage Foundation.

Kivisto, Peter. 2001. "Theorizing Transnational Immigration: A Critical Review of Current Efforts." *Ethnic and Racial Studies* 24, no. 4 (July): 549–77.

Koechlin, Valerie and Gianmarco Leon. 2006. "International Remittances and Income Inequality: An Empirical Investigation." Working Paper 57. Washington, DC: Inter-American Development Bank. http://idbdocs.iadb.org/wsdocs /gtedocument.

Krull, Catherine and Audrey Kobayashi. Forthcoming. "Shared Memories, Common Vision: Generations, Socio-political Consciousness and Resistance among Cuban Women." *Sociological Inquiry* 79.

Krull, Catherine et al. 2003. *La Vida de Mujeres en San Isidro: Patrones de Tiempo y Espacio en una Cultura de Resistencia.* Publicación de la Catedra de la Mujer. Havana: Universidad de Habana, 1–16.

Kuhn, Philip. 2008. *Chinese Among Others: Emigration in Modern Times.* Boulder, CO: Rowman and Littlefield.

Kuhn, Thomas. 1996. *The Structure of Scientific Revolutions.* Chicago: University of Chicago Press.

Kunz, E. F. 1973. "The Refugee in Flight: Kinetic Models and Forms of Displacement." *International Migration Review* 7: 125–46.

———. 1981. "Exile and Resettlement: Refugee Theory." *International Migration Review* 15: 42–51.

Kyle, David. 2000. *Transnational Peasants: Migrations, Networks, and Ethnicity in Andean Ecuador.* Baltimore, MD: Johns Hopkins University Press.

Landolt, Patricia, Lilian Autler, and Sonia Baires. 1999. "From Hermano Lejano to Hermano Mayor: The Dialectics of Salvadoran Transnationalism." *Ethnic and Racial Studies* 22: 290–315.

LeoGrande, William. 2008. " 'The Cuban Nation's Single Party': The Communist Party of Cuba Faces the Future." Pp. 50–62 in Philip Brenner, Marguerite Rose Jiménez, John Kirk, and William LeoGrande (eds.), *A Contemporary*

Cuba Reader: Reinventing the Revolution. Lanham, MD: Rowman and Littlefield.

LeoGrande, William and Julie Thomas. 2002. "Cuba's Quests for Economic Independence." *Journal of Latin American Studies* vol. 34, part 2 (May): 325–64.

Lessinger, Johanna. 1995. *From the Ganges to the Hudson: Indian Immigrants in New York City.* Boston, MA: Allyn and Bacon.

Levine, Robert. 2002. *Secret Missions to Cuba: Fidel Castro, Bernardo Benes, and Cuban Miami.* New York: Palgrave Macmillan.

Levitt, Peggy. 2001. *Transnational Villagers.* Berkeley: University of California Press.

Levitt, Peggy and Mary Waters (eds.). 2002. *The Changing Face of Home: The Transnational Lives of the Second-Generation.* New York: Russell Sage Foundation.

Levitt, Peggy and Nina Glick Schiller. 2004. "Conceptualizing Simultaneity: A Transnational Social Field Perspective on Society." *International Migration Review* 38, no. 3: 1002–39.

Lieberson, Stanley. 1985. "Unhyphenated Whites in the United States." *Ethnic and Racial Studies* 8, no. 1: 159–80.

Light, Ivan. 1984. "Immigrant and Ethnic Enterprise in North America." *Ethnic and Racial Studies* 7, no. 2: 195–216.

Light, Ivan and Stavros Karageorgis. 1994. "The Ethnic Economy." Pp. 647–71 in Neil Smelser and Richard Swedberg (eds.), *Handbook of Economic Sociology.* Princeton, NJ: Princeton University Press.

Lin, Nan. 2001. *Social Capital: A Theory of Social Structure and Action.* Cambridge: Cambridge University Press.

Linz, Juan. 1975. "Totalitarian and Authoritarian Regimes." Pp. 175–411 in Fred Greenstein and Nelson Polsby (eds.), *Handbook of Political Science*, vol. 3: *Macropolitical Theory.* Reading, MA: Addison-Wesley.

Logan, John, Richard Alba, and Thomas McNulty. 1994. "Ethnic Economies in Metropolitan Regions: Miami and Beyond." *Social Forces* 72: 691–724.

Mahler, Sarah. 1995a. *Salvadorans in Suburbia: Symbiosis with Conflict.* Boston, MA: Allyn and Bacon.

———. 1995b. *American Dreaming: Immigrant Life on the Margins.* Princeton, NJ: Princeton University Press.

———. 1998. "Theoretical and Empirical Contributions Toward a Research Agenda for Transnationalism." *Comparative Urban and Community Research* 6: 64–102.

———. 2000. "Migration and Transnational Issues: Recent Trends and Prospects for 2020. Washington, DC: Inter-American Dialogue, www.thedialogue.org/publications/country_studies.

Mahler, Sarah and Katrin Hansing. 2005. "Toward a Transnationalism of the Middle: How Transnational Religious Practices Help Bridge the Divides between Cuba and Miami." *Latin American Perspectives* 30, no. 1 (January): 1–26.

Mannheim, Karl. 1952. "The Problem of Generations." In P. Keckskemeti (ed.), *Essays on the Sociology of Knowledge.* New York: Oxford University Press.

Marquetti Nodarse, Hiram. 1996. "Evolución del sector industrial en 1996." Pp. 44–67 in *La Economía Cubana en 1996: Resultados, Problemas y*

Perspectivas. Havana: University of Havana, Centro de Estudios de la Economía Cubana.

Martínez, Milagros et al. 1996. *Los Balseros Cubanos: Un estudio a partir de las salidas ilegales.* Havana: Editorial de Ciencias Sociales.

Massey, Douglas. 1995. "The New Immigration and Ethnicity in the United States." *Population and Development Review* 21, no. 3: 631–52.

———. 1985. "Ethnic Residential Segregation: A Theoretical Synthesis and Empirical Review." *Social Science Research* 69: 315–50.

Massey, Douglas, Jorge Durand, and Luin Golding. 1987. *Return to Aztlan: The Social Process of International Migration From Western Mexico.* Berkeley: University of California Press.

———. 1994. "Continuities in Transnational Migration: An Analysis of Nineteen Mexican Communities." *American Journal of Sociology* 99: 1492–1533.

———. 1998. *Worlds in Motion: International Immigration at the End of the Millennium.* Oxford: Oxford University Press.

Massey, Douglas, Jorge Durand, and Nolan Malone. 2002. *Beyond Smoke and Mirrors: Mexican Immigration in an Era of Economic Integration.* New York: Russell Sage Foundation.

Masud-Piloto, Felix. 1996. *From Welcome Exiles to Illegal Immigrants: Cuban Migration to the U.S., 1959–1995.* Baltimore, MD: Rowman and Littlefield.

Mathews, Herbert. 1970. *Fidel Castro.* New York: Simon & Schuster.

Mauss, Marcel. 1967. *The Gift: Forms and Functions of Exchange in Archaic Societies.* New York: Norton.

Mayer, Karl Ulrich and Johannes Huinink. 1990. "Age, Period, and Cohort in the Study of the Life Course: A Comparison of Classical A-P-C-analysis with Event History Analysis, or Farewell to Lexis?" Pp. 211–32 in David Magnuson and Lars Bergman (eds.), *Data Quality in Longitudinal Research.* Cambridge: Cambridge University Press.

McHugh, Kevin, Ines Miyares, and Emily Skop. 1997. "The Magnetism of Miami: Segmented Paths in Cuban Migration." *Geographical Review* 87, no. 4: 504–19.

Mello Veiga, Fernanda. 2008. "Internet Access in Cuba—Maybe in 2010." *Havana Journal* (May 23): 2.

Menéndez, Ana. 2001. *In Cuba I Was a German Shepherd.* New York: Grove Press.

Menjívar, Cecilia. 2000. *Fragmented Ties: Salvadoran Immigrant Networks in America.* Berkeley: University of California Press.

Mesa-Lago, Carmelo. 2000. *Market, Socialist, and Mixed Economies.* Baltimore, MD: Johns Hopkins University Press.

———. 2004. "Economic and Ideological Cycles in Cuba: Policy and Performance, 1959–2002." Pp. 25–41 in Archibald R. M. Ritter (ed.), *The Cuban Economy.* Pittsburgh: University of Pittsburgh Press.

Milán, Guillermo and Moraima Díaz. 2000. "Sociedad Cubana y Emigración: Una aproximación en la última década del siglo XX." Unpublished manuscript.

Molyneux, Maxine. 1999. "The Politics of the Cuban Diaspora in the United States." Pp. 289–310 in Victor Bulmer-Thomas and James Dunkerley (eds.), *The United States and Latin America: The New Agenda.* Cambridge, MA, and London: David Rockefeller Center for Latin American Studies, Harvard University and the Institute of Latin American Studies, University of London.

Monreal, Pedro. 1999. "Las Remesas Familiares en la Economía Cubana." *Encuentro* 14 (Fall): 49–63.

———. 2004. "Globalization and the Dilemmas of Cuba's Economic Trajectories." Pp. 91–118 in Jorge Domínguez, Omar Everleny Pérez Villanueva, and Lorena Barberia (eds.), *The Cuban Economy at the Start of the Twenty-First Century*. Cambridge, MA: David Rockefeller Center Series on Latin American Studies, Harvard University.

Morawska, Ewa. 2003. "Immigrant Transnationalism and Assimilation: A Variety of Combinations and the Analytic Strategy It Suggests." Pp. 133–76 in C. Joppke and E. Morawska (eds.), *Toward Assimilation and Citizenship: Immigrants in Liberal Nation-States*. Hampshire: Palgrave Macmillan.

Moreno, Dario. 1997. "Cuban American Political Empowerment." In Chris García (ed.), *Latinos and the United States Political System*. Notre Dame, IN: University of Notre Dame Press.

———. 2005. "Politics and Ethnic Change in Florida." Unpublished paper.

———. 2006. "Cuban American Political Power: Challenges and Consequences." *Cuban Affairs* 1, no. 4 (October).

———. n.d. "Exile Political Power: Cubans in the United States Political System" (metropolitan.fiu.edu/downloads/exile%/exile%20political%20political) [or: http://metropolitan.fiu.edu/about_us/dario.htm]

Moreno, Dario and Nicole Rae. 1992. "Ethnicity and Partisanship: The Case of the 18th Congressional District in Miami." Pp. 186–203 in Guillermo Grenier and Alex Stepick (eds.), *Miami Now!* Gainesville: University Press of Florida.

Moreno, Dario and Christopher Warren. 1995. "The Conservative Enclave Revisited: Cuban-Americans in the 1992 Election." In Rudy de la Garza and Luis DeSipio (eds.), *Ethnic Ironies: Latino Politics in the 1992 Election*. Boulder, CO: Westview Press.

Moreno, Dario and Christopher Warren. 1998. "Cuban-Americans in the 1996 Election." In Rudy de la Garza and Luis DeSipio (eds.), *Latinos in the 1996 Election*. Boulder, CO: Westview Press.

Morley, Morris and Chris McGillion. 2002. *Unfinished Business: America and Cuba after the Cold War, 1989–2001*. Cambridge: Cambridge University Press.

Multilateral Investment Fund (MIF)/Inter-American Development Bank (IDB). 2002. "Remittances to Latin America and the Caribbean." Washington, DC: MIF/IDB (February).

Nordlinger, Jay. 2003. "Meet the Díaz-Balarts: A Couple of Castro's 'Nephews'— in Congreso—Lincoln and Mario Díaz-Balart." *National Review* March 10. http://articles.findarticles.com/p/articles/mi_m1282/is_4_55/ai_97937295

Oficina Nacional de Estadísticas (ONE). 2001. *Anuario Estadístico de Cuba 2000*. Havana: ONE.

———. 2005. *Anuario Estadístico de Cuba 2005*. www.one.cu.anuariopdf2005.

Ojito, Mirta. 2005. *Finding Mañana: A Memoir of a Cuban Exodus*. New York: Penguin Press.

Oppenheimer, Andres. 1993. *Castro's Final Hour: The Secret Story Behind the Coming Downfall of Communist Cuba*. New York: Simon & Schuster.

Orozco, Manuel. 2001. "Family Remittances to Latin America: The Marketplace and Its Changing Dynamics." Paper delivered at the Inter-American Development Bank Conference, "Remittances as a Development Tool." May.

————. 2002a. "Challenges and Opportunities of Marketing Remittances to Cuba." Washington, DC: Inter-American Dialogue (July) www.thedialogue.org/ publications.html.

————. 2002b. "Globalization and Migration: The Impact of Family Remittances to Latin America." *Latin American Politics and Society* (Summer).

————. 2002c. "Money, Markets and Costs." Washington, DC: Inter-American Development Bank/International Monetary Fund. www.thedialogue.org/ publications.html.

————. 2003a. "Hometown Associations and Their Present and Future Partnerships: New Development Opportunities." Washington, DC: Inter-American Development Dialogue. www.thedialogue.org/publications.

————. 2003b. "Worker Remittances, Transnationalism and Development." Paper presented at the International Conference on Migrant Remittances: Development Impact, Opportunities for the Financial Sector and Future Prospects, London.

————. 2003c. "Changes in the Atmosphere? Increase of Remittances, Price Decline, and New Challenges" (March). www.thedialogue.org/ PublicationsFiles/chanes%20in%20markets.pdf.

————. 2004. *The Remittance Marketplace: Prices, Policy and Financial Institutions.* Washington, DC: Pew Hispanic Center Report. www.pewhispanic.org.

————. 2005. "Remittance Recipients in Cuba." Washington, DC: Inter-American Dialogue, May 25.

————. 2007. "Remittances and Social Development: The Latin American Experience." Washington, DC: Inter-American Dialogue.

Orozco, Manuel et al. 2005. "Transnational Engagement, Remittances and their Relationship to Development in Latin America and the Caribbean." Final Report Submitted to the Rockefeller Foundation. Washington, DC: Institute for the Study of International Migration, Georgetown University.

Ostrower, Francie. 1995. *Why the Wealthy Give: The Culture of Elite Philanthropy.* Princeton, NJ: Princeton University Press.

Parrenas, Rhacel Salazar. 2001. *Servants of Globalization: Women, Migration, and Domestic Work.* Stanford, CA: Stanford University Press.

————. 2005. *Children of Global Migration: Transnational Families and Gendered Woes.* Stanford, CA: Stanford University Press.

Pearson, Ruth. 1997. "Renegotiating the Reproductive Bargain: Gender Analysis of Economic Transition in Cuba in the 1990s." *Development and Change* 28: 671–705.

Pedraza, Silvia. 1985. *Political and Economic Migrants in America: Cubans and Mexicans.* Austin: University of Texas Press.

————. 1996. "Cuba's Refugees: Manifold Migrations." Pp. 263–79 in Silvia Pedraza and Rubén Rumbaut (eds.), *Origins and Destinies: Immigration, Race, and Ethnicity in America.* Belmont, MA: Wadsworth Publishing.

————. 2007. *Political Disaffection in Cuba's Revolution and Exodus.* New York: Cambridge University Press.

Pérez, Lisandro. 1992. "Cuban Miami." Pp. 83–108 in Guillermo Grenier and Alex Stepick (eds.), *Miami Now! Immigration, Ethnicity, and Social Change.* Gainesville: University of Florida Press.

————. 2001. "Growing Up in Cuban Miami: Immigration, the Enclave, and New Generations." Pp. 91–126 in Rubén Rumbaut and Alejandro Portes (eds.), *Ethnicities: Children of Immigrants in America*. Berkeley and New York: University of California Press.

Pérez, Louis A. 1999. *On Becoming Cuban: Identity, Nationality, and Culture*. Chapel Hill: University of North Carolina Press.

Pérez Mok, Moisés and Alfredo García. 2000. "Reformas económicas en Cuba, Turismo: Retos, Posibilidades y perspectivas." Paper presented at the Latin American Studies Association Meeting, Miami.

Pérez Villanueva, Omar Everleny. 1996. "El comercio exterior y la inversión extranjera en la economía Cubana en 1996." Pp. 25–33 in *La Economía Cubana en 1996: Resultados, Problemas y Perspectivas*. Havana: University of Havana, Centro de Estudios de la Economía Cubana.

———. 2004. "The Cuban Economy Today and Its Future Challenges" and "The Role of Foreign Direct Investment in Economic Development: The Cuban Experience." Pp. 49–90 and 161–98 in Jorge Domínguez, Pérez Villanueva, and Lorena Barberia (eds.), *The Cuban Economy at the Start of the Twenty-First Century*. Cambridge, MA: David Rockefeller Center for Latin American Studies, Harvard University.

Pew Hispanic Center. 2006. "Fact Sheet: Cubans in the United States." (August 25). www.pewhispanic.org/files/factsheets/23pdf

Pieke, Frank et al. 2004. *Transnational Chinese: Fujianese Migrants in Europe*. Stanford, CA: Stanford University Press.

Population Reference Bureau (PRB). 1991. *World Population Data Sheet of the PRB*. Washington, DC: PRB.

Portes, Alejandro. 1996a. "Transnational Communities: Their Emergence and Significance in the Contemporary World System." Pp. 151–68 in Roberto Patricio Korzeniewicz and William C. Smith (eds.), *Latin America in the World Economy*. Westport, CT: Greenwood Press.

———. 1996b. "Self-Employment and the Earnings of Immigrants." *American Sociological Review* 61, no. 2: 219–30.

———. 1998. "Social Capital: Its Origins and Applications in Modern Sociology." *Annual Review of Sociology* 24: 1–24.

———. 2000. "The Two Meanings of Social Capital." *Sociological Forum* 15, no. 1: 1–12.

———. 2005. "The Cuban-American Political Machine: Reflections on the Origins and Perpetuation." Pp. 269–92 in Joseph Tulchin, et al. (eds.), *Changes in Cuban Society since the 1990s*. Washington, DC: Woodrow Wilson International Center for Scholars.

Portes, Alejandro and R. Bach. 1985. *Latin Journey: Cuban and Mexican Immigrants in the United States*. Berkeley: University of California Press.

Portes, Alejandro, Luís Guarnizo, and Patricia Landolt. 1999. "The Study of Transnationalism: Pitfalls and Promise of an Emergent Research Field." *Ethnic and Racial Studies* 22, no. 2: 217–37.

Portes, Alejandro, William Haller, and Luís Guarnizo. 2002. "Transnational Entrepreneurs: An Alternative Form of Immigrant Economic Adaptation." *American Sociological Review* 67 (April): 278–98.

Portes, Alejandro and Bryan Roberts. 2005. "Free Market City." *Studies in Comparative International Development* 40, no. 1: 43–82.

Portes, Alejandro and Rubén Rumbaut. 2001. *Legacies: The Story of the Immigrant*

Second Generation. Berkeley: University of California Press and New York: Russell Sage Foundation.

Portes, Alejandro and Julia Sensenbrenner. 1993. "Embeddedness and Immigration: Notes on the Social Determinants of Economic Action." *American Journal of Sociology* 98, no. 6: 1320–50.

Portes, Alejandro and Steven Shafer. 2007. "Revisiting the Enclave Hypothesis: Miami Twenty-Five Years Later." *Sociology of Entrepreneurship, Research in the Sociology of Organization* 25: 157–90.

Portes, Alejandro and Alex Stepick. 1993. *City on the Edge: The Transformation of Miami.* Berkeley: University of California Press.

Portes, Alejandro and Min Zhou. 1993. "The New Second Generation: Segmented Assimilation and Its Variants Among Post-1965 Immigrant Youth." *Annals of the American Academy of Political and Social Sciences* 530: 74–98.

Putnam, Robert. 2000. *Bowling Alone: The Collapse and Revival of American Community.* New York: Simon & Schuster.

Ragin, Charles. 1994. *Constructing Social Research.* Thousand Oaks, CA: Pine Forge.

Riley, Matilda and Anne Foner, et al. 1972. *Aging and Society.* New York: Russell Sage.

Ritter, Archibald. 2004. "The Cuban Economy in the Twenty-First Century: Recuperation or Relapse?" Pp. 3–24 in Ritter (ed.), *The Cuban Economy.* Pittsburgh: University of Pittsburgh Press.

Ritter, Archibald and Nicholas Rowe. 2002. "Cuba: From 'Dollarization' to 'Euroization' or 'Peso Re-Consideration'?" *Latin American Politics and Society* (Summer): 99–123.

Rodríguez Chávez, Ernesto. 1996. "El patrón migratorio cubano: cambio y continuidad." *Cuadernos de Nuestra América* 9, no. 1 (January–June): 77–95.

Roman, Peter. 1999. *People's Power: Cuba's Experience with Representative Government.* Boulder, CO: Westview Press.

Rose, Nicholas and Ana Julia Yanes Faya. 2004. "Cuban Monetary Policy: Peso, Dollar, or Euro?" Pp. 45–58 in Archibald Ritter (ed.), *The Cuban Economy.* Pittsburgh: University of Pittsburgh Press.

Ruggles, Steven and Mathew Sobek, et al. 2003. *Integrated Public Use Microdata Series (IPUMS), Version 3.0.* Minneapolis: Historical Census Projects, University of Minnesota. www.ipums.org.

Rumbaut, Rubén. 2002. "Severed or Sustained Attachments? Language, Identity, and Imagined Communities in the Post-Immigrant Generation." Pp. 43–95 in Peggy Levitt and Mary Waters (eds.), *The Changing Face of Home: The Transnational Lives of the Second Generation.* New York: Russell Sage Foundation.

————. 2004. "Ages, Life Stages, and Generational Cohorts: Decomposing the Immigrant First and Second Generations in the United States." *International Migration Review* (September) 38, no. 3: 1160–1205.

————. 2005. "Immigration, Incorporation, and Generational Cohorts in Historical Context." In K. Warner Schaie and Glen Elder (eds.), *Historical Influences on Lives and Aging.* New York: Springer Publishing.

Russell, Sharon Stanton. 1986. "Remittances from International Migration: A Review in Perspective." *World Development* 14, no. 6: 677–96.

Ryder, Norman. 1965. "The Cohort as a Concept in the Study of Social Change." *American Sociological Review* 30, no. 6 (December): 843–61.

Sahlins, Marshall. 2004. *Apologies to Thucydides: Understanding History as Culture and Vice Versa.* Chicago: University of Chicago Press.

San Martin, Nancy. 2003. "Wary Exiles: A Challenge for Dissident's Cuba Project." *Miami Herald* (January 10). www.cubanet.org/CNews/y03/jan03/10e3.htm)

Sánchez, Ray. 2008. "Telephone Service in Cuba." *Sun-Sentinel.com* (July).

Sánchez-Egozcue, Jorge Mario. 2003. "Cuba: los desafíos de la inserción en el comercio Caribe-EE.UU." Paper delivered at the Latin American Studies Association Meeting, Dallas (March).

———. 2004. "Challenges of Cuba's Intersection in Caribbean-U.S. Trade." Pp. 119–60 in Jorge Domínguez, Omar Everleny, Pérez Villanueva, and Lorena Barberia (eds.), *The Cuban Economy at the Start of the Twenty-First Century.* Cambridge, MA: David Rockefeller Center for Latin American Studies, Harvard University.

———. 2007. "Economic Relations Cuba-U.S.: Bilateralism or Geopolitics?" Paper presented at the Latin American Studies Association Congress, Montreal, September.

Sanders, Jimy and Victor Nee. 1992. "Problems in Resolving the Enclave Economy Debate: Comment on Portes and Jensen." *American Sociological Review* 57: 415–18.

Sassen, Saskia. 2006. *Cities in a World Economy.* Thousand Oaks, CA: Pine Forge Press.

Sawyer, Mark. 2004. *Racial Politics in Postrevolutionary Cuba.* Cambridge: Cambridge University Press.

Schoultz, Lars. 2009. *That Infernal Little Cuban Republic: The United States and the Cuban Revolution.* Chapel Hill, NC: University of North Carolina Press.

Scott, James C. 1985. *Weapons of the Weak: Everyday Forms of Peasant Resistance.* New Haven, CT: Yale University Press.

———. 1990. *Domination and the Arts of Resistance: Hidden Transcripts.* New Haven, CT: Yale University Press.

Shapiro, Johanna et al. 1999. "Generational Differences in Psychosocial Adaptation and Predictors of Psychological Distress in a Population of Recent Vietnamese Immigrants." *Journal of Community Health* 24, no. 2 (April): 95–113.

Shelley, N. Mark. 2001. "Building Community from 'Scratch': Forces at Work among Urban Vietnamese Refugees in Milwaukee." *Sociological Inquiry* 71, no. 4 (Fall): 473–92.

Sills, David. 1957. *The Volunteers: Means and Ends in a National Organization.* Glencoe, IL: Free Press.

Skerry, Peter. 1993. *Mexican Americans: The Ambivalent Minority.* New York: The Free Press.

Skrentny, John. 2002. *The Minority Rights Revolution.* Cambridge, MA: Belknap Press of Harvard University Press.

Smith, Robert. 2006. *Mexican New York.* Berkeley: University of California Press.

Smith, Tony. 2000. *Foreign Attachments: The Power of Ethnic Groups in the Making of American Foreign Policy.* Cambridge, MA: Harvard University Press.

Spadoni, Paolo. 2003. "The Role of the United States in the Cuban Economy."

Papers and Proceedings of the Thirteenth Annual Meeting of the Association for the Study of the Cuban Economy (ACSE). Lanic.utexas.edu/project/asce/ pdfs/volume 13.

———. 2004. "The Current Situation of Foreign Investment in Cuba." Papers and Proceedings of the Fourteenth Annual Meeting of the Association for the Study of the Cuban Economy (ACSE). Lanic.utexas.edu/project/asce/pdfs/ volume 14.

Stach, John and Christopher Warren. 1990. "Ethnicity and the Politics of Symbolism in Miami's Cuban Community." *Cuban Studies* 20: 11–28.

Stark, Oded and David Bloom. 1985. "The New Economics of Labor Migration." *American Economic Review* 75: 173–78.

Stepick, Alex, Guillermo Grenier, Max Castro, and Marvin Dunn. 2003. *This Land is Our Land: Immigrants and Power in Miami.* Berkeley: University of California Press.

Suro, Roberto. 1998. *Strangers Among Us: How Latino Immigration Is Transforming America.* New York: Alfred A. Knopf.

———. 2003. *Remittance Senders and Receivers: Tracking the Transnational Channels.* Washington, DC: Multilateral Investment Fund and Pew Hispanic Center.

Swanson, Ian. 2007. "Hard-line Cuba PAC Makes Inroads with House Freshmen." *thehill.com* (September 21): 1–3.

Swartz, David. 1997. *Culture & Power. The Sociology of Pierre Bourdieu.* Chicago: University of Chicago Press.

Symmes, Patrick. 2008. *The Boys from Dolores: Fidel Castro's Schoolmates from Revolution to Exile.* New York: Vintage Books.

Tamayo, Juan. 2002. "CANF Affirms Power Despite Struggles." *Miami Herald.* March 28. http://64.21.33.164/CNews/y02/mar02/28e6.htm.

Thomas, W. I. and Florian Znaniecki. 1996. *The Polish Peasant in Europe and America: A Classic Work in Immigrant History,* edited by Eli Zaretsky. Urbana: University of Illinois Press.

Togores, Viviana and Anicia García. 2004. "Consumption, Markets, and Monetary Duality in Cuba." Pp. 245–96 in Jorge Domínguez, Omar Everleny, Pérez Villanueva, and Lorena Barberia (eds.), *The Cuban Economy at the Start of the Twenty-First Century.* Cambridge, MA: David Rockefeller Center for Latin American Studies, Harvard University.

Torres, Maria de los Angeles. 2003. *The Lost Apple: Operation Peter Pan, Cuban Children in the U.S., and the Promise of a Better Future.* Boston: Beacon Press.

Tufte, Edward. 1978. *Political Control of the Economy.* Princeton, NJ: Princeton University Press.

Tulchin, Joseph, Lilian Bobea, Mayra Espina Prieto, and Rafael Hernández (eds.). 2005. *Changes in Cuban Society since the Nineties.* Washington, DC: Woodrow Wilson International Center for Scholars.

Tweed, Thomas. 1997. *Our Lady of the Exile: Diasporic Religion at a Cuban Catholic Shrine in Miami.* New York: Oxford University Press.

United Nations Population Fund (UNFPA). 1990. *State of the World Population 1990.* New York: UNFPA

United States Bureau of the Census (USBC). 1981 to 2000. *Statistical Abstract of the U.S.* Washington, DC: Bureau of the Census, U.S. Department of Commerce, Economics and Statistics Administration. http://www.census.gov.

————. 2006. *American Community Survey.* Washington, DC: USCB. www.census.gov/acs.

United States Coast Guard (USCG). 2006. "Alien Migrant Interdiction." Washington, DC: Coast Guard Office of Law Enforcement. www.uscg.mil/ hq/g-o/g-opl/amio/FlowStats/CY.htm.

United States Department of Commerce, United States Census Bureau. 2001. *Profile of the Foreign-Born Population in the United States: 2000.* Washington, DC: U.S. Census Bureau, December.

United States Department of Homeland Security (USDHS). 2003, 2006. *Yearbook of Immigration Statistics.* (Washington DC: USDHS (see also http:// www.immigration.gov/graphics/shared/aboutus/statistics/index.htm and www.dhs.gov/ximgtn/statistics)

United States Department of Justice (USDJ), Immigration and Naturalization Service (INS). 1990–2002. *Statistical Yearbook of the Immigrant and Naturalization Service.* Washington, DC: INS. http://www.ins.usdoj.gov/graphics/ aboutins/statistics.

United States Department of State (USDS), Bureau of Western Hemisphere Affairs (BWHA). 2004. Commission for Assistance to a Free Cuba. Report to the President. May. Colin Powell, Secretary of State, Chairman. www.uscubacomimssion.org/history5.html.

Uriarte, Miren. 2008. "Social Impact of the Economic Measures." Pp. 285–91 in Philip Brenner et al. *A Contemporary Cuba Reader: Reinventing the Revolution.* Lanham, MD: Rowman and Littlefield.

U.S.-Cuba Trade and Economic Council (UCTEC). 2002. "Economic Eye on Cuba." (March 17). http://www.cubatrade.org.

U.S. Government Accountability Office (USGAO). 2006. *Foreign Assistance: U.S. Democracy Assistance for Cuba Needs Better Management and Oversight.* November. www.gao.gov/new.items/d07147.pdf.

————. 2007. *Economic Sanctions: Agencies Face Competing Priorities in Enforcing the U.S. Embargo on Cuba.* November. Washington, DC: USGAO. www.gao.gov/new.items/d0880.pdf.

Verba, Sidney, Kay Lehman Schlozman, and Henry Brady. 1995. *Voice and Equality: Civic Voluntarism in American Politics.* Cambridge, MA: Harvard University Press.

Wald, Karen. 1978. *Children of Che: Child Care and Education in Cuba.* Palo Alto, CA: Ramparts Press.

Waldinger, Roger. 1993. "The Ethnic Enclave Debate Revisited." *International Journal of Urban and Regional Research* 17, no. 3: 428–36.

————. 1994. "The Making of an Immigrant Niche." *International Migration Review* 28, no. 1: 3–30.

Waldinger, Roger and Cynthia Feliciano. 2004. "Will the New Second Generation Experience 'Downward Assimilation'? Segmented Assimilation Re-assessed." *Ethnic and Racial Studies* 27, no. 3: 376–402.

Wallerstein, Immanuel. 1974. *The Modern World System.* New York: Academic Press.

————. 1979. *The Capitalist World-Economy.* Cambridge, Eng: Cambridge University Press.

Waters, Mary. 1990. *Ethnic Options: Choosing Identities in America.* Berkeley: University of California Press.

Waters, Mary and Tomas Jiménez. 2005. "Assessing Immigrant Assimilation: New Empirical and Theoretical Challenges." *Annual Reviews of Sociology* 31: 16.1–16.21.

Weber, Max. 1978. *Economy and Society: An Outline of Interpretive Sociology*, edited by Guenther Roth and Claus Wittich. Berkeley: University of California Press.

Werlau, Maria. 2003. "U.S. Travel Restrictions to Cuba: Overview and Evolution." *Cuba in Transition* 13. Washington, DC: Association for the Study of the Cuban Economy. http://lanic.utexas.edu/project/asce/publications/proceedings.

William C. Velasquez Institute. 2004. "Florida Cuban American Survey." www.nowaroncuba.org/documentation/new_poll/poll_results.pdf.

Wilson, K. and Alejandro Portes. 1980. "Immigrant Enclaves: An Analysis of the Labor Market Experiences of Cubans in Miami." *American Journal of Sociology* 86 (September): 295–319.

World Bank. 1995. *World Tables*. Baltimore, MD: Johns Hopkins University Press.

———. 1997. *World Development Report*. New York: Oxford University Press.

———. *World Development Indicators 2006* (web.worldbank.org).

———. 2001–2007. *World Development Indicators*. Washington, DC: World Bank and "Quick Query" (www.web.worldbank.org/WBSITE/external/datastatistics.

Wuthnow, Robert. 1991. *Acts of Compassion: Caring for Others and Helping Ourselves*. Princeton, NJ: Princeton University Press.

Yanez, Luisa and Nancy San Martin. 2001. "20 on CANF Board Resign." *Miami Herald*. August 8. Cubanet-Cubanews. http://64.21.33.164/CNews/y01/ago01/08e7.htm.

Zeitlin, Maurice. 1970. *Revolutionary Politics and the Cuban Working Class*. New York: Harper.

Zhou, Min. 1992. *New York's Chinatown: The Socioeconomic Potential of an Urban Enclave*. Philadelphia, PA: Temple University Press.

Index